Science and Religion
Baden Powell and the Anglican
Debate, 1800-1860

Science and Religion
Baden Powell and the Anglican debate, 1800-1860

PIETRO CORSI

Università di Cassino

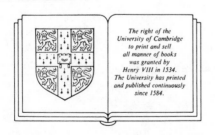

The right of the
University of Cambridge
to print and sell
all manner of books
was granted by
Henry VIII in 1534.
The University has printed
and published continuously
since 1584.

CAMBRIDGE UNIVERSITY PRESS

Cambridge
New York   New Rochelle
Melbourne   Sydney

Published by the Press Syndicate of the University of Cambridge
The Pitt Building, Trumpington Street, Cambridge CB2 1RP
32 East 57th Street, New York, NY 10022, USA
10 Stamford Road, Oakleigh, Melbourne 3166, Australia

© Cambridge University Press 1988

First Published 1988

Printed in Great Britain by the University Press, Cambridge

BL
245
.C67
1988

British Library cataloguing in publication data
Corsi, Pietro
Science and religion: Baden Powell and
the Anglican debate 1800–1860.
1. Powell, Baden 2. Great Britain –
Intellectual life – 19th century
I. Title
941.07′3   DA533

Library of Congress cataloguing in publication data
Corsi, Pietro.
Science and religion.
Includes index.
1. Religion and science – 1800–1859. 2. Powell,
Baden, 1796–1860. I. Title.
BL245.C67   1988   261.5′5   87-13845
ISBN 0 521 24245 2

CONTENTS

PREFACE

The research for this study started in 1972, when I was a graduate student at the Scuola Normale Superiore of Pisa. In 1973, a Lord Florey European Studentship at the Queen's College, Oxford gave new impulse to my work. I was then able to exploit the resources of the Bodleian Library, the manuscript collections of several Colleges – Oriel and Manchester in particular – and of Pusey House. Mr Francis Baden Powell kindly put at my disposal the important collection of papers in his possession. I also enjoyed the hospitality of the Wellcome Unit for the History of Medicine, and I greatly profited from the advice of Dr Charles Webster, its Director.

The first draft of this monograph was submitted in August 1980 to the History Faculty at Oxford University in the form of a D.Phil. dissertation. Further research on early nineteenth-century English philosophy of science, with particular reference to the debates on the epistemological status of theories in political economy, was undertaken at King's College, Cambridge, where I served as Senior Research Associate during the academic year 1980–1. I enjoyed there the comradeship and intellectual stimulation of the members of the Research Centre engaged in the 'Political economy and society, 1750–1850' project.

The years 1981–3 were spent deepening my understanding of the early history of evolutionary ideas in France and England. The resources of the National Library of Florence were particularly relevant for the revision of the fourth part of the present study. Pietro Omodeo, a pioneer of contemporary studies of Lamarck and French science in the early nineteenth century has offered constant advice and encouragement.

The difficulty of living and teaching in different countries, and the need not to impose upon one's family the burden of one's choices, have delayed the publication of this work. A sabbatical leave from Harvard University, and a last-minute invitation by the Ecole des Hautes Etudes en Sciences Sociales in Paris have allowed me to complete the revision of this monograph. Prof. Paolo Galluzzi, Director of the Museo e Istituto di Storia della Scienza of Florence, kindly put at my disposal the facilities of his institution. I wish to thank all the above-mentioned colleagues and institutions for their trust and their help over many years.

Since 1980, numerous important studies have been published dealing with crucial features of English intellectual life in early and mid-Victorian England. I have found a basic agreement with most of the recent historiographical production, while I have noted my differences with a minority of authors. It is clear that scholars are looking with new eyes to the period examined in this study. They are progressively abandoning ready-made, highly ideological and reductive interpretative simplifications for a richer appreciation of the problems faced by a society subjected to radical transformations.

The intellectual career of Baden Powell, from his participation in the activities of the ultra-conservative Hackney Phalanx, to his contribution to *Essays and Reviews*, represents a fascinating case-study of the relationship between cultural and political change. Baden Powell's voyage through early nineteenth-century British culture and Anglican apologetic in particular unveils dimensions of contemporary debates often neglected by historians of the period. It imposes a reconsideration of long-cherished historiographic myths such as the role of the so-called Broad Church movement in fostering British science, or the existence of a phantasmic entity called 'Anglican orthodoxy'. New evidence is also offered on the vexed, and often specious question of whether the complex, and constantly shifting relationship between science and religion can be interpreted in terms of inevitable conflict, or of constitutional harmony, as a new wave of revisionist historiography has been claiming in the last few years.

My own journey through early nineteenth-century British culture owes a great deal to the patience and understanding of the staff at the Bodleian Library, the University Library, Cambridge, the Widener Library, Harvard, the Biblioteca Nazionale, Florence, and of the librarians in charge of manuscript collections at the Bodleian Library, the National Library of Wales at Aberystwyth, the University Library, Liverpool, University College in London, the Devon Record Office in Exeter, Lambeth Palace, the British Library, Oriel College, Manchester College, Keble College and Pusey House in Oxford, Trinity College in Cambridge.

I have discussed – at times without convincing or being convinced – parts of my work with several colleagues. I would like to thank, among others whose work I have discussed in my work, J. H. Brooke, R. Burckhardt, Y. Conry, R. Cooter, J. Garnett, C. C. Gillispie, M. Gowing, S. Gould, J. Greene, B. Hilton, J. Hodge, I. Hont, L. Jordanova, D. Kohn, C. Matthew, E. Mayr, J. Moore, D. Outram, G. Pancaldi, J. Roger, G. Rowell, S. S. Schweber, J. Walsh, P. Weindling, D. Yule.

My greatest debt is to Dr Charles Webster and Margaret Pelling, who have assisted me in many ways since my early days in Oxford. Without their constant intellectual stimulation and moral support, I would not have been able to overcome the daunting difficulties facing a career devoted to research in my own country. To my parents, and to Marica and Elena this product of a common effort is dedicated.

PIETRO CORSI

ABBREVIATIONS

A.S.	*Annals of Science*
B.C.	*British Critic*
B.J.H.S.	*The British Journal for the History of Science*
B.M.	*Blackwood Magazine*
C.R.	*Christian Remembrancer*
E.R.	*Edinburgh Review*
J.H.B.	*Journal of the History of Biology*
Q.R.	*Quarterly Review*
R.R.E.	*Rational Religion Examined*
W.R.	*Westminster Review*

PART I

BIOGRAPHICAL INTRODUCTION

The aim of this study is to assess the contribution of Baden Powell (1796–1860) to debates on the methodology of science, natural theology and the question of species, within the context of contemporary Anglican debates. The three topics have been selected out of a wide range of issues with which Baden Powell was concerned in the course of his life. His intellectual career covered many fields of inquiry. He devoted attention to experimental research on optics and radiant heat, to ecclesiastical history, the history of science, educational reform and theological and philosophical debates. He was an extremely prolific author, the great majority of his works being anonymous contributions to periodicals. Secondary sources have made only incidental reference to Baden Powell, usually confining themselves to consideration of his last publications. There is no systematic analysis of Baden Powell's contribution to nineteenth-century culture available. The most significant comment on his ideas is the Cambridge doctoral dissertation by John David Yule on the 'Impact of science on British religious thought' (1976). Yule's reconstruction of the early phases of Baden Powell's career will be examined in detail. Reference to relevant secondary literature will be given when appropriate.

The issues selected for detailed examination in this study represent Baden Powell's main concerns. It will be shown that his consideration of the philosophical foundation of scientific and religious knowledge guided his approach to the wide spectrum of specific issues upon which he touched. The present monograph is mainly concerned with illustrating significant phases of Baden Powell's intellectual biography with an emphasis on the relevance of some neglected features of English, and specifically Anglican, intellectual life for the understanding of our author's ideas. Biographical details will be mentioned only when relevant to appreciating the importance of personal events in Baden Powell's intellectual development. It is therefore appropriate to provide the reader with an annotated synopsis of Baden Powell's life and to specify in some detail the criteria which have guided the choice of the issues selected for analysis.

Particular attention will be devoted to Baden Powell's family background. None of the biographers or historians who have written on Baden Powell mentions the close links of his family with the group of High Church activists known as the 'Hackney Phalanx' or 'Clapton Sect'. Baden Powell's early outlook was profoundly influenced by the Hackney standpoint. He was educated privately in Hackney and absorbed the views of his relatives respecting the means best suited to revive the declining fortunes of the Anglican Church.

Baden Powell's early education focused on the liberal disciplines required for admission to the English universities. On 24 April 1814 he became a commoner of Oriel College, though he started his period of residence in January 1815. The teaching of the Oriel dons, known as the 'Oriel Noetics', represented the second major influence on Baden Powell's intellectual development. It is emphasized that in the early phase of his contribution to contemporary debates the young author attempted a synthesis of Hackney and Oriel views. In later years, however, he abandoned the Hackney standpoint, and became an original interpreter of the Noetic theological and philosophical approach.

On 12 December 1817 Baden Powell obtained his B.A. with first class honours in mathematics. His manuscript journal, kindly put at my disposal by his descendants, records the increasing interest of the young student in scientific subjects, geometry and experimental researches on light in particular. Baden Powell also attended lectures on geology by William Buckland, and on chemistry by Charles Daubeny. His ecclesiastical career started on 19 December 1819, when he was ordained Deacon of the Church of England and appointed Curate to the parish of Midhurst, Sussex. The incumbent of the living, the Reverend Richard Lloyd, was an ally of the Hackney leaders.

In October 1820 Baden Powell took his M.A., and was shortly afterwards introduced to the Reverend William Rowe Lyall, then editor of the *British Critic*, the journal financed by the Hackney Phalanx. The manuscript notes in Baden Powell's journal permit the identification of several of his contributions to the *Critic* and to the *Christian Remembrancer*, another journal sponsored by the Phalanx. Baden Powell's early writings have been overlooked by historians, and the author himself never mentioned his involvement with the Hackney editorial activities for reasons which will be examined in some detail.

Baden Powell contributed several papers on optics and radiant heat to various scientific journals. It is noted that his early experimental work represented his only original contribution to science. Even though Baden Powell published in his life more than one hundred and twenty papers on scientific subjects, as well as several surveys of scientific debates, his work was increasingly devoted to popularizing the result of current research. Theological polemics, educational reform and the defence of scientific pursuits against epistemological and theological criticism characterized his publications from the early 1820s. Baden Powell's inability to update his scientific notions to meet the growing specialization of physical sciences will be documented and discussed in detail.

He married his first wife, Eliza Rivaz, on 17 July 1817. In January 1821 his relatives offered him the living of Plumstead, Kent, and on 4 May 1821 he was ordained Priest of the Church of England. At his vicarage Baden Powell pursued his experiments on light and heat. On 29 May 1824 he became a Fellow of the Royal Society. He also devoted much time to philosophical and theological studies. In June 1824 he held a meeting with the editor of the *Critic* and became a regular reviewer for the journal. In February 1825 he conceived the project of a book against theological rationalism. *Rational Religion Examined* appeared on 11 March 1826. Only a few months earlier Baden Powell's views on the sabbath, printed in the *Christian Remembrancer*, aroused criticism and suspicion concerning the reliability of his theological standpoint. The synthesis of Oriel and Hackney approaches published by him in March 1826 rehabilitated the young author.

With the help of the Hackney and Oriel influence, Baden Powell was appointed Savilian Professor of Geometry in February 1827. He immediately concentrated his efforts on raising the standards of mathematical studies at Oxford and took an active part in the debate on the reform of the statutes. His involvement in academic politics was of crucial relevance to Baden Powell's intellectual development. He was persuaded that the Anglican Church was reluctant to come to terms with new intellectual trends. He also realized the limits of the reforming impulse of his Oriel colleagues and friends. Baden Powell did not take part in the debate on the reform of the Royal Society, nor in the debate on the decline of science in Britain. He held views on both subjects, but he was too absorbed in the dramatic events at Oxford to play a major rôle in those issues.

The debate on the reform of the curriculum and the heated controversy over the admission of Dissenters into English universities were two key issues in Baden Powell's development. His apologetic stance changed into a severe criticism of the university and the conservative factions of the Anglican Church. He found the theological approach of his Noetic friends particularly effective in dealing with the intellectual advances of the time, even though several members of the Oriel group refused to subscribe to all the conclusions deduced by Baden Powell from their standpoint. By the early 1830s the basic elements of his later approach to philosophy, theology and science were fully developed.

Baden Powell became an active supporter of the Ashmolean Society, the Oxford organization for the promotion of scientific studies which he helped to establish in 1829. He also took an active part in the proceedings of the British Association for the Advancement of Science (1831) and of the Society for the Diffusion of Useful Knowledge (1826). He wrote for the *Journal of Education*, the magazine sponsored by the S.D.U.K., and edited by the mathematician Augustus de Morgan, a lifelong friend of Baden Powell. In 1832 he published his lecture on *The Present State and Future Prospects of Mathematical and Physical Studies in the University of Oxford* and in 1833 his sermon *Revelation and Science*. In 1834 he contributed *An Historical View of the Progress of the Physical and Mathematical Sciences* to the *Cabinet Cyclo-paedia*. The three works forcefully emphasized Baden Powell's belief that the development of modern science was obstructed by well-meaning but misguided theologians, who were afraid of the impact of scientific advance on religious feelings. Baden Powell found himself under attack from the *British Critic* and his Hackney relatives. His family ceased to give him financial support, and he thus found himself forced to multiply his literary efforts.

In 1837 he contributed several papers to and edited the shortlived *Magazine of Popular Science*. In 1838 he discussed with the publisher Parker the possibility of launching a new quarterly, open to the forward-looking factions of the Anglican Church and the laity. The project failed, even though Baden Powell was powerfully supported by his former Oriel teacher, Richard Whately, Archbishop of Dublin since 1832. The links between the two men were reinforced by Baden Powell's second marriage, Eliza, his first wife, having died on 13 March 1835. On 27 September 1837 he married Charlotte Pope, the younger sister of Whately's wife Elizabeth.

The situation in Tractarian Oxford became difficult for Baden Powell, who progressively increased his contacts with intellectual and scientific circles in the capital. On 17 May 1837 he became a member of the Geological Society and took an active part in its meetings. On 14 December 1838 he became a member of the Astronomical Society. The question of the epistemological status of geology and of its relevance to the Genesis narrative of creation attracted great attention in the 1830s. Baden Powell felt that the issue deserved a thorough investigation. He was also persuaded that the debate on geology represented a crucial test of the capacity of Christian apologists and natural theologians to adapt their arguments to the intellectual and scientific priorities of the time. From November 1836 he was engaged in writing his second major work, *The Connexion of Natural and Divine Truth*, which was published in February 1838.

The years 1838–41 were the most prolific of Baden Powell's career. In January 1839 he published *Tradition Unveiled*, a polemical examination of the Tractarian emphasis on Church authority. The book was highly successful. A *Supplement* was published in 1840, and an American edition appeared in Philadelphia in 1841. In 1840 Baden Powell also entered the debate on popular education and advocated the principle of non-denominational state education in a pamphlet on *State Education*. In 1841 he published *A General and Elementary View of the Undulatory Theory, as Applied to the Dispersion of Light*, where he surveyed the debate on the theory of light and his own contribution to the subject – mainly translations of memoirs by the French physicist Augustin-Louis Cauchy. From 1841 Baden Powell contributed a considerable number of papers to various journals.

He increasingly regarded himself as a Christian philosopher who surveyed the development of scientific, philosophical and theological knowledge. During the 1840s he became a well-known figure in metropolitan social and intellectual circles. He was a frequent guest at soirées organized by the Marquis of Northampton, the President of the Royal Society, and at parties given by Charles Lyell, Roderick Impey Murchison and Charles Babbage. On 24 October 1844 his second wife, Charlotte, died. On 10 March 1846 Baden Powell married Henrietta Grace Smyth, daughter of Captain William Henry Smyth and sister of the astronomer Charles Piazzi Smyth. The new well-connected family circle raised Baden Powell's social status.

During his frequent visits to London, Baden Powell came into contact with representatives of liberal and radical theology. He became acquainted with the Baron von Bunsen, an active supporter of German higher criticism. He was also on close terms with the classicist and radical theologian Francis Newman. The circle of Baden Powell's new friends included the physiologist William Benjamin Carpenter, Henry Thomas Buckle, Robert Chambers and George Henry Lewes. We will discuss in detail the relationship of Baden Powell with the metropolitan radical theologians and philosophers active in the late 1840s and the early 1850s.

In the late 1840s Baden Powell took a prominent part in the campaign for the reform of the universities. He was a member of the deputation to Lord John Russell which on 10 July 1848 submitted the petition for a University Commission of Inquiry. Eventually in 1850 the Commission was established, and on 20 August 1850 the Savilian Professor was asked to become one of its members. It is appropriate to emphasize that in 1835 Baden Powell had been the first Oxford professor to insist that only Parliament was capable of overcoming the resistance to change displayed within the universities of Oxford and Cambridge. He put forward his views on university reform in the section which he contributed to the final Report of the Commission (1852). We will not expand upon Baden Powell's involvement in university politics in the 1850s, since he simply restated the arguments elaborated by him in the early 1830s, which will be examined in detail.

In the early 1850s Baden Powell discovered that his ideas were now accepted by many of his London friends. He therefore decided to give publicity to his views by publishing a series of essays on the methodology of science and the question of species. The publication of the anonymous *Plurality of Worlds* – immediately ascribed to William Whewell – forced Baden Powell to include a further essay on the astronomical controversy. The *Essays on the Spirit of Inductive Philosophy, the Unity of Worlds and the Philosophy of Creation* was published in April 1855. The book was an immediate success. The Savilian Professor was invited to preach at Kensington Palace. The sermons he delivered before the royal family were published as a second series of essays, with the title *Christianity without Judaism* (1856).

Baden Powell's last work, *The Order of Nature*, appeared in 1859. The advanced theological views put forward in his last writings provoked an open

Science and religion

confrontation with Whately, who severely criticized the ideas of his former pupil. Baden Powell retorted to Whately's criticism in his contribution to the *Essays and Reviews*, the collective volume which gave rise to one of the most famous theological controversies of the century. In his essay 'On the Study of the Evidences of Christianity' Baden Powell questioned the credibility of miracles and praised Darwin's *On the Origin of Species*. He had become the most outspoken representative of liberal theology and the evolutionary approach to natural history. His sudden death, on 11 June 1860, deprived him of the possibility of linking his name with the evolutionary debate as the first outspoken theological supporter of Darwin's theory.

The Hackney Phalanx: a family network

Baden Powell was born at Stamford Hill, Hackney, on 22 August 1796.[1] To state the place and the date of his birth is not, in this case, an instance of biographical pedantry. Indeed, Hackney, in those days a village north-east of London, and the rôle several families living there played in the social and cultural life of early nineteenth-century England, are of particular relevance to an understanding of Baden Powell's early intellectual career. It is the more interesting to pursue and describe our author's family connections, as we become aware of the fact that both Baden Powell himself and historians who have been concerned with his work, or with the activities of members of his family, have systematically failed to make clear the links between the much discussed figure of the Savilian Professor of Geometry at Oxford and the Hackney Phalanx, the famous High Church group of staunch supporters of the Constitution in Church and State during the early nineteenth century.[2] Baden Powell, who was otherwise in the habit of indulging in copious references to his earlier works and ideas, persistently avoided mentioning his earliest contributions to the activities of the Hackney Phalanx. Mrs Baden Powell, who in 1866 published a sketch of her husband's life, omitted to list in the otherwise satisfactory bibliography of Baden Powell's works all the books and papers discussing theological and philosophical doctrines which he published before 1830.[3]

In an impressive thesis on natural theology in the early decades of the nineteenth century, J. D. Yule analysed Baden Powell's early ideas on the relationship between science and religion.[4] Unfortunately he ignored Baden

---

[1] D.N.B.; D.S.B.; obituary notice in *Proceedings of the Royal Society*, 11 (1860–2), xxvi–xxix; W. Tuckwell, *Pre-Tractarian Oxford* (1909), pp. 165–225; O. Chadwick, *The Victorian Church*, pt.I (1966), pp. 553–5; J. D. Yule, 'The impact of science on British religious thought in the second quarter of the nineteenth century', (Ph.D. thesis, Cambridge University, 1976).

[2] J. H. Overton, *The English Church in the Nineteenth Century* (1894), ch. 2; B. R. Marshall, 'The theology of Church and State in relation to the concern for popular education in England, 1800–1870' (D.Phil. thesis, Oxford University, 1956), ch. 6; J. K. B. Jones, 'Anglican theological thought, 1750–1833, with especial reference to the pre-Tractarians' (Ph.D. thesis, Leeds University, 1968).

[3] H. G. Baden Powell, *Notices of the Life of the Reverend Baden Powell* (n.d.) [1886].

[4] Yule, 'The impact of science', pp. 85, 110.

Powell's numerous anonymous contributions to the *British Critic* and the
Christian Remembrancer, two magazines sponsored in different ways by the
Hackney Phalanx. As a consequence, he inevitably misunderstood the rationale
of the problems Baden Powell and his associates were discussing. This failure
cannot be attributed to Dr Yule's lack of interest in the early stages of Baden
Powell's intellectual development, but to the reluctance of primary and
secondary sources seriously to investigate Baden Powell's family and intellectual background. A. B. Webster, author of a modern biography of Joshua
Watson (1771–1855), the organizing spirit of the Hackney Phalanx, did mention
Professor Baden Powell as being one of the youngest members of the Phalanx
'who ultimately abandoned the Hackney standpoint'. However, he clearly
failed to distinguish between Baden Powell senior, of Langton, Kent, and
Baden Powell the Oxford professor. As far as Baden Powell's family relations
were concerned, Webster stated that Baden Powell was 'a distant cousin' of
Watson. As with Yule's dissertation, Webster's lack of accuracy is easily
explained. Most of his information on the Watson family was taken from the
Memoir of Joshua Watson, a nineteenth-century biography of the father figure
of the Hackney circle published in 1861 by Edward Churton (1800–74).

Churton expanded upon Watson's activities and repeatedly emphasized the
family links which bound together several families who took an active part
in promoting the Phalanx plans. When describing the charitable enterprises
initiated by Watson, Churton mentioned the generous contributions of Baden
Powell senior. However, he avoided making a single reference to the rôle
played by Baden Powell in the editorial and general cultural activities of the
Phalanx during the early 1820s. Indeed he simply ignored Baden Powell
altogether.[5] This is the more surprising in view of the close family links
between Churton and Baden Powell. Edward Churton's wife was a daughter
of John James Watson (1770–1839), brother of Joshua. In 1807 he married
Caroline Powell, a sister of Baden Powell senior. Thus, Baden Powell the
Savilian Professor was in fact a cousin of Edward Churton's wife. Clearly, it
was a matter of policy which made Churton ignore the activities and family
connections of the notorious Professor Baden Powell. When Churton's
biography of Watson appeared in 1861, the Savilian Professor had died recently
(June 1860), thus escaping being the first in the list of candidates for prosecution among the authors who contributed to the *Essays and Reviews*.[6]

It is not surprising, therefore, that Churton preferred not to mention his
hero's connection with an acknowledged leader of the infidel party within the
Anglican Church. Yet, Churton's scrupulous and detailed account of the life
of Watson allows the patient reader to find his way through the intricacies

---

5 A. B. Webster, *Joshua Watson* (1954), pp. 27, 28, 69, 175; E. Churton, *Memoir of Joshua
   Watson*, 2 vols. (1861), vol. i, pp. 85, 149, 221; vol. ii, pp. 220–1, 231, 265.
6 Baden Powell's contribution to the *Essays and Reviews* was probably the one which most
   shocked contemporary churchmen and parish priests. On the several angry comments on
   Baden Powell's denial of the physical possibility of miracles see I. Ellis, *Seven against Christ*
   (1980), and below, ch. 12.

of the family tree. By patching together passing allusions to Watson's relatives it was possible to reach the conclusion that Baden Powell, whom Edward Bouverie Pusey (1800–82) doubted had died a Christian, was closely related to the central figures of the ultra-orthodox Hackney Phalanx. Indeed, J. J. Watson, Henry Handley Norris (1771–1850), and Thomas Sikes (1767–1834) the leaders of the Hackney group, were Baden Powell's uncles.[7]

Further inquiry stimulated by the surprising result of the analysis of Churton's work, made it possible to trace a *Pedigree of the Powell Family*, privately printed in 1891. This richly documented history throws much needed light upon Baden Powell's family connections. In 1797 Thomas Sikes, Vicar of Guilsborough and author of the once famous *Discourse on Parochial Communion* (1812), married Susanna Powell, sister of Baden Powell senior. Sikes was a nephew of Charles Daubeny (1745–1827), the ultra-Tory High Churchman whose *Guide to the Church* (1798) was a favourite work among the Hackney group and English conservative circles. In the same year, 1797, Joshua Watson married Mary Sikes, sister of Thomas. In 1805 Henrietta Catherine Powell (1773–1854), another of Baden Powell senior's sisters, married Henry Handley Norris, later Vicar of South Hackney. Norris was a leading figure in the Society for Promoting Christian Knowledge; his influence on the government regarding matters of Church politics, gained him the sobriquet of 'Bishop-maker'. In 1807 Caroline Powell (1775–1865) – the future mother-in-law of Edward Churton – married John James Watson, brother of Joshua and Rector of Hackney.[8]

The network of family links between the Norrises, Watsons and Powells was favoured by the fact that all lived in the same London suburb. Baden Powell had a house in Upper Homerton, five minutes' walk from H. H. Norris's chapel, and from Clapton, where Joshua Watson came to live in 1811. The Powells contributed generously to the building of new churches, a characteristic feature of the religious and social activities of the Hackney Phalanx. In 1802 this group of friends launched a subscription to build two new chapels of ease in Hackney. One was to be built in Wells Street, the other in Shacklewell, two populous districts of London's expanding suburbs. Donations by the Norrises and the Powells were munificent, especially on behalf of the Wells Street project. The chapel so built, St John's, was given into the care of H. H. Norris, who officiated there as Curate to his brother-in-law, J. J. Watson. In later years, the chapel was transformed into a vicarage and H. H. Norris became the Rector of South Hackney.[9]

7 Churton, *Memoir of Joshua Watson*, vol. i, pp. 46–7, 97; vol. ii, pp. 220–1. On Churton's conservative theological leanings, see (Anon.), *A Short Memoir of Archdeacon Churton* (1861).

8 B. Powell, *The Pedigree of the Powell Family* (1891). I wish to thank Mrs. Muriel Powell Baker for her assistance.

9 W. Robinson, *The History and Antiquities of the Parish of Hackney*, 2 vols. (1842), vol. i, pp. 173–8; D. Lysons, *Supplement to the first edition of the Historical Account of the Environs of London* (1811), pp. 163–75; see also Webster, *Joshua Watson* and Churton, *Memoir of Joshua Watson*.

It could be argued that the zeal these families showed in building new churches during the early 1800s and in promoting the cause of Church popular education, was related to the peculiarity of the Hackney situation. For many decades during the second half of the eighteenth century, Hackney had been a convenient country resort for a number of wealthy families; bankers and merchants predominated among the parish aristocracy. During the closing decades of the eighteenth century and the first years of the nineteenth, their religious and political outlook was not always in tune with the policies pursued by the Tory government and the Church of England. Moreover, the populous sectors of the parish housed working-class families, especially artisans, and were a prolific seed-bed for radical activities and propaganda.

Homerton was a locality particularly dear to the Dissenting party, since it housed Homerton College, the oldest educational institution of the Independents. Even more worrying to and detested by Anglican churchmen was the shortlived presence in Hackney of the Unitarian New College. The defiant radicalism and Jacobinism of students and teachers there brought to an end the experiment of Unitarian higher education in Hackney.[10] However, the leader of the Unitarian movement after the death of Joseph Priestley (1733–1804), Thomas Belsham (1750–1829), was a tutor at the College and kept his residence in the parish until a few months before his death.[11] His works caused great alarm and aroused apprehension in conservative Anglican circles. The learning displayed by Belsham could hardly have been matched by High Church Anglican divines.

A work by Belsham called forth a learned reply from the pen of the Dissenting minister John Pye Smith (1774–1851), another Hackney intellectual of high prestige. Smith was resident tutor at Homerton College from September 1800 and theological instructor in the same establishment from 1806. His *Scripture Testimony to the Messiah* (1812) contained, together with a refutation of Belsham's principles, one of the first detailed analyses of recent developments in German theology.[12] It was a meagre consolation to see a learned 'infidel' production disputed by an even more impressive disquisition by a Dissenter; the Hackney leaders probably felt that the Anglican Church had very little to say on theological and exegetical issues. Undeterred by Anglican invectives, the Unitarians made significant progress in Hackney as in Britain

[10] On Homerton College see Robinson, *History and Antiquities*, vol. i, pp. 278–89, and A. Lincoln, *Some Political and Social Ideas of English Dissent, 1763–1800* (1937), p. 88; on the Unitarian New College, C. G. Bolam *et al.*, *The English Presbyterians* (1968), p. 237; on the Unitarian Academy established in 1811 see R. Aspland, *Memoir of the Life, Works and Correspondence of the Rev. Robert Aspland* (1850), pp. 303–30; B. Simon, *Studies in the History of Education* (1960), pp. 66–70.

[11] *D.N.B.*; J. Williams, *Memoirs of the Late Reverend Thomas Belsham* (1833). On the anxiety caused by Belsham's editorial activities, see J. W. Burgon, *Lives of Twelve Good Men* (1888), p. 69.

[12] J. Medway, *Memoirs of the Life of John Pye Smith* (1853). J. Hunt, *Religious Thought in England in the Nineteenth Century* (1896), pp. 82–3.

as a whole. In 1809 they were building a new meeting house on the side of Paradise Field. Various Dissenting groups were also active in building chapels and organizing schools at Hackney.[13]

The Hackney cultural life was characterized by a wide spectrum of religious, educational and editorial activities. This social and cultural commitment was at variance with the policy of relative inactivity adopted by the hierarchies of the Established Church and the State. The Norrises, Watsons and Powells perceived that by their intellectual activity and their capacity for adapting to the needs of an expanding urban population, the non-conformists in Hackney presented a challenge of worrying dimensions to the Anglican Church. In response they built new churches at their own expense and founded new schools. In 1805 H. H. Norris personally financed the establishment of a new school and in later years he also built and endowed a school for girls.[14]

Outside of Hackney and away from the rapidly changing religious and political atmosphere of industrial urban settlements, it was probably difficult to appreciate the need for such a display of pastoral and educational zeal. There is some evidence suggesting that the activities of the Hackney Phalanx were looked at with a certain degree of hostility within ultra-reactionary circles. The Hackney plan to convince the Church and the State of the need to gain ideological and institutional control over the popular education movement, for instance, succeeded in winning a cautious and qualified approval only after considerable debate. It was difficult to persuade the strong anti-Jacobin party – of which the Hackney group was itself a very active faction – that Sunday schools were not synonymous with 'nurseries of sedition' or the diffusion of popular culture the chief engine of social unrest.[15]

There is indirect evidence suggesting that representatives of the Anglican

---

[13] R. B. Aspland, *Memoir of Robert Aspland*, p. 255; J. Sellers, 'Political and social attitudes of representative English Unitarians (1795–1850)' (B.Litt. thesis, Oxford University, 1956). Aspland, 'Oratio delivered by R. Aspland', British Library, Hone Papers, Ms Add 40120, fol. 84. Aspland's congregation was one of the most prosperous and active in England, see (Anon.), 'Unitarianism in England', *British Magazine*, 3 (1833), 209–10. A. Ruston, 'Radical Nonconformity in Hackney, 1805–1845', *Transactions of the Unitarian Historical Society*, 14 (1955), 1–9.

[14] It was from Hackney that Aspland edited the *Monthly Repository* and the *Christian Reformer*; see J. R. Beard (ed.), *Unitarianism Exhibited* (1846), p. 132, and F. E. Mineka, *The Dissidence of Dissent. The Monthly Repository 1806–1838* (1940). In 1807 Aspland started a series of very successful weekly conferences at the Gravel Pit chapel: see R. B. Aspland, *Memoirs* p. 165, who also noted (p. 176) that Hackney was 'the residence of several persons of high cultivation'. Among the latter, it is sufficient to mention Francis August Cox (1783–1853), founder of the *Baptist Magazine*, and one of the instigators of the *Encyclopaedia Metropolitana*.

[15] Churton, *Memoir of Joshua Watson*, vol. i, p. 103; S. C. Carpenter, *Church and People* (1933), pp. 68–88; Marshall, 'Theology of Church and State'. For an epigraphic statement of the Hackney interpretation of the aim of popular education, see (Anon.), 'The scandals of impiety and unbelief', *B.C.*, 2 (1820), 413–30, and in particular p. 430: 'The superior is no longer respected, because he is a superior in rank; he must prove himself also a superior in knowledge and virtue. The proof can only be comprehended by such as are not absolutely ignorant, and we must consequently instruct the poor, that we may be able to convince them.'

Church regarded with hostility even the idea of refuting the tenets of Dissenters and Unitarians on theological grounds. To discuss with the heretics and the infidels was in their eyes to acknowledge their existence and their cultural identity. It is interesting to point out that in 1805 William Van Mildert (1765–1836), the theological spokesman of the Phalanx, felt it necessary to justify his severe critique of contemporary non-Anglican theological standpoints, which he equated with infidelity and social subversion. He could not agree, Van Mildert wrote, with those who believed that the very fact of attacking the tenets of the enemies with a detailed and well argued criticism was in itself a dangerous exercise.[16]

The social and political events of the 1810s and the 1820s convinced the more reluctant that the old world could not be saved without concrete and positive effort, and indeed without adopting the organizational skills of the adversary. The pressure exercised by the Hackney Phalanx was the chief factor in the creation, in 1811, of the National Society for the Education of the Poor. It was specifically established to counter the successful Dissenting enterprises in the field of popular education. In 1818, a few months after the institution of the Church Building Society at the instigation of the Phalanx, Parliament voted a one million pound grant for the purpose of providing the newly expanded towns with adequate church facilities.[17]

In the first two decades of the nineteenth century the Hackney Phalanx constituted the only active group within the ranks of the High Church aware of the need for positive policies to be used in preference to purely repressive ones – even though the latter were not at all excluded and indeed often welcomed. Complete control over society and the preservation of privileges and inequality were aims the Hackney leaders had in common with the more conservative forces in Church and State. Yet, the experience they had of middle-class economic, religious and intellectual activities made them aware of the need for competitive policies. These were to be pursued in the same crucial sectors in which the adversaries had chosen to undermine the presence and the authority of the Anglican Church in English society.

It needs to be pointed out that all the families in the Hackney Phalanx group were of mercantile extraction. The wars with the colonies and France offered many openings to private profiteers and the families demonstrated their ability to take full advantage of these opportunities, redoubling their capital several times during the years of conflict. The financial and organizational skills underlying their economic success were successfully redeployed to implement political and religious programmes.[18]

[16] W. Van Mildert, *An Historical View of the Rise and Progress of Infidelity*, 2 vols. (New edn., 1831), vol. i, p. 448.

[17] H. J. Burgess and P. A. Welsby, *A Short History of the National Society* (1951); Churton, *Memoir of Joshua Watson*, vol. i, pp. 102–17; M. H. Port, *Six Hundred New Churches* (1961). J. H. Overton, *The English Church in the Nineteenth Century* (1894), p. 240; F. K. Brown, *Fathers of the Victorians* (1961), pp. 352–3.

[18] Webster, *Joshua Watson*, pp. 28–9.

Notwithstanding the many successes achieved at financial and institutional levels, the leaders of the Hackney Phalanx were painfully aware that Parliament and the law could not deal with more fundamental weaknesses currently afflicting the religious Establishment. Qualities other than financial skills were needed to bridge the gap between the cultural equipment of the parson and the intellectual challenge of the day. The theological instruction of the clergy was practically nonexistent, nor did the Church as a whole distinguish itself for learning or aggressive theological proposals. Charles Daubeny's and Van Mildert's writings were sufficiently belligerent, but only at the level of invective. As a distinguished visitor pointed out, the Anglican Church had in the early nineteenth century 'few accomplished theologians'.[19] Furthermore, the learning of the few active theologians was more adapted to anti-deistic controversy than to biblical criticism or scholarly exegesis.

The education of the average parish priest was scarce on specific theological subjects. Those few clergy who had attended Oxford and Cambridge, were more familiar with Greek orators and Latin historians than with patristic literature or elementary biblical exegesis. As H. H. Norris remarked, the country clergy were 'constant readers of the *Gentleman's Magazine*, deep in the antiquities of the signs of inns, speculations as to what becomes of swallows in winter, and whether hedge-hogs, or other urchins, are most justly accused of sucking milch-cows dry at night'. The problem was therefore twofold. On the one hand, there was the question of the education of the clergy. On the other, it was essential to raise the theological standards of the active clergy and of the lay supporters of the Establishment.[20]

As far as the question of providing the clergy with basic theological literacy was concerned, individual efforts were made during the 1810s and the 1820s to raise theological standards in both universities. In 1814 Van Mildert, a close friend of Joshua Watson, was made Regius Professor of Divinity at Oxford, where he lectured with satisfactory regularity. He was succeeded by another friend of the Phalanx, Charles Lloyd (1784–1829), later Bishop of Oxford. Lloyd took private pupils, and delivered lectures on a wide though traditional range of topics to pupils like Pusey and John Henry Newman (1801–1890).[21]

---

[19] John Henry Hobart, Archbishop of New York; see Churton, *Memoirs of Joshua Watson*, vol. i, p. 245; F. W. B. Bullock, *A History of the Training for the Ministry of the Church of England* (1955), pp. 38–9.

[20] H. Marsh, *An Essay on the Usefulness and Necessity of Theological Learning to Those who Are Designed for Holy Orders* (1792), pp. 1–2: 'though the greatest number of students in the two universities is designed for orders, the study of divinity is regarded as a secondary consideration'. Churton, *Memoir of Joshua Watson*, vol. i, p. 277.

[21] *D.N.B.*; on Van Mildert, see Churton, *Memoir of Joshua Watson*, vol. i, pp. 62–79, E. S. Ffoulkes, *A History of the Church of St. Mary the Virgin* (1892), pp. 371–84 and W. H. Mackean, *The Eucharist Doctrine of the Oxford Movement* (1933), p. 15. For a summary of Lloyd's lectures, see Ffoulkes, pp. 400–5. F. Newman, *Contributions chiefly to the Early History of Cardinal Newman* (1891), pp. 39–40, p. 40: 'I now learned from Baden Powell that he [Lloyd] was learned in German theological literature, and felt it a scandal that in Oxford there was a

Herbert Marsh, probably the most learned Anglican divine of the early nineteenth century, delivered a series of lectures at Cambridge. Marsh's teaching aroused considerable apprehension on account of its favourable reference to German theological studies, and to the works of Michaelis in particular. Marsh was one of the very few English divines conversant at a scholarly level with the problem of the scriptural canon. Of a more orthodox tenor were the lectures delivered at Cambridge by Thomas Rennell (1787–1824) and Hugh James Rose (1795–1838), in their capacity of Christian Advocates. However, as Rose himself remarked, their efforts were followed by scarcely noticeable results. The fortunes of Anglican theological learning and teaching were even lower at Cambridge than at Oxford.[22]

On the whole, despite the lack of immediate results, the prospects for theological teaching in the universities looked slightly brighter. The question which increasingly worried the Hackney leaders was the problem of securing a qualified presence of sound High Church principles in theological and political debates. Since the beginning of the nineteenth century there had been a constant increase in the number of magazines and reviews. As is well known, the press was not always friendly to the entrenched interests of the more conservative sectors within the Church and the State. The Hackney leaders fully appreciated the importance of press campaigns and of party organs of opinion in influencing the public mind. They had gained considerable experience in organizing pro-establishment political publications since the time of their involvement in the *Anti-Jacobin Review* and the *Scholar Armed*.[23]

The ever-increasing pugnacity of Dissenting organizations and expanding Unitarian intellectual activity convinced the Hackney friends of the need to give a pronounced Church and State tone to the *British Critic*, a monthly magazine established in 1793 to fight the influence of the radical *Monthly Repository*. Joshua Watson and H. H. Norris bought the magazine at the end of 1811. Van Mildert and Rennell were the first editors. They were followed

total absence of solid learning as to the origins and history of the separate books of our Scriptures'. In a letter to Lord Melbourne, R. Whately made interesting comments on theological teaching at Oxford, and was severely critical of Lloyd's competence and achievements.

22 Marsh was a cousin of William Frend (1757–1841), the mathematical tutor expelled from Cambridge in 1793 for his political ideas, whose daughter married Augustus de Morgan. On Marsh, see J. Hunt, *Religious Thought in England in the Nineteenth Century* (1896), pp. 30–6, Brown, *Fathers of the Victorians*, pp. 309–10. See also Overton, *The English Church*, pp. 176–7, on the war of pamphlets which followed Marsh's 1801 *Origin and Composition*. Bishop Randolph of Oxford was a firm opponent of Marsh. However, the merits of the latter's pro-Hackney political activities imposed a restriction on the attack: see for instance the respectful disagreement expressed by J. J. Conybeare in his 1824 Bampton Lectures. Yet, suspicion of Marsh's pro-German sympathies survived decades after his death, and was frequently voiced in private correspondence among High Churchmen in the aftermath of the publication of *Essays and Reviews*: cf. Ellis, *Seven against Christ*. On Rennell see Hunt, pp. 46–7. On Rose see D. M. B. Snow, 'Hugh James Rose Rector of Hadleigh, Suffolk' (B.Litt. thesis, Oxford University, 1960).

23 Churton, *Memoir of Joshua Watson*, vol. i, pp. 28–9.

by a series of Hackney appointees, which included Thomas Fanshaw Middleton (1769–1822), later Bishop of Calcutta, and William Rowe Lyall, later Dean of Canterbury. Moreover, when in 1818 the Reverend Frederick Ironmonger started the *Christian Remembrancer*, Van Mildert was asked to give his advice. There is indirect evidence suggesting that the Hackney leaders had a financial concern in the *Remembrancer* and were influential in appointing its editors.[24]

The *British Critic* and the *Christian Remembrancer* both failed to satisfy their owners and inspirers. This was partly because it was difficult to find contributors sufficiently equipped to further the programme of the editors and partly because the reviews had to follow the taste of the public if the journals were to pay their way. The *British Critic*'s editorial policy during the 1810s and the 1820s, relevant to our study of Baden Powell's early activity and of Anglican views of the relationship between science and religion, was characterized by different phases, up to the issue of a third series of a more pronounced theological character in 1827. A glance at the indexes of the first fifteen years of the life of the *British Critic* under direct Hackney editorship reveals that the new magazine hardly escaped the kind of criticism made by H. H. Norris against the *Gentleman's Magazine*.

Several papers reviewed popular books on travels or reported on miscellaneous scientific subjects. Ample space was also given to scientific curiosities or to scientific disciplines fashionable at the time, such as geology, astronomy, anthropology and entomology. An equal number of contributions were devoted to commenting on sermons and speeches on the questions of the day by bishops and churchmen supported by the Hackney group. The alliance between the Church and the State was uniformly upheld. Unitarians and Dissenters were regularly abused. Social and political issues were also considered. It was typical of the *British Critic*'s editorial line to link theological, philosophical or scientific debates to the social and political preoccupations of the upper classes.

Thus, the repeated attacks against the British and Foreign Bible Society, established in 1804, were motivated by theological considerations, but reviewers were careful to point out the subversive implications of the Society's programme. As is well known, the British and Foreign Society was designed to promote the reading of the Bible at home and in the colonies. In order to achieve the maximum result, the Society was ecumenical and non-denominational. It enjoyed the highest patronage and succeeded in establishing branches throughout the country.[25]

The Hackney leaders disliked the very idea of working with Dissenters and

[24] Churton, *Memoir of Joshua Watson*, vol. i, pp. 96, 276–85; Overton, *The English Church*, pp. 44, 200–2. W. R. W. Stephens, *Life and Letters of W. H. Hook* (1878), p. 144: 'Joshua Watson and Mr. Norris encouraged Mr. Ironmonger to start the *Christian Remembrancer*'; Mineka, *The Dissidence of Dissent*, p. 53.

[25] Brown, *Fathers of the Victorians*, pp. 244–5, 255–8, 314–5.

Unitarians or even with Anglican evangelical brethren. Dissenters were heretics and traitors. It was difficult to draw a line between their policy and the subversive plans of the radicals or even the Jacobins. The local committees established by the Society to reach the lower strata of the population were organized according to detestable democratic principles. It was often the case that a barber or a bank accountant dared to preach the gospel and Christian duty to his superiors. The Hackney leaders pointed out that to teach self-organization to the lower classes was to lower the social barriers, and to open the gates to the formation of revolutionary movements.[26]

Entrenchment was the programme of the Hackney leaders. Yet their first-hand experience of the social and cultural activities of their enemies had made them aware that invective was powerless to stop the downward trend of the old political and religious establishment. It could be argued that their social and political instincts were more developed than their theological and intellectual ones.

The Hackney leaders unsuccessfully tried to revive Hutchinsonianism and proposed the Caroline divines as guides to the times. Young Baden Powell was advised to read the non-juror authorities most valued by the Hackney leaders. His relatives and mentors often visited Nayland to pay their respects to William Jones (1726–1800), the Hutchinsonian theological inspirer of the Phalanx.[27] During the 1820s and the 1830s, the Phalanx leadership failed to impose a coherent theological line on the journals it controlled. Their scholarship and theological learning was amateurish and old-fashioned. Significantly, in the late 1830s they progressively gave way to Newman's manoeuvres to obtain control of the *British Critic*, though they could not agree with or were unable fully to understand the theological consequences of Newman's standpoint.[28]

It would be wrong, however, to ascribe failure solely to the old fashioned theology or philosophy of the Phalanx. The educational and theological short-comings that the Hackney leaders engaged to improve were the result of deep institutional weaknesses of the Anglican establishment. No solution was possible without reforming the organizational structure of the Church. Ironically, but

[26] H. H. Norris, *A Practical Exposition of the Tendency and Proceedings of the British and Foreign Bible Society* (1814), pp. 206–12, 286, 407, 413. Norris hinted that the B.F.B.S. could be equated with the conspiratorial activities of pre-revolutionary *illuminati*; see also (Anon.), *B.C.*, 8 (1817), 541–2: 'we wish to see the labouring man at no other place but at his work, at his chapel, and at his home. Neither his education nor his habits fit him for what may be termed society; and we are persuaded that when the lower orders meet at any other place, excepting the three which we have mentioned, they meet to gather only for mischief'. (T. Sikes), *An Humble Remonstrance to the Bishop of London* (1806); see copy in Bodleian Library, Oxford (133 e 723 (1)) for a manuscript account of a meeting between Sikes and Bishop Porteus on the B.F.B.S., where Sikes expressed his horror at the growth of Dissent and of the Society.

[27] Marshall, 'Theology of Church and State', p. 324; Churton, *Memoir of Joshua Watson*, vol. i, p. 58.

[28] Marshall, 'Theology of Church and State', pp. 500–8.

not surprisingly, the major ambition of the Hackney leaders, to revive Anglican theology, fell victim to their obsessive defence of the institutional *status quo*. The contemporary Anglican Church was a federation of parishes and dioceses. Nepotism, pluralism and absenteeism were deadly plagues of the establishment, which the Hackney leaders went to extreme lengths to defend. These typical *ancien régime* features were clearly among the chief factors which made theological proficiency inferior to wealth and connection, when promotion was concerned. A bishop or the owner of a patronage, appointing his son or nephew to a living, cared but little for the actual theological ideas, or lack of them, demonstrated by the relatives they chose to appoint.[29]

Furthermore, the awareness of their relative isolation on theological and philosophical grounds (as Hutchinsonians), made the Hackney leaders less severe than expected in judging theological differences, albeit only within High Church circles. The chief criterion for alliance was the stand taken by the various theological factions on specifically political grounds. Thus, Marsh's theology could well be dangerous, but his marked and outspoken denunciation of the Cambridge Evangelicals and the British and Foreign Bible Society made him a good ally in the eyes of the Hackney friends. It was possible for Hutchinsonians of the Hackney Phalanx to respect such fierce theological opponents as Bishop Horsley (1733–1806) since the chief goal of their activities was the defence of the *status quo* in Church and State.

The accident of birth placed Baden Powell at the centre of an interesting and original movement pursuing cultural and political activities of great relevance to the fortunes of the Anglican Church in contemporary Britain. The familiar intercourse with men fully aware of the complex relationship between cultural and political developments alerted him to the necessity of relating social and political action to sophisticated intellectual standpoints. The conservative and indeed reactionary instincts of his relatives had positive connotations of great formative significance to the young Baden Powell. From his early years at Hackney, he learned that the movements of the enemy had to be carefully watched. The time of King and Church mobs was over. It

<hr>

[29] J. Wade, in his extremely successful *Black Book* (1820, 1832 edn.), p. 21, reported that Bishop Hobart of New York was shocked by the number of livings for sale listed in contemporary newspapers. A safer authority, J. Hunt, in a paper published in the *Contemporary Review* of 1870 (reprinted in *Contemporary Essays*, 1873, p. 13) bitterly complained that 'the traffic in Church livings has not ceased'. On Church patronage and 'the sale of souls', see M. J. D. Roberts, 'Private patronage and the Church of England, 1800–1900', *Journal of Ecclesiastical History*, 32 (1981), 199–223: in 1821, out of 10,693 benefits, 6,619 had private patrons. Of the irrelevance of theological training and private theological opinion for obtaining the required testimonials from the Bishops, see Bullock, *History of the Training for the Ministry*, p. 73. The consequence of structural malpractice on theological learning and doctrinal cohesion within the Anglican Church is a point often overlooked. Notwithstanding the inflationist use of the term 'orthodox Anglican theology' by historians and nineteenth-century polemicists, it is clear that it is impossible to provide a clear-cut definition of the expression for most of the nineteenth century. See the excellent discussion of this point in Ellis, *Seven against Christ*, pp. 121, 146, 150, 151.

was increasingly counterproductive to ignore the theological and intellectual liveliness of Dissenters, Unitarians and radicals. The organizational structure of the Anglican Church left the expanding urban areas a vacuum which was being filled by all sorts of social and religious movements often decidedly opposed to the Anglican Church and the unreformed Parliament.

Baden Powell's relatives devoted all their efforts to counteracting the pressure from below. Mass popular education on Church principles and the building of new churches were measures providing defence against the threat of number. Yet, the threat of ideas had few valid opponents within the Anglican Church. Thus Baden Powell was sent to Oriel, the rising college in Oxford, where a group of dons were making a name for themselves, on account of their determination to meet the adversaries of the Church on theological, philosophical and scientific grounds. It was his relatives' hope that in providing young Baden Powell with the best education available, they would help breed a generation of High Churchmen capable of giving intellectual prestige to the Anglican Church.

How it could happen that the ultra-conservative Hackney leaders sent one of their sons and pupils to a college made famous by the Oxford Movement leaders and their historians as the hotbed of 'daring liberalism' is a question which will force a deep re-examination of long established views of political and ideological allegiances in early nineteenth-century Britain. It is appropriate firstly to provide a detailed examination of Baden Powell's early contributions to the *British Critic* and to the *Christian Remembrancer* and of his first major work, *Rational Religion Examined* (1826). A consideration of the epistemological and theological issues approached by Baden Powell, the Hackney protégé and pupil of the Oriel Noetics, as the Oriel dons were named, will provide material for reassessing interesting developments in Oxford intellectual life during the 1820s and the early 1830s. Traditional and recent reconstructions of intellectual life in early and mid-Victorian England have customarily taken the years of the Reform Bill debate, of the birth of the Oxford Movement and of the writing of John Stuart Mill's *System of Logic* as the starting point for their interpretation of theological, philosophical and scientific debates. The investigation of the tenets put forward by Baden Powell and his allies during the 1820s and the early 1830s will open up new interpretative perspectives on this crucial period in the history of modern England.

2

Baden Powell's early theological papers

A series of entries in Baden Powell's manuscript journal covering the years between 1823 and 1826 help in establishing the authorship of reviews on theological subjects Baden Powell contributed to the *British Critic* and the *Christian Remembrancer*.[1] In the former magazine Baden Powell published articles on Van Mildert's edition of Daniel Waterland's works, on John Davison's (1777–1834) *Discourses on Prophecy* and on John Davies's *Inquiry into the Limits of Reason in the Investigation of Divine Truth*. All these reviews appeared in 1824. During the closing months of 1824, and in early 1825, the magazine underwent a period of prolonged crisis. Publication was suspended until January 1827, when the third series of the *British Critic* appeared.

During the closure Baden Powell sent his contributions to the *Christian Remembrancer*, a journal edited at the time by Renn Dickson Hampden (1790–1864), later the controversial Professor of Divinity at Oxford. Hampden was a cousin of the economist Nassau William Senior (1790–1864) and a lifelong friend of Richard Whately (1787–1863). In 1814 Hampden was elected Fellow of Oriel College. The circle of his intimates included Joseph Blanco White (1775–1841), the Spanish ex-Catholic priest, Philip Nicholas Shuttleworth (1782–1842), the Whig president of New College, Philip Bury (1772–1863) and John Shute Duncan. Through his friendship with Whately, William Bishop and Edward Copleston (1776–1849), Hampden was a frequent visitor to the Oriel common room, even after resigning his fellowship following marriage. His family, like Senior's, was linked to West Indian landed and commercial interests. It is worth mentioning that the *Christian Remembrancer*, the High Church journal edited by Hampden from 1825 to 1826, was established with strong financial support from West Indian merchants.[2]

Baden Powell was well acquainted with Hampden. Apart from the obvious Oriel connection, he probably met Hampden when the latter served as a

---

[1] Baden Powell Papers, Baden Powell Manuscript Journal 1816–60, henceforth B.P.J. See bibliography for the list of papers Baden Powell contributed to the *British Critic* and the *Christian Remembrancer*.

[2] H. Hampden, *Some Memorials of Renn Dickson Hampden* (1871); S. Leon Levy, *Nassau W. Senior* (1970), p. 56; Yule, 'The impact of science', p. 85; Tuckwell, *Pre-Tractarian Oxford*, pp. 128–64.

Curate to H. H. Norris. The personal links between the Oxford 'liberal' most hated by the Tractarians and by the *British Critic* reviewers of the early 1830s, and the ultra-High Church Hackney leaders need some explanation. Thomas Mozley, the highly partisan chronicler of the Oxford Movement, felt the need to justify this embarrassing connection, and briefly commented that Hampden's curacy at Hackney simply indicated the occasional 'strange mishaps' of the old men of the Phalanx.[3] The relationship between Hampden and the Hackney leaders was far from being the result of mere 'mishaps', but revealed instead the complexity of High Church alignments in the 1820s. The analysis of Baden Powell's early theological works will provide material towards identifying crucial features of High Church theology and politics in the early 1820s.

Between 1825 and 1826 Baden Powell contributed seven papers to the *Christian Remembrancer*. These essays are of considerable importance, since they contained the first hints of a parting of the ways between the author and his Hackney relatives, as well as between the Oriel Noetics and the traditional High Church party. However, as we shall argue below, it is revealing that Baden Powell was sincerely convinced that his treatment of the question at issue – the theological foundation for the observance of the sabbath – in no way contradicted the teaching of Van Mildert and of other theological representatives of the Hackney Phalanx.

Baden Powell believed that his solution of the sabbath question represented a perfectly coherent development of Oriel and Hackney Christian apologetic. Furthermore, it is also to be emphasized that the tone of his three contributions to the *British Critic* unambiguously expressed his conviction that Hackney and Oriel were two expressions of the same effort to restore Anglican intellectual and spiritual supremacy in British society. Thus, he welcomed with equal enthusiasm the edition of Waterland's works by Van Mildert and Davison's essay. It is useful to recollect that Van Mildert was, and is, persistently represented as the major interpreter of High Church 'orthodoxy', whereas the latter has been credited with being a central figure in the 'unorthodox' Noetic group.[4]

Davison's *Discourses on Prophecy* and Baden Powell's review of this work, provide the starting point for a first glance at theological concerns and the cultural priorities within High Church circles in the early nineteenth century. As is well known, the French Revolution and the European wars led to a renewed interest in prophetic literature. Millenarian hopes characterized working-class culture; millenarian fears equally appealed to High Church prelates and the clergy in general. The kind of prophetic exercise favoured

3 T. Mozley, *Reminiscences Chiefly of Oriel College*, 2 vols. (1882), vol. i, p. 339.
4 (Baden Powell), 'Works of the Rev. Daniel Waterland', *B.C.*, 21 (1824), 624–38; (*idem*), 'Davison's *Discourses on Prophecy*', *B.C.*, 22 (1824), 368–89. R. Soloway, *Prelates and People* (1969), pp. 41, 90. W. H. Mackean, *The Eucharist Doctrine of the Oxford Movement* (1933), p. 15.

by the Hackney group was related to the complex rules of Hutchinsonian scriptural exegesis. This had survived well into the nineteenth century thanks to the efforts of churchmen, laymen and naturalists linked to the Hackney families. William Kirby, a friend of Jones and Watson whose entomological works were read and admired by generations of British naturalists, was a keen student of scriptural prophecies and millenarian chronology.[5]

Several scholars active in the 1790s and early 1800s applied a well-established prophetic tradition of millenarian computation in order to come to terms with the eschatological significance and import of the French Revolution and of Napoleon's dominion over Europe. Bishop Horsley, a figure of great authority with the Hackney friends despite his anti-Hutchinsonianism, spent the last years of his life in prophetic lucubrations. His catastrophic forecasts probably convinced him that the best thing to do was to spend the few years still available enjoying the full comforts of civilization, to the discomfort of his ruined heirs. Baden Powell senior himself had been enlisted to gather information confirming Horsley's and Kirby's prophetic hypothesis that Bonaparte, the leading candidate for Antichrist, was planning to restore the Jewish kingdom in Palestine: a sign widely regarded as the announcement of the millennium.[6]

The concern with the prophetic interpretation of European and English political events did not vanish with the defeat of Napoleon and revolutionary France. It survived well into the 1820s, though strict millenarianism was progressively abandoned within High Church circles. The *British Critic* editors gave ample space to reviews of prophetic commentaries. However, the tone of many articles grew increasingly sceptical regarding unguardedly detailed predictions. The concern with prophecies also had intellectual connotations wider than the popular hopes for a millenarian emancipation or the social anxiety of the rich and the powerful. Recent commentators on prophetic literature in the early nineteenth century have failed to mention that the apologetic appreciation of prophecy loomed large in the long tradition of the search for evidence for Christianity.[7] The supporters of the Lockean theme of the reasonableness of Christianity argued that the fulfilment of prophecies was one chief assurance of the divine inspiration of the Old and New Testaments.

Prophetic evidence probably enjoyed a status of reliability (to a certain extent) superior to that of miracles. Indeed, the credibility of miracles involved the question of the reliability of the witness, a topic of considerable philosophical

5 J. Freeman, *Life of the Rev. William Kirby* (1852), pp. 165–8, 235–6.
6 *D.N.B.*; S. Horsley, *Biblical Criticism of the First Fourteen Historical Books of the Old Testament*, 4 vols. (1820); Soloway, *Prelates and People*, pp. 39–41; J. Freeman, *Life of Kirby*, pp. 238–41. On the tradition of prophetical exegesis in Britain see C. Webster, *The Great Instauration* (1975).
7 W. H. Oliver, *Prophets and millennialists* (1978); J. F. C. Harrison, *The Second Coming: popular millenarianism* (1979); D. M. Valenze 'Prophecy and popular literature in Eighteenth-Century England', *Journal of Ecclesiastical History*, 29 (1978), 75–92.

debate in the closing decades of the eighteenth century. Prophecies could claim history and historically ascertained facts as their witness. The early Noetics made ample use of the evidential argument. They stressed that the Lockean tradition was a safe *via media* between what was regarded as the fanaticism of Dissenters and the daring rationalism of the Unitarians. The brand of prophetic inquiry advocated by the Hackney Phalanx was probably less sensitive to the result of the emphasis on prophecy as evidence for Christianity pointed out by Copleston, Whately and Davison. Yet the Hackney leaders themselves, together with wider sectors of the High Church party, had many reasons to welcome Davison's learned *Discourses on Prophecy*.

Davison's work was viewed as a successful attempt at regaining the intellectual superiority of traditional High Church Christian apologetics and at vindicating the study of prophecy among the learned. The extravagant popular millenarianism, and implicitly the indulgence in millenarian exercises by leaders of the Church, represented, according to Davison, a perversion of the actual import and value of scriptural prophecies. Davison's treatise represented a significant step towards abandoning prophecies as instruments for the analysis of the contemporary world within High Church circles and the Hackney Phalanx in particular. Kirby himself, after devoting long years to unravelling prophetic riddles, eventually chose to keep to himself the result of his inquiries.

The Hackney leaders were well informed of Davison's work, and of developments within prophetical literature. There is biographical evidence suggesting that from the early 1810s Van Mildert, the theological spokesman of the Hackney Phalanx and from 1814 Regius Professor of Divinity at Oxford, represented a channel of communication between Copleston, Whately and Davison – the rising generation of High Church intellectuals – and the Hackney men. The very fact that the *British Critic* published a very favourable review of Davison's work, written by Baden Powell, the young Oxford scholar of the Phalanx, clearly implied approval of the *Discourses on Prophecy*.

Davison, the leading scholar of the early Noetic group, left the Oriel common room in 1817 and lived in relative isolation. Yet, like Copleston and Whately, he was active in discussing political and social issues. He took part in the 1819 debates on the reform of the Poor Laws and published a dialogue meant to provide a suitable antidote to the inroads made by radical culture among artisans. The crowning achievement of his scholarly career was the treatise Baden Powell reviewed. Davison's *Discourses*, severed from the background of the 1820 debates, have been almost totally neglected by historians writing on the Oxford Movement.[8] Instead of entering the field of prophetic speculation concerning the future of English or European society, Davison submitted the whole body of Old Testament prophecies to a critical analysis.

[8]   J. Davison, *Remains and Occasional publications of the late Rev. John Davison* (1840), *Considerations on the Poor Laws* (1817), and *Discourses on Prophecy* (1824); J. R. Poynter, *Society and Pauperism* (1969), pp. 233–4.

The Lockean theme of the reasonableness of Christianity was coupled with the Butlerian didactic insight that there were as many mysteries and difficulties in human affairs and knowledge as in the revealed word. Thus, it was not surprising that commentators often found it difficult to explain prophetic passages. Indeed, this very difficulty reinforced the conviction that the scriptures contained much matter above the capabilities of the human understanding. The acknowledgement that there were prophecies unfulfilled, did not mean that Davison was convinced that the prophetic evidential argument was a weak one. He stressed that the fulfilment of the great majority of the scriptural prophecies decidedly proved the divine inspiration of the Bible. Davison was not particularly concerned with the precise chronological accuracy of prophetic predictions. His design was to emphasize the 'spiritual' and moral features of prophecies. He argued that at the time of the Jewish dispensation, enforced by the Mosaic law, the prophetic writings prefigured the spiritual dispensation to be delivered by Christ. According to Davison, prophets pointed the way towards a spiritual, individual religion, markedly different from the secular one sanctioned by the Jewish law.

This interpretation of the role of prophetic writings derived from Davison's reflection upon the progressive nature of revelation. He argued that the Old Testament contained the history of the Jews from the harshness of the law – indispensable for ruling primitive societies – to the spiritual liberty of the Gospel.[9] Bishop Stillingfleet, Baden Powell remarked, had already pointed out the intermediate place occupied by prophets between the Mosaic law and the Gospel. Davison was, however, the first nineteenth-century High Church commentator who put forward a fully developed theory of the progressive character of revelation. The scriptural emphasis on the observance of rituals gradually gave way to the emphasis on the spiritual, inward acceptance of revealed truth. As Baden Powell recapitulated, 'the fullest prophetic discoveries of Christ and his spiritual Kingdom were made concurrent with the decline and fall of the temporal kingdom of Israel... when the first dispensation began to be shaken, the objects and promises of the second began as it were to be substituted in its place.'[10]

The concept of a radical differentiation between the Old and the New Testament was to play a considerable role in Baden Powell's intellectual development. It allowed him to define every passage or doctrine of the Old Testament narrative which appeared to contradict modern ethics, philosophy, or natural knowledge, as features of revelation necessarily adapted to primitive

---

[9] Davison, *Discourses on Prophecy*, pp. 54, 302, 381.

[10] (Baden Powell), 'Davison's Discourses', p. 383. Davison's work was held in high esteem by Samuel T. Coleridge, Thomas Arnold and John H. Newman. As late as 1891, in his *Contributions chiefly to the Early History of Cardinal Newman*, Francis Newman remembered (pp. 128–9) the impression made upon him by the *Discourses*. See also F. W. Macran, *English Apologetic Theology* (1905), p. 84, and E. L. Williamson, *The Liberalism of Thomas Arnold* (1964), p. 36.

social conditions and beliefs. Thus, according to Baden Powell, those who defended uncritical literal adherence to the letter of the Old Testament deeply misunderstood the different functions of the two dispensations. They were guilty of Judaizing tendencies, since they rejected the spiritual religion of Christ.

However, during the 1820s Baden Powell had not yet developed all the conclusions he was ultimately to derive from Davison's remarks on the progressive character of revelation. In his review of John Davies's *Inquiries into the Limits of Reason in the Investigation of Divine Truth*, Baden Powell insisted that the solidity of the evidence provided by miracles and prophecies compelled the rational Christian, and indeed all rational beings, to take the scriptures at their face value and to endorse the theory of the plenary inspiration of the Bible. As we shall argue below, Baden Powell was already trying to keep one door open in order to accommodate science with revelation. He therefore joined the chorus of commentators maintaining that the scriptures were not designed to teach philosophy or natural science, but the way to salvation. It is however to be emphasized that this view was put forward with extreme caution. No one within Church circles, Baden Powell included, insinuated or believed that there was any fundamental discrepancy between the Old Testament and modern natural sciences.

In later years, Baden Powell became convinced that such a discrepancy existed. This conclusion led him to widen the gap between the Old and the New Testament, thereby enlarging the scope of Davison's original theory. The interesting point is that Baden Powell was unaware of the analogous conclusions reached by German philosophers and theologians. Davison's remarks on the progressive nature of the Christian dispensation originated from the English exegetical tradition, as Baden Powell himself pointed out. In later years, when the German higher criticism became known in Britain, and Baden Powell became acquainted – albeit often at second hand – with German theology, he had no difficulty in endorsing the view of the progressive enlightenment of the human race from the obscurity of paganism to the philosophical disclosures of modern times.[11]

Baden Powell's review of John Davies's work on the relationship between reason and religion has been mentioned above. There is no need at this stage to enter into a detailed examination of the apologetic scheme put forward by Davies and endorsed by Baden Powell. Indeed, the theme of the reasonableness of Christianity was fully developed in his *Rational Religion Examined* (1826), a work I shall later consider in some detail. I need only observe here that Davies's book represents a further confirmation of the popularity of the Locke-Butler apologetic tradition in contemporary High Church circles.

---

[11] O. Pfleiderer, *The Development of Theology in Germany Since Kant and its Progress in Great Britain Since 1825* (1890). On Baden Powell's relationship with German theology, see below, and ch. 12.

It is clear that the Oxford Noetics and the young Baden Powell had more
llies than hitherto supposed or acknowledged. It would be more correct to
ay that the 'reasonableness of Christianity' theme was widely discussed and
pheld by several sections of the Church of England. The Locke-Butler
radition was seen as a viable approach to an intellectually aggressive Christian
pologetic, powerful enough to scorn Unitarian pretences at the monopoly of
ational and philosophical views on religious matters. Davies's pedantic and
lidactic treatise – a good commonplace dissertation, Baden Powell called it –
eceived a prize from the Society for the Promotion of Christian Knowledge
nd Church Union of the Diocese of St David's.

The Bishop of St David's, Thomas Burgess, was a staunch High Churchman
nd a vigorous opponent of the Unitarian aggression. He was a friend of
Charles Daubeny and a frequent visitor at Hackney. Needless to say, he was
he inspirer and leader of the diocesan S.P.C.K., and approved of Davies's
lissertation. Thus, once again the apologetic strategy privileged by the Noetics
ound supporters in ultra-conservative sectors of the High Church. Baden
Powell, still regarded as a member of the Hackney Phalanx, pointed out that
he true 'rational religion' approach formulated by the Reverend Davies was
apable of providing effective checks against 'that sort of religion which makes
o great pretensions to the exclusive title of a rational faith'. Contemporary
eaders had no difficulty in understanding that the Unitarians were the target
f Baden Powell's ironic remark.[12]

Baden Powell himself took an active part in the anti-Unitarian campaign.
This was hardly surprising, in view of the deep anxiety the Unitarian revival
rovoked amongst his Hackney relatives and within High Church circles. As
ointed out when discussing the general features of the *British Critic*'s and
Christian Remembrancer's editorial policies in the 1810s and the 1820s, Unitar-
ans were a constant target of reviewers and commentators contributing to
he two papers. It could be argued that the success of the early Noetic
heological and philosophical standpoint was partly due to the ability the group
howed in counteracting Unitarian philosophical arguments. Baden Powell
liscussed the cultural dimension of the Unitarian threat in a series of papers
n theological subjects he contributed to the *Christian Remembrancer*. The
ccasion for his three 'Letters to the Editor' was provided by the Unitarian
laim that Sir Isaac Newton and John Locke advocated principles of theological
nquiry and doctrine not dissimilar from those defended by contemporary
British Unitarians.

The questionable features in Newton's and Locke's theological standpoint
ould be easily explained by referring to the culture of their times; moreover,
Baden Powell argued, the tenor of all their writings contradicted the false
ationalism advocated by the Unitarians. Both thinkers actually insisted on

² J. S. Harford, *The Life of Thomas Burgess* (1840), pp. 227, 293, 353, 473; (Baden Powell),
'Davies's Inquiry', p. 457.

the reasonableness of acknowledging mysteries in revelation. The classic fundamental assumption of Socinians, Baden Powell pointed out, was that the human
mind, 'enlightened by science in physical things, must be guided by analogy
and congruity, and depend upon its own resources in the search after religious
truth'. The Unitarian confidence in the powers of the human mind was not
shared by those who spent years in scientific inquiries. The serious and
dedicated pursuit of science induced habits of rigorous and cautious reasoning
which disproved the rash conclusions of Unitarian and Socinian philosophers.[1]

The question of the role of rational sophistication and philosophy in religious
inquiries was different from the question of the misapplication of rational
tools in religious debates and literature. Thus, Baden Powell took an interesting
position in the debate on Unitarianism and German theology which characterized the middle 1820s. Indeed, the denunciation of the fallacies of
Unitarianism loomed large in his review of Rose's *Discourses* on German
theology and theological rationalism. In the late 1820s, Rose, the Christian
Advocate at Cambridge, became acquainted with the Hackney Phalanx leaders.
The more Van Mildert retired from scholarly pursuits – his edition of Waterland's works was his last literary effort – the more Rose took a leading role
in the Hackney propaganda effort.[14]

Baden Powell was certainly acquainted with Rose and probably discussed
theological and philosophical matters with him. There was undoubtedly much
in Rose's *Discourses* to elicit his approval. He quoted at great length Rose's
remarks on the fundamental difference between scientific and theological
inquiries, a theme Richard Whately dwelt upon in similar terms. No new
discovery was to be expected from scriptural exegesis. Rose argued that it
was methodologically wrong to maintain that 'the theologian must *mine* for
the long hidden treasure of truth, and like the naturalist must make new
discoveries, and modify his beliefs accordingly'. Baden Powell was in entire
agreement with Rose's theoretical approach to contemporary theological debates.
He also praised Rose's denunciation of current trends in German theology,
in particular their critique of miracles.[15]

Baden Powell knew very little of German theology, and in this he was no
exception in early nineteenth-century England. He never made reference to

[13] (Baden Powell), 'Philosophy and Socinianism', *C.R.*, 8 (1826), 106; see also *C.R.*, 7 (1825)
      566–75, and 7 (1825), 701–12; Yule, 'The impact of science', pp. 82–5.
[14] Christopher Wordsworth, Master of Trinity, acted as intermediary between Rose and the
      Hackney Phalanx. He supported Rose against Hare in the 1825 competition for the chair of
      Greek at Cambridge. See Burgon, *Lives of Twelve Good Men* (1888), pp. 62–146, and
      N. M. Distad, *Guessing at Truth* (1979), pp. 50–1. In 1828 Archbishop Howley appointed
      Rose his chaplain, at the suggestion of Joshua Watson; the latter also financed the *British
      Magazine*, the quarterly Rose launched in 1832. Rose was a close friend of Bishop Hobart
      of New York, whom he met in Rome, in 1824.
[15] H. J. Rose, *The State of the Protestant Religion in Germany* (1825), pp. 5–6; Churton, *Memoir
      of Joshua Watson*, vol. i, p. 260; R. Whately, *The Use and Abuse of Party Feelings in Matters
      of Religion* (1822), pp. 79–80.

the works of Marsh, nor ever displayed any acquaintance with problems like the canon of the scriptures, or the authorship of Genesis. The reading of Rose's critique of German standpoints on miracles only gave him the occasion for comparing German theology with contemporary British Unitarianism, that is, for launching a new attack against the worst enemies of the Church. He did not deny that Unitarians never questioned the credibility of miracles, but argued that logical consistency might, and indeed would, have led their theology towards this inevitable outcome. Unitarians questioned the doctrine of incarnation and the atonement, though they professed belief in the resurrection of Christ. However, their *a priori* rejection of mysteries in Christianity was seen by Baden Powell as contradicting the belief in any form of miracles. The *via media* Unitarians proposed was therefore untenable.[16]

The review of Rose's *Discourses* represented the point of Baden Powell's strictest adhesion to the Hackney position. His enthusiasm for Rose's unsophisticated critique of German theology provides further insight into the complexity of theological alignments in the 1820s. Baden Powell approved of Rose's work. Whately, the alleged leader of the 'liberal party' within the Anglican Church, deeply disliked German theology and philosophy. On the other hand, Pusey, in later years the leader of the Anglo-Catholic movement, left Britain for Germany to see for himself how much truth there was in Rose's account of German theological studies. He came back convinced that the Christian Advocate had done little justice to theological inquiries carried on in the German universities.[17]

It is fair to point out that Rose's design was not to provide a critical and scholarly account of recent developments in German theology, but to emphasize the need for Church discipline against excessive freedom of inquiry. His aim was to define in a restrictive way the right of private judgement, a factor of notorious centrality in Protestant theology, by pointing out the excesses to which the principle had been carried. Furthermore, Rose wanted to stop the penetration of German theology at Cambridge, where Connop Thirlwall (1797–1875), Augustus William (1792–1834) and Julius Charles Hare (1789–1855) were looking with increasing sympathy to German philosophy and theology. Not wishing publicly to censure his friends, Rose chose to criticize German theology in general.[18]

---

[16] (Baden Powell), 'State of Protestant Religion in Germany', *C.R.*, 8 (1826), 65–81.

[17] E. B. Pusey, *An Historical Enquiry into the Probable Causes of the Rationalist Character Lately Predominant in the Theology of Germany* (1828); it should be pointed out that Pusey himself limited his defence of German theology to the literal translation of long passages from the lectures of his friend and teacher Friedrich August Tholuck (1799–1877). In the second edition of his work, Rose accused Pusey of plagiarism: see also (Anon.), *B.C.*, 6 (1829), 469–85. D. W. Forrester, 'The intellectual development of E. B. Pusey, 1800–1850' (D.Phil. thesis, Oxford University, 1967).

[18] In the preface to the first edition of his work, Rose also attacked Arnold's defence of Niebuhr; see also A. P. Stanley, *Life of Arnold* (1890 edn.), p. 45, letter dated 15 October 1825: 'it does grieve me to find persons of his standing quarrelling with their friends when there are

Baden Powell did not doubt the accuracy of Rose's report. In his review he borrowed Rose's arguments against German rationalistic theology as ammunition for his own anti-Unitarian campaign. Yet, Baden Powell's whole-hearted support for Rose's *Discourses* was limited to the approval of the polemical side of the Christian Advocate's denunciation of modern rationalism. Baden Powell shared Rose's preoccupation with the inroads 'the rationalistic system' was making in contemporary culture, but he was not convinced that the right answer to this phenomenon was to stress the need for Church authority. On the contrary, he thought it imperative to preserve 'the purity in doctrine' by carefully distinguishing divine revelation from human opinion, church formularies and rituals, which were justifiable only on traditional grounds. Clearly, Baden Powell was convinced that his reasonableness-of-Christianity approach, based on the evidential value of miracles and prophecies, was a sufficient guarantee of the credibility of the scriptures.

Scriptural literalism and religion could both be defended by deploying the sophisticated epistemological and logical tools elaborated by Dugald Stewart or Copleston, rather than by appealing to Church authority. If this was the case, the insistence on Church authority was indeed tending to weaken the position of Christianity in a time dominated by scientific and philosophical advance. Thus, he set out to give a concrete instance of what he regarded as the correct procedure to adopt against critics and enemies. The application of his theological approach to specific doctrinal or liturgical issues led Baden Powell into difficulties with the more conservative sectors of the High Church and with his Hackney relatives.

Richard Lloyd (d.1834), the pluralist Rector of Midhurst, Sussex, under whom Baden Powell served as curate, published in 1825 a treatise on preaching. Lloyd lamented the lack of observance of the sabbath. He argued that the sabbath prescription emanated from divine authority, and should have been enforced with greater efficiency by Church and State. Baden Powell agreed that the breaking of sabbath regulations had reached worrying dimensions. Yet, he was also convinced that Lloyd's approach to the question represented a good instance of the habit of defending Christian practices by claiming for them 'an authority which they really do not possess'. The habit of overstating one's own reasons was conducive to much harm, especially at a period when Socinians were asking for the suppression of the sabbath regulation, on the score that no scriptural authority, they argued, justified the transition from

more than enough of enemies in the world for every Christian to strive against!'. J. J. Perowne and L. Stokes, *Letters, Literary and Theological, of Connop Thirlwall* (1881), pp. 52–90. Trinity College, Cambridge, William Whewell Papers, correspondence with H. J. Rose and with Hare. It should be noted that Whewell kept an ambiguous middle ground between the two friends, letting Hare believe that he shared his views of German theology, but siding with Rose on conservative ecclesiastical and university policies. It is also important to emphasize that representatives of the so-called 'Cambridge network' avoided public discussion of their theological and philosophical standpoints and differences: a fact often and wrongly interpreted as indication of identity of views. Rose had learned German during evening sessions with Whewell and Thirlwall, under the guidance of Hare.

the Jewish sacred day to the Christian Sunday. On the opposite side of the theological spectrum, the 'fanatics', a name Baden Powell employed to describe Evangelicals, Methodists, and Dissenters of various denominations, were increasingly driving towards 'puritanical moroseness' in their obsession with the sabbath. They were convinced that the rules of the Jewish sabbath fully applied to the Christian Sunday.[19]

It was therefore urgent to establish the authority of the sabbath prescription on sound and unequivocal grounds. Baden Powell did, however, fail to specify the grounds for sabbath rules. Indeed, his paragraph only stressed the need for a careful apologetic strategy to counteract sophisticated adversaries like Thomas Belsham or Unitarian intellectuals in general. Baden Powell otherwise felt it necessary only to state that 'the authority of the Church ... is fully sufficient to enforce' the observance of the Christian Sunday regulations. However, contemporary readers and High Churchmen in particular perceived that he denied the divine institution of the Christian Sunday, without giving the indispensable justification for his assertion. Baden Powell's methodological remark that 'in the present age, when sober religion is assailed on all sides' it was extremely dangerous 'to *assert* as scripture what is, in truth, *not scripture*', failed to satisfy convinced sabbatarians. Baden Powell needed to explain his position.[20]

In a later contribution he acknowledged that 'we have of late been so unfortunate as to fall under the censure of some of our correspondents in a more than ordinary degree'. From the outset of his thorough discussion of defences of the sabbath, Baden Powell reassured the readers that his goal was to strengthen the Christian faith, by warning against self-defeating arguments often employed to defend crucial religious doctrines. It is noteworthy that the tone of Baden Powell's paper was anything but apologetic. His criticism of traditional sabbatarianism betokened a mood of self-confidence. He defiantly applied the Noetic intellectual approach to heap scorn on his evangelical and High Church critics.

The interpretation by Copleston and Whately of John Locke's and Stewart's philosophy provided the justification for Baden Powell's conclusion that strict sabbatarianism failed to comply with elementary rules of correct reasoning. Sabbatarians neglected 'the very necessary step of setting out with a definition of the terms employed, and equally essential rule of keeping to that definition throughout'. Sabbatarians failed to pay attention to the context in which the scripture passages referring to the sabbath occurred. They overlooked the fundamental difference between the Jewish and the Christian dispensations.[21]

---

[19] R. Lloyd, *Inquiry into Two Important Questions* (1825), p. 126; (Baden Powell), 'Lloyd on Preaching', *C.R.*, 7 (1825), 635–6.

[20] (Baden Powell), 'Lloyd on Preaching', *C.R.*, 7 (1825), 636.

[21] (Baden Powell), 'The Christian sabbath', *C.R.*, 8 (1826), 192–6. For a discussion of Stewart's influence at Oxford, see below, ch. 3. It is important to stress that High Churchmen and the Oriel dons in particular deeply appreciated the apologetic potential of the epistemological critique of modern science put forward by the Scottish philosopher.

Applying for the first time in his own works Davison's theory of the progressive nature of revelation, Baden Powell pointed out that the Christian dispensation superseded the Mosaic law, thereby abolishing the civil enforcement of religious practices. It was incumbent upon the Christian apologist to restore the purity of Christ's teaching by clearing away 'those incrustations which are formed around it, as it were, from alluvial depositions of the antiquated system of Judaism'. Thus, amateurish dialectic procedures and ignorance of biblical exegesis made sabbatarians forget the essential distinction between 'a positive divine institution' – the Jewish sabbath – and a 'moral commandment' – the prescription of keeping one day in the week for religious practices. Sabbatarians were unwarranted in applying the scriptural ordinance relating to the Jewish sabbath to the apostolic and early Christian custom of setting apart Sunday, the first day of the Jewish week and the day of Christ's resurrection, for religious ceremonials.[22]

Contrary to his statement in the April contribution to the *Christian Remembrancer*, Baden Powell gave no prominence to the concept of Church authority. Obedience to the sabbath prescription, as to other precepts of the Mosaic decalogue, was due on account of their 'substance and spiritual force, and not in all their circumstantial particularity'. Only when defending himself from the charge of indirectly endorsing the infringement of the sabbath law, he mentioned 'the indispensable *obligation*, under which all members of the Christian Church lie, of observing with religious exactness the institutions of that Church'. Evidence below suggests that sabbatarians failed to appreciate Baden Powell's attempt at stating the 'abstract principle' on which the sabbath prescription rested.[23]

Copleston had been the first member of the Oriel community who criticized the common view that the authority of the sabbath rested on a definite divine prescription. Copleston's remarks appeared in his review of William Buckland's (1784–1856) *Reliquiae Diluvianae* (1823), where he criticized those who adopted a literal interpretation of the days of creation, because they felt that an allegorical interpretation would have shaken the scriptural foundation of the sabbath. Copleston argued that Christians were in fact breaking the Old Testament law, since they rested on the first day of the week, and not on the day originally chosen by God to contemplate his creative effort. Copleston, as Baden Powell was to do three years later, gave no further detail of his view on the sabbath. He simply stated that the authority of the Sunday prescription rested on a traditional rule which had 'been allowed gradually to supersede a positive command'.[24]

---

22 (Baden Powell), 'The Christian sabbath', *C.R.*, 8 (1826), 196.
23 'The Christian sabbath', pp. 204–7.
24 (E. Copleston), 'Buckland – *Reliquiae Diluvianae*', *Q.R.*, 29 (1823), p. 164. Note that Baden Powell had employed a geological metaphor, when discussing current misconceptions on the sabbath, as if he was referring to Copleston's review of Buckland.

I have found as yet no evidence of negative reaction to Copleston's remarks. However, when Copleston canvassed to be appointed Bishop of Oxford, it was reported that his theology had given occasion of suspicion of heterodoxy.[25] The fact that the authorship of the paper on Buckland was certainly known in literary and Church circles would provide support for the hypothesis that it was the denial of the scriptural foundation of the Christian Sunday which displeased conservative High Churchmen, let alone the Evangelicals. Three years later Baden Powell was attacked for maintaining analogous views. Indeed, it is fair to argue that Baden Powell was influenced by Copleston. He obviously did not learn to question the common view on the divine authority of the sabbath observance from his vicar Richard Lloyd, or from his Hackney relatives.

A close analysis of Baden Powell's two papers reveals the extent of his debt to Copleston. Moreover, Copleston had a long-standing interest in the sabbath question. A passage in Copleston's diary suggests that the Provost of Oriel was evaluating the grounds of authority of the sabbath prescription from the early 1810s. Thus, the fact that Baden Powell had access to the *Quarterly Review* paper on Buckland – an author he admired – as well as to the conversation of the Provost of Oriel, would substantiate the claim that his self-confident tone derived not only from the consciousness of his philosophical superiority over his adversaries, but also from his awareness that he was relying upon an authoritative precedent.[26]

It is interesting to point out that the interpretation of the sabbath put forward by Baden Powell failed fully to satisfy his teachers, Whately in particular. In 1828, a few months after Copleston's failure to be elevated to the Oxford see, Richard Whately published his essay on the Epistles of St Paul, which contained a long footnote on the sabbath. Copleston was known to hold questionable views on the sabbath, and, according to the suggestion put forward above, his remarks on the Christian Sunday were held against him. Baden Powell, a pupil of the Noetics, caused considerable apprehension by expanding upon Copleston's remarks. Furthermore, the friendship of the editor of the *Christian Remembrancer* with the Oriel philosophers was well known in High Church circles. By printing Baden Powell's first and second paper on the sabbath, Hampden was open to the charge of endorsing the opinion of the contributor. There was sufficient ground to speculate that the Oriel Noetics were anti-sabbatarians, and indeed the charge was later publicized in a letter printed in *John Bull* considered below.[27]

Richard Whately thought it advisable to point out that the Noetic criticism of sabbatarianism was designed to put the sabbath prescription on an unassailable foundation. He also set out to correct some of the conclusions reached

[25] N. Gash, *Mr. Secretary Peel* (1961), p. 408.
[26] W. J. Copleston, *Memoir of Edward Copleston* (1851), p. 77.
[27] *John Bull*, 10 (1830), 141. See also Stanley, *Life of Arnold*, pp. 206–7, on Arnold's formulation of the Noetic standpoint on the Sabbath.

by Baden Powell, though he never mentioned his pupil by name. The latter had stressed apostolic tradition and Church practice as the proper justification for the prescription. He also mentioned Church authority, but without further specification. Whately felt that this was precisely the point which needed to be clarified with the utmost urgency. The observance of the Sunday was of divine origin because Christ had given his Church full authority on matters of ritual and ceremonial. The Sunday prescription enjoyed the highest authority, as emanating from a Church empowered by Christ to regulate the collective observance of God's commandment.

With Copleston and Baden Powell, Whately repeated that no direct scriptural command could be quoted in support of the change from the Jewish sabbath to the Christian Sunday. Understandably, those who objected to Baden Powell's formulation of the Noetic critique of the sabbath failed to be satisfied by Whately's remarks on the foundation of Church authority. The point at issue was not, according to many contemporary churchmen, whether the Church had or had not the power to ordain rituals and ceremonies, but whether the sabbath prescription rested on scriptural authority. It was clear that the Oriel school thought it did not.[28]

The consideration of the debate on the sabbath has brought our analysis of the context of Baden Powell's early theological productions to the late 1820s. The parting of the ways between Hackney and Oriel was partly due to the polemic over the interpretation of the sabbath. Yet, as will become apparent, more dramatic events were responsible for bringing to the forefront theological differences within the High Church party. It will be argued below that theological differences became crucial only as a consequence of serious splits at a political level.

It is indeed interesting that in the short term Baden Powell's interpretation of the sabbath did not produce major tensions with his Hackney relatives and his Oriel teachers. A few weeks after the publication of the second paper on the sabbath, Van Mildert wrote to Baden Powell approving the comments on Locke's and Newton's orthodoxy, and he did not mention the sabbath issue. On 5 December 1826, Edward Copleston wrote to Baden Powell inviting him to stand for the Savilian chair of Geometry. According to a later comment by Baden Powell his standpoint on the sabbath did not satisfy his relatives and teachers, who nevertheless regarded the matter as non-essential and strongly supported his application for the chair.[29]

Baden Powell's early theological papers revealed his sincere commitment to the Hackney cause and indicated his attempt at applying the apologetic tools elaborated by Van Mildert, Copleston, Davison and Whately to contemporary theological debates. It could be argued that he applied the Hackney strategy of fighting the enemy on its own grounds to the philosophical and

[28] R. Whately, *Essays on Some of the Difficulties in the Writings of St. Paul* (1828), pp. 163–8.
[29] B.P.J., February 1826; 5 December 1826.

theological confrontation with the Unitarians. Thus, from the early phases of his intellectual development Baden Powell approached contemporary cultural debates with the sense of realism which characterized the Hackney leaders' approach to the contemporary social and political tensions. Purely repressive measures were ineffective and impracticable, as the various prosecutions against political and theological radicals abundantly proved.

The Hackney leaders opposed the spread of Dissenting and Unitarian religious and educational enterprises by actively promoting appropriate organizational countermoves. Baden Powell felt that the same strategy was effective at the theological and philosophical levels. In this, as it is already clear, he was not original. In the 1820s the attempt at opposing the Unitarian aggression with the help of the reasonableness of Christian tradition represented a move shared by many churchmen, from Van Mildert to Copleston and Whately.

Baden Powell's concern with contemporary cultural events was not limited to the theological dimension. From the early years of his literary career, the consideration of contemporary science played a crucial role in Baden Powell's intellectual upbringing. His reflection on science and its epistemological and educational relevance reflected a further fundamental feature of Baden Powell's interpretation of the Hackney and the Noetic strategy. From his Hackney relatives he learned to pay close attention to the contemporary social and intellectual scene, in order to be ready to counteract any move unfavourable to Christianity and the Anglican Church. From his Noetic teachers he learned how to fight the apologetic battle at the level of highly sophisticated theological and philosophical concepts. Science and the philosophical dimension of scientific research provided crucial elements to Baden Powell's strategy.

3

Baden Powell's reflections on science in the early 1820s

Between 1823 and 1825 Baden Powell published in the *British Critic* ten papers on scientific subjects. Books on zoology, astronomy, scientific biography, transactions of learned societies, magnetism, geology, chemistry, hydrostatics and animal behaviour were in turn scrutinized in his contributions to the magazine. The great majority of Baden Powell's scientific contributions to the *British Critic* were generally concerned with summarizing the contents of the books under review. More relevant to the purpose of the present study were his observations on science, its methods and place in contemporary culture and academic education. The frequent remarks on the epistemological bearing of the scientific research under discussion, or introductory paragraphs of a philosophical drift, revealed interesting elements in his early reflections on science.

Baden Powell's campaign on behalf of the introduction of scientific subjects into the university curriculum is also of great historical interest. As it will be shown in chapter 9, the Oxford debate on the reform of the statutes in which Baden Powell participated during the 1820s was characterized by an insistence on the speculative and philosophical dimensions of scientific pursuits. As is well known, the concept of a liberal, non-professional education dominated the educational policies of both English universities. Scientific pursuits, with the exception of the 'liberal' mathematical disciplines at Cambridge, were thought to be unfitted for undergraduate studies, although it was acknowledged that the gentleman scholar could find it instructive and amusing to take some interest in chemistry or mineralogy.

Baden Powell certainly felt he had to convince reluctant academic authorities that modern natural investigation required high levels of intellectual and philosophical sophistication. His first goal was therefore to dispose of the traditional and popular view that scientific activities were only concerned with mechanical manipulation and aimed at purely practical results. Baden Powell did not deny the relationship between science and *praxis*. Thus, for instance, he acknowledged the importance of Peter Barlow's studies on the influence of the iron parts of ships on nautical compasses. He praised the useful application made possible by Barlow's discovery. In an interesting review of Robert

Woodhouse's *A Treatise on Astronomy*, Baden Powell also mentioned the contribution of astronomical observation to the art of navigation. Yet the passages considering the application of science to practical ends were significantly the ones in which the 'liberal' features of scientific investigation were stressed.

The appreciation of Barlow's practical contribution to oceanic navigation gave occasion for a spirited defence of the speculative theoretical dimensions of the study of magnetism. Baden Powell focused on the second part of Barlow's book, where the scientist put forward his theory of magnetism. He pointed out that the theoretical parts of the work were less important from the practical point of view, but were nevertheless the most interesting, on account of 'the beauty and universality of the analytic formulae deduced, and . . . the profound skilfulness and fertility of invention displayed in the mathematical reasoning'. An emphasis on the aesthetic and intellectual potentialities of the physico-mathematical sciences characterized also the concluding remarks on Barlow's researches. Baden Powell expressed his conviction that, independent of the practical application of Barlow's theories, their elegance recommended them to the 'philosophical student, whose enquiries are stimulated by the intrinsic beauty of scientific truth, rather than by the practical advantages to which it may be made subservient'.[1]

The remarks on the usefulness of astronomy for the art of navigation were significantly qualified by the comment that theoretical astronomy had actually fulfilled its duties towards the art. Historically speaking, the end of the techno-logical utility of astronomical investigations had not meant the end of the science. Indeed, the reverse had been the case. Recent advances in mathe-matical sciences and improved instruments increasingly added to the precision and scope of astronomical observation. Theoretical astronomy in particular, as Laplace's work had recently demonstrated, was immensely helped by the refinement of mathematical methods. Baden Powell did not deny that the development of astronomy would have helped towards the solution of intricate problems in the field of plane and physical astronomy. Philosophical commen-tators, however, agreed that any significant progress in theoretical astronomy was to be evaluated in terms of the intellectual advance it represented. Indeed, 'the utility of every fresh accession to knowledge, as it tends to exalt and improve the mental faculties, must surely be admitted by every reflecting mind'.[2]

Baden Powell tried to convince his academic readers that the utility of astronomical discoveries was intellectual, not practical. If this was the case, then disciplines like astronomy or physics were entitled to a better place and higher consideration within the ideology of liberal education. There was no

---

[1]   (Baden Powell), 'Woodhouse's *Treatise on Astronomy*', *B.C.*, 20 (1823), 155–6; (*idem*), 'Barlow on magnetic attractions', *B.C.*, 19 (1823), 168, 177.
[2]   (Baden Powell), 'Woodhouse's *Treatise*', p. 156.

contradiction, in Baden Powell's eyes, between the pursuits of modern science and the aims of liberal education; the votaries of the latter claimed to be concerned with the general training of the mental faculties, the teachers of the former actually contributed to their development.

One of Baden Powell's most cherished schemes, the adaptation of the academic curriculum to the intellectual priorities of the time, found expression in these early publications. The tone of his remarks, and the tactics he pursued, were significantly different from his later aggressive standpoint on this issue. Forced to abandon any hope of achieving appropriate reform by working from within, during the 1830s Baden Powell supported the proposal of opening the university to Parliamentary inquiry and intervention. In the early 1820s there seemed, however, to be no reason why reform could not be achieved by operating within the institution.

To some extent, Baden Powell was following a policy he learned at Hackney. His relatives had to fight hard to convince their friends and Anglican brethren that mass education could not be opposed but had instead to be directed and supervised. Baden Powell was convinced that scientific knowledge was increasingly becoming a crucial element of the modern world view. It was therefore appropriate that the Anglican universities made a positive effort to gain control of the scientific movement in its most 'philosophical' dimensions. The plan he devised received help from the very animosity displayed by the radical critics of the Established Church.

The attacks launched from various quarters against the lack of educational and specifically scientific contribution made by the English universities to contemporary culture, gave by reaction considerable publicity to the few examples of scientific life within the universities, particularly achievements at Cambridge in mathematics. Baden Powell himself, in his review of *The Life and Remains of the Reverend Daniel Clarke* praised the efforts which led to the establishment of the Cambridge Philosophical Society. The society's activities met the approval of the friends of science throughout Britain, Edinburgh reviewers included. Thus, the insistence on the scientific reliability of the research pursued at Cambridge fulfilled functions wider than the justification of science. It gave occasion for polemical remarks against the 'northern calumniators and ignorant political economists', as Baden Powell put it.[3]

Attacks against the academic reputation of Oxford and Cambridge were becoming a common feature of the activities of a host of reformers and radicals. The *Edinburgh Review*, the successful *Black Book* by the Benthamite John Wade (1788–1875), and the extreme radical publications by Richard Carlile (1790–1843), though differing on many substantial points, agreed in condemning the inactivity of the unreformed religious and educational establishment. As might be expected, the editors of the *British Critic* supported the efforts made

---

3 (Baden Powell), '*Life and Remains of the Rev. E. D. Clarke*', B.C., 22 (1824), 519; (*idem*), 'Hydrostatics, mechanics and dynamics', B.C., 23 (1825), 163.

to defend the honour of the universities and of their scientific record. Typically, Baden Powell's review of physical textbooks published at Cambridge opened with an indignant defence of the universities from the accusation of being 'content to grow old and fat in the errors and prejudices of former ages, and never manifest any of the spirit of improvement so rigorously and continually exerted in all other places and all other institutions, and which form the characteristic boast of modern times'.[4]

Baden Powell argued that the presence of the Whewells, the Peacocks and the Herschels at Cambridge showed that the attacks were unjustified. Yet there were no comparable examples to be quoted on behalf of Oxford. His general defence of the universities turned into a denunciation of the educational and scientific shortcomings at Oxford. Baden Powell compared the vitality of Cambridge with the stagnation prevailing in his university. In past centuries, he pointed out, the Radcliffe Observatory had been made famous by the activities of astronomers like Wallis, Halley and Bradley. In modern times, 'how little, even of their names is known', he sadly commented. Notwithstanding his fame, the present Professor of Astronomy was rarely able to collect a class. When he was fortunate enough to arouse the interest of a few young students, the number of those attending kept falling as mathematics was increasingly required to follow the train of the demonstrations. Thus, Baden Powell concluded, the success of scientific disciplines in modern universities could not be left to the individual efforts of enthusiastic practitioners: 'It is in vain that at the *Observatory* every explanation, encouragement, and invitation is afforded, if there be no corresponding stimulus in the *schools*'.[5]

Baden Powell's insistence on the liberal dimension of science was related to his awareness of the need for deep and substantial reform of the curriculum. Yet it would be wrong to reduce his emphasis on the liberal features of scientific pursuits to merely academic, or politically motivated manoeuvrings. Such a conclusion would prevent a right appreciation of Baden Powell's

---

4 J. Wade, *The Black Book; or, Corruption Unmasked!* (1820); R. Carlile, *An Address to Men of Science* (1821); (Anon.), 'Calumnies against Oxford', *E.R.*, 16 (1810), 158–9; (Baden Powell), 'Hydrostatics', p. 163.

5 (Baden Powell), 'Woodhouse's *Treatise*', p. 145. Baden Powell was clearly limiting his remarks to the state of physico-mathematical disciplines at Oxford. The geological lectures delivered by Buckland, and the ones on chemistry by Charles Daubeny attracted considerable attention. Yet, the audience was almost exclusively composed of dons and visitors. Moreover, at the time there was little prospect of including geology and chemistry in the university curriculum, whereas elements of mathematical and physical knowledge were part of the examination system. This fundamental distinction between disciplines within the curriculum, and the ones which were excluded, is often overlooked in the literature. See for instance Rupke, *The Great Chain of History* (1983). On Buckland's lectures, see J. M. Edmonds and J. A. Douglas, 'William Buckland...and an Oxford Geological Lecture', *Notes and Records of the Royal Society*, 30 (1976), 141–6, and Edmonds, 'The founding of the Oxford readership of geology', 34 (1979), 33–51; on Daubeny's lectures, see D. R. Oldroyd and D. W. Hutchings, 'The chemical lectures at Oxford of Charles Daubeny', *Notes and Records of the Royal Society*, 33 (1979), 217–59.

reflections on the role of modern mathematics in the future prospects of physical investigation. He sincerely believed that the more exciting developments of modern science derived from the investigation of highly speculative questions in contemporary analytics.

In his review of Barlow's book the mathematical excellency of modern physical sciences was recommended to the attention of the philosophical student. Baden Powell described the progress of the inquiry which had led Barlow to propose the somewhat heretical concept of a tangential force at variance with the rectilinear action of orthodox Newtonian forces. The concept of tangential action was proposed by Barlow in order to explain the rotatory effect induced in a magnetized needle by a wire conducting galvanic electricity and placed at an appropriate distance. Barlow's formula, representing the angular variation of the needle's position with respect to the wire, excited Baden Powell's admiration for the power of analytic procedures, which 'in an expression composed of four algebraic terms, can sum up a statement of every possible case, and concentrate in general terms, what it actually requires the three following pages of the volume... to explain, in the detail of ordinary language'.[6]

Baden Powell's appreciation of the theoretical and mathematical features of contemporary physical inquiry derived from his deep admiration for the work of the younger generation of Cambridge mathematicians. We have already mentioned his early contacts with the Cambridge theological and scientific milieu. Hugh James Rose and Christopher Wordsworth (1774–1846) were frequent visitors to the Hackney families and relied on their support for their ascent in the religious and the academic establishment. Wordsworth's appointment to the prestigious position of Master of Trinity College in Cambridge was due to the influence of his Hackney mentors. His obsessive concern for his health forced him slowly to give up active duty, thus favouring the emergence at Trinity of an active group of young mathematicians and naturalists, which maintained the name of the College. Rose, who later in life developed a positive dislike for what he regarded as the pretence of physical and natural sciences to philosophical and cosmological status, in his early days at Cambridge paid amateurish attention to mathematical subjects, though according to Whewell with poor results.[7]

As is well known, mathematical concerns were favoured at Cambridge by the Newtonian tradition. Mathematical proficiency was often the road to academic prestige and church preferment. Baden Powell probably enjoyed many opportunities of gaining first-hand knowledge of the new trends developing in Cambridge scientific studies, particularly in mathematics. It should also be mentioned that Rose was a close friend of Whewell, and represented for

[6] (Baden Powell), 'Barlow on magnetic attractions', pp. 175, 176.
[7] Webster, *Joshua Watson*, p. 26; Churton, *Memoir of Joshua Watson*, *passim*; British Library, Wordsworth Papers, Ms Add 43.136, fols. 182–204; Trinity College, Cambridge, C. Wordsworth Diary; I. Todunter, *William Whewell*, 2 vols. (1876), vol. ii, p. 15.

Baden Powell a privileged channel of communication with Cambridge. Furthermore, as already pointed out, the *British Critic*, under the editorship of the Hackney appointees, was actively publicizing and patronizing the scientific achievements of the universities.

There is little doubt that the scientifically oriented atmosphere of the sister university exercised a deep influence on young Baden Powell. He had early contacts with Whewell and Herschel on account of his own experimental researches on light and heat.[8] He was easily won to the side of the scientific reformers. His youthful enthusiasm for the potentialities of the new mathematical methods also characterized most of the papers on physical subjects he contributed to the *British Critic*. When reviewing Miles Bland's work on hydrostatics and Whewell's textbook on mechanics and dynamics, Baden Powell engaged in interesting, albeit parochial reflections on the advantages and shortcomings of the French methods. He warned that the undisputed merits of the French school did not justify an eager adoption of foreign style by the British mathematicians. The tendency to fall into a trivial habit of imitation was to be checked by producing 'good and extensive works in our own language'.

Baden Powell reproached the French school of the Pronys, Poissons and Ampères for tiresome diffuseness and lack of geometrical concision in their exposition. This last remark would certainly have sounded odd to his French colleagues, as it does to modern readers. Yet, the reviewer conceded that the elegance of French mathematical writings was indisputable. English scientific productions, Baden Powell remarked, 'have till of late seemed as if designed for the workshop'. He predicted that taste would be brought to bear on the stylistic treatment of the mathematical portion of physical research. After all, as he pointed out, 'the language of analysis is as much under the dominion of laws of good taste as ordinary language'.[9]

Baden Powell's stress upon the rules of symmetry and upon the formal simplicity of the mathematical expression of experimental data was not, however, dictated by mere considerations of taste or by the wish to emphasize the 'liberal' nature of scientific investigation. The discussion of the merits of the analytical treatment of experimental findings had theoretical as well as pedagogical implications. According to Baden Powell, the qualities of the mathematical treatment of experimental data helped the student to grasp the essential elements of the inquiry. It also led the naturalist to consider the possibility of combining together, with the help of the analytic methods, the results of single experiments, thus proceeding towards a more general theory.

Baden Powell regarded mathematics as the key towards higher intellectual

[8] B.P.J., 1818–30.
[9] (Baden Powell), 'Hydrostatics', pp. 166, 163–4, 171, 168. For relevant background information and bibliography, see M. Crosland and C. Smith, 'The transmission of physics from France to Britain, 1800–1840', *Historical Studies in the Physical Sciences*, 9 (1978), 1–61.

and aesthetic dimensions of scientific investigation. The use of differential calculus produced results unattainable by the old fluxional methods. The refinement of mathematics made it possible to produce comprehensive and highly abstract physical theories. It was his conviction that mathematics would eventually establish the title of the physical sciences to a place in the liberal curriculum.

A further, powerful source of inspiration to young Baden Powell's reflections on science and its methods was Dugald Stewart's *Elements of the Philosophy of the Human Mind*. There is no comprehensive study of the influence of Stewart on British philosophy in the early nineteenth century. The almost exclusive focus on figures like Samuel Taylor Coleridge or Jeremy Bentham has till very recently prevented a detailed analysis of a wide range of philosophical ideas debated by English intellectuals of the first three decades of the nineteenth century. Of the major streams of thought which characterized this period, Stewart's philosophy certainly constituted one essential tributary, particularly as far as High Church circles were concerned. W. R. Lyall, a close friend of the Phalanx, wrote two interesting reviews of Stewart's works for the *Quarterly Review*. Stewart's *Elements* was also extensively quoted by Copleston and Whately.[10]

As far as Baden Powell was concerned, the influence of Stewart was of primary importance to his early reflections on science. Baden Powell met W. R. Lyall when the future Dean of Canterbury was the editor of the *British Critic*, and discussed with him his own subsequent contribution to the magazine. Lyall, though increasingly critical towards Stewart on account of the latter's defence of Hume, still admired the *Elements*. It is however significant that Baden Powell started a systematic reading of Stewart's work in the early months of the year 1822, as if he desired to confer philosophical dignity upon his scientific contributions to the *British Critic*. The only other philosophical work which received special mention in Baden Powell's journal was, in later years, John Stuart Mill's *System of Logic*.[11]

The influence of Stewart upon Baden Powell was particularly marked with respect to two major points of his early reflections on science: his emphasis on the philosophical relevance of scientific technical language and his critical remarks on the role of hypothesis in science. Both were clearly derived from

---

[10] D. Stewart, *Elements of the Philosophy of the Human Mind*, vol. i (1792), vol. ii (1814), vol. iii (1827): quotations will be from Sir W. Hamilton edn. (1854–60); (W. R. Lyall), 'Stewart's *Philosophical Essays*', *Q.R.*, 6 (1811), 1–37; (*idem*), 'Stewart's *Philosophy of the Human Mind*', *Q.R.*, 12 (1815), 281–317; E. Copleston, *An Enquiry into the Doctrine of Necessity and Predestination* (1821), p. 12; on Copleston and Stewart see E. Copleston (ed.), *Letters of the Earl of Dudley to the Bishop of Llandaff* (1840), pp. 16, 21–2, 191: J. W. Ward, Lord Dudley, had been a pupil of both Stewart and Copleston. On the Copleston–Stewart relationship, see P. Corsi, 'The heritage of Dugald Stewart', paper read at King's College Cambridge, July 1981, forthcoming in *Nuncius. Annali di Storia della Scienza*, 2, no.2 (1987), 89–144; R. Whately, *The Right Method of Interpreting Scripture* (1821), pp. 84, 87, 106, 119–20 and *Remains of the Late Edward Copleston* (1854), pp. 99–102.   [11] B. P. J., January 1822.

his reading of Stewart's work. The consideration of the linguistic features of philosophical, theological, or scientific debates was not a novelty at Oxford, nor in English culture of the late eighteenth and early nineteenth century.

A tradition wider than that represented by the single figure of Dugald Stewart made linguistic and even etymological considerations the key element of philosophical and theological polemics. However, Stewart provided in his *Elements* an updated historical and critical assessment of these issues. Moreover, in his attempt to vindicate the superiority of the philosophy of the human mind, and of philosophers, over the physical sciences and the scientists, Stewart provided a detailed account and critique of French debates on science.[12]

Contemporaries on both sides of the Channel regarded the scientific revolution promoted by Lavoisier and Haüy, Laplace and Cuvier as the clear indication that a new era had started in the history of humanity, and philosophy. The inquiries of Locke and Condillac suggested new ways of conducting scientific investigation, based on sophisticated logical and linguistic considerations. In their turn, the results obtained in modern disciplines like chemistry and crystallography, comparative anatomy and taxonomy vindicated the validity of the method, and suggested its application to all intellectual enterprise, from theology to political economy. Stewart did not agree that the philosophy of the human mind had to give way to pure epistemology. In order to vindicate his views, however, he was forced to engage in lengthy discussion of contemporary science and epistemology. It was this feature of the *Elements* that made the book attractive to readers as different as James Mill and Copleston, David Ricardo and W. R. Lyall, Nassau Senior and John Stuart Mill.[13]

Relevant features of Stewart's analysis of philosophical and scientific language deeply influenced Baden Powell's teachers at Oriel. As I have shown elsewhere, Copleston and Whately often quoted from the *Elements* when discussing the problem of the epistemological foundation of modern theories in political economy. The methodological priorities which made Nassau Senior insist upon

---

[12] For an impressive account of debates on the philosophy of language in England from 1780 to 1860 see H. Aarsleff, *The Study of Language in England* (1967), where detailed attention is paid to the work of Stewart. For Prof. Aarsleff's valuable studies on English and European philosophy in the eighteenth and nineteenth centuries, see his *From Locke to Saussure* (1982).

[13] On the French debate on the role of language, and linguistic combinatory procedures, in modern science, see P. Corsi, 'Models and analogies', in G. Montalenti and P. Rossi (eds.), *Lazzaro Spallanzani* (1980), pp. 381–96 and *Oltre il Mito. Lamarck e le scienze naturali del suo tempo* (1983), ch. 1; on the relationship between Stewart and French science, and on the influence exercised by the second volume of the *Elements* on thinkers such as James and John Stuart Mill, see P. Corsi, 'The heritage of Dugald Stewart'. The thesis that Stewart was a central, albeit controversial, figure in early nineteenth-century philosophical debates has recently been confirmed in studies by R. Yeo, 'An idol of the market-place', *History of Science*, 23 (1985), 251–98, and B. M. Fontana, *Rethinking the Politics of Commercial Society* (1985). N. De Marchi has written on the influence exercised by Stewart on debates on the method of political economy. S. Rashid, a pioneer of studies on the Noetics and their philosophical outlook, is not aware of the extent of Stewart's influence at Oxford: see his recent 'Dugald Stewart's "Baconian" methodology and political economy', *Journal of the History of Ideas*, 46 (1985), 245–57.

the axiomatic nature of political economy as a science, different from the realm of concrete political application, also derived from Stewart's discussion of the status of credibility and of the epistemological reliability of physical and natural sciences. As we shall consider below, the religious formulation of Stewart's linguistic analysis by the Noetics deeply influenced Baden Powell's early theological outlook. The young scholar was however the first member of the Oriel group systematically to deploy Stewart's ideas in his epistemological reflections.[14]

Stewart wrote interesting passages on the role of technical terminology in science, a point French scientists following the lead of Condillac had placed at the forefront of epistemological debates. A keen reader of contemporary scientific literature, Stewart argued that the introduction of technical words into the vocabulary of any science indicated that a notable step forward was being made in the progress of that science. Indeed, he claimed, the more the scientific terminology diverged from the popular use of language, the more precise and unambiguous the meaning of the single terms would become. In a paragraph of the second volume of the *Elements* headed 'Of Language Considered as an Instrument of Thought', Stewart insisted that it was essential to embark upon a close analysis of 'the branch of logic which relates to the use of words'. He also warned that the neglect of this crucial aspect of scientific procedures would have serious consequences on the progress of scientific research.[15]

Following Stewart's remarks, Baden Powell praised the philosophical caution showed by Woodhouse in his *Treatise on Astronomy*, where the astronomer constantly linked the new terms introduced to the relevant specific passage of the inquiry. In this way, the reader was appropriately and philosophically introduced 'to those technical words, which it is necessary for the student to take out of the ordinary acception, and limit to the designation of some peculiar ideas belonging alone to the phenomena under consideration'.[16]

According to Baden Powell, modern geology suffered because of the scant attention paid to the relationship between technical terminology and theory. Having considered controversies on the attribution of strata to different formations, Baden Powell granted that such discussions originated from specific technical reasons. However, they also 'frequently arise merely from that want of due discrimination in the use of terms, from that most common source of dispute, the neglect of definition'.[17] The value of Conybeare's and Phillips's geological inquiries was increased by their correct appreciation of the relation-

[14] P. Corsi, 'The heritage of Dugald Stewart'.
[15] D. Stewart, *Elements*, vol. i, p. 51; vol. ii, pp. 97–113, 100.
[16] (Baden Powell), 'Woodhouse's *Treatise*', p. 146.
[17] (Baden Powell), 'Geology of England and Wales', *B.C.*, 20 (1823), 288; W. D. Conybeare and W. Phillips, *Outlines of the Geology of England and Wales* (1822).

ship between theory and technical terminology. Having paid 'a close attention to the perspicuity of terms', the two authors made use of generalizations 'only in reference to their most proper and legitimate objects'.

Though a very young science, geology quickly became a very popular branch of scientific inquiry. As typical with many sciences in their infancy, the reviewer explained, geology had been characterized by a succession of controversial theories struggling for supremacy. Baden Powell believed that most disputes were due to the fact that 'different parties have given names borrowed from their peculiar theoretical views, and often conveying descriptive ideas, which are far from being universally applicable'. The inductive procedure had been reversed, greatly damaging the prospects of scientific progress in geology. The only safe way towards the building of theories was by proceeding through carefully defined steps, thus avoiding the inertial effect of careless definition. Thoughtless definitions were considered by Baden Powell, as well as by Stewart, to be highly misleading, especially when they became incorporated into a theoretical framework interpreting classes of phenomena.[18]

His insistence on the necessity of following a cautious path of induction did not mean, however, that Baden Powell concurred in the 'prevailing spirit' of opposition to the use of hypotheses and hypothetical theories in contemporary geology and in science in general. A *British Critic* reviewer maintained that 'geologists have gradually relinquished theory and gained ground in real knowledge. Discovery has, in a great measure, banished the intrusive spirit of hypothesis from our class-rooms, our memoirs, our transactions, and essays'.[19]

The identification of theory with hypothesis which emerged from this passage, and the condemnation of both theory and hypothesis as synonymous with bad science, seemed to be rather popular in the 1810s and the early 1820s. Moreover, the weight of a traditional interpretation of the Newtonian orthodoxy – whatever Newton himself thought on the subject – gave authority to the emphasis on the correlation between scientific progress and the abandonment of hypothesis in science.

With his usual display of sound learning, Stewart authoritatively tackled this crucial and delicate issue. He stressed the heuristic value of hypotheses, even of false ones. He also contested the philological accuracy of regarding the famous Newtonian *Scholium* as the sacred origin of the denunciation of hypotheses. Newton, Stewart pointed out, probably had Descartes's vortices in mind, when he declared 'Hypotheses non fingo'. Authorities ranging from David Hartley (1705–59) to Ruggiero Giuseppe Boscovich (1711–87) and James Gregory (1753–1821) were marshalled to support the conclusion that 'although a knowledge of facts must be prior to the formation of legitimate

[18] (Baden Powell), 'Geology of England and Wales', pp. 287–90.
[19] (Anon.), 'Boué's Essay on the Geology of Scotland', *B.C.*, 16 (1821), 652.

theory; yet a hypothetical theory is generally the best guide to the knowledge of connected and of useful facts'.[20]

This was also Baden Powell's opinion. In his paper on geology he declared his opposition to the building of theories unsupported by inductive procedures. However, he also expressed his strong disapproval of the current dogmatic attitude against hypotheses. The historical development of science offered, he argued, numerous instances in which 'valuable facts have often been elicited in the ardent pursuit of a most visionary theory, and discoveries of real importance, cast aside in the enthusiasm of following up some fanciful hypothesis, have been subsequently treasured up, and found to possess infinitely more value than the speculations which gave them birth'.[21]

A further interesting reflection developed from these considerations. Baden Powell wondered whether the increasing number of gentlemen geologists, enthusiastically collecting facts, were really helping the advance of science. It was indisputable that the diffusion of a general taste for geological observation was bound to advance the process of collecting data. Nevertheless, this very positive feature of the popularity of the subject obscured the crucial role of 'bold and original ideas' in the progress of scientific discovery. In this respect too Baden Powell was following the lead of the Scottish philosopher and of his Oriel teachers. Stewart, Copleston and Whately extolled the indispensable 'philosophical' dimension of science, and the consequent superiority of the philosopher over the mere practitioner.

It should be pointed out that Baden Powell's emphasis on the role of ideas and hypotheses in science was not limited to the vindication of academic and genteel science in general. Important in his early reflections on science was a refusal to regard scientific progress as a function of the summation of data derived from elementary observations. Awareness that science cannot be reduced to a simple manipulation of data, and the acknowledgement of the role of hypothesis in science, guided Baden Powell's later epistemological reflections. His realistic attitude towards the sinuous ways of scientific knowledge also provided the spur for his acceptance of less orthodox scientific hypotheses and doctrines, such as the theories of evolution put forward from the early 1800s to explain the succession of beings throughout the ages of the earth.

The analysis of Baden Powell's early papers on scientific subjects provides

---

[20] Stewart, *Elements*, vol. ii, pp. 402, 406. For a recent comment on Stewart's defence of hypotheses in science, and for the relevant bibliographical information, see Yeo, 'An idol of the market-place'. A point which still needs further investigation is the relationship between the intense debate on the role of hypothesis and hypothetical theories which characterized the French scientific and cultural periodical literature of the years 1796–1820 on the one hand, and Dugald Stewart on the other. Systematic investigation of contributions to periodicals on both sides of the Channel is proving particularly rewarding. It is my intention to publish a study on this subject.

[21] (Baden Powell), 'Geology of England and Wales', pp. 285–6; cf. Conybeare and Phillips, *Outlines of Geology*, p. xliv.

material for a brief consideration of the first stage of his intellectual development. Baden Powell had early and strong views on the subject of science as an educational and cultural practice. His remarks on the role of mathematics in modern physical sciences and on the increasingly liberal nature of the highly abstract physico-mathematical sciences, together with his vindication of the philosophical dimension of scientific discourse, reveal the complex but integrated nature of his early views on science. It would be misleading, therefore, to emphasize any one dimension as exclusively oriented by philosophical or political or pedagogical aims, or as simply stemming out of his scientific concerns. His comments reveal awareness that the modern calculus, as applied to physics by the French school, was changing the nature and the image of the physico-mathematical disciplines.

Baden Powell was convinced that scientific procedure – and indeed, the very popularity of scientific disciplines – was becoming a central feature of contemporary culture. The apologists of science were giving clear warning that they would not accept the intellectual leadership of Anglican academics who knew little and cared less for science. With these factors in mind he argued for improving the standards of scientific education at Oxford and recommended suitable changes in the curriculum and the examination system. At the same time, he stressed the élitist nature of scientific investigation and of theoretical activity. Science had to be cultivated in the universities, but there was to be no doubt that the layman could not judge the sophisticated fabric of science. In this too he was a pupil of Stewart, who had scorned those who opposed the successes of physical sciences to the alleged lack of progress in mental philosophy. For Stewart and for Baden Powell the Christian philosopher aware of science was to occupy the highest place in the hierarchy of intellectual authority. He was to lead the Church through the dangers of the pride of science, of demagogical appeals to reason, of attacks against the credibility of revelation launched in the name of science. This was the programme the young Oxford man had in mind for himself, and for his academic colleagues.

The relationship between Baden Powell's attitude towards science and what his Hackney relatives thought on the subject is also worth comment. There is minimal information which might allow a positive identification of the views on science held by the leaders of the Phalanx. However, the evidence does suggest that the Hackney men took a keen interest in science and technology. They toured the factories around London and were eager to visit workshops where new production techniques were applied. Some of their inspirers and allies were active in debating scientific issues. Bishop Horsley, a favourite authority with the Hackney leaders, produced an edition of Newton's work. William Jones of Nayland and William Kirby propagated a revised version of eighteenth-century Hutchinsonian natural history.

A considerable number of papers on scientific subjects were published in the *British Critic*, a clear indication of the curiosity evoked by science in the journal's editors and clergymen readers. Indeed, it can be proved that the *British Critic* was from its inception one of the better informed periodicals on new developments in English and French science: a point worth a separate investigation, in view of the fact that even works by well-known Jacobins were favourably reviewed, and this in a magazine which wholeheartedly embraced the conspiratorial doctrine of Barruel and Robison. Yet, the changes which affected the British social and intellectual scene during the first decades of the nineteenth century also affected the rôle of science in contemporary debates and polemics, thereby forcing intellectual and religious circles to revise their standpoint on science. As I shall argue in the next chapter, during the late 1810s radical agitators and leading cultural figures, such as Carlile, William Lawrence (1783–1867), Sir Thomas Charles Morgan (1783–1843) and Wade, appealed to men of science to shake off old prejudices and reject Church sectarian control of research. The concept of a free science, uncensored by religious or metaphysical preconceptions, was opposed to the trite and static culture of the Anglican universities, monopolized by the most reactionary sectors of the Anglican Church.

The fear that science could become a key factor in an all-out assault against the Anglican universities and Anglican Christianity worried many clergymen. The Hackney leaders were not alone in opposing contemporary naturalists who purported to substitute a lay vision of nature for the traditional religious one. By the late 1820s the Hackney leaders increasingly sympathized with the stance adopted by men like Rose, who denounced the dangers of the excessive attention to science paid at Cambridge. The plan of showing that the English universities were capable of keeping pace with scientific advance risked backfiring. At Oxford and Cambridge, several dons were convinced that scientific subjects should be included in the curriculum, and not just reserved for public lectures, to be quoted with pride in polemical pamphlets against the *Edinburgh Review*.

Baden Powell's interest in science was stronger than his Hackney relatives' curiosity about technology and natural rarities. He was convinced that science progressed and that scientific advance was bound to influence all aspects of social and cultural life in contemporary Britain. At the same time, he shared the preoccupation of his relatives and friends with the consequences to be expected from a confrontation between science and revealed religion. Baden Powell studied and wrote with the aim of defending the Anglican Church and of implementing at a scholarly and philosophical level the religious policies of his Hackney relatives and his Oriel teachers. It was therefore unavoidable that he should approach the question of the relationship between science and the scriptures and state the case of science in its relation with modern Christian apologetic.

4

Science and religion in the 1820s

In Chapter 1 I examined the considerable effort made by the Hackney friends to alert the clergy and the Anglican intelligentsia to the necessity for a better understanding of theological issues, and particularly for a more serious commitment to the study of Anglican theology. However, the lack of a well-defined canon of Anglican doctrine and of a coherent grouping of professional theologians was reflected in the plurality of views expressed by the contributors to the *British Critic*, the journal controlled by the Hackney leaders. Agreement on a broad spectrum of political questions made theological differences a matter of secondary importance. Moreover, the absence at this time of any sustained attempt to develop a systematic approach to theological studies and doctrines made even more remote the possibility of clashes on purely theological issues. In the course of this study, it will become apparent how, with the outbreak of serious political contention within the High Church party, theological differences tended to come to the forefront of the tense debates which characterized the late 1820s and the early 1830s.

The lack of agreement on several points of crucial theological relevance (in particular on the character and extent of the divine inspiration of the Bible) had obvious and important effects on the solutions put forward in the *British Critic* regarding the relationship between science and the scriptures. A survey of reviews on scientific subjects published in the magazine during the 1810s and the early 1820s reveals that suspicions about the actual or potential danger of scientific inquiry from the religious point of view were voiced along with firm reassurances as to the intrinsic safety of natural and physical researches.

James Cowles Prichard (1786–1848) opened his *Researches into the Physical History of Man* (1813) by declaring that the truth of the scriptures was not involved in the discussion of the question of whether mankind had been generated from a single pair or many original pairs, the parent stock of the different races of man. Prichard's views were widely shared. His work was favourably reviewed in the *British Critic*. However, there was some dissension over the degree to which science should be independent of the scriptures.

49

Cautious as it was, the formulation of the problem by Prichard met with a severe warning from an otherwise indulgent *British Critic* reviewer.

The anonymous commentator conceded that the ultimate goal of the naturalist was the reconciliation of Genesis with recent researches into physical anthropology. He was also far from recommending 'the *circular* mode of argumentation, or requiring that he [Prichard] should first take the authority of the scripture for concluding that the whole race of men descended from one common ancestor'. Yet, surreptitiously reintroducing the very circularity he had just discarded, he warned Prichard to remember that 'upon the conclusions [of his inquiries] rests the validity of our holy faith'. The reviewer implicitly argued that the results of any scientific inquiry relevant to the contents of scriptural passages were bound to be taken as proof or refutation of the veracity of revelation. Viewed in this light, scientific activities and publications should be carefully supervised by churchmen and theologians, in order to detect and counteract in advance any presumptuous declaration of the independence of science from revelation or, even worse, atheistic and materialistic infection.[1]

Without openly discussing the concept of plenary inspiration implicit in the above position, but actually allowing for a certain latitude of interpretation of the character and extent of Bible inspiration, the great majority of contributors to the *British Critic* insisted that science itself was safe: 'the fault is in the man, not in the subject'. This remark applied equally to geology and to physiology, the two disciplines at the centre of the debates on the relationship between science and the scriptures in the early nineteenth century. Essential and significant differences characterized the approach to the two subjects. No inquiry into the spectrum of positions on the science-religion debate in the 1810s and early 1820s can ignore that physiological researches were seen as far more dangerous than geological ones.

Geology was rapidly increasing in popularity among the clergy, probably helped by the fact that in Anglican circles it was generally regarded as a safe science. Many Anglican clergymen and university dons had recently entered the field and with notable success. On the other hand, physiological inquiries were suspect, being stamped by open defiance of established religious and political beliefs. Indeed, Lawrence's and Sir T. C. Morgan's works contained much to substantiate the worst fears, provoking almost unanimous opposition to physiological materialism. However, even in this case, an examination of

---

[1] J. C. Prichard, *Researches into the Physical History of Man* (1813), p. 3; see also second edn., 2 vols. (1826), vol. i, pp. 6–8; (Anon.), 'Prichard's *Physical History of Man*', *B.C.*, 3 (1815), 293. See also *B.C.*, 7 (1828), 33–61, and *B.C.*, 13 (1831), 440–59. Prichard was particularly worried by materialist developments in French science; on the plurality of monogenist and polygenist options discussed in France – then the leading country of physical anthropology – and well known to Prichard, see C. Blanckaert, 'Monogénisme et polygénisme' (1981); on the theological and philosophical dimensions of Prichard's work, see W. Bynum, 'Time's Noblest Offspring' (1974).

the reviews devoted to the discussion of this controversial issue reveals significant differences of emphasis.[2]

Thomas Rennell, the Hackney protégé who in those years edited the *British Critic*, was the most active opponent of Lawrence's ideas. In his pamphlet, *Remarks on Scepticism*, Rennell maintained that physiological researches, and science at large, could easily follow a course that would fully develop their unchristian tendency. In any case, their pursuit was distracting man's mind from the contemplation of God. Underlying Rennell's severe strictures upon physiological materialism was the conviction that 'the "laws of nature", the "vital properties", the "energies of the mind", are among the mysterious phantoms which are to supersede the will and the wisdom of God'. His belief that the impious doctrines of the physiological materialists were far from being the only danger to revealed religion emerges clearly. The fervour with which 'the laws of nature' were currently investigated was to him the symptom of a subtler but no less sinister attempt to eliminate God from the natural scene.[3]

Rennell's position was neither isolated, nor ephemeral. It was taken up by Rose in the commencement sermon we will examine below, as well as by William Kirby and Thomas Chalmers in their Bridgewater treatises. According to Kirby, even meteorological inquiries indicated the intention of excluding God's direct intervention in atmospheric phenomena. Rennell argued that he was not asking moral and natural philosophers to refer at every step of their researches to the inspired word. Yet, he too advocated the principle that in scientific inquiry 'the mind should be led upwards to discern the intimate connection and absolute dependence of all things upon God'.[4]

Baden Powell praised Rennell's decided opposition to physiological materialism, though he himself emphasized the benefits rather than the dangers of scientific inquiry. The elucidation of natural phenomena, he argued, was bound to increase our admiration for the creator of nature. Furthermore, a truly scientific method was always characterized by a great caution, especially in inquiries touching on so complex a question as the functions of organic life or the brain–mind relationship. Briefly reviewing contemporary contributions to geological and physiological studies Baden Powell discussed the relationship between the results of current scientific research and the portion of the scriptural narrative concerned with the description of natural phenomena. His comments on the import of geological and physiological doctrines for the

[2] W. Lawrence, *Lectures on Physiology, Zoology and the Natural History of Man* (1819); Sir T. C. Morgan, *Sketches of the Philosophy of Life* (1818); O. Temkin, 'Basic science, medicine, and the romantic era', *Bulletin of the History of Medicine*, 37 (1963), 97–129; K. D. Wells, 'Sir William Lawrence (1783–1867)', *J.H.B.*, 4 (1971), 319–61; L. S. Jacyna, 'Immanence or transcendence: theories of life and organization in Britain, 1790–1835', *Isis*, 74 (1983), 311–29.

[3] T. Rennell, *Remarks on Scepticism* (1819), pp. 8–9.

[4] Rennell, p. 9; W. Kirby, *On the Power, Wisdom and Goodness of God as Manifested in the Creation of Animals and in their History, Habits and Instincts*, 2 vols. (1835), vol. i, pp. xc–xciii.

acceptance of revealed religion followed the approach adopted by several *British Critic* reviewers in the late 1810s and early 1820s.

The reconciliation of geology with the scriptures was not seen as a major problem. For instance, a reviewer argued that geology could, and indeed had been used to undermine belief in the inspiration of the scriptures but this fault was not to be imputed to the science itself; after all, astronomy, comparative anatomy, even optics had been forced to serve infidelity in its assaults upon Christianity. In addition, Baden Powell approvingly emphasized that according to Phillips and Conybeare 'the establishment of physical truths is not the proper province of revelation', since the primary concern of the scriptures is 'the history of the divine dispensation to man'.[5]

Various contributors to the *British Critic* during the 1810s and 1820s shared this point of view, though there were some dissenting voices. The reviewer of Prichard's work quoted above, or Rennell and Rose, would have felt strong reservations as to the true extent to which this principle could be safely carried. However, sympathizers with the approach expressed by Baden Powell made themselves heard. Severely critical of Granville Penn's treatise on Mosaic geology, a reviewer confidently argued that the scriptures 'were not meant to convey to mankind a system of philosophy': the book of Genesis could not be read as a manual of astronomy or geology. This view was echoed in a paper published by the *Christian Remembrancer* of 1826. The contributor called attention to the fact that the Bible did not teach 'the structure of the earth, but the way to heaven'.[6]

Baden Powell had something to add. He argued that the cautious path followed by the inductive inquirer into geological phenomena could have made this science subservient to the teaching of the way towards salvation. Though irrelevant to doctrinal theology, which could find its light only from the scriptures, geology had auxiliary functions to perform in support of natural theology. Natural sciences and geology *in primis*, confuted the materialistic belief in the eternity of the universe and were providing the student with clear indications of a divine teleology presiding over the succession of natural events.[7]

Notwithstanding the avowal that revelation was not designed to teach natural science, Baden Powell conceded that a confrontation between geology and revelation was possible on two particular questions: the Noachian deluge and the antiquity of the earth. On the first issue, his position reflected the confident mood of the period: on geological grounds, the question was seen as settled

5 (Anon.), 'Boué's *Essay on Geology*', p. 653; (Baden Powell), 'Geology of England and Wales', p. 297.
6 (Anon.), 'Penn's Mineral and Mosaical Geologies', *B.C.*, 21 (1824), 387; (P. N. Wilton), 'Misapplication of geology to scripture', *C.R.*, 8 (1826), 211; the identification of Wilton as the author of the review is by Dr Yule, 'The impact of science'. On Mosaic geology, see the classic study by C. C. Gillispie, *Genesis and Geology* (1959), M. Millhauser, 'The scriptural geologists', *Osiris*, 11 (1954), 65–86 and Yule, 'The impact of science'.
7 (Baden Powell), 'Geology of England and Wales', 298.

and the historicity of Noah's flood irrefutably established. The *British Critic* reviewer of Buckland's *Reliquiae Diluvianae* triumphantly declared that

if infidel surmises should be hazarded anywhere, in books or in lectures, respecting the narrative contained in our more ancient scriptures, and doubts thrown out as to the accuracy of the historian who describes the Mosaic deluge; let Mr. Buckland gird on his orthodox armour, and plant his foot on the disputed field.[8]

The tone of this review shows how in the early 1820s those Anglicans utilizing geology for demonstrating the relations between science and religion were confident that they were treading on safe ground. Opposition to the scientific and historical reliability of the sacred writings came from highly disreputable quarters, such as Elihu Palmer's reissues of eighteenth-century materialistic cosmogonies or the publications sponsored by Carlile. At a more serious level, though equally disqualified in the eyes of Anglican High Churchmen, Lawrence in his *Lectures on Physiology* of 1819 expressed qualified doubts as to the inspiration of Genesis. Last but not least Belsham, the acknowledged leader of British Unitarians in the 1810s and the 1820s delivered a lecture in which he maintained that the Mosaic account of creation could not be substantiated on scientific grounds. Belsham's critical strictures were founded on old astronomical objections. He was clearly unaware of recent geological discoveries proving the contrary of his thesis. Thus, it is not surprising that the *British Critic* reviewer of the *Reliquiae Diluvianae* saw Buckland's work as an adequate answer to recently renewed attacks against the scientific reliability of Genesis.[9]

The strategy of Unitarians, physiologists and radical Paineite publishers of the school of Richard Carlile occasioned worries on theological and social grounds. However, several Anglican apologists felt that to confront opponents with geological arguments was to fight a battle already won. The consideration of this wider dimension of the debates on the relationship between geological doctrines and revelation helps in explaining the success of geological inquiries even within reactionary Anglican circles. It could be argued that it was by extolling the apologetic import of geological research that the friends of the new science obtained access to Oxford University. Even those who were still suspicious about science in general could not deny that the leading geologists of the day and of the past decades – Déodat de Dolomieu (1751–1801), Jean-André Deluc (1727–1817), Georges Cuvier (1769–1832), Adam Sedgwick (1785–1873) and Buckland – authoritatively confirmed the substantial veracity of the scriptural accounts of geological phenomena.

[8] 'Geology of England and Wales', 298. (Anon.), 'Buckland's *Reliquiae Diluvianae*', *B.C.*, 20 (1823), 608.

[9] E. Palmer, *Principles of Nature* (1823); Lawrence, *Lectures on Physiology*, pp. 247–9, 254; T. Belsham, *Reflexions upon the History of Creation in the Book of Genesis* (1821), pp. 26–8; J. Garbett, *The Book of Genesis and the Mosaical History of the Creation Vindicated* (1821); C. C. Gillispie, *Genesis and Geology* (1959).

Baden Powell referred to the geological inquiries of the naturalists mentioned above, to conclude that 'the geological argument for the credibility of the Mosaic accounts of the deluge [is] most abundantly substantiated'. The coincidence between the independent researches of modern geologists and the Mosaic narrative had significant implications for the question of biblical inspiration. Baden Powell did not expand upon the subject but expressed his firm conviction that the matter should be re-examined in a systematic way. Such an inquiry, he argued, 'would not fail to place Moses's claims to divine inspiration in a striking point of view'.[10]

The second point at which a comparison between the Genesis narrative of creation and the findings of modern geology imposed itself on the attention of contemporary commentators was the question of the antiquity of the earth. On this point too Baden Powell adopted an approach widely shared by many *British Critic* contributors in the early 1820s. However, on this issue even the authorities already called upon to confirm the coincidence between the Noachian deluge and geology were offering only partially satisfactory indications. The *British Critic* reviewer of Granville Penn's treatise unguardedly compared the ideas – 'reveries', he specified – of the Mosaic geologist with Hutton's 'eternal renovations' and Cuvier's 'numerous debacles'; thereby acknowledging that such a safe authority as Cuvier concluded that the natural history of the earth could have developed for a period of time longer than the biblical chronology reckoned.[11]

In order to explain this discrepancy, the reviewer of Boué's work on the geology of Scotland suggested that the first verse of Genesis referred to the originally created universe, evolving for indefinite periods of time. The remaining part of the narrative referred to the final intervention of God in the six days' operations and its consequences. This exegetical proposal was put forward with the cautionary remark that 'this is, no doubt, a mere hypothesis, and which will, of course, be received or refused, according to the particular principles of biblical interpretation by which it shall be tried. Still, there is certainly no impiety in the supposition'.[12]

Following an analogous approach, Phillips and Conybeare had two more hypotheses to put forward. They argued that the 'days' of creation could be safely interpreted as periods of indefinite length, or alternatively that it was possible to match the findings of geology with the literal interpretation of the Genesis narrative. The last proposal – the 'safest' of all – was put forward as one among many possible explanations.[13]

[10] (Baden Powell), 'Geology of England and Wales', 299.
[11] (Anon.), 'Penn's *Mineral and Mosaical Geologies*', 392.
[12] (Anon.), 'Boué's *Essay on Geology*', 655.
[13] Conybeare and Phillips, *Outlines of Geology*, pp. ix–xi. It is noted that both the reviewer of Boué's work and the authors of the *Outlines* considered the possibility of several interpretative approaches to scripture, a stand which reflected the actual state of affairs within the Anglican

Baden Powell summed up the conclusions of Phillips and Conybeare on the subject of the relationship between geology and the scriptures. He too specified that the exegetical proposals suggested were hypotheses. The scriptures were designed to teach spiritual truth and not geology. Thus, all that was required was the *possibility* of reconciling geological findings with the general outline of the Genesis narrative of creation. No strict literal coincidence was required. Baden Powell severely commented upon the productions of the Mosaic geologists. These authors pretended to force geological findings into a word-for-word agreement with the sketchy and often impressionistic biblical account of creation. Yet, it is important to stress Baden Powell's confidence that the general compatibility of the scriptures with geology had been established and, on specific points such as the Noachian deluge, triumphantly proved. The progress of the science was bound to bring further confirmation of the coincidence between God's revelation and the results of geological inquiries.[14]

It is somewhat ironical that geology, the safe science of the early 1820s, was going to cause serious problems in the next decades, whereas physiology, which in the early 1820s was seen as the most dangerous attempt at giving renewed impulse to physiological and psychological materialism, abandoned unsafe ground and developed through the 1830s and the 1840s in relative obscurity. At the end of the 1810s and in the early 1820s, the physiological and especially psychological materialism preached by Lawrence, or even Daniel Pring (1789–1859), Franz Joseph Gall (1758–1828) and Johann Christoph Spurzheim (1776–1832), was at the centre of a violent debate in which the *British Critic* reviewers played an active role.[15]

It was the editor of the journal at the time, Rennell, who actually started the debate with a severe attack on Lawrence's work of 1816 on comparative anatomy. Lawrence's adherence to the doctrine that thought was the product of the nervous system, the result of a physiological function performed by the brain, represented a provocation which Rennell could not let pass unnoticed. Even before Lawrence published his more outspoken and politically committed

Church. This situation of plurality of biblical interpretations was bound to last for a long time: cf. Ellis, *Seven against Christ*. Recent attempts at providing a definition of nineteenth-century Anglican orthodoxy, or the assumption that it existed, do not appear to be warranted by a close examination of theological and natural theological debates of the time. For a recent assessment of the relationship between geology and scripture at Oxford, limited to the ideas of W. Buckland, see Rupke, *The Great Chain of History* (1983), pp. 205, 217.

[14] (Baden Powell), 'Geology of England and Wales', p. 300.

[15] Daniel Pring, *A View of the Relations of the Nervous System* (1816), and *General Indications which relate to the Laws of the Organic Life* (1819). On Gall and Spurzheim and the early, aggressively materialistic phases of phrenology in England, see R. Cooter, *The Cultural Meaning of Popular Science* (1984). On physiology in the early decades of the nineteenth century see Temkin, 'Basic science, medicine, and the romantic era', 97–129, Goodfield-Toulmin, 'Some aspects of British physiology', *J.H.B.*, 2 (1969), 283–320, and Jacyna, 'Principles of General Physiology' (1984), 47–92.

Lectures on Physiology (1819) Rennell launched a major offensive against physiological and psychological materialism in his *Remarks on Scepticism*.[16]

Much has been written on the famous debate which followed and which forced Lawrence to resign his chair at the Royal College of Surgeons. Scientific, theological and philosophical features of this polemic have been highlighted in recent publications and studies. Various commentators have pointed out that the multiform dimensions of this dramatic debate can only be understood within the context of English social, political and intellectual life at the end of the Napoleonic wars. Concentration upon Lawrence's work, however, has often prevented a comprehensive assessment of the question and the acknowledged need for taking into account the wider intellectual dimensions of the debate has not yet been fulfilled.[17]

In the light of our present concern, it is important to emphasize some of the reasons why the *British Critic* group and the Hackney leaders became the most active parties in the debate. It is relevant that Lawrence's *Lectures* were seen by members of the Hackney group as an authoritative re-publication of the Priestleian materialism they politically defeated in the 1790s and the early 1800s. Rennell himself explicitly acknowledged the connection between past and present materialism, when he remarked that the ideas put forward by Lawrence were far more dangerous than anything Hartley himself dared to maintain. Rennell was painfully aware that physiological and psychological materialism as cultural forces had survived the political defeat of Priestley and his friends.

A long list of Unitarian publications had been devoted to the discussion of materialism and necessitarianism, the more specifically philosophical features of Unitarian materialism. Even within Unitarian circles there was dissatisfaction with the dangerous philosophical tenets of some of the historical leaders of the movement. Yet, the dissension helped to keep the debate alive among Unitarians. It is furthermore significant that Stewart, the leading philosophical authority of the day, acknowledged the vitality of the materialist tradition by devoting one of his *Philosophical Essays* (1810) to refuting physiological and psychological materialism.[18]

---

[16]   W. Lawrence, *An Introduction to Comparative Anatomy and Physiology* (1816), reviewed anonymously by T. Rennell in *B.C.*, 8 (1817), 63–73; authorship acknowledged by Rennell, *Remarks on Scepticism*, p. 136. W. Bynum, 'Time's noblest offspring', ch. 3.

[17]   The work of such interesting a figure as Daniel Pring, or the discussion of physiological, anatomical and anthropological issues in medical magazines and literature deserves closer attention. The diffusion of French collective works such as the *Dictionnaire des sciences médicales* in medical and naturalistic circles, giving publicity to ideas High Churchmen equated to atheism, should also be considered. See below, Part IV, ch. 15.

[18]   (Anon.), 'Somatopsychoonologia', *B.C.*, 22 (1824), 225–45; (Anon.), 'On Scepticism', *C.R.*, 1 (1819), 427–48; on Unitarian debates on materialism see T. Belsham, *A Letter to the Unitarian Christians in South Wales* (1816), pp. vi–viii; D. Stewart, *Philosophical Essays* (1810, W. Hamilton edn.), 'Essay Fourth', pp. 127–45; see also *The Monthly Repository* for the years 1806–20. Necessitarianism was slowly abandoned within Unitarian philosophical circles, though it survived through the work of authors like Charles Bray. On developments within

Rennell, an expert in anti-Unitarian polemic, realized the wide implication of Lawrence's physiological teaching and of Morgan's defence of philosophical necessity. To him, Lawrence's 'vitalism' was only a camouflage under which dangerous tenets could be introduced. The above remarks on current Unitarian debates make it understandable that physiological materialism was not the major worry Rennell had. The assertion that the mental faculties were the result of the organization of the brain was the real point at issue, the subversive core of the cultural and philosophical proposal publicized by Lawrence. Psychological materialism was bound, in Rennell's eyes, to become the scientific support of the doctrine of philosophical necessity, that is, of the central philosophical tenet of the Unitarian school. Furthermore, it was Rennell's conviction that current intellectual debates had political connotations. It was not by chance that he referred to Gall and Spurzheim as 'the German Illuminati', an expression clearly taken from John Robison (1774–1805), the major theoretician of the participation of philosophers, scientists, and reading societies in the revolutionary events of the 1790s.[19]

To a generation obsessed by the belief that the social and intellectual components of the French Revolution were still active and ready to produce their explosive mixture again, the diffusion of the popular press, the birth of the working-class movement, the daily confirmation of Anglican and Tory weakness and the defiant posture of middle-class intellectuals like Lawrence and Morgan were clear indications of an approaching violent conflict. The political overtones of the writings by Lawrence and Morgan and the allies they found during the dispute, ranging from the detested Carlile to the Roman Catholic Thomas Foster (1789–1860), reinforced Rennell's belief that science had once again become the spearhead of an ideological strategy which had obscure but imaginable ends.[20]

Baden Powell entered the debate on the Lawrence affair with a review of John Fleming's *Philosophy of Zoology*. His paper was in fact an excuse for a tirade against the unsound doctrine of physiological and psychological materialism. Baden Powell himself was engaged in the anti-Unitarian controversy. It is not surprising, therefore, that he too regarded psychological materialism, the 'scientific' side of philosophical necessitarianism, as a far

British Unitarianism, with particular reference to philosophic and scientific issues, see T. L. Alborn, 'The York Unitarians' (B.A. thesis, Harvard University, 1986).

19 T. Rennell, *Animadversions on the Unitarian Translation or Improved Version of the New Testament* (1811) and *Remarks on Scepticism*, pp. 133–5; J. B. Morrell, 'Professor Robison and Playfair, and *Theophobia Gallica*', *Notes and Records of the Royal Society*, 26 (1971), 43–63. The *British Critic* extensively reviewed the works of Robison, Moulnié, Barruel and other minor supporters of the conspiracy theory. See also N. U. Murray, 'The influence of the French Revolution on the Church of England and its rivals, 1789–1802' (1975), and Overton, *The English Church*.

20 P. Hollis, *The Popular Press* (1970); E. P. Thompson, *The Making of the Working Class* (1963); K. R. Webb, *The British Working Class Reader* (1955); M. J. Thomis and P. Holt, *Threats of Revolution in Britain, 1789–1848* (1977).

more important issue than physiological materialism. Indeed, after a few opening paragraphs in praise of Fleming's contention that 'the vital principle must be something more than a mere result of organization', the reviewer argued that 'the question of the connection between the organization and mind' was the 'most generally interesting part' of the whole debate. He briefly alluded to the various theories put forward in order to explain the intellectual faculties and functions in physiological terms. Then, after mentioning the theories of Gall and Spurzheim, Baden Powell concluded that

All theories of this kind appear to us extremely liable to degenerate into dangerous errors. Considered in themselves, they may be harmless speculations; but they are always liable to take a particular tone and character from the minds of those who adopt them;...they may very easily convert the visionary views of some speculative physiologist into the vehicles of most fatal error, productive of the worst practical consequences, and spreading far and wide their insidious infection.[21]

Baden Powell's main contention was that these doctrines were scientifically and philosophically incorrect. Serious mistakes at factual and logical levels made the doctrines endorsed by Lawrence and his friends totally untenable. He seemed to offer little more than a summary of Rennell's *Remarks on Scepticism*, and also adopted the violent and vituperative tone of that pamphlet. Yet, it would be wrong to identify Baden Powell's reaction to psychological materialism with Rennell's. It is indeed understandable why the young reviewer expressed himself so decidedly on this issue. The Lawrence affair constituted a serious blow to those Anglicans who cherished hopes for the future of scientific inquiries in the British universities. It revived and indeed reinforced the old suspicions and hostility towards scientific pursuits. Rennell's adoption of the epithet 'illuminati' to describe famous naturalists was in itself indicative of the extent and determination of his opposition to independent scientific inquiry.

It is not surprising that many Anglican naturalists became the most severe critics of Lawrence. Several *British Critic* reviewers, however, continued to issue reassurances as to the intrinsic Christian merits of science. In the midst of the storm raised by the Lawrence affair Buckland, in works published in 1820 and 1823, did his best to present geology as a safe science. Such efforts may be seen as endeavouring to dissociate scientific pursuits from the ominous spell of pre-revolutionary materialist natural philosophy and from contemporary revivals of challenging philosophical and scientific theories.

In his intellectual approach Baden Powell placed a high value upon scientific interests and advocated the extension of scientific studies at Oxford. He himself was a scientific amateur. It was crucial to his strategy to dissociate himself and the scientific interests he championed from the kind of proposals put

²¹ (Baden Powell), 'Fleming's *Philosophy of Zoology*', *B.C.*, 21 (1824), 150, 151, 153.

forward by Lawrence and his allies. Thus, his opposition to physiological and psychological materialism was expressed in very incisive terms. The materialist view was that thought and the moral faculties, which Christians believed to be of spiritual origin, were the product of mere physiological organization. This conclusion, Baden Powell remarked, was bound to have dangerous consequences from a religious point of view. On the other hand, those who believed that thought was the effect of an immaterial spiritual agent, but still pretended to assign to it 'a physical space', were contravening elementary rules of consistent philosophizing. Thus, he concluded, psychological materialists of all schools 'are not content with rejecting revelation, but must also pervert philosophy; they not only offend against religion, but think to excuse it by an equally outrageous offence against all sound principles of reasoning'.[22]

It was clear that the approach adopted in surveying the points of contact between geology and revelation could not be applied to the critical examination of physiological and psychological materialism. As far as the latter case was concerned, there was no question of calling upon the principle 'Revelation does not teach natural sciences', since psychological materialism involved a fundamental doctrinal element concerning God's dispensation to man. The relationship between mind and body was complex, indeed mysterious. God revealed the immortality of the human spiritual principle precisely in order to provide secure guidance and a firm certainty as to the eternal destiny of man.[23]

Baden Powell expressed the conviction that recent allegations against scientific pursuits originated from the fact that accusers improperly confounded true science with the impious speculations of the psychological materialists. Scientific research, when conducted in accordance with a correct methodology, was bound to provide much support to the cause of revealed religion. The evidence it afforded of design and purpose in creation reinforced the credibility of the existence of a creator. Furthermore, scientific pursuits made the Christian naturalist aware of the limits of the human understanding, thereby preparing the human mind for the reception of the revealed mysteries.

Baden Powell's early reflections on the relationship between physiological materialism and the revealed doctrines of the immortality of the soul, were characterized by intellectual, political, and specifically theological concerns.

---

[22] 'Fleming's *Philosophy of Zoology*', 156.

[23] The debate on Lawrence and on psychological materialism was particularly tense at Oxford, and within the Noetic circle; Nassau Senior supported the doctrine that the mind was the product of nervous functions, and died with man. It was this condition that made the doctrine of resurrection and immortality a crucial point of Revelation. Senior was asked by his friends to recant, and to put in writing a declaration of faith. See National Library of Wales, Senior Papers, C.493: 14 July 1827. Charles Daubeny wrote a pamphlet, *A Letter to the Reverend Thomas Rennell, concerning his remarks on scepticism, from a graduate in medicine* (1819) where he vindicated freedom of research, defended the legitimacy of phrenological investigations, and denied that Rennell represented the majority of Anglican opinion. For authorship, see Daubeny Papers, Magdalen College, Oxford.

In view of the later development of Baden Powell's ideas on the Genesis-geology debate, his early standpoint on this controversial issue deserves further mention. He accepted the methodological guideline according to which 'Revelation does not teach science'; yet, he was equally convinced that it was possible to emphasize the basic agreement between the scriptural narrative of creation and the findings of modern geology. Moreover, he hinted that the geological confirmation of the historical truth of the Noachian deluge reinforced Moses's claim to divine inspiration. Whenever such a close coincidence between geological discoveries and the relevant scriptural passages could not be established, cautious exegesis was capable of providing various conciliatory hypotheses.

The theme of the limits of the human mind, fully developed in the 1826 essay on *Rational Religion* examined below, laid the foundation for Baden Powell's remarks on the humility and caution required for scientific research. A mature and philosophically aware science either proved the coincidence of revealed religion with sound inductive inquiries, or it declared the insufficiency and the hypothetical status of those doctrines which could not be made to serve apologetic purposes. Thus, according to young Baden Powell, it was only a preconceived moral – or immoral – choice which made infidel philosophers so self-assured in pointing out or devising scientific theories apparently contradicting the scriptures.

Few of the certainties and hopes that Baden Powell shared with his *British Critic* colleagues in the early 1820s survived the intense theological, philosophical and political debates of the next decade.

5

'Rational Religion Examined'

Rational Religion Examined was the first major production by Baden Powell. It was not a work which influenced contemporary debates nor was it widely read or commented upon – none of these qualifications would apply to Baden Powell's early writings – but it undoubtedly epitomized the complex theological and philosophical scene of its day. Viewed in the right historical perspective, this text provides interesting new insights into neglected features of Oxford and English intellectual life in the 1820s. It also shows that the clear-cut division customarily made between the Hackney Phalanx and the Oxford Movement on the one hand, and the Noetic circle on the other is without factual basis. The failure to appreciate first the actual terms of agreement, and then the dynamics of the widening gap between the two approaches, has prevented a clear appreciation of important philosophical and theological issues debated in the first decades of the nineteenth century.

Several of the themes Baden Powell dwelt upon in his contributions to the *British Critic* and the *Christian Remembrancer* featured prominently in *Rational Religion Examined*, and became essential parts of a systematic treatise on the philosophy of belief. The very systematic character of this work represents a further element of interest to the historian of philosophy and theology. It also provides the historian of science with a closer insight into the dimensions of contemporary epistemological debates. Though the book was professedly a critical analysis of the theological systems 'which discard reason', namely Unitarianism, Roman Catholicism, and various Dissenting doctrines, more than two-thirds of the treatise was in fact devoted to the refutation of the Unitarian doctrine.

The authors Baden Powell quoted in support of his critical remarks were equally worried by the intellectual aggressiveness of contemporary Unitarians. It will be recalled that the editorial policy of the *British Critic* in the 1810s and the 1820s was a counter to the Unitarian threat. Reviews of Unitarian publications appeared frequently in High Church periodicals, and these works received a degree of attention at odds with the actual numerical strength of Unitarianism at the period. The question of the Unitarian intellectual revival was also central in the papers on theological subjects Baden Powell wrote between 1824 and 1826. In *Rational Religion Examined* he gave an interesting explanation of the care with which the progress of Unitarianism was monitored and vigorously denounced. Baden Powell argued that 'the number...of those professing actual Unitarianism is small, but its leading principle...is more or less adopted, with various shades of difference, by great numbers, many of whom in outward profession are supporters of established opinions and institutions'.[1]

Thus, Baden Powell's early theological production confirms the view that in the 1820s a considerable sector of the High Church party, ranging from the Hackney Phalanx and the Bishop of St Davids to Whately, Copleston and their school, considered Unitarianism as the major threat to Anglican doctrine. Moreover, members of the Hackney circle who distinguished themselves in fierce opposition to any form of alliance between Anglicans and Dissenters thought that in the theological fight against Unitarianism it was admissible to join hands with eminent Dissenting scholars. Rose and Baden Powell quoted with approval Smith's work against German 'rationalistic' theology. Baden Powell also remarked that he was actually engaged in unravelling the erroneous philosophical presuppositions of German theological trends already denounced by Rose and Smith. He clearly regarded German 'rationalistic' theology as an expression of the same philosophical and theological fallacies preached by Unitarians at home.

The Anglican reaction against the Unitarians lacked originality and inventiveness. Few leaders of the Church who engaged in the debate examined the Unitarian doctrine on its own terms. The Unitarians were *tout court* assimilated with European Socinians and the English Deists of the late seventeenth and the eighteenth centuries. Since Unitarianism was regarded as a resurgence of older deistic theology, it was thought appropriate to produce new editions of works by former champions of Anglicanism who fought bravely in the eighteenth-century debate against deism. Van Mildert published an edition of Waterland's works. The Oxford University Press was producing new editions of works by Joseph Butler (1692–1752) and Whately edited the *Discourse on Predestination* by William King (1650–1729).[2]

The revival of the Lockean theme of the reasonableness of Christianity is to be understood within this context. As mentioned above, the philosophy of Dugald Stewart was widely popular in the 1810s and the 1820s amongst

---

[1] J. R. Beard (ed.), *Unitarianism Exhibited in its Actual Condition* (1846), p. 149; (Anon.), 'Unitarians in England', *British Magazine*, 3 (1833), 209–10; A. D. Gilbert, *Religion and Society in Industrial England* (1976), pp. 40–1; Baden Powell, *Rational Religion Examined* (henceforth *R.R.E.*), pp. 51, 234, and 'Notes', pp. 185–256.

[2] Garbett, *The Book of Genesis*, pp. 4, 8; Whately (ed.), *The Right Method*; J. Butler, *The Analogy of Religion, Natural and Revealed* (1820). It has often been stated that Whately and his friends belonged to the eighteenth-century tradition of Christian apologetic. It is important to stress that this was not the result of acquiescence in tradition, but of a conscious decision determined by their assessment of contemporary threats to the Anglican Church.

Anglican intellectuals; the *Quarterly Review* and the early Noetics united in the praise of Stewart. However, the increasingly critical tone of Scottish academic culture towards the English universities caused alarm and ill feeling. Stewart's philosophy was thought to provide the intellectual scheme of reference for Scottish Whiggery as represented by the *Edinburgh Review*. Though several tenets of Stewart's philosophy still found upholders in England, and at Oxford in particular, the philosophy of John Locke was seen as a more appropriate and safer intellectual tool against contemporary challenges.

A secondary figure such as Richard Lloyd well expressed the feeling of a High Churchman in search of a theologically reliable philosophical authority. Lloyd confessed to admiring the 'multifarious learning' displayed by Stewart; yet, 'the lights it communicates are by no means proportionate to the splendid expectations it excites; I cannot but own, that I rose from the perusal of it with an increased attachment to Locke'. Stewart demonstrated the limits of human reason, which he regarded as capable of reaching universal and necessary truths only in deductive systems such as mathematics, with no contacts with natural objects. Copleston, Whately, Lloyd, and Baden Powell were looking for a deductive demonstration of the authority of the scriptures. Their aim was a concept of reason which asserted that the human understanding had nothing to say about revelation, but that God's word had to be accepted without further or indeed any question. Many felt that Stewart indeed provided such a concept of the human understanding, but that he refused to turn his philosophical sophistication into a system of Christian apologetic. Locke's theme of the reasonableness of Christianity provided a suitable corrective to Stewart's otherwise fully adequate philosophical exercises.[3]

Baden Powell's attitude towards the limitations of reason in religious matters moved from the cultural premises summarized above. He criticized what he considered to be the philosophical fallacy of Unitarian deism by stressing the reasonableness of conceiving the contents of the scriptures as above the reach of human reason. Furthermore, in characteristic Noetic and Stewartian fashion, he also argued that the debates between Deists and orthodox Anglicans often arose out of a persistent refusal on both sides to adopt rigorous rules of reasoning. The lack of clear definitions of the concepts employed was particularly deplorable in Baden Powell's eyes. The defect was to be accounted for on historical grounds, though it is significant that he laid much blame on the traditional system of English higher education.

The English universities, Baden Powell argued, offered students little

---

[3] Lloyd, *Two Important Questions*, p. 32. Though Prof. Aarsleff is right in pointing out the growing dissatisfaction with Locke in early nineteenth-century England, it is suggested that several Anglican divines carefully studied his works, and professed their acceptance of several features of his philosophical reflections. See W. R. Fey, 'J. H. Newman, empiricist philosophy and the certainty of faith' (D.Phil. thesis, Oxford University, 1977); Ellis, *Seven against Christ*.

encouragement in pursuing a thorough investigation of the methodology of the curricular disciplines, divinity among others. The persistent institutional disregard for sound philosophical education was seen by Baden Powell as favouring the contemporary success of the Unitarian doctrine, as well as the numerous secessions from the Anglican Church into Dissenting bodies. He was also convinced that the time for piecemeal counterattacks was over: the strength and number of the adversaries of the Anglican doctrine required a more sophisticated strategy. It was his declared intention to provide the philosophical basis for a comprehensive system of Christian Anglican apologetic.[4]

Baden Powell considered the existence of God and the truth of revelation as non-contentious issues. This assumption was justified by the fact that all the active non-Anglican religious denominations – Dissenters, Unitarians, Roman Catholics – obviously agreed that there was a god and that the scriptures represented his word. In the 1820s atheism or extreme forms of deism were politically defeated and were living a clandestine life helped by the circulation of works by Volney, d'Holbach, Carlile and Paine. The aggressive secularism of the late 1840s and the agnosticism of the 1850s and 1860s were yet to come. At the end of the Napoleonic wars there were few signs of a large-scale attack on the credibility of revelation coming from the 'educated' section of the British population. The theological situation of the late 1810s and early 1820s also explains why Baden Powell's contributions to Anglican journals were almost silent on the subject of natural theology.

In *Rational Religion Examined* the theme of natural theology was briefly considered but only in order to remark that it proved an effective argument against the atheist, in so far as it provided testimonials of the existence of a supernatural designing mind. Contemporary theological debates, Baden Powell explained, did not assign a central role to natural theology. This was because the polemic with the opponents of the Church, even radical Unitarians, was not about the existence of God or revelation, but was instead concerned with the different answers given to the questions: 'Where is the precise record and depository of this revelation? In what manner is it to be received and understood? By what principles are we to proceed in examining and interpreting its purport? In what sense are we to regard its declarations?'[5]

The various religious denominations claimed that their doctrine and exegesis represented the only possible interpretation of the scripture and Christian truth. Baden Powell was, however, convinced that the key point of Christian apologetic was not the sophistication of the doctrine, but the question of the applicability of reason to matters of religion. Once the methodological guidelines for theological inquiry were established, then it was possible to counteract prevailing error and to show that Anglican teaching was 'the very model of caution and discrimination'.

⁴ *R.R.E.*, pp. 5, 24–7.   ⁵ *R.R.E.*, pp. 22, 37.

Baden Powell followed Locke in maintaining that revelation implied the communication of truth otherwise unattainable by man. Mere common sense was sufficient to suggest that matters involving the nature of the deity and the scheme of his dispensation to man, by far exceeded the powers of human understanding. No concept of authoritative teaching or articles of faith were required for a man to be convinced of this fact. Indeed, it was sufficient briefly to consider the limits of human reason to perceive that human standards of truth were not applicable to judging the credibility of the scripture.

A survey of the subjects upon which human intellectual powers were engaged revealed that the mind was capable of two kinds of knowledge. The first was described by Baden Powell as characterized by the possibility of apprehending the 'ultimate principle' of the subject under investigation. The second and by far the most common kind of knowledge available to man was defined by the impossibility of obtaining any final insight into the essential features of the object investigated. Baden Powell repeated with Stewart and Whately that *knowledge* in the full sense of the word was attainable only in deductive systems not dealing with matters of fact, but with pure creations of the intellect, such as mathematical and geometrical objects. In pure axiomatic reasoning, the definitions which constituted the starting point of the chain of deductions were 'ultimate principles'.

Not surprisingly, Baden Powell repeated with Stewart that geometry and mathematics were the model of perfect knowledge. In these branches of science, man's inquiries attained the maximum degree of certainty and consistency. In geometrical and mathematical reasoning the definition of an object coincided with its existence: geometrical objects, for instance, were 'the creatures of our intellect'. Geometrical entities, Baden Powell argued, existed 'solely by virtue of... definition. ... Setting out from this definition, therefore, we may proceed to show that it will involve such and such properties, and that such and such assertions respecting it will involve contradictions'.

However, in the majority of cases in which men were engaged in understanding reality, imprecision and fundamental difficulties prevented them from attaining conclusions comparable to geometrical truth. Even when the utmost care was taken in defining the terms and the concepts employed, the definition conveyed nothing more than a description, however accurate, of the properties immediately accessible to man's limited faculties. Baden Powell conceded that it was indeed possible to expand upon these partial definitions by following a pattern of rigorous deduction, analogous to the procedure adopted in geometrical reasoning.

The conclusions reached by applying axiomatic procedures to our definitions of natural objects did not escape the daunting imprecision which characterized the premisses of the deductive train. No necessary truth could be reached when dealing with matters of fact. The inherent partiality of any such conclusions was a warning to the rational inquirer to proceed with the utmost care when attempting to 'ascend towards the higher principle' from the data at his disposal. Thus, it was imperative to state all the foreseeable and actual exceptions to any general conclusion which appeared to account for a number of phenomena:

> If we know the ulterior principle, then we may perhaps reduce those exceptions to their proper place, and regard them as in fact all parts of one great system. But if we have not this knowledge, the utmost we can do is carefully to state those exceptions, as modifying the general truth; and though we do not pretend to understand how they are to be reconciled to each other, yet still we do not think that a reason for overlooking the apparent difficulty, or endeavouring to explain it away by artful subtleties and fanciful refinements.[6]

Theories in particular were bound to influence the judgement of the inquirer. Indeed, the most daunting feature of scientific inquiry was the problem of keeping a careful balance between facts and theories:

> In philosophical inquiries it is often a matter of greater difficulty for an ill-instructed mind to admit a number of simple facts, than to apprehend an abstruse theory. In the latter there is generally something to captivate the imagination; whilst the former have a harsh, and perhaps incongruous appearance; they are multifarious and unconnected, and the apprehension does not readily collect and combine them.[7]

A theory 'pleases by seeming to reduce all the facts to their common first principle'. However, the well-instructed mind knew that the validity of a theory was open to an indefinite number of falsifications, equal at least to the number of facts it pretended to explain. Within the limits of the conditions of observation, the 'fact' was regarded as certain, whereas the theory was *a priori* uncertain. Theories were based on the assumption that the definition of the fact under observation was capable of including all its relevant properties, and that the several facts the theory was assumed to explain had relevant properties in common. It was not in the power of the inquirer to prove either of those two points.[8]

This expression of caution regarding the use of theories in the natural and the physical sciences could be seen as partly revising the ideas on the positive role of hypotheses and theories in science Baden Powell put forward in his early contributions to the *British Critic*. Furthermore, the definition of 'scientific facts' was rather cavalier, since Baden Powell simply distinguished between the apprehension of a phenomenon at the level of observation, and the formulation of a definition of it, without expanding at all on so crucial an epistemological issue.

---

[6] *R.R.E.*, pp. 25–7, 173; Stewart, *Elements*, vol. ii, pp. 203–43; on necessary and contingent truth in Stewart, see Corsi, 'The heritage of Dugald Stewart'; Whately acknowledged his debt to Stewart for the definition of necessary and contingent truth, *The Right Method*, p. 87; Stewart's discussion of necessity and contingency constituted the basis for the discussion of the issue by authors like W. Whewell, J. F. Herschel, W. R. Lyall and John Stuart Mill.

[7] *R.R.E.*, p. 175.   [8] *R.R.E.*, p. 175.

In *Rational Religion Examined* Baden Powell was primarily concerned with sketching the epistemological premisses for his denunciation of Unitarian theological rationalism. His aim was to charge the Unitarians with disregarding the 'facts' of revelation in order to favour partial though somewhat attractive general theories. Thus, since he wanted to extol the epistemological status of the 'facts' of the scriptures, he avoided discussing the philosophical status of 'facts' in general. Indeed, the theological preoccupation underlying Baden Powell's analysis of human knowledge in the 1826 work made him both insist on the primacy of facts in science, and emphasize the danger of theories rather than their heuristic value.[9]

Baden Powell still argued that scientific progress was not characterized by mere accumulation of data. The building of theories was still seen as an essential and legitimate feature of science. Theories led to the formulation of general principles, which constituted the broad theoretical guidelines of science. The history of the physical sciences, from the time when Bacon and Newton established the correct experimental foundation of science, demonstrated the point: the more men discovered increasingly abstract principles connecting together numerous classes of phenomena, the more they were convinced of the uniformity and simplicity of the natural order. In other words, it was possible to frame broad conceptions of the course of nature as a whole. He did however stress that the epistemological status of broad theoretical principles was extremely weak, when compared with the far stronger status of the 'fact' immediately apprehended in experiment or observation. Thus, even though scientific progress allowed the inquirer to argue that natural phenomena were governed by criteria of uniformity and simplicity, it was wrong to assume this conclusion as a dogmatic guideline in future research.

Baden Powell insisted that it was not the simplicity of a theory that necessarily recommended it as the correct explanation of experiments and observations. Had scientists assumed a criterion of geometrical simplicity in astronomical inquiries, they would have been led to conclude that planets were describing circular orbits, and would have opposed the correct elliptical theory of planetary motion. Baden Powell argued that failure to appreciate the provisional character of general scientific principles could in fact represent a serious obstacle towards the further development of science. The consideration of the rôle of general theories in science reinforced the conclusion that hypotheses or theories which rejected parts of the observations or experiments under consideration, could not be adopted without seriously impairing the whole inquiry. The only correct way of producing a theory, Baden Powell

---

9 The consideration of scriptural passages as 'facts' the deep nature of which was for ever unknown to man, and the consequent conclusion that theological statements could not be taken for absolutely reliable representations of revealed doctrine were at the basis of Hampden's Bampton Lectures. Hampden too was an admirer of Stewart, and wished to apply the latter's critique of science to the critique of dogmatic theology; see below, Part II, chs. 7 and 8.

concluded, was 'to frame it upon the general expressions of all the particular facts'.[10]

The epistemological reflections Baden Powell embarked upon were designed to confer philosophical authority upon his approach to contemporary theological debates. In line with the reasonableness-of-Christianity tradition fully endorsed by the Noetics and by wider circles of contemporary High Churchmen, he assumed that miracles and prophecies attested the supernatural origin of the scriptures. When the divine origin of the testaments was established, it was but logical to emphasize that the content of revelation was to be approached with the utmost caution. Baden Powell stressed the difference between his brand of Christian apologetic and the one represented by the natural theology tradition. The concept of God framed through reflection upon the natural order was a false yardstick against which to judge scriptural narrative, nor could the attributes of the divine creative mind be deduced from natural phenomena.[11]

The existence of evil in nature and in human society was considered by Baden Powell as a particularly pertinent illustration of this point. One of the major conclusions of natural theologians was the acknowledgement of God's benevolence displayed throughout the natural and the moral world. However, according to Baden Powell, it was equally true that there was in nature much evil which was not tending towards any foreseeable good. To many minds, the presence of such unjustified or unjustifiable evil clearly contradicted the concept of God's perfect benevolence. To Baden Powell's mind, the difficulty of explaining the existence of evil only proved the philosophical weakness of human theories when applied to judging the eternal design. Furthermore, he pointed out that terms such as 'benevolence', 'wisdom', or 'power' used to describe God's attributes were derived by analogy from human behaviour. This was indeed a further major weakness of natural theologians, who assumed that the conclusions reached through the contemplation of human ethical propensities or phenomenology could be employed in describing the attributes of God.[12]

Baden Powell's remarks on the existence of evil in nature and on the weak epistemological status of natural theology were conclusions faithfully repeating reflections by Van Mildert, Copleston and Whately on the subject. Expanding upon Van Mildert's criticism of natural theology, Copleston added a note of philosophical sophistication to the Hackney disregard for natural theology. Copleston discussed the question of the existence of evil in nature in order

---

[10] *R.R.E.*, p. 175.

[11] *R.R.E.*, p. 134. The same astronomical example was later used by (W. Whewell), 'Modern Science – Inductive Philosophy', *Q.R.*, 45 (1831), 401; for Stewart's ideas on the misleading concept of theoretical simplicity, see *Elements*, vol. ii, ch. 4, sect. iv. *R.R.E.*, pp. 70–4.

[12] *R.R.E.*, pp. 76–8. for a summary of contemporary debates on the existence of evil, see Forrester, 'Development of Pusey', pp. 44–7.

to explain that social injustice and human suffering could not be seen as disproving or contradicting the benevolence of the creator.

Copleston's considerations were part of his indirect defence of Malthusian population laws. Though he disagreed with certain features of the Malthusian view of human society, Copleston accepted the basic theory of the *Essay on Population*. A recent authoritative commentator has argued that Copleston failed to notice that Malthus 'raised the question of overpopulation and divine forethought' and attempted to formulate his population theory in providential terms. It could be argued on the contrary that Copleston was fully aware of Malthus's justification of his own theory. Copleston's silence was designed to avoid open disagreement with an author whose views he accepted, and for the sake of making his own philosophical strategy more acceptable. According to Copleston, the Malthusian population law could not be seen as questioning God's benevolence. On the contrary, it revealed the unreliability of human reason when engaged in inquiries so far above its powers. It was as wrong to deny God's benevolence because of the existence of evil as it was to expand upon explanations which would eventually cause more confusion than conviction. Malthus's view that struggle and strife were providentially arranged to develop man's faculties, could not be endorsed by Copleston.[13]

As contemporaries were quick to point out, Copleston's approach revealed a weak flank, since it was undermining too great a portion of Christian ethical thought. If analogies from human behaviour were not to be applied to religious discourse, in what terms were Christians to preach God's parental care for his creatures? The brand of Christian agnosticism elaborated by Copleston was treading on very dangerous ground, since it could have been construed as describing a god too remote from human ethical concerns to be a guide for Christians in living: 'it would destroy the confidence of prayer, and the ardour of devotion'.[14] Baden Powell and the *British Critic* reviewer who commented on the debate did not accept this criticism. Baden Powell followed Copleston's approach with enthusiasm. He considered the establishment of methodological guidelines in theological inquiry a more important task than the preservation of popular religious views, which only too often proved liable to fanaticism and extravagance.[15]

Baden Powell's description of Anglican Christianity exemplified the tone and the order of priorities of Noetic thinking and contemporary High Church religious thought in general. Thus, for instance, he defined Anglican worship as 'a worship of reason, and does not derive its life and support from mere

---

[13] Van Mildert, *Historical View of Infidelity* (1806), vol i, pp. 3–7; on Archbishop King's views on evil see pp. 53–64. Copleston, *Enquiry into Necessity*, pp. 53–64; Whately (ed.), *The Right Method*, pp. 105–26; Soloway, *Prelates and People*, p. 102. On Malthus's theology, see Soloway, and J. M. Pullen, 'Malthus's theological ideas and their influence on his principle of population', *History of Political Economy*, 13 (1981), 39–54.

[14] E. W. Grinfield, *Vindiciae Analogicae* (1822), p. 39.

[15] (Anon.), 'Copleston on Predestination', *B.C.*, 28 (1822), 3–32.

impressions on the senses, or mere impulses on the feelings'. When confronted with the shocking conclusions of Malthusian political economy, those Christians whose faith was based on feeling were often left to doubt the benevolence of the creator or to embark upon extravagant speculations in order to explain away the difficulty. The rational Anglican Christian, on the other hand, knew that his inductive inferences concerning the attributes of God had an extremely weak epistemological status. It was the rational Christian who felt irresistibly impelled to rely upon the scriptures as the sole source of advice and guidance in religious matters.[16]

The question of the presence of evil in nature highlighted the general case of apparent contradictions between human concepts of God and the often obscure or contradictory passages of revelation dealing with the attributes of God. As was the case with the question of the existence of evil in nature, theologians and philosophers often attempted to be 'wiser than the word' and put forward explanatory theories which appeared to provide a satisfactory solution for the alleged contradiction. Unitarian theology, according to Baden Powell, presented dramatic instances of the consequences of approaching the scriptures with preconceived ideas about the personality and the attributes of God.

He raised the specific case of the passages in the scriptures which spoke of the divinity of the Father, the Son and the Holy Spirit, though other statements could be found stressing the unity of God. Baden Powell argued that those statements could not be reconciled, by whatever effort of ingenuity. He considered that there was undoubtedly a higher philosophical category capable of embracing both classes of passages in a logical harmony. Yet, this higher principle was clearly beyond man's rational capabilities and scripture itself left men in total obscurity on the subject. The solution offered by the Unitarians was incorrect from the epistemological point of view. Their insistence on the unity of God was based on a theory which provided a satisfactory account of passages of the scriptures dealing with the personality of God, at the price of disregarding other passages of a different nature.

The Unitarians disregarded the simplest rules of inductive reasoning: they accepted as true a theory which failed to account for all the 'facts' of revelation. The Anglican doctrine, creeds and formularies were framed according to the collected evidence provided by the scriptures on crucial features of the revealed message. Baden Powell agreed that the Anglican articles themselves were to be thought of as 'theories' built upon the 'facts' of the scriptures, and were therefore inevitably framed 'in terms of human origin'. However, Anglican theologians took every possible step to restrict and define the meaning of the terms employed 'to express in one word the doctrine of scripture, which otherwise would require much circumlocution...; in using such terms we have a due regard not to attaching any meaning to them beyond that of their being the representatives of scriptural ideas'.[17]

A distinction was maintained between Church doctrine – inevitably framed in human language – and the 'facts of revelation' – the literal formulation of a communication from God. This theme was further illustrated when the Unitarian attitude towards the nature and attributes of God was compared with the Roman Catholic approach to the subject. According to Baden Powell, Unitarians presumed to harmonize contradictory statements of the scriptures in a single incomplete theory, whereas the Roman Catholics were guilty of the opposite mistake. Roman Catholic theology was seen by Baden Powell as characterized by a tendency to overcharge the plain meaning of scripture with sophisticated philosophical hermeneutics. The Church of Rome had been 'the parent, or at least the patroness of the scholastic theology'. Van Mildert's remarks on the rôle of scholastic philosophy in Roman Catholic theology were quoted with approval by Baden Powell, who acknowledged his debt to the professor of divinity of his undergraduate days.[18]

Supported by Van Mildert's authority, Baden Powell went on to argue that doctrines and formularies of the Church of England represented a successful attempt at restoring the 'facts' of revelation, which had been perverted by centuries of confusion between the word of God and dogmatic theology. According to Baden Powell, the advancement of philosophical and scientific studies after the Reformation helped make clear the characteristic capabilities and limitations of human reason. The growing intellectual enlightenment had nothing to do with attempts at undermining belief in the scriptures. Indeed, it provided the intellectual tools for a more aggressive Christian apologetic, capable of exposing the unphilosophical, irrational presuppositions of the self-styled advocates of rational religion. The more philosophy advanced, the more it became clear that the revealed word was incommensurable with man's intellectual powers.[19]

Rational Religion Examined was a work which pleased the early Noetics and the Hackney leaders. The authorities Baden Powell relied upon were representatives of both schools. Works by Rose, Van Mildert, and indeed even Jones of Nayland and H. H. Norris, were quoted together with the more recent productions by Copleston and Whately. As a concrete sign of approval, Van Mildert and Copleston exercised their influence to have Baden Powell elected Savilian Professor of Geometry at Oxford a few months after the publication of the book. The young author pleased Copleston and Whately by advocating the necessity of following strict rules of induction in theological inquiries. He also pleased Van Mildert by his critique of natural theology.

[17] *R.R.E.*, pp. 79–81. It is important to stress that Baden Powell was the first member of the Noetic group explicitly to theorize an inductive approach to theology grounded on the epistemology of Stewart: a fault later attributed to Hampden.
[18] *R.R.E.*, pp. 95, 196–9.   [19] *R.R.E.*, pp. 211–12, 216–18.

Rose expressed in print his approval of the first literary production by the youngest member of the Phalanx.[20]

Baden Powell expressed the hard-line approach of the Hackney leaders towards the claims of Dissenters and Roman Catholics in a language and philosophical style strongly influenced by the Oriel teaching. He clearly thought that the Noetic school had elaborated a successful philosophical approach to the theological and cultural problems which had engaged the attention of his Hackney relatives from the early 1800s. In an age characterized by growing social, economic and cultural progress, it was natural that the enemies of religion should refurbish the old arguments against the scriptures and the Anglican Church in accordance with the prevalent taste and the cultural priorities of the time. The Oriel leaders were opposing with the utmost vigour the tenets of these adversaries, in particular the Unitarians, by showing the philosophical fallacies at the basis of their arguments. At the same time, the Oriel Noetics could claim that they avoided discrediting the ideas of their opponents by resorting to political alarmism, invective, or ecclesiastical authority. It was on the ground chosen by their opponents that the Noetics were meeting them, and with appreciable results.

[20] (Anon.), 'Powell's *Rational Religion Examined*', *Quarterly Theological Review*, 4 (1826), 185–93; B.P.J., 5 Dec, 1826, 'Letter from the Provost of Oriel proposing the Sav. Professorship'; British Library, Peel Papers, Ms Add 40.390, fol. 204: letter from Van Mildert to Sir Robert Peel, 11 Dec. 1826. H. J. Rose, *State of the Protestant Religion in Germany* (1829 edn.), p. xxiv. See also Ellis, *Seven against Christ*, pp. 217–22

6

Baden Powell between Oriel and Hackney

The preceding chapters have drawn attention to the relevance of Baden Powell's early literary output to the understanding of Oxford and English intellectual life in the 1820s. Historians have customarily opposed traditional High Church theology and the Oxford Movement to the daring 'liberalism' of the Noetics. The term 'liberal' in this context has been grossly misused. A mistaken analogy with the meaning of the term in the later decades of the nineteenth century has biased the assessment of intellectual and religious movements in the early decades of the century. Thus Edward Sillem, the learned editor of Newman's philosophical notebooks, described Hume, Bentham and Locke as the prophets of the 'liberal world' in the eyes of British intellectuals active in the first quarter of the nineteenth century.[1]

The analysis of Baden Powell's early works demonstrates that the philosophy of John Locke admitted of more traditional and conservative uses in High Church circles. Many clergymen viewed the revival of the Lockean theme of the reasonableness of Christianity as a major success in the fight against Unitarianism and 'liberalism'. Sillem also described the 'Liberal Enlightenment' as a movement which 'would lead Anglicans like Whately towards... enforcing the principle that articles of faith can be passed as credible on the sole condition that they can survive the severest logical test as satisfactorily as any purely mathematical theorem'. W. R. Fey has recently argued that the 'Noetics... concluded that the truths of faith like those of mathematics should be immediately compelling to an honest mind'.[2]

The early works by Copleston and Whately show that the Noetics made considerable efforts to prove that the reverse was true. Certainly they thought that the evaluation of the evidence for the credibility of scripture was to be grounded on rigorous intellectual procedures. Yet, they also insisted that the scriptural doctrines called for total and unconditional acceptance. They maintained that no criterion of human rationality could possibly have applied to judge such mysterious revealed truths as the Unity and Trinity, the Atonement, or the promise of an eternal life. Reason, far from pretending to evaluate

---

[1] E. Sillem, *The Philosophical Notebook of John Henry Newman*, 2 vols. (1969), vol. i, p. 27.
[2] Sillem, vol. i, p. 164; Fey, 'J. H. Newman', p. 7.

the credibility of scriptural doctrine or scrutinize the realm of faith, was capable of proving that the Christian truth had to be accepted even *against* reason, since there was little doubt that the revealed message was by definition above reason.

During the 1820s the emphasis on this brand of Christian apologetic was not peculiar to the Oriel circle, though it could be claimed that the Noetic reformulation of the reasonableness-of-Christianity tradition was particularly sophisticated. The constant reference by the early Noetics to the economic, social and intellectual debates of the time appealed to the intelligentsia of the country. Even the *Edinburgh Review* was forced to admit that the 'school of speculative philosophy' at Oxford was a marked and positive novelty within the High Church cultural scene.[3]

The epithets 'Noetic' and 'Oriel school' are, however, misleading when applied without further qualification to Copleston's early works or to later publications by Hampden, Blanco White and Whately. A more precise definition must therefore be attempted. The first part of this study referred to Copleston, Davison and Whately as representatives of the early Noetic school. The first section of the second part will be devoted to assessing the central features of the late Noetic school, or more accurately, of Whately's school.

As far as the early Noetic school is concerned, in the 1810s and the early 1820s Copleston was undoubtedly the acknowledged leader of the group. Whately's early thought was clearly influenced by Copleston. A detailed analysis of the early Noetic outlook, and of Copleston's leadership and literary performance, far exceeds the scope of the present study. However, the study of Baden Powell's early theological and philosophical standpoint substantiates the general conclusion that the so-called Oriel 'liberalism' and the Hackney conservatism had crucial common features which historians have been extremely reluctant to acknowledge. It is for this reason that it will be important to consider key themes within the Noetic outlook.[4]

A brief consideration of Baden Powell's university education provides further evidence of the political and intellectual alignments within High Church circles and in Oxford during the 1810s and the early 1820s. Van Mildert, as the acknowledged guide of the Hackney group in theological matters and the unquestioned champion of High Church conservatism, advised Baden Powell senior to favour Oxford rather than Cambridge for his son's education. The Cambridge intelligentsia were more concerned with mathematical proficiency than with theology. Furthermore, in Van Mildert's eyes, evangelicalism was stronger at Cambridge than at Oxford. Baden Powell was sent to Oriel, which,

---

3 (J. Mackintosh), 'Stewart's *Introduction to the Encyclopaedia*', *Q.R.*, 36 (1821), p. 254; R. J. Mackintosh, *Memoirs of the Life of the Rt. Hon. Sir James Mackintosh*, 2 vols. (1836), vol. i, pp. 426, 435.

4 Sillem, *Notebook of Newman*; J. Tulloch, *Movements of Religious Thought in Britain during the Nineteenth Century* (1885), ch. 2; Jones, 'Anglican theological thought', ch. 4.

of all the Oxford colleges, was described in the 1810s as the successful rival of Christ Church and the new centre of influence in Oxford intellectual life.

There was no reason why Copleston's writings or his efforts to restore academic standards, should have aroused suspicion. On the contrary, his essays on necessity and predestination furnished philosophical proof of a favourite point among High Church polemicists, namely that Methodism and Dissenting theology in general had marked features in common with open infidelity. Copleston distinguished himself by opposing the *Edinburgh Review* in defence of the elegance, dignity, and propriety of liberal studies at the English universities. He strongly denied current allegations that the only occupation of the Anglican intelligentsia was the parasitical enjoyment of privilege, and that the English universities were irreversibly out of touch with the pressing cultural demands of modern society. Copleston proved well aware of the economic and social questions of the day and was fully equipped to deal with them. He produced able disquisitions on crucial contemporary issues such as the bullion debate and Poor Law reform.[5]

Whately's first book, the *Historic Doubts relative to Napoleon Buonaparte* (1819) shocked a few pious minds. To many High Churchmen, Whately's witty narrative of Napoleon's military successes in a language imitating the style of the scriptures was painfully evocative of the blasphemous paraphrases of the Bible and the liturgy produced by the notorious William Hone. However, the book proved extremely successful, and attracted more sympathy than the apocalyptic denunciations by clergymen calling upon the government to repress every form of political and religious dissent.[6]

The claim that the Oriel brand of Christian and Anglican apologetic was tolerated if not actually endorsed by the Hackney leaders is supported by further evidence than that provided by an analysis of the philosophical and theological themes discussed by Davison, Copleston, Whately, Baden Powell and Van Mildert. The major works by the early Noetics were favourably reviewed in the *Quarterly Review*, the *British Critic*, and the *Christian Remembrancer*. When Copleston's essay on necessity and predestination was attacked by Edward Grinfield, the *British Critic* reviewer – certainly a member of the Oriel community – made sarcastic comments on the provincial clergyman who dared to intervene in debates so far above his accomplishments.

5 (E. Copleston), *A Reply to the Calumnies of the Edinburgh Review* (1810) and *A Letter to the Right Hon. Robert Peel on the Pernicious Effects of a Variable Standard of Value* (1819); Soloway, *Prelates and People*; B. Hilton, *Corn, Cash and Commerce* (1977), pp. 44, 94, 309; P. Corsi, 'The heritage of Dugald Stewart'.

6 (R. Whately), *Historic Doubts* (1819), and (Anon.), *C.R.*, 1 (1819), 302–7; on W. Hone see *D.N.B.* British Library, Hone Papers, and Aspland, *Memoir of Robert Aspland*, pp. 386–7. Copleston thought the prosecution of Hone inexpedient, see Copleston (ed.), *Letters of Dudley to Llandaff*, p. 190; Lord Dudley often expressed to Copleston the pre-occupation of conservative politicians and aristocrats that Oxford was unable to put a remedy to low academic and ethical standards.

At a more concrete level, protégés of Whately and Copleston were helped by the Hackney leaders in finding temporary employment as curates at Hackney. Hampden was appointed editor of the *Christian Remembrancer* in 1825, a position he could not have obtained without the approval of the Hackney men. A brief comment on the complexity of the contemporary theological scene is appropriate in order to explain how the differences which did exist between Oriel and Hackney – for instance, the Oriel dons did not share the Hackney fury against the Bible Society though they themselves opposed evangelicalism – were not an obstacle to co-operation between the two groups. It is well known that the High Church party and the episcopacy of the Anglican Church of the early 1800s lacked a unified theological and philosophical outlook, a not uncommon feature in the Anglican tradition. Later events, the debates over the establishment of the Jerusalem episcopate, the Gorham judgement and *Essays and Reviews* in particular, proved how difficult it was to formulate the official Anglican view of crucial Christian and Church doctrines.

As far as the Hackney group was concerned, it has been shown above that in the 1810s and the 1820s the Hutchinsonianism inherited from the Nayland group was modified if not progressively abandoned by Norris and Watson. The Hackney men increasingly concentrated on Church policy and parliamentary manoeuvrings. The intellectual side of their religious and cultural policy was acknowledged to be rather weak. Thus, the benevolence and indeed the approbation evinced towards the early Noetic publications is not surprising; the Oriel men proved extremely effective in exorcising the pretended intellectual superiority of the Unitarians.

At a more sophisticated level, a close analysis of the Hackney and the Oriel theological productions reveals that several themes Van Mildert dwelt upon in his Boyle and Bampton lectures – the criticism of reversion to *a priori* philosophical categories in the interpretation of the scriptures, the condemnation of scholastic theology and philosophy, the critique of natural theology – were central features in early publications by Copleston and Whately. It may be anticipated that the critique of the influence of scholastic philosophy upon Roman Catholic theology, and on theology in general, was a topic also debated within Whately's school, and one which became the guiding principle of the much abused 1832 Bampton lectures by Hampden. The elaboration of sophisticated theological and epistemological considerations to prove the necessity of a literal acceptance of the scriptures or the Noetic insistence on the incommensurability between revelation and the human reason, appealed to the basic Hutchinsonian literalism of the Hackney leaders.

The eclectic marshalling of the philosophies of Stewart, Locke and Butler made the Noetic approach all the more attractive to contemporary readers. Bishop Butler's *Analogy* was a text the early Noetics viewed with particular favour. Direct reference to Butler's work was as prominent as quotations of texts by Stewart or Locke. The comments by Butler on the uncertainty of human knowledge, on the difficulty of fully understanding the revealed message as well as the natural and moral worlds, were understandably appealing to the apologetic aims of Copleston, Whately and Baden Powell.

A commentator has recently argued that Newman 'found in Butler a fresh alternative to the artificial reasoning of the Noetics'. The view that the Noetics were anti-Butlerians is not new. As early as 1821 Grinfield accused Copleston of subverting the Butlerian tradition by his critique of natural theology. Grinfield argued that the discussion of the role of analogical reasoning in natural theology by Copleston was undermining a cornerstone of Christian apologetic. Analysis of Copleston's works reveals that the Provost of Oriel College was on the contrary a keen follower of Butler. Copleston had no intention of questioning *in toto* the possibility of applying analogies from man's intellectual and moral experience to God's operations in the natural and the moral world.[7]

His aim was to counteract the tendency to make human analogies the standard by which God's works had to be judged. Analogical comparison between God's and man's behaviour had a practical import and a legitimate place in Christian thought. However, according to Copleston, these analogies had no cognitive or normative value. The only source of man's knowledge of God was in the scriptures. In his reply to Grinfield's criticism (1822), the Provost of Oriel took great care to prove that his argument did not contradict the Butlerian brand of Christian apologetic: 'in pursuing the argument of my own discourses, the work of this excellent author was always present to my mind'.[8]

The *British Critic* reviewer agreed with Copleston that his approach to theology was unmistakably Butlerian. Early works by Davison, Whately and Baden Powell repeatedly emphasized the Butlerian theme of the inherent uncertainty and limited power of human knowledge. Man's pretence at judging the difficulties and apparent contradictions of revelation was based on gross epistemological misunderstanding. The question of the actual debts of the early Noetics towards the philosophical relativism and probabilism of Butler, and indeed the general question of the influence exercised by Butler on early and mid nineteenth-century thought, certainly requires closer analysis. Yet, there is enough historical evidence to leave little doubt as to the feelings of the Noetics towards Butler. Hampden publicly claimed that he had proposed inclusion of the *Analogy* in the list of compulsory reading for Oxford under-graduates.[9]

The relationship between Hackney and Oriel is relevant to any investigation

---

[7] R. J. Mackintosh, *Memoirs*, vol. ii, pp. 426–35; Fey, 'J. H. Newman', p. 23; W. de Smet, *L'influence de Butler sur la théorie de la foi chez Newman* (1963), p. 34; Grinfield, *Vindiciae Analogicae*, pp. 22, 48 and *Vindiciae Analogicae Part Second* (1822), pp. 72–87.

[8] E. Copleston, *Remarks upon the Objections Made to Certain Passages in the Enquiry Concerning Necessity and Predestination* (1822), pp. 72–87.

[9] (Anon.), 'Copleston on Predestination', 30–1; R. D. Hampden, *Introduction to the Second Edition of the Bampton Lectures of the Year 1832* (1837), p. 37.

of the defensive intellectual strategies produced within High Church circles in the 1810s and the 1820s. A comprehensive study of the intellectual movements briefly described here will provide much needed insight into the actual state of affairs in philosophical and theological debates at the period: analysis of the intellectual, social and political events of the first and second decades of the century has generally been an uncritical endorsement of the view later generations and historians had of their past. This practice has, however, produced serious distortions in the historical assessment of crucial features of early nineteenth-century intellectual life.

Educated at the core of the Hackney Phalanx, Baden Powell came to Oxford well equipped to evaluate the approach to contemporary theological and philosophical debates elaborated by his Oriel teachers. Placed under the protection of Van Mildert, Baden Powell started his period of residence at Oriel College in January 1815.

His contacts with the early Noetics were deeper than those of an ordinary undergraduate. Apart from the obvious patronage of his Hackney relatives, Baden Powell also enjoyed the friendship of William Law Pope and Henry Bishop, two fellow students closely linked with the Oriel leaders. Pope was the brother of Elizabeth, Whately's fiancée. Pope's father was living at Tunbridge Wells, the fashionable spa town where Baden Powell senior had a house and where he lived part of the year. Baden Powell's father was very active in supporting local schemes for extending church facilities. It is safe to assume that a common background of Church activities made Baden Powell's family well acquainted with the Popes. The friendship between Pope and Baden Powell was fostered by college life and periods of vacation spent at Tunbridge Wells.

Henry Bishop's older brother, William, had been a fellow of Oriel before being offered the living of Upton in Buckinghamshire. William Bishop was a friend of Copleston and Whately and was particularly close to Joseph Blanco White. It is however improbable that at the time of his residence at Oriel Baden Powell enjoyed any informal association with the early Noetics. He was taught by them, but it is safe to assume that a pupil–tutor relationship characterized such contacts. The close personal friendship with some of the Noetic leaders developed only in the late 1820s.

The analysis of Baden Powell's early publications shows that the young author fully endorsed the intellectual outlook of his teachers. It is also important to stress that he gave early warnings of an original elaboration of the Oriel standpoint. On theological grounds, Baden Powell proved reluctant to accept Whately's view that Church formularies and articles enjoyed derivative but secure divine origin. More important was the different emphasis Baden Powell and his teachers put on the role of science in the university curriculum. Admittedly Baden Powell's interest in scientific subjects was certainly more determined than his teachers'. Whately regarded logic as a subject of research far more important than mathematical or experimental science. Copleston had strong views on how the scientific disciplines taught at Oxford had to be advanced and advised Baden Powell not to spend too much time in promoting academic science.

The different evaluation of the import of modern science for contemporary thought marked a major difference between the Noetics and Baden Powell. It could be argued that the Hackney training taught him to pay close attention to contemporary intellectual priorities. He agreed with his teachers that the natural sciences enjoyed a weak epistemological status. However, he was also convinced that the development of science was enhancing both the quantity and quality of human information on natural phenomena. Moreover, from the point of view of the intellectual approach best equipped to meet contemporary challenges to the Anglican religion, the relevance of science was even greater. Scientific findings were acquiring unprecedented cultural authority and were bound to influence the attitude of the masses towards religion and its evidence. A modern Christian apologetic could not ignore the consequences of the spread of scientific education and values for traditional religious beliefs.

The emphasis on deductive systems as models of perfect science allowed Baden Powell further to elaborate on the Butlerian theme of the uncertainty of human knowledge. In characteristic Noetic fashion, he regarded questions of philosophical or epistemological import as relevant in approaching contemporary theological debates, though on no account was this intellectual strategy to be construed as implying that articles of faith and religious beliefs in general were to be judged according to the rules of logical consistency.

On 5 February 1827 Baden Powell was elected Savilian Professor of Geometry at Oxford. Early in October he came to live in Oxford, and started lecturing at the Ashmolean Museum. The pressure of political and social events was already producing considerable effects on theological and political alignments. Whately's school and the traditional High Church party were increasingly at odds in their interpretation of contemporary ills and on the remedies most appropriate to cure them.

PART II

BADEN POWELL AND THE NOETIC
SCHOOL

Before discussing the relevance of the late Noetic school to Baden Powell's intellectual development, it is necessary to consider whether it is legitimate to refer to a 'late Noetic school' at all. A corollary to this is the question of Whately's leadership. It could indeed be argued that Whately's essays, notwithstanding their author's claim that he was approaching his subjects systematically, were in fact occasioned by contemporary and often ephemeral debates.[1] It could also be said that the works by members of the group reveal at times significant differences of emphasis and of approach.

As far as the first point is concerned, it has already been made clear that Whately's approach to themes on which he touched evolved out of a sophisticated and coherent theological and philosophical culture. His contributions to a variety of topics have a common denominator in an intellectual programme that has been ignored by past and present historians. As far as the second point is concerned, it is undoubtedly true that there were differences within the Noetic group. Nevertheless, theologians, historians, and naturalists linked with Whately and his friends at Oriel were described by contemporaries as members of a well-defined political and cultural circle. Furthermore, historians have often overlooked the fact that the Noetics made a serious and determined effort to extend their influence on both academic and public opinion. In this context the publication of the *London Review* in the summer of 1828 should be mentioned. This editorial venture was designed to provide the late Noetics with a means of promoting their social, philosophical and theological programme.

The *Review* was edited by Blanco White and financed by a group of London intellectuals headed by Nassau Senior and Herbert Mayo (1796–1852). The intention of the editor and proprietors was that the journal should be a forum for debating intellectual and social issues facing contemporary England. It was to be open to Anglicans of various theological and political opinions. The attempt failed, mainly because of the lack of contributors. The heightened tension within Church parties in the course of 1829 made it difficult for the

---

[1] Tulloch, *Movements of Religious Thought*, p. 53.

editor to find contributors willing to identify themselves with the catholic aims of the *London Review*. It is however undeniable that the journal represented a highly significant move in the intellectual and political scene of the day.

The broadly conceived plan of the *Review* well represented the approach to contemporary issues adopted by Whately and his friends. It could be said that the guiding principle of the *London Review* was Whately's often repeated invitation to agree to disagree: the problems to be faced were of such magnitude that tangential flights towards the left or the right of the political and theological spectrum would only have worsened an already dangerous situation. Contributors ranging from Whately, Blanco White and John Henry Newman, to Baden Powell, Mayo and Edwin Chadwick (1800–90) represented often diverging interpretations of the intellectual, political and social condition of the country, though the editor hoped that all could put forward a constructive and non-partisan point of view.[2]

The detailed analysis of the events and problems mentioned above deserves a separate study. It is appropriate here to expand upon the central features of the late Noetic intellectual standpoint, in particular that of Richard Whately, in order to provide adequate background information for an understanding of Baden Powell's crucial political shifts and intellectual development during the decade 1826–36. It is also necessary to detail the succession of events which led to the breaking of the alliance between the Oriel group and other sectors of the High Church party, the Hackney Phalanx in particular. These developments provide essential insights into Baden Powell's ideas on the relationship between science and revelation, and on the role of the Anglican universities in contemporary society.

---

[2] Numbers I and II only of the first volume of the *London Review* were published: see W. E. Houghton (ed.), *The Wellesley Index to Victorian Periodicals*, vol. ii, pp. 522–8; Oriel College, Hawkins Papers, letters from Blanco White to Hawkins, 1.92: 19 August 1828; 1.94: 27 October 1828; Lambeth Palace, Whately Papers, letters from Blanco White to Whately, 2164, fols. 214–15: 9 September 1828; fols. 216–17: 6 December 1828.

7

The teaching of Richard Whately

During the 1820s Whately's reputation grew steadily in Oxford and throughout Britain. His famous *Historic Doubts relative to Napoleon Buonaparte* (1819) was followed by a flow of publications which established Whately as one of the most prolific Anglican authors of the third decade of the century. Copleston increasingly devoted his time to political manoeuvring and to London social life: ill health and his 'natural indolence' made him unwilling to embark upon any major literary project. Whately was thus the only member of the early Noetic school still actively engaged in theological and philosophical debate. Furthermore, after 1825 several pupils and friends of Whately were coming back to Oxford to occupy positions of prestige and academic influence.

In 1825 Whately was appointed Principal of St Alban Hall. The plan of taking over one of the small colleges in order to circumvent resistance to change and improvement was an old idea of Copleston's. As was often the case with Copleston's programmes, it was Whately who realized the plan. Whately proved to be a very able principal. The academic record of St Alban Hall underwent a dramatic change. In his work of reform Whately was helped by J. H. Newman, one of his most promising pupils.[1]

In 1825 Nassau Senior, a former pupil and lifelong friend of Whately, was elected first Drummond Professor of Political Economy. Senior lectured in Oxford to a disappointingly decreasing audience till 1829, the year in which Whately decided to place his reputation at the service of the newly established academic discipline. In 1826 Blanco White, a friend of Whately from the early 1810s, obtained an honorary M.A. as reward for his *Evidences against Catholicism*. Blanco White came to live in Oxford and was admitted to common-room rights at Oriel. He took lodgings near Whately's house, which he visited

---

[1] For Copleston's earliest and last recommendation to Lord Grenville on behalf of Whately's appointment to St Alban Hall, see British Library, Ms Add 59416, fol. 90r: 10 Dec. 1821 and fol. 98r: 9 March 1825. For the Dudley–Copleston correspondence, see Copleston (ed.), *Letters of the Earl of Dudley* (1840), pp. 7, 235–8; Dudley was convinced that 'improvement must be forced upon them [the university]'. He was preaching to Copleston the 'adapt institutions to the state of the country' creed of Stewart. Dudley also believed that 'if Adam Smith and Gibbon had not attacked them – to say nothing of twenty less celebrated persons, and if the world had not began to cry out shame, you ever would have had the new statute!' (p. 6)

daily. He was also on terms of close friendship with Newman, Hurrel Froude, Nassau Senior, Pusey and Hampden.[2]

In 1827 Samuel Hinds (1793–1872) came into residence at Oxford. He was a close friend of Whately, and was a member of the Oriel group with West Indian connections, which included Nassau Senior and Hampden. Hinds was appointed Vice Principal of St Alban Hall, a position left vacant by Newman when the latter was appointed tutor of Oriel in 1826. In the spring of 1827 Baden Powell came to live in the house in New College Lane allocated to the Savilian Professor of Geometry. Hampden was the last to join his friends in Oxford. In 1829 he was appointed to the board of examiners on which he served for three years, the first step of a rapid, problem-ridden academic career.[3]

The change of leadership at Oriel from Copleston to Whately was favoured by the elevation of the Provost of Oriel to the Bishopric of Llandaff in 1827. Copleston's visits to Oxford became rare. Of the early Noetics, Arnold alone was a figure of major standing in Oxford. However, he cannot be credited with an intellectual penetration or philosophical perspicuity comparable to that of Whately, and his visits to Oxford were as rare as Copleston's. Moreover, Arnold himself was to some extent under the influence of Whately. Hawkins, who succeeded Copleston as Provost of Oriel (31 January 1828) with the support of a still compact Oriel common room, was a secondary figure in intellectual matters.[4]

Hawkins clearly resented Whately's superiority. The latter was unquestionably the dominant and often domineering personality of the Oriel community. Hawkins was eager to keep his distance from Whately, especially after the publication of the *Letters on the Church. By an Episcopalian*, a much discussed work in which Whately paid him the dubious compliment of quoting with approval his sermon on authoritative tradition. Thus, Whately found himself at the head of a group of Oriel men, many of whom had been his pupils. None of the other dons represented a threat to his influence in Oriel. Opposition to Whately did not gain momentum until Newman's full 'conversion', the events following the passing of the Catholic Reform Bill, and, of course, Whately's departure for Dublin.[5]

When Baden Powell came to live in Oxford in 1827, the divergence of the

---

[2] W. J. Copleston, *Memoir of Edward Copleston* (1851), p. 104; Levy, *Nassau Senior* (1970), pp. 52–3; Tuckwell, *Pre-Tractarian Oxford*.

[3] Hinds, a contemporary of Hampden, was, like his friend, born in Barbados.

[4] Copleston was offered the see of Llandaff and the Deanery of St Paul on 30 Nov. 1827; see W. J. Copleston, *Memoir*, p. 116.

[5] (R. Whately), *Letters on the Church. By an Episcopalian* (1826), p. 67. Oriel College, Hawkins Papers, letters from Whately to Hawkins, 4.348: n.d. (1826); 4.349: 3 Dec. 1826; 2.177: 17 Aug. 1829; 2.180: 23 Nov. 1830; 2.182: 11 Oct. 1831. For an epigraphic assessment of Whately's leadership of the late Noetic school, see Overton, *The English Church* (1894), p. 119: 'Whately was beyond a doubt the leading spirit of that rising party which never rose, but which for a short time appeared likely to do for the Church what Earl Gray and his friends did for the State'.

Oriel men from the traditional High Church party, and from the Hackney Phalanx in particular, was well under way. In 1826, the year in which Baden Powell set out to prove the coincidence between the Oriel intellectual standpoint and the political and religious strategy planned at Hackney, Whately published an anonymous pamphlet, the *Letters on the Church*. Though Whately never avowed the authorship of the essay, rumours as to the identity of the 'Episcopalian' spread immediately, and the book was readily ascribed to the Principal of St Alban Hall.

The Hawkins papers and Whately's correspondence with Nassau Senior substantiate the attribution of the *Letters* to Whately. Furthermore, notwithstanding the assertion by John Hunt that the *Letters* were unlike anything Whately had already written or was to publish in later years, a careful internal analysis of the text confirms that Whately was the author of the Episcopalian pamphlet.[6]

The central theme underlying the *Letters on the Church* was that the Church had to regain independence from a state that was undergoing radical change. There were clear signs that in the near future the State could be dominated by forces hostile to the Anglican Establishment. Since the danger of reform being imposed by political and religious opponents was a real one, Whately believed it was safer to act promptly while the settlement was likely to be to the advantage of the Church.

Deeply impressed by the success of the American Episcopalian Church, Whately proposed a form of disestablishment by which the Church would retain all its property and economic privileges. The Episcopalian pointed out that a planned disestablishment would allow the Church to enforce uniformity of creed and practices, without incurring the increasingly common accusation of being a tyrannical religious monopoly which enforced superficial doctrinal acquiescence upon members fearful of sacrificing social and political privileges.

The theme of the distinction between the Old and the New Dispensation, already developed by Davison and fully accepted by Baden Powell, reinforced at an exegetical level the essentially political proposal put forward by Whately. The Church established by Christ was different from the Jewish church. Christianity forfeited all links with the temporal power. It was a mistake, though perhaps a historical necessity, that after a few centuries the early Church assumed a political role. According to Whately, the Church was a society of Christians who subscribed to its articles and accepted the formularies and the liturgy of their community: a society independent of the invidious coercive power or the 'protection' of the State.

The Church, like any other voluntary organization, should exercise its power

---

6 National Library of Wales, Senior Papers, C.492: Whately to Senior, 1826. Lambeth Palace, Whately Papers, 2164, fols. 139–41: 8 Oct. 1829, Whately to Senior; Oriel College, Hawkins Papers, 4.348: (1826), Whately to Hawkins, and 4.349: 3 Dec. 1826. Hunt, *Religious Thought*, pp. 55–8. Internal and linguistic analysis of works by Hinds gives plausibility to the hypothesis that he might have been assisting Whately in the drafting of the *Episcopalian*.

and corporate right to exclude from its community those persistently disagreeing upon doctrinal and liturgical questions. Such a procedure of excommunication would not impinge upon the civil rights of the members of the society, but would simply represent the decision of a voluntary organization to exclude a member who did not accept its rules.[7]

Whately conceived the Church as invested by Christ with the power of establishing rituals and directing the forms of devotion of its members. However, he denied that the Church articles or formularies enjoyed divine authority. It was thus unavoidable that the human interpreters of the scriptures should disagree among themselves: the history of theology amply illustrated the point. Yet, the acknowledgement of differences of opinion on historical and theoretical grounds was made by Whately with important limitations and essential quali-fications. A Christian who believed that the doctrinal system of his Church diverged in substantial points from scripture, was free to discuss the matter with his brethren in order to forward his pious wish of restoring what he regarded to be the true meaning of revelation. On the other hand, the Church was free to exclude from its community those who persisted in maintaining doctrines not warranted by the interpretation of the revealed message provided by official Church theology.

Though Whately saw the articles and formularies as divested of divine authority, he nevertheless insisted that every member of a Church was compelled either to accept them in their literal sense or to abandon the Church. Whately's so-called 'liberalism' did not acknowledge the right to a plurality of inter-pretations and doctrines within the same Christian body, a point later made by Baden Powell. The question of the epistemological status of doctrines and articles of faith was at the centre of late Noetic thought. The solution put forward by Whately was designed to avoid latitudinarianism and disruptive pluralistic tendencies: the authority of Church doctrine should be a matter of agreement, the test of membership of a Christian community. However, Whately's secular interpretation of the articles was designed to *reinforce* the doctrinal authority of the Church and not to weaken it.[8]

In many respects, this favourite topic of discussion within the late Noetic circle represented a logical development of observations by the early Noetics

---

[7] Whately probably met Archbishop Hobart of New York; see Ker and Gornall, *Letters and Diaries of Newman*, vol. iv, p. 173. On the wide interest aroused by Hobart's activities, see (Anon.), 'State of the Episcopalian Church in the United States of America', *B.C.*, 17 (1822), 540–55, and 579–95. In his letter to Senior (National Library of Wales, C.492) Whately referred to his *Episcopalian* pamphlet as 'the address to the American episcopalians'. (Whately), *Letters on the Church*, pp. 32–3, 66–71, 84, 136, 150, 170–1.

[8] (Whately), *Letters on the Church*, pp. 61–6. Commentators who have attributed a key role to Whately in the framing of the so-called Broad Church theology, have often overlooked the fact that the Archbishop of Dublin was not prepared to tolerate plurality of doctrines within the Church, was deeply shocked by the inroads made by German theology in the 1840s and 1850s and like his friend Hampden detested *Essays and Reviews*: see below, Part III, ch. 14.

and Van Mildert. During the 1810s and the early 1820s the theological spokesman of the Hackney Phalanx and the Oriel leaders advocated the principle of the literal interpretation of the scriptures, in order to avoid superimposing fallible human concepts or philosophical categories upon the revealed doctrines. The crucial difference between the early Noetics and the Hackney Phalanx on the one side and the late Noetics on the other, was disagreement as to the applicability of the critical tools originally devised to oppose Unitarians and Calvinists. Whately, and Baden Powell with him, believed that in times of growing popular literacy and of pressure from a variety of rival religious organizations it was counterproductive to resort to polemics without being prepared to submit one's own beliefs to the tests imposed upon one's adversaries.

Failure to inquire into the doctrinal status of Church articles and of the authority upon which they rested, would have put very effective weapons in the hands of opponents, who could then claim that there was no reason why their interpretation of scripture was wrong and the Anglican one right. Both sets of doctrines were formulated in terms of human origin, terms which were not to be found in scripture. Both made use of terms and conceptual abstractions which were bound to say either more or less than the revealed passages of the scriptures which the articles were supposed to clarify or to expand upon. In *Rational Religion Examined* Baden Powell argued that the Anglican articles were the expression of a human interpretation of scripture, though he emphasized with understandable vigour that the Anglican doctrine was the result of the best possible application of a sound inductive method to scriptural exegesis.

In the early 1820s Baden Powell's interpretation of the articles was acceptable to the various sectors of the High Church party. The mounting tension of the late 1820s and the early 1830s convinced many Anglican apologists that their defence of the articles undermined the argument for Church authority. The Hackney leaders and the Oriel men gathering around Newman were terrified by the prospect that the Anglican Church could fall victim to Dissenters in the reformed Parliament. They strove for a solution, a *via media* which would allow them to maintain the title of Protestant against the claim to infallibility by the Roman Catholic Church but at the same time would enable them to express a new and stronger emphasis on the divine authority of the Church. They argued that the rights, privileges and property of a divinely appointed institution could not be alienated in order to pacify Dissenters, nor the Irish bishoprics abolished in order to avoid a civil war in the island. The very concept of parliamentary intervention in the affairs of the Church was obviously blasphemous, since any measures taken would apply to an institution established by God.[9]

9 G. J. T. Machin, *Politics and the Churches* (1977); G. F. A. Best, 'The constitutional revolution', *Theology*, 62 (1959), 226–34; E. Hughes, 'The bishops and reform', *English Historical*

In 1825 Rose insisted that the only appropriate check against rationalism, social insubordination and middle-class political reformism was to emphasize the idea of the divine origin of the Church. He also asked for a restriction of the traditional Protestant right to private judgement. Rose argued that private judgement was the prerogative of the Church, not of the individual. Whately did not disagree with the substance of Rose's point. Indeed, he concurred with Rose and the more conservative Anglican faction in the view that Church doctrinal decisions were strictly binding upon the faithful. Whately was however convinced that the God-given authority to enforce uniformity of practice and doctrine did not confer divine authority on the doctrine itself: scripture alone was the source of doctrinal truth. Church doctrine simply represented the best possible interpretation of the truth and could never be truth in itself. The same kind of argument applied to the organization of the Church, the ceremonies and the liturgy. God invested the Church with authority to establish rituals, but rituals of any specific historical or geographical church could not be seen as established by God.[10]

This fine theoretical difference, a trifle to the modern, secular mind, provided the basis for Whately's political speculation and practice. The kind of Church authority he advocated allowed sufficient flexibility for a considerable amount of political change and adjustment. The institution of the Church had been established by God, though the actual organizational structure of historically given churches was bound to change, and indeed did change over the centuries. No one could have denied a well-established historical fact or that changes had often been for the worse.

In Britain the Reformation had made the Church an instrument of the State. The Anglican Church was still suffering from the consequences of meddling with the temporal power. Whately was fully aware of the pressure to reform the Church and of the serious shortcomings of the Anglican Establishment. This conviction did not make him a 'liberal' reformist. Indeed, the Hackney leaders themselves agreed that positive action was to be taken in order to save the Church. Whately was convinced that the Church could not be reformed externally by Parliament, but only by internal change. For this reason he insisted on the necessity of reviving Convocation, as the only means of achieving an efficient self-government.

According to Whately, the correct emphasis Rose placed on the authority of the Church ended in the wrong claim that every single organizational detail of the Anglican Church, from the political Establishment down to cathedral

Review, 56 (1941), 459–90, for documents on the opposition to the Irish Temporalities Bill by Van Mildert and Joshua Watson. See also Trinity College, Cambridge, the Whewell–Rose correspondence on the fears aroused by the readiness with which the Oriel leadership accepted and indeed favoured the bill on the Irish Church. On reactions at Oxford, see J. Ker and T. Gornall, *Letters and Diaries of Newman*, vol. iv, pp. 23–6.

10 Rose, *State of the Protestant Religion*, pp. 11, 23–4, 106–7.

talls and sinecures was established by God and could on no account be
eformed. The form of disestablishment he himself proposed was in Whately's
yes the only way to save and indeed reinforce the authority of the Church.
'aced by the challenges of the day, Anglicans had to decide whether they
vere to fall back into some form of Romanism, as many were already doing
t the theological level, or accept the changed political situation and react by
estoring the God-given spiritual authority of the Church.

The themes and differences sketched above were to develop during the late
820s and through the 1830s. Opposition to Whately's ideas mounted only
vhen concrete political differences emerged within the High Church party
nd the Oriel common room. Thus, Whately himself was surprised that
eaction to the ideas put forward in his *Letters on the Church* was slow to
ome. Consideration of the sequence of events between 1826 and 1832 might
•rovide an explanation for the belated response which Whately lamented. In
826 Oriel had not yet taken sides on the Test and Corporation Bills, and
ave united support to the annual anti-Catholic petition by the University.
Blanco White's book against Roman Catholic theology pleased many at Oxford
nd at Hackney. White's anti-Catholic tirade proved that the Oriel men
aithfully opposed the claims of the Romanists.[11]

The anonymous pamphlet on the state of the Church by Whately was
egarded as an eccentric production of no particular consequence. In 1828
vents took a dramatic turn. The Test and Corporation Acts were passed
mid the relative indifference of the country, but evoked an infuriated reaction
rom the Hackney leaders and conservative High Churchmen. The split within
he Tory party over the issue made it clear that the passing of a Catholic
Relief Bill of some kind was a question of time – of months rather than years.
The Catholic Bill of 1829 sharply and openly divided the former allies. The
British Critic reviewers attacked the 'divinity of a certain school' represented
•y Thomas Arnold and the 'Episcopalian'. The editors and theological
nspirers of the *British Critic* became aware that the speculative reflections of
he 'Episcopalian' were providing the theoretical foundation for the political
•peration mounted by the Peelites in Oxford and throughout the country.[12]

It was from Oxford, the citadel of Anglican political orthodoxy, that the
Noetics were putting forward the view that while the Anglican articles were
nore sophisticated than the ones upheld by Methodists, Roman Catholics
ind Unitarians, the actual status of the various sets of doctrinal pronounce-
nents was equally doubtful. Clearly, since there was no theological justification

---

* Lambeth Palace, Whately Papers, 2164, fols. 139–41: 9 Oct. 1829, Whately to Senior. Blanco
White, *Evidences against Catholicism* (1825); the book did not please White's Whig friends
and patrons: see Liverpool University Library, Blanco White Papers, I B 6: 25 May 1825,
John Allen to Blanco White. G. J. T. Machin, *The Catholic Question* (1964); E. R. Norman
(ed.), *Anti-Catholicism in Victorian England* (1967).

² Gash, *Mr. Secretary Peel*, pp. 460–6; Churton, *Memoir of Joshua Watson*, vol. i, pp. 292,
298–300; (Anon.), 'Arnold's Sermons', *B.C.*, 12 (1829), 265, 280–1.

for defending the Anglican Establishment, then the growing political and
economic power of Dissenters and a state of virtual civil war in Ireland made
it impossible not to relinquish the political privileges of the Church. This
interpretation of the Noetic approach to theology and Church politics gave
many churchmen reason for concern. Where was the process of reform to
stop? Was disestablishment the next item in the agenda of dissenters and
radicals? Was it not true that Whately was ready to concede it without debate
and indeed was he not boldly advocating such a measure?

Thousands of clergymen, who for decades had enjoyed sinecures or the
comfortable peace of rural livings, were now troubled by increasing resistance
to the collection of tithes, by the danger of a *bellum servile*. Their only hope
was that the might of the State guaranteed their economic and social privileges.
Events proved however that the protection of the State could not be taken
for granted. It is not surprising that such a theoretical disquisition as Whately'
on the Church as a spiritual, non-political organization was bound to be
regarded as a blasphemous expression of extreme liberalism, or, at best, as
senselessly playing with a highly explosive situation.[13]

The Noetics did of course disagree with what they considered to be a
misinterpretation of their tenets. It is however true that the wide-ranging
implications and the political context of their speculations on theology or
Church policy were closely scrutinized by the Noetics themselves. The theme
of the political and social condition of contemporary Britain was central to
Whately's works, as well as to those of Baden Powell, Senior and Arnold.
Indeed, it was not far from the surface of theoretically or historically oriented
essays by Hinds, Hampden and Blanco White. The radicalization of political
and social affairs after 1829 made the practical consequences of theological or
philosophical proposals increasingly apparent. Political and ideological
considerations emerged at the forefront of intellectual debates. Though it is
essential not to describe complex intellectual developments as the univocal
function of historically given political or social conditions, it is equally essential
fully to appreciate that the intellectual options debated at this period cannot
be seen except within the context of a dramatically evolving situation.

Many portrayed contemporary social and political affairs as the ruinous and
unalterable course towards revolution. Even though it would be an exaggeration
to describe the years between 1829 and 1832 as a period of *grande peur*, there
were certainly enough catastrophic forecasts abroad to urge many to think
carefully over the consequences of their thoughts and writings. Arnold and
Baden Powell, as well as Newman, Rose and Pusey, were not scholars secluded
in cloisters. Rather, they were, and regarded themselves as, 'gentlemen' of
their times, who discussed and theorized upon the close relationship between

[13] (Anon.), *B.C.*, 12 (1829), 267–8, 271. '*Bellum servile*' is the expression used by Blanco White
in a letter to Whately, Lambeth Palace, Whately Papers, 2164, fols. 220–1: 26 Nov. 1830,
commenting on rural revolt.

academic education and social status, theological doctrines and political rights
or economic privileges. It could be argued that the crucial difference between
the early and the late Noetics, and between them and their opponents, originated from the modified political context in which the late Noetics formulated
their proposals.[14]

Many controversial tenets upheld by Whately between 1826 and 1832 had
much in common with what he wrote in earlier years or with what Copleston
and Van Mildert taught between 1810 and 1825. Whately's 'liberalism' could
be better defined as a sophisticated form of political opportunism of a basically
conservative kind. His intellectual vigour was consciously directed to counteracting new social and intellectual ferments forcefully emerging at the surface
of British society. He strongly opposed new concepts of social organization
with middle- and working-class origins, and seemed indifferent to appeals
asking for concrete and practical social meaning to be given to the concept
of Church charity. Thus, his political economy was designed to show that
inequality was a natural state of society, and indeed the only state in which
it was possible to organize efficient human communities, by means of the
division of labour. This became one chief 'evidence of Christianity', a further
proof of God's intervention in human affairs. Once God's creative act was
accomplished, then the organism of civil society could develop according to
the laws of its constitution and could become the subject-matter of science.[15]

Whately repeated with Copleston that the existence of evil in nature and
in society was an unavoidable and theologically incomprehensible fact, though
he increasingly allowed that a tendency towards progress and amelioration in
the social and the natural scheme bespoke God's benevolence. His concern
for university and popular education professedly aimed at restoring on the
cultural plane the inequalities it was no longer possible to preserve at a political
level by the use of physical force or legal repression. The masses, he argued,
helped by industrial and urban concentration, were increasing the means of

[14] Churton, *Memoir of Joshua Watson*, vol. i, pp. 323–4; vol. ii, p. 7; Webster, *Joshua Watson*,
    p. 23. A. De Morgan, *A Budget of Paradoxes*, 2 vols. (1915), vol. i, p. 187. Ker and Gornall,
    Letters and Diaries of Newman, vol. iii, and vol. iv. For a vivid account of the fears aroused
    by English and European political events of 1830, see (T. De Quincey), 'The French Revolu-
    tion', *B.M.*, 28 (1830), p. 555: 'the waters of the great abyss are again abroad: one deep is
    calling to another. Trepidation and panic are spreading over the thrones of Europe: the
    friends of real liberty are perplexed and uncertain of the course before them: no William
    Pitt is at hand to guide us: no great leading angel arises to dictate the destiny of Europe'.
    See also (A. Alison), 'On Parliamentary Reform and the French Revolution', *B.M.*, 29 (1831),
    429–46, 745–62, 919–35. On the political dimension of theological debates at Oxford, see
    H. C. G. Matthew, 'Edward B. Pusey', *Journal of Theological Studies*, 32 (1981), 101–24.
[15] R. Whately, *Introductory Lectures on Political Economy* (1831), pp. 111, 115–16, 122, 140–8,
    217–20, 236; M. Berg, *The Machinery Question and the Making of Political Economy* (1980),
    pp. 293–4; Hilton, *Corn, Cash and Commerce*, pp. 307–10; Soloway, *Prelates and People*, pp.
    162–4; Poynter, *Society and pauperism*, pp. 311, 315, 316, fails to distinguish between Thomas
    Whately, minister of Cookham in Berkshire, famous parish Poor Law reformer, and his
    brother Richard, the Professor of Political Economy at Oxford.

reciprocal intercourse. They were reflecting upon their condition and were clearly eager to increase their capacity to understand political and cultural affairs.[16]

Faced with this new and dangerous situation, the higher classes of society needed to establish and make felt their intellectual superiority. They should become the leaders, patrons and proprietors of the education movement. As Whately pointed out in a vigorous and lucid sermon preached in 1830, the question as he saw it was not whether the working classes should or should not be educated but by whom and for what purpose. The danger was that middle-class radicals had assumed the leadership of the popular education movement in order to replace the higher classes at the head of the State and British society.[17]

In his *Remarks on Scepticism* Thomas Rennell singled out the lower departments of professional life – surgeons, accountants, etc. – as the strongholds of modern scepticism and social subversion. Rennell accordingly set out to charge the social and intellectual class represented by Carlile, Lawrence and Morgan with heresy, atheism, revolutionary tendency and conspiracy to subvert the State. By contrast, Whately advocated a better university education, capable of sending forth into the world gentlemen well equipped to lead the professional life. Rennell, according to Whately, was right in his analysis of the ills, but wrong in the remedy – legal and political repression. Both were already impracticable.[18]

Whately's effort to promote the teaching of science at Oxford, political economy included, as integral parts of the curriculum for higher degrees, was motivated by his desire to see the universities performing essential functions of ideological supervision in contemporary society. Though he remained faithful to the emphasis placed by Copleston on the liberal nature of academic pursuits, he stressed the need to include in the curriculum disciplines which would provide a 'liberal' overview of professional and scientific culture. The Anglican gentleman wishing to supervise the professional or the scientific community did not need to be acquainted with boring technical details, though it was clearly his duty to be aware of and to comment on the 'principles' of each discipline applied to professional and scientific practices.

Whately moved from the defence of logical studies at Oxford to the promotion of academic political economy. A practitioner of neither discipline, he became an able apologist for both in terms he thought acceptable to his audience. He pointed out that the peculiarity of modern infidelity was the

[16] For a contemporary discussion of these issues, very similar to the reflections put forward by Whately, see the series of articles by D. Robinson in the *B.M.* devoted to the 'Condition of England', and in particular 'The Repeal of the Combination Laws', 17 (1825), 20–31, 'The Combinations', 18 (1825), 463–78, 'Brougham and the Education of the People', 18 (1825), 534–51.

[17] R. Whately, *The Duty of those who Disapprove the Education of the Poor* (1830), p. 17.

[18] Rennell, *Remarks on Scepticism*, pp. 12–13.

intellectual sophistication of its professors. The new middle-class intelligentsia were not to be converted by declamations or appeals to tradition.[19]

Whately never questioned the superiority of the Anglican faith (of his own brand of it, at least) nor the need to defend the social status and the economic privileges of the Anglican clergy. He was nevertheless convinced that positive action needed to be taken in order to save the Church from the many impending dangers. Purely defensive action was in his judgement politically and theologically dangerous. It is not surprising that Baden Powell saw in the strategy developed by Whately the logical development of the policies pursued by his Hackney relatives. Unfortunately however, the Hackney leaders themselves and the dons around Newman did not share the views of Whately and Baden Powell. They came to believe that Whately and his friends were pushing the policy of positive action and timely concession to the point of giving up the Church and its theology for the sake of saving it. 'Everything was to be removed which gave offence to anybody' was said to be the political guideline of Whigs and Noetics.[20]

[19] Whately, *Introductory Lectures*, p. 236, and *Elements of Logic* (1826), pp. xx–xxi, xxviii–xxix.
[20] Ker and Gornall, *Letters and Diaries of Newman*, vol. iv, p. 127.

8

The collision

The theological doctrines of the Noetics collided with the increasing conservatism of several factions within the High Church party when the Oriel approach to theology and philosophy came to be regarded as the theoretical basis for political subversion. It is, however, interesting that while the *British Critic* in 1829 started a campaign against the anonymous 'Episcopalian' and launched open and veiled attacks against Whately and his friends, in Oxford itself the situation remained relatively calm. Notwithstanding the sharp division on the Peel re-election affair, evidence suggests that in the university at large and in Oriel the atmosphere was less tense than expected. Copleston was reassured by Hawkins that the split within the Oriel community left scarcely perceptible ill feeling. Whately conveyed the same impression to Sir Robert Peel. Blanco White sensed a change of attitude on the part of some of his closest friends after he had voted for Peel, but could not report any perceptible estrangement. When in 1831 Whately left for Dublin, he asked Hawkins to take care of pending business relating to St Alban Hall and suggested Newman as the second best choice.[1]

Beneath the official calm, a change had indeed occurred. Newman's attitude towards his friends, or, at first, towards their ideas, underwent a revolution. The Peel affair, the confrontation with Hawkins on the reform of the tutorial system at Oriel proposed by Newman, and matters of academic policy and jealousy widened the gap between Newman, Froude and Keble and the group of the friends and disciples of Whately. It could be argued that Baden Powell directly contributed to 'opening' Newman's eyes as to the inevitable outcome of Whately's teaching.

The newly elected Savilian Professor of Geometry was selected to preach the official University Sermon for Easter 1829. Baden Powell thought the reaction to his preaching on the relationship between science and revelation so significant as to deserve a telegraphic but highly revealing entry in his

[1] Oriel College, Hawkins Papers I.1: Hawkins to Copleston, 1 Mar. 1829; British Library, Peel Papers, 40.399, fols. 9–12: 1 Mar. 1829, Whately to Peel; Pusey House, Pusey Correspondence, B3: 21 Feb. 1829, letter of Blanco White to Pusey; Oriel College, Hawkins Papers, 2.184: 18 Dec. 1831, Whately to Hawkins.

journal: 'Preached at St. Mary's. Newman odd'. In 1833 the sermon was revised for publication and, as will be shown, it represented the *casus belli* for the confrontation between Baden Powell and the *British Critic*. The sermon contained a solution to the religion–science debate which Newman was not ready to accept and indeed regarded as positively heretical; Baden Powell's ideas reinforced Newman's worst fears as to tendency and actual consequences of the Noetic teaching.[2]

A few years later it was the debate on the admission of Dissenters at Oxford and Cambridge which confirmed Newman's conviction that the political opportunism of the Noetics was leading his friends towards extreme doctrinal positions. In the eyes of the orthodox supporters of the Establishment, the radicalization of the political situation and the social unrest accompanying the parliamentary progress of the Reform Bill added a worrying new dimension to the logically meticulous approach to theology elaborated by the Noetics. As one *British Critic* reviewer pointed out in July 1831, 'we greatly fear that the most luminous and elaborate lecture . . . will do but little for the relief of *tender* consciences which are scandalized and afflicted by the exaction of tithes and fees'. Whately, the target of this sarcasm, preached against the human tendency to fall into the errors of Romanism, into a superstitious and authoritarian view of religion.[3]

To Whately's psychological worries, the reviewer objected that the danger was of a completely different nature. The real threat was in fact the attempt allegedly made by the Mechanics' Institutes, the Society for the Diffusion of Useful Knowledge and the Unitarian philosophers to suppress 'all reverence for sacred things'. Pious frauds and a moderate degree of popular superstition were better left alone: 'We are far from certain that it is, *in all* cases, required of us to unsettle the thoughts of ill-informed people.'[4]

The election of Whately to the see of Dublin imposed understandable curbs to the attacks upon him in the High Church press. It is noteworthy that his appointment did not provoke that manifestation of hostility which was to follow the appointment of Hampden to the incomparably less important chair of divinity at Oxford. Keble expressed to Newman the fear that Whately had been forced into a secret deal, engaging himself to reform the Irish 'temporalities', but nonetheless asked his friend to congratulate Whately on his behalf for accepting the burden of the Irish Church. Newman was then completely confident that his friend would handle the Irish situation with firmness and courage, but was soon disillusioned by Whately's approval of the Irish Temporalities Bill and his speech on behalf of the Jewish claim for political equality.[5]

[2] B.P.J., Easter Day, April 1829.
[3] (Anon.), 'Whately's *Romish Errors*', *B.C.*, 19 (1831), 22, 11.
[4] 'Whately's *Romish Errors*', 13, 18.
[5] Keble College, Oxford, Keble Correspondence, A.1: 21 Sept. 1831 (?), Keble to Newman. Ker and Gornall, *Letters and Diaries of Newman*, vol. iv, p. 23 and *passim*.

At Oxford, in the five years between Whately's accession to Dublin and the Hampden affair of 1836, the debate on the admission of dissenters provoked the definitive split between the late Noetics and their former allies and friends. The debate also made theological differences a matter of national policy and gave the newly created Tractarian party its first chance to rally around its banner an increasingly large sector of Church opinion. Since the 'Episcopalian' jealously preserved his anonymity, the only charge against Whately which could be understood by the public at large was to cast doubt on his views on the sabbath. In 1830, Whately republished in pamphlet form the long footnote in the *Essays on St Paul* of 1828 with firm apologetic additions. His views on the sabbath put him in a difficult position with respect to his academic colleagues and his Anglican brethren.[6]

In 1829, Whately thought it advisable to pay a visit to Norris in order personally to explain to the 'Bishop-maker' the actual strategy underlying his remarks on the sabbath. The *British Critic* reviewer of his *Essays on the Writings of St Paul*, who very likely expressed the official Hackney point of view on the subject, accepted the substance of Whately's self-defence. The reviewer acknowledged that Whately was 'an acute, vigorous and independent thinker', but found in his works 'too much artificial nicety and precision': 'we cannot discern the wisdom of perplexing him [the believer] with doubts', the reviewer concluded.[7]

The debate over the admission of Dissenters at Oxford and the theoretical justification of the measure allegedly or actually offered by Noetics like Hampden and Baden Powell, provided the opponents of Whately with sufficient ammunition for a determined and dramatic confrontation with his pupils. As many saw it, the question was no longer one of 'perplexing men with doubts': the very foundation of Church doctrine was at stake. The theological substance of the clash was the contraposition between the lucid Noetic criticism of dogmatic theology, and the High view of Church doctrine and sacraments advocated by the High Church and the Tractarian party, and endorsed, albeit with increasing reluctance, at Hackney and Cambridge. The concrete political issue of the admission of Dissenters into the English universities made clear even to the country clergyman the far-reaching dimensions of the dispute.[8]

We have seen that during the 1810s and the early 1820s the Noetics insisted that the fault common to all the opponents of the Anglican Church – Unitarians and rationalists *in primis* – was the lack of a sound inductive method in theology. The methodological approach to the theology of the adversary inevitably raised

---

[6] On the contemporary, widespread pro-sabbath action by conservative and evangelical clergymen see E. Hughes, 'Bishops and Reform', 459–90.

[7] Oriel College, Hawkins Papers, 2.177: 13 Aug. 1829, Whately to Hawkins; (Anon.), 'Whately, on *St. Paul*', *B.C.*, 5 (1829), 389, 379.

[8] On the early worries by the Hackney men and Rose that the young Tractarians were taking too high a view of Church authority, tradition and the sacraments, see Burgon, *Lives of Twelve Good Men* (1888), pp. 62–146.

the wider question of the status of all doctrinal statements. It was clearly difficult to refuse the conclusion that all articles and dogmas were inevitably expressed in terms differing from the actual wording of the scriptures. Thus historical and theoretical considerations were provided to explain the origin of the many dogmatic deviations from the revealed truth.

In his *History of the Rise and Early Progress of Christianity* (1828), Samuel Hinds gave a historical explanation of the rise of dogmatic theology. Error spreading within the primitive church made the framing of creeds and symbols of faith a condition for survival. The obvious consequence of the rise of dogmatic theology had been the creation of a technical language. Hinds repeated Dugald Stewart's remark that the introduction of technical terms into the language of science was designed to develop an unambiguous terminology capable of faithfully representing the natural phenomena under observation. Hinds commented that the opposite was the case with theology. Technical terms derived from analogy with human feelings and behaviour or were taken from the 'jargon' of metaphysical speculation.

The great majority of technical terms employed in dogmatic theology had nothing to do with scriptural 'facts' or truth. Dogmatic theologians super-imposed the equivocal vocabulary of ordinary human language to interpret the chosen and inspired words of revelation. Though he never denied the doctrinal necessity and the pedagogical expediency of collecting the exegetical tenets of a church in articles and formularies, Hinds argued that it was nevertheless essential not to forget the historical and epistemological nature of all theological statements. No divine authority was attached to them. A close collaborator of the 'Episcopalian', and probably one of the few friends who discussed with Whately the contents of the *Letters on the Church*, Hinds maintained that the articles of a church 'constitute the marks which distinguish that church from all other Christian bodies that are so at variance with it, as to be excluded from its communion'.[9]

In 1827 another member of the late Noetic group, Blanco White, submitted to Whately for comment a sermon he had written for St Mary's pulpit. White argued that creeds and theological symbols were 'tokens' of the scriptural truth, but were far from enjoying the authority of revelation. Whately's margin-alia substantiate the claim that White, often described as the inspirer of the Noetic anti-dogmatic standpoint, was in fact learning from his Oriel friends.[10]

Hampden, the alleged 'pupil' of Blanco White, published in 1828 a volume of parochial sermons, in which the Noetic standpoint on creeds and articles of faith was again insisted upon. In passages strongly evoking Baden Powell's

9 S. Hinds, *History of the Rise and Early Progress of Christianity*, 2 vols. (1828), vol. i, p. 253, and 'Appendix', vol. ii, pp. 339–41; idem, *An Inquiry into the Proofs, Nature and Extent of Inspiration* (1831), pp. 178–9.
10 Liverpool University Library, Blanco White Papers, iii.1: 'Various Sermons preached in or around Oxford', 1826–30, N. 10.

defence of the Anglican doctrine in *Rational Religion Examined*, Hampden pointed out that the article expressing the Anglican belief in the unity and trinity of God differed substantially from the analogous article of the Roman Catholic faith. The Catholic theologians assumed that the word of the scripture was to be interpreted according to the subtle distinctions of scholastic philosophy. The Anglican theological definition of God, according to Hampden, 'simply notes and records what Scripture reveals, and it delivers no opinion whatever concerning the matters revealed and there specified...it brings together points which are scattered throughout Scripture'.[11]

Hampden's famous Bampton Lectures of 1832 described the historical process by which metaphysical speculations had invaded Christian theology and had thereby relegated to a secondary role the proper and only foundation of the Christian truth, the word of scripture. Whately was very pleased with the work of his friend. As he wrote to Macvey Napier (1776–1847), he did not doubt Hampden's lectures were 'a work which must sooner or later attract general attention'. Whately was indeed a good prophet, though a few years later he was less than pleased with the actual fulfilment of his prediction.[12]

Hampden's reluctance to quote works by his friends led contemporary commentators (and many historians with them) to accept the allegation by Hampden's enemies, that Blanco White (the ex-Catholic priest, ex-Anglican minister, converted in 1835 to Unitarianism, and allegedly on the way to Spinozan pantheism) was the inspirer of the Bampton Lectures. The political motives behind this allegation are too evident to deserve detailed comment. An analysis of works by Van Mildert, Copleston, Whately, Baden Powell and Hinds shows that the Bampton Lectures were in fact a systematic development of themes often touched upon by High Churchmen and Noetic thinkers in the 1810s and the 1820s. As Whately himself commented in a letter to Hawkins, 'he [Hampden] and I have gone over much the same ground, in opposite directions; I, conjecturally, upwards, and he, historically, downwards'.[13]

The eighth and final lecture of the Bampton series 'The Nature and Use of Dogmatic Theology', emphasized Hampden's intellectual allegiances. Hampden denied the right to human reason to inquire into the 'facts' of revelation, that is the words or, at times, the apparently contradictory passages

[11] R. D. Hampden, *Parochial Sermons* (1828), pp. 27, 36.
[12] Hampden, *The Scholastic Philosophy* (1833). British Library, Napier Correspondence, 34.616, f. 165: 3 Oct. 1833, Whately to Napier.
[13] Oriel College, Hawkins Papers, 2.193: (answered 15 Apr. 1832), Whately to Hawkins. The thesis that Blanco White had substantially helped Hampden in writing the Bampton Lectures goes back to William Palmer's *A Narrative of Events* (1843), and his article on 'The Tendencies towards the subversion of faith', *English Review*, 10 (1848), 399–444. The allegation has been uncritically repeated several times. See for instance T. Mozley, *Reminiscences* (1882), vol. i, pp. 353–4; G. C. Richards, 'Oriel College and the Oxford Movement', *The Nineteenth-Century Review*, n. 676 (1933), p. 730; R. D. Middleton, *Newman at Oxford* (1950), p. 39; Sillem (ed.), *The Philosophical Notebook*, vol. i, p. 169. For a contrary opinion, see H. Hampden, *Life and Letters* (1871), pp. 28–9, and Distad, *Guessing at Truth*, p. 171.

of scripture. Together with his Oriel friends and teachers, Hampden acknowledged the usefulness and indeed the necessity of humanly framed summaries or exegetical commentaries on the scriptural truth. His task, he declared, was to establish 'the importance and proper truth' of creeds and articles.[14]

Hampden stressed that the Anglican creeds and articles were open to the same critical approach employed to question the reliability of the theological formularies of rival religious societies. However, Hampden maintained that the inductive theology he elaborated, and which he claimed had always been at the basis of the Anglican approach to theology, was restoring the balance between the 'facts' of revelation and the 'theories' so dear to theologians. He conceded that in science as well as in theology theories were often useful and indeed indispensable. Hampden commented that men were naturally inclined to speculation and to expressing their knowledge in systematic form. For this reason too he wanted to make clear that all conflict between humanly-framed systems of knowledge – scientific theories or theological doctrines – was only a conflict of opinion: the final light on any such dispute could only be obtained by an appeal to the 'facts' of nature or revelation.[15]

The Bampton lecturer was careful to point out that the analogy between scientific and theological procedures did not imply any deep similarity between the two fields of inquiry. He repeated with Whately that science was searching for new discoveries, whereas theology had to restore the 'facts' of revelation in their purity. The dominion of scientific facts was continually expanding, whereas the 'revealed facts' were once and for all entrusted to the books of the scriptures.[16]

Notwithstanding the marked similarity between the ideas of Hampden and the tenets put forward by his Noetic friends, there was a question of form, rather than substance, which made the Bampton Lectures different, and almost offensive in the eyes of many High Churchmen. Baden Powell, Whately, Hinds and Hampden himself in his early works developed their criticism of dogmatic theology as part of a wider plan, and always directed their criticism against the theology of Dissenters, Roman Catholics, or Unitarians. In his Bampton Lectures, Hampden dealt systematically with the question of the role and status of dogmatic theology in the Christian religion as a whole. Furthermore, the practical deductions Hampden drew or appeared to draw from his anti-dogmatic standpoint were far more daring than anything the Noetics had yet cared to propose.

Hampden was the first member of the Noetic group who publicly appeared to deploy the theoretical arsenal of his school to support a controversial political

---

[14] Hampden, *The Scholastic Philosophy*, pp. 353–4.
[15] Hampden, *The Scholastic Philosophy*, pp. 370–1. The theme of man's natural inclination to theorizing was fully discussed by Stewart in the second volume of his *Elements* and in the polemical *Ninth Lecture* Whately appended to his lectures on political economy, to answer the attacks by Richard Jones and William Whewell: see P. Corsi, 'The heritage of Dugald Stewart'. [16] Hampden, *The Scholastic Philosophy*, p. 376.

measure, the admission of Dissenters to university degrees. Many who in 1832 took offence at passages of Hampden's lectures but considered the work a harmless, tedious and scarcely noticed scholarly exercise were forced in the years 1834–5 to reconsider their judgement. The Noetics, and Hampden in particular, were increasingly represented as the allies of the reformed Parliament in the attempt to force changes upon the university and the Church.[17]

It could be argued that the aims of the Noetics were different from those ascribed to them by their adversaries. Thus, the proposal originally put forward by Hawkins, for substituting a generic declaration of loyalty to the Church of England for the subscription to the articles, was intended as a limited peace offer to the victorious forces of political and religious dissent. Hawkins expressed his amazement at the bitter reaction his plan met with in Oxford. His proposal would exclude Dissenters as effectively as did subscription, since a conscientious Dissenter who refused to sign the articles would hardly be prepared to sign a declaration of loyalty to the Church of England.[18]

In 1834 Parliament was discussing matters of university policy and rumours spread that Wellington himself was in favour of some liberalization of access to the universities. Hawkins thought it was essential to show that the university authorities were open to constructive discussion. *A priori* refusal to take external pressure into consideration could have endangered the future independence of the Anglican academies. Whately lucidly summed up the Noetic point of view in a letter conveying to Hawkins his opinion on the current Parliamentary debates: 'I think the same of it (the admission of Dissenters) in one respect as I did of the Roman Catholic Relief: viz: that it will be carried, and that therefore it is better to make terms early, least you have to buy one Sibyl's book at the price of three'.[19]

The political opportunism of Whately and Hawkins did not appeal to High Churchmen and young dons galvanized by the prospect of defending Oxford as the last bastion of Anglican Christianity. The support that the Tractarians marshalled in the country was hardly motivated by spiritual considerations. Yet, it was equally clear that the combined forces of sincere conservative Anglican Christians and sincere lovers of clerical privilege had to be countered with more convincing arguments than the crude political realism of Whately and Hawkins. Indeed, many Anglicans were convinced that political expediency had already sold the Anglican parliamentary monopoly to dissenters and Roman Catholics and that they had in addition paid the unacceptable price of several Irish bishoprics – a 'National apostasy', Keble called the measure.[20]

---

[17] (Anon.), 'Hampden's Bampton Lectures', *B.C.*, 14 (1833), p. 150: Hampden's views were basically sound, but 'are pushed to an extravagant length, and thus become liable to interpretations which were probably never contemplated by the author'.

[18] W. R. Ward, *Victorian Oxford* (1965), pp. 87–98.

[19] Oriel College, Hawkins Papers, 3.204: 6 Apr. 1834, Whately to Hawkins.

[20] Ker and Gornall, *Letters and Diaries of Newman*, vol. iv, pp. 239, 364, 374.

Hampden entered the debate on the admission of dissenters with two pamphlets in which he deployed his criticism of dogmatic theology in support of the proposal put forward by Hawkins. The Provost of Oriel soon perceived that Hampden's theoretical justification was used against his measure and wrote a pamphlet declaring that there was no connection between the proposal of the declaration and Hampden's theology. It was however too late. As in the case of the Peel re-election affair, the Noetics failed to evaluate correctly the capacity of the entrenchment party to unite a wide spectrum of previously divided forces.

Hampden's justification of the move favouring the admission of Dissenters stressed that all Christians in England sincerely professed their belief in the truth of scripture. The only divergence, though an important one, Hampden conceded, was on theological grounds. Yet, in some sense at least, those theological differences were not as crucial as they appeared. Faith in formularies and creeds was not the *conditio sine qua non* for salvation, but only for the membership of a church. Hampden did however specify that dissenters had no *right* of admission and firmly maintained that Parliament could not interfere with the university.

The theological teaching of the university could in no way be modified in a latitudinarian sense in order to accommodate the Anglican doctrine to the taste of the Dissenters. Hampden refused to sign the declaration of 24 April 1834 expressing the opposition of the Oxford tutors to any form of concession to the Dissenters, but, significantly, he signed the declaration of 2 May 1834 opposing Parliamentary interference in university matters. He insisted that the question of the admission of dissenters had to be discussed within the university and the Church, not in the country or in Parliament.[21]

Hampden's specifications failed to convince those who opposed the measure. Many at Oxford became convinced that the Noetics adapted their theological speculations to the political requirements of the day. Newman, Keble, Froude and their allies felt that their colleagues were falling victim to the very intellectual sophistication they successfully deployed against Unitarians and Calvinists. Pusey, who kept for years a middle course between the Noetics and Newman, was probably forced to re-examine his own beliefs on the relationship between dogmas and scripture by the debates on the admission of Dissenters. He progressively shifted the emphasis from revelation to dogma. He now maintained that however weak the epistemological status of articles and dogmas, they had to be accepted and obeyed. Epistemological weakness

---

[21] Hampden, *Observations on Religious Dissent* (1834), pp. 4–8, 28–30, 33–5, 39–40. Hampden signed the declaration of 2 May 1834 drafted by the Heads of Houses and the Proctors. He did not sign the 'General Declaration of April 24', because he did not think it right 'that hostility to dissent should form a bond of union among our members': see footnote p. 40. Ward, *Victorian Oxford*, p. 93, refers to the passage above, but concludes that Hampden 'concurred in the tutors' declaration'. Hampden, *A Postscript to Observations on Religious Dissent* (1835).

was the sign that human reason had nothing to offer to the religious mind, but doubts and confusion.[22]

A dramatic confirmation of the tendency of Noetic teaching came from Blanco White's sudden conversion to Unitarianism in 1835. Pusey was deeply affected by the defection. Whately pointed out that the letter Pusey wrote to White represented a clear change in Pusey's thought. Newman pondered the implications of White's conversion to Unitarianism and expressed his deep sorrow to the 'lost' friend. The unremitting intellectual inquiry into the grounds of belief and doctrine had proved its destructive power. Keble's *Christian Year*, with its pious and intellectually unimaginative poetry, touched the hearts of many. So too had the logical acuity of Whately, but with opposite and disastrous results. The approach to theology and Anglican apologetic favoured by Whately, Hampden and Baden Powell now stood more clearly than ever in dramatic contraposition to the stance of Keble and his friends. At Oxford the increasingly isolated Noetic group, deprived of the vigorous personality of Whately, was left to contend with the growing influence of Newman, undoubtedly the most acute of Whately's pupils.[23]

Between 1826 and 1834 Baden Powell changed many of his ideas. He was greatly disappointed by the failure of many leading Anglican churchmen to promote the best interests of the Church and of the nation. The Anglican academies, according to Baden Powell, refused to provide the intellectual guidance much needed by contemporary society; the universities turned against the times, in the pursuit of ideas and ideals that he felt were totally out of touch with contemporary ethical and intellectual tensions.

Baden Powell accepted the substance of the Noetic criticism of dogmatic theology, but also admired Arnold's ideas on matters such as Church government, the constitutional status of the universities, and the question of the inspiration of scripture. In some respects Baden Powell applied the method of theological inquiry he learned at Oriel more systematically and coherently than many of his friends and teachers. Arnold's brand of latitudinarianism and the criticism of dogmatic theology by Whately and Hampden were combined to build an intellectual system which was to develop along lines that increasingly diverged from the less pliable standpoints of his former teachers.

Baden Powell's appreciation of the importance of scientific ideas emanci-

22 (E. B. Pusey), *Questions Respectfully Addressed to the Members of Convocation* (1835), pp. 5, 7–8 and *Subscription to the Thirty-Nine Articles: Questions Addressed to Convocation on the Declaration Proposed as a Substitute for Subscription. By a Bachelor of Divinity [E. B. Pusey]* with answers by a Resident Member of Convocation [E. Hawkins] and brief notes upon those answers by the Bachelor of Divinity (1835).

23 On Blanco White's defection see Oriel College, Hawkins Papers, 1.100, 2.101, 2.103, 2.104, 3.208, 3.209. Lambeth Palace, Whately Papers, 2164, fols. 230–1, 232–3, 328–9, 240–1, 242–3. Pusey House, Pusey Correspondence, B.3: 23 Apr. 1835, and 5 May 1835, letters from Blanco White to Pusey. See comments by Whately on Pusey's letters, Oriel College, Hawkins Papers, 3.214: 25 Oct. 1835, Whately to Hawkins. See also H. P. Liddon, *Life of E. B. Pusey*, 4 vols. (1893–7), vol. i, p. 315.

pated him from the cautious approach followed by Hawkins, Hampden and Whately on questions such as the reform of the university statutes and the admission of Dissenters. It is indeed noteworthy and revealing that Baden Powell's unconditional approval of the admission of Dissenters was closely linked to his conviction that the university curriculum needed to include elements of the scientific culture so validly advanced by eminent Dissenters and the social classes they represented. To open the university to scientific subjects became in Baden Powell's eyes synonymous with opening the gates at Oxford to the middle-class intelligentsia.

Thus, the years of the confrontation between the Noetics and their former allies at Oriel and the university also witnessed many changes in Baden Powell's outlook. The debates he took part in, concerning such matters as the relationship between science and revelation or the reform of the statutes, had a lasting influence on his intellectual development. The analysis of this period of his activities emphasizes the links between his personal intellectual growth and the social, political and educational debates of the time.

9

Science and academic politics at
Oxford: 1825–1835

In his learned and thorough investigation of Victorian university politics, W. R. Ward felicitously described the debates on the reform of the statutes as 'the burning domestic question at Oxford in the 'twenties'. Ward's detailed reconstruction of the main phases of the Oxford debate on the reform of the university curriculum makes it possible to concentrate upon Baden Powell's participation in the academic politics of the time.[1] His personal library, donated to the Bodleian Library in 1972, contains important manuscript material largely unavailable to Ward. A critical evaluation of the documents, marginalia and pamphlets of this collection will contribute a significant appendix to Ward's reconstruction of Oxford academic alignments in the years 1825–35.

Professor Ward stressed the relevance of the Noetic involvement in the drafting of several reform projects during this crucial decade. However, Ward's account was limited to the more immediate academic issues. He did not expand upon the general theme of Noetic political and cultural manoeuvres with relation to the reform of the university, nor did he monitor in detail the marginal and substantial differences which emerged in those years within the Noetic group itself. The strain of the Peel re-election affair and the debates on the Reform Bill which affected relations amongst the Oriel dons equally affected the circle of friends gathering around Copleston and Whately.

The parting of ways between the Noetics and the younger dons like Newman, the Wilberforces, or Froude has been described in some detail by several historians. However, the divergence of opinion on many political and educational issues which emerged within the Noetic circle, still awaits assessment. It is true that the differences which divided Hawkins from Arnold, Copleston from Hampden, or Baden Powell from Hawkins, Copleston and Whately, had less dramatic consequences than the split between Newman and Whately. Even Baden Powell's occasional expression of impatience towards what he regarded as the political timidity and shortsightedness of some of his Noetic friends produced no serious rifts in the short term. Yet the theological and

[1] Ward, *Victorian Oxford*, p. 56.

political conflicts of the 1830s demonstrated the limits of the reforming intents of some Noetic leaders and indicated far deeper divergences which manifested themselves in the course of the following decades.[2]

The main political and theoretical developments which led to the open clash between the traditional High Church party and the Oriel school have already been described. It has also been pointed out that on the theological front the open conflict was delayed until the early 1830s, even though elements of tension had been perceptible since the Peel re-election affair and the publication of the *Letters on the Church* by the anonymous 'Episcopalian'. We have also seen that the national political debate on the Reform Bill had far-reaching consequences on crucial features of the Oxford intellectual and theological debates. An analysis of Baden Powell's activities as university reformer will illustrate a further consequence of the Reform Bill agitation: the defeat of the movement for educational reform at Oxford.

The first reviews on scientific subjects published by Baden Powell in the *British Critic* voiced the author's concern for the institutional fortunes of academic science. Baden Powell advocated a substantial effort by the university to revive the tradition of Oxford science. The young reviewer touched upon many topics. He appealed to the intellectual pride of his colleagues. He exploited the eternal rivalry between Oxford and Cambridge. He embarked upon a philosophical disquisition on the speculative, liberal dimension of mathematical physics.

During the late 1820s Baden Powell was almost exclusively engaged in asserting the rights of scientific subjects, particularly mathematics, in the university curriculum. Significantly, he almost completely abandoned his theological activities and ambitions between 1826 and 1834. *Rational Religion Examined* was the only extended theological work he published in his youth. The anonymous contributions to the *Christian Remembrancer* were the last comments upon any theological subject he published until the appearance in 1833 of *Revelation and Science*, the controversial sermon he preached at Easter 1829. This seeming lack of interest in theological issues coincided with Baden Powell's devotion to academic politics and the debate on educational reform.

As already suggested, there is positive evidence that Baden Powell's standpoint on the sabbath displeased his Hackney relatives, as well as many of his Oxford colleagues. The claim that our author abandoned theological speculation because his interpretation of the Oriel approach to the sabbath met with a cool, if not hostile, reception, is confirmed by the contents of a polemical

---

[2] On the formation of the Tractarian party, and on the widening gap between Whately and the group gathering around Newman, see the excellent D. Newsome, *The Parting of Friends* (1966). The highly partisan Burgon, *Lives of Twelve Good Men*, is still the best printed source for the Hackney attitude towards the young Oxford men; see also B. R. Marshall, 'The theology of Church and State' (1956).

exchange of letters between Baden Powell and a correspondent to *John Bull,* almost ten years after the sabbath debate.

In May 1836 *John Bull,* then actively engaged in a violent campaign of character assassination against Hampden and his few friends, reproached Baden Powell for having betrayed the trust of his Oxford teachers and Hackney relatives. The anonymous contributor to the journal alleged that Baden Powell led his friends to believe he was an orthodox defender of the Anglican doctrine and establishment, in order to gain their support in his candidature for the Savilian Chair of Geometry. In his answer addressed to the editor of *John Bull,* Baden Powell denied he had receded from supposedly sounder opinions, and confessed: 'I held those same heterodox views (the rejection of the Sabbath) many years ago; and ... those excellent friends ... *regarding me as heterodox,* consistently with their own views, felt that here was an appointment unconnected with such questions, to which they could conscientiously recommend me'.[3]

This attack by *John Bull* and Baden Powell's defence provide indirect confirmation for the thesis that the *summa* of Hackney and Noetic tenets produced by Baden Powell in *Rational Religion Examined* was regarded as orthodox. It is somewhat surprising that the *John Bull* correspondent thought so in 1836, at a time when it should have been clear that the theological ideas put forward by Hampden in his Bampton Lectures closely resembled the themes which characterized Baden Powell's former 'orthodoxy'.

The election to the Savilian Chair opened to Baden Powell a seemingly less controversial field of action. He was now responsible for the mathematical teaching of the university. Even at this early date, minor differences of emphasis with respect to educational policy emerged between Baden Powell and Copleston, the leader of the early Noetic school. The newly-elected professor of geometry wrote to the Provost thanking him for his support and asking advice. Copleston's answer revealed the limits of his reforming zeal. Though he had been the promoter of the early Noetic teaching, Copleston was also the first of the Noetics to recede towards safer and more conservative standpoints on Church policy and the extension of the curriculum. His advice to Baden Powell, written in 1827, contained a significant indication of a basically propagandistic view of modern academic disciplines, scientific subjects in particular.

The Provost of Oriel had made a name for himself in countering the criticism of the Edinburgh reviewers by instancing the mathematical examination and the new scientific chairs at Oxford. He also reviewed Buckland's *Vindiciae Geologicae,* asserting the vitality and orthodoxy of academic science. However, he could not see how either new or old specialized scientific subjects could

3 'Oxoniensis', 'Letter to the Editor', *John Bull,* 16 (8 May 1836), 149–50; Baden Powell, 'Letter to the Editor', *John Bull,* 16 (15 May 1836), 148. The quotation is from Baden Powell, 'Letter to the Editor', p. 173.

find a place in the undergraduate curriculum. Early specialization, he repeated, was detrimental to the harmonious development of man's intellectual faculties.[4]

The examination statutes approved by Convocation in 1825 sanctioned the constitution of a separate board of mathematical examiners. In 1826 an amendment introduced an interval of three weeks between the examination for honours in classics and the one in mathematics. It should be pointed out that the two provisions were approved on grounds of expediency, rather than as a step towards raising the dignity and importance of mathematical studies. Many dons felt that provisions for a single board of examiners for both classics and mathematics imposed burdensome duties that made it difficult to find examiners to sit on it. For Copleston the measure had purely technical connotations. In any case, he was convinced that the 1825 and 1826 concessions to the mathematical examiners were to be regarded as final.[5]

Consistently with this view, Copleston dissuaded Baden Powell from delivering public inaugural lectures on the subject of mathematical studies and from giving gratuitous publicity to mathematical teaching at Oxford. Copleston praised the young professor's wish to promote mathematical proficiency at Oxford. Yet, he also reminded his zealous colleague that 'the credit of the University will be chiefly consulted by such philosophical essays and scientific researches as form your principal employment'. It is not difficult to perceive that Copleston cared more for the public image of the university, than for the actual state of health of scientific disciplines. The duty of the Savilian Professor of Geometry was to give elementary courses, to avoid publicity about them and to publish 'from time to time', as Copleston specified, the results of his research.[6]

Copleston's attitude towards mathematical studies and applied mathematics in particular had an epistemological and broadly philosophical foundation. His concept of liberal education, apart from the obvious emphasis on classics, relied more on logic than on mathematics as far as the 'philosophical' attainments were concerned. Copleston had been the promoter of logical studies at Oriel. He trained Whately to become his substitute. He convinced many Oriel and Oxford colleagues that a course of study centred upon the idea of a 'liberal education' would accord logic the first place, while relegating physical sciences to a secondary position.

Arnold, the educational reformer who never provided for systematic scientific teaching at Rugby, lucidly expressed the early Noetic view: 'Logic must be beyond all comparison more valuable than the Elements of Mathematics'. The study of Euclid, for instance, was seen by Arnold as providing the student with *examples* of rigorous reasoning, whereas logic was teaching him 'the

---

4 (E. Copleston), *Reply to the Calumnies of the Edinburgh Review* (1810), p. 176.
5 Ward, *Victorian Oxford*, pp. 58–60.
6 Copleston, *Memoir of Edward Copleston*, pp. 114–15, 330–40. Baden Powell, *The Present State and Future Prospects of Mathematical and Physical Studies* (1832), pp. 30–8.

principles of reasoning'. Baden Powell was on the contrary convinced that mathematical studies were an important part of a liberal education, since they trained the mind of a student in the contemplation of general truths.[7]

There is however no reason to believe that Baden Powell totally disagreed with the educational views of his Oriel teachers and friends. His emphasis on the liberality of scientific studies did not prevent him from following Copleston's advice. He refrained from giving publicity to his courses in print. Yet his personal views on the role of mathematical studies prevented him from restricting the interpretation of his academic duties to the limits outlined by his Provost.

Between 1827 and the late 1830s, Baden Powell published a series of textbooks designed for the use of students seeking mathematical honours. He promoted the practice of printing the questions of the mathematical examiners, an initiative that revealed his admiration for his Cambridge colleagues, who were already doing so as a means of raising the standards of their students. Baden Powell also became the most determined and active reforming member of the board of mathematical examiners. As the drafts of memoranda, letters and speeches preserved in the Baden Powell collection show, the Savilian Professor was pursuing a carefully planned strategy.[8]

His proposals aimed at achieving the complete independence of the mathematical examiners and examinations from their classical counterparts. Once a complete separation between the two had been achieved, then the mathematical examiners would be free to make the best possible use of their discretionary powers. They could impose higher standards for the honours examination in mathematics by introducing criteria of proficiency and competition.

In June 1828, only a year after his election, Baden Powell wrote the draft of a memorandum addressed to the Hebdomadal Board, which was signed by all the mathematical examiners. He asked that the day for the examination in mathematics should be fixed independently, to avoid the impression that the mathematical examination was simply an appendix to the classical. In December 1828 the mathematical examiners felt they could ask even more. They proposed that a permanent location for the mathematical examination should be established. They insisted that the three weeks' interval between the two examinations was deterring students from seeking honours in mathematics, and proposed that the examination in their subject should be held one or two terms after the classical examination.[9]

---

7 (T. Arnold), *Address to the Members of Convocation* (1824), pp. 2–3; for authorship, see copy in Bodleian Library, G.A. Oxon C. 40 (23). See also T. W. Bamford, *Thomas Arnold* (1960), p. 117.

8 B.P.J., May 1828, 'Math. Examinations – the questions printed for the first time at my suggestion'. For the main body of Baden Powell's manuscripts on the examination statutes, and important marginalia commenting on contemporary debates on university reform, see Bodleian Library, Baden Powell 31 and 32.

9 Bodleian Library, Baden Powell 31 (7), draft of a memorandum to the Vice-Chancellor, dated

The most important clause was the proposal that the order of classification of students who obtained honours in mathematics should be different from the order followed in the classical examination. This apparently obscure concluding demand was in fact designed to provide the necessary discretionary power to introduce a listing following the order of merit within each class, as was the practice at Cambridge. Baden Powell was convinced that the success of mathematical studies at Cambridge was due to the competition amongst candidates and to the academic honours and Church preferments accorded to those who earned the top positions in the merit list.

The requests of the mathematical examiners were moderate and avoided all declaration of principle. They were keen to convey the impression that the success of mathematical studies at Oxford could be achieved through mere technical adjustments of the examination statutes. Baden Powell and his colleagues were obviously persuaded that much could be gained by avoiding all explicit reference to projects of reform. This cautious attitude was shared by intellectuals favouring a policy of sound but moderate reform. In his interesting account of English universities Charles Lyell expressed his conviction that 'our universities are called upon to make no daring inroads upon their ancient constitution': 'no extensive or violent changes are required, in order to accommodate, in a very short time, the institutions of Oxford and Cambridge to the wants and the spirit of the present age'. Lyell praised the separation of the mathematical examination from the classical one achieved at Oxford in 1826 and advocated analogous steps for the natural sciences.[10]

In his paper on modern mathematical inquiries which he contributed to the *London Review* Baden Powell wrote optimistically on the prospects of mathematical studies in the English universities. Cambridge, he conceded, had undoubtedly taken the lead. The printed mathematical questions revealed the high level of proficiency required to earn a place in the honours list at Cambridge. Oxford too was on the move: 'The number of mathematical aspirants in that distinguished seat of learning will continue . . . progressively to advance'.[11]

In the polemical lecture he printed in 1832, Baden Powell maintained the opposite thesis that the number of students achieving mathematical honours actually decreased over the years. This conclusion obviously contradicted the 1829 statement and was reached by stressing the decreasing ratio between the number of students taking mathematical honours and the total number of students completing their studies in the same year. The statistical manipulation of the data reveals a deep change in Baden Powell's assessment of the situation.

9 June 1828, signed by Baden Powell, Robert Walker, and Augustus P. Saunders, and Baden Powell 31 (8), draft of a memorandum to the Vice-Chancellor, dated 6 Dec. 1828, signed by 'The Examiners'.

10 (C. Lyell), 'State of the Universities', *Q.R.*, 36 (1827), 274, 257.

11 (Baden Powell), 'Elementary Mathematical Treatises', *London Review*, 1 (1829), 481.

It is essential to account for the transition from the optimism of 1829 to the pessimism of 1832 and for the complete change his tactics underwent during the same years.[12]

In 1829 Baden Powell's confidence was certainly justified. The years 1825 to 1829 represented the peak of the Noetic influence at Oxford. In March 1829 the Hebdomadal Board instituted a committee to consider the short-comings of the examination statutes, and the various proposals of improvement put forward. The Board felt that the debates of the past years were causing ungentlemanly division within the academic body. In order to avoid further and bitter splits in Convocation, and the renewal of the 1824–6 battle of pamphlets, memoranda and declarations, the committee was to report to the Board on the best way to reconcile the projects of reform currently discussed by the different factions within the university. The Noetics exercised a significant influence on the committee.[13]

The committee suggested, among other measures, that mathematics should be offered as an option, replacing logic. The move, inspired by Whately, was certainly seen by Baden Powell as a relaxation of the intransigent defence of logic by the Noetics. As Whately authoritatively pointed out in the preface to his popular textbook on logic, the compulsory study of the discipline produced little positive results. Compulsion made logical propositions, requiring the full exertion of the reasoning powers, the object of mechanical repetition. The mathematical examiners too were consulted by the committee. They repeated the requests formulated in the earlier memorandum, though they compromised on the merit list: a mark of distinction in the alphabetical arrangement represented a sufficient distinction for the particularly deserving candidate.[14]

The deterioration of the political and the social situation of the country was already affecting the prospects of reform at Oxford. W. R. Ward has ably described the explosion of dissatisfaction with the 'old Oriel heresy that the Schools were a test of intellectual excellence'. The proposals put forward by the mathematical examiners, by Baden Powell in particular, were clearly designed to increase the competitiveness of the examination system. Thus, this group of reformers and Baden Powell were singled out for special censure by the faction opposed to all change.[15]

[12] Baden Powell, *The Present State and Future Prospects*, pp. 38–9.
[13] Ward, *Victorian Oxford*, p. 58. See Bodleian Library, Oxford University Archives, Hebdo-madal Board Minutes, 1823–33, fol. 101: 23 March 1829, for the establishment of the committee. The Dean of Christ Church, the Principal of Brasenose, the Warden of New College, the Provost of Oriel, the President of St John's and the Principal of St Alban Hall were selected to serve on the committee.
[14] *To the Board of Heads of Houses and Proctors. The Report of the Committee Appointed by the Resolution Dated March 23, 1829*, printed copy, Bodleian Library, G.A. Oxon b 21, p. 3. Whately, *Elements of Logic*, pp. xiii–xiv. 'Examination Statutes. Suggestions', Bodleian Library, Ms. Top. Oxon d 15, fols. 36–9, 41–7. See draft of the suggestions by the mathematical examiners in Bodleian Library, Baden Powell 31 (10).
[15] Ward, *Victorian Oxford*, p. 59.

The author of the *Address to the Members of the Lower Division of Convocation* – a pamphlet attributed to Baden Powell, to the latter's amazement – spoke of the mathematical school as an anomaly to be readily corrected. A separation of the mathematical and classical schools implied an unacceptable partition of learning. Those who dared to request a separate honour list for the mathematical examination, the author argued, clearly failed to understand that the institution of the board of mathematical examiners was no more than tolerated by the majority of the university. As a matter of fact, in recent years the division had become intolerable: 'Some', the author complained, 'have advocated the narrow, illiberal, and ungentlemanlike idea of a classification in order of merit', 'a monstrous notion' indeed.[16]

The Oriel common room itself was divided on the reform of the examination system. On 11 November 1830 Robert Wilberforce published a pamphlet in which he advocated the abolition of a separate examination in mathematics, a practice which he thought gave undue importance to the subject. Wilberforce attempted a theoretical justification of his position. He compared modern with ancient mathematics, particularly geometry. Modern mathematics, he argued, was characterized by the mechanical repetition of a few simple formulae, which hardly favoured the full exertion of the reasoning faculties. Proficiency in the discipline required a kind of 'dexterity exactly like that of the banker's clerk in arithmetic, or a sailor's in astronomy'. Thus, ancient mathematics only and the model reasoning procedures invented by Euclid were worthy of inclusion in a liberal education. Wilberforce pointed out that ancient geometry was a branch of *litterae humaniores*. As such, proficiency in Euclid's geometry should be assessed by the examiners of the classical board.[17]

The concentrated attack on the proposals put forward by the mathematical examiners accelerated as the scientific culture became identified with the reformist ideologies of the middle classes and the Dissenters. The deterioration of the political situation was also opening serious breaches in the ranks of the reforming party. Augustus Page Saunders, who in 1828 signed the memorandum drafted by Baden Powell, published in 1830, a few days before Wilberforce's, a conciliatory pamphlet. Saunders conceded to the adversaries of reform that the mathematical examination should not be separated from the classical one,

---

16 (Anon.), *Address to the Members of the Lower House of Convocation* (1830), pp. 12, 9–11. The mounting tide of opposition to university reform deeply affected the committee appointed in 1829. The 'Suggestions' to the committee (see note 14 above) contain several expressions of approval for the proposal by the mathematical examiners to introduce an order of merit within each class, the only contrary voice being the one of the Dean of Ch. Ch., who felt 'at loss to know how positive degrees of merit can in practice be fairly assessed' (fol. 2). Yet, when the committee finally submitted its report to the Hebdomadal Board on 9 December 1829, it advised that the examinations for honours in classics and mathematics should be taken on the same day, and pointed out 'strong objections on moral grounds' 'against the plan of arranging the names according to personal relative merit' (Ms. Top Oxon b 21, fols. 6–7).

17 (R. J. Wilberforce), *Considerations Respecting the Most Effectual Means of Encouraging Mathematics* (1830), pp. 9–11; authorship attributed by Baden Powell, copy in Bodleian Library, Baden Powell 31 (32).

since the two branches of knowledge had to go hand in hand. He was thus abandoning the cornerstone of Baden Powell's strategy for the mathematical examiners. The separation of the boards and of the dates of the examination was the institutional instrument essential to full independence from the more conservative board of classical examiners.[18]

Wilberforce was ready to take advantage from Saunders's retraction, and approved of the latter's 'judicious and well timed' proposals. The mathematical examiners felt the political and psychological blow of Saunders's defection. A memorandum signed by the mathematical examiners and addressed to the Vice-Chancellor on 11 November 1830 contained a considerably reduced list of requests. The plea for a longer interval between the mathematical and classical examinations was not mentioned. The only request the mathematical examiners put forward was the listing in order of merit of the students examined for the mathematical honours. On 23 November 1830 the proposals put forward by the committee appointed in 1829 were finally approved, though deeply modified by Convocation.[19]

The proposals put forward by the mathematical examiners were flatly rejected. In one respect, the November 1830 statutes represented a 'retrograde move', as Baden Powell put it. Even though students examined for the B.A. degree were offered mathematics instead of logic, the statutes also prescribed a minimum requirement of four books of Euclid to satisfy the examiners. This clause had the obvious effect of restricting the 'scientific' side of the curriculum to the mechanical repetition of a few geometrical definitions and theorems. Wilberforce's view on the superiority of Euclid over the modern mathematics was thus fully endorsed by Convocation.[20]

On 1 December 1831, a year after the passing of the above statutes, the mathematical examiners were again on the move. This time, Saunders agreed to rejoin his colleagues in petitioning the Hebdomadal Board. The examiners requested that the names of the fifth class, the pass men, should be printed. This measure was designed to confer higher dignity upon the newly introduced fourth class. They also asked that each class be subdivided according to the order of merit and that logic should not be compulsory for students seeking honours. With the single exception of the insistence on the order of merit for the mathematical honour list, it was clear that the requests by the mathe-

[18]   A. P. Saunders, *Observations on the Different Opinions Held as to the Changes Proposed in the Examination Statutes* (1830), pp. 6, 9, copy in Bodleian Library, Baden Powell 31 (28).

[19]   (R. Wilberforce), *Considerations*, p. 8; Baden Powell, 'Copy of the Memorial sent to the Vice-Chancellor, 11 Nov., 1830', in Bodleian Library, Baden Powell 31 (31). For the official memorial, see Bodleian Library, Vice-Chancellor Papers, Ms. Top. Oxon b 23, fols. 298-9. For the drafts of the various *Examination Statutes* circulated in printed form and discussed in Convocation, see Bodleian Library, Oxford University Archives, Register of Convocation 1829-1837, fols. 69 *et. seq.*, 84 *et seq.*, 140 *et seq.*

[20]   Baden Powell, *The Present State and Future Prospects*, p. 39.

matical examiners were only minor adjustments of the statutes passed in November 1830.[21]

As was expected, on 30 January 1832 the Council of the Heads of Houses resolved that 'the examination statute having been too recently enacted, it is not expedient to propose to Convocation any alteration in its details'. The obvious need to face the Board with proposals unanimously supported by the examiners, forced Baden Powell to formulate very moderate and almost insignificant aims. On the other hand, the timidity of the requests, limited to matters of detail as the Hebdomadal Board pointed out, was sufficient to exclude the possibility of a debate in Convocation. The confidence of the previous years was shattered, and Baden Powell became convinced that little was to be achieved by working from within. He wrote to the Vice-Chancellor: 'Being by experience now perfectly satisfied that no exertion on the part of the examiners can produce any effectual diminution of those evils ... I can no longer continue to discharge the office of examiner, and beg to take this mode of tendering my resignation.'[22]

The time of internal reform was over. Baden Powell realized that only pressure from cultivated public opinion could restore the balance between reformers and conservatives at Oxford. Until 1832 he followed Copleston's advice on the subject of the inaugural lecture he delivered every year at the beginning of his course. In 1832 he decided to publish his lecture for the Easter term. The Oxford meeting of the British Association for the Advancement of Science (1832) represented the ideal occasion for giving the maximum of publicity to his protest.[23]

The debate on the decline of science in Britain and Professor Moll's remarks on the deficiency of academic science in England provided the friends of science at Oxford with a further stimulus to the full expression of their frustration. Professor Moll alleged that the Oxford professors of mathematics and astronomy 'seldom or never lecture', and 'often do not reside at all at the University'. Baden Powell replied that the guilty party was not the professoriate but the system of university education. It was a difficult task to collect a class, he added, since the university did not compel attendance, and many colleagues positively discouraged students from hearing public lectures on scientific subjects.[24]

21 *Reasons for the Suggestion of certain Alterations in the Examination Statutes, by the Public Examiners* (1832), see copy in Bodleian Library, Baden Powell 32 (2), where Baden Powell states that he received assistance from A. P. Saunders drafting the pamphlet.

22 Vice-Chancellor Papers, fols. 557–8; for a draft of Baden Powell's letter, see Bodleian Library, Baden Powell 32 (4).

23 On the preparation of the B.A.A.S. Oxford meeting see J. B. Morrell and A. Thackray, *Gentlemen of Science* (1981); Baden Powell was the least active of the local secretaries, though he wholeheartedly supported the Association from its inception: it is however clear that he regarded the reform of the statutes a matter requiring immediate and exclusive attention.

24 Baden Powell, *The Present State and Future Prospects*, pp. 29–30. On the debate on science

The 1832 pamphlet on the state of mathematical studies at Oxford prompts a general consideration of the development of Baden Powell's position during the three years between 1829 and 1832. The 1832 pamphlet was an outspoken, well-argued and documented denunciation of the insensitivity of the academic authorities towards mathematical and physical disciplines in particular. Baden Powell defended the liberality of mathematical and physical studies. He maintained that the cultivation of scientific disciplines had a beneficial influence upon the development of the student's mental faculties. As far as the mathematical subjects were concerned he acknowledged the superiority of tutorial teaching over the professorial. However, he also emphasized 'the absolute necessity for an attendance on public experimental lectures' for the cultivation of the natural sciences. For the first time Baden Powell advocated a 'judicious and *systematic combination* of the tutorial and the professorial systems of instruction'.[25]

The pamphlet contained proposals and themes typical of the Noetic approach to the role of the Anglican universities in times of social and political crisis, albeit interpreted by Baden Powell with considerable originality and occasional crudity. He repeated Whately's complaint about the lack of adequate elementary education of students entering the universities. He also deployed the arguments put forward by Whately to defend academic logic or political economy and pleaded the case for physical and mathematical studies. Baden Powell sought to impress his colleagues by explicitly linking the educational debate as it related to science to the political convulsions of the day: 'Scientific knowledge is rapidly spreading among *all classes* EXCEPT THE HIGHER, and the consequence must be, that that Class *will no longer remain* THE HIGHER. If its members continue to retain their superiority, they must preserve a real *preeminence in knowledge*, and must make advances at least in proportion to the Classes which have *hitherto* been below them'.[26]

in the early 1830s see G. A. Foote, 'The Place of Science in the British Reform Movement', *Isis*, 42 (1951), 192–208; N. Reingold, 'Babbage and Moll on the Decline of Science in Great Britain', *B.J.H.S.*, 4 (1968), 58–64; S. F. Cannon, *Science in Culture* (1978), ch. vi.

[25] Baden Powell, *The Present State and Future Prospects*, pp. 18–20.

[26] *The Present State*, pp. 24–5, 38–9. Morrell and Thackray have argued that Baden Powell's lecture was ill-judged: the occasional intemperance of the language employed, and the vehement critique of academic authorities was bound to doom to failure his reforming intents. It is noted that the lecture represented the last, desperate move when all internal manoeuvring had already failed. It should also be pointed out that even the more moderate William Buckland and Charles Daubeny, who carefully avoided taking side in the dispute between the mathematical examiners and the University, after 1832 decided to appeal to cultivated public opinion. See for instance C. Daubeny, *An Inaugural Lecture* (1834), and the favourable review of it, severely critical of university education, in *Athenaeum*, n.344 (31 May 1834), 401–2. A certain degree of coolness in the relationship between Baden Powell on the one hand, and Buckland and Daubeny on the other, is inferred from the latter's failure to mention the statistics of attendance to lectures put forward by the Savilian Professor in the pamphlets Daubeny devoted to university reform. Buckland, according to Mrs E. O. Gordon *(Life and Correspondence*, 1894, p. 24) was in favour of a liberal education based on the study of classics, and thought that natural sciences should occupy 'a subordinate part in the university curriculum'.

Baden Powell's complaint about the state of mathematical and physical studies at Oxford attracted some attention and even support. Robert Walker published a more moderate pamphlet in defence of his colleague's lecture. Walker too insisted on the social relevance of the debate on the extension of the curriculum. In an age like the present, he concluded, 'when every mechanic is taught to think, and to read', the public seminaries of education ought to have made every effort to gain cultural ascendance and respectability. Walker's was the only favourable public answer to Baden Powell's proposals. As a 'Master of Arts' pointed out in a venomous attack, 'the Professor well knows he is in a minority in Oxford on the points in question. He has often tried it, and found it so'.[27]

Significantly, none of Baden Powell's Noetic friends came to his rescue. Moderate as they were, Baden Powell's proposals for extending the curriculum to include the first elements of mathematical and physical sciences were not seen as a priority by many of his Oriel colleagues. Furthermore, developments in Church and State absorbed the attention of the majority of his friends. The more conservative academics were obviously opposed to any innovation aimed at introducing scientific subjects or competition in the examination system. On the other hand, the Noetics were not convinced that the battle fought by Baden Powell was a vital one, nor were they sure that a successful Anglican cultural strategy needed to inscribe the word 'science' on its banners.

By publishing his polemical lecture to coincide with the British Association meeting at Oxford, Baden Powell risked excluding himself from academic respectability. As adversaries were ready to point out, the pamphlet published by their colleague was designed to stir up educated public opinion against the academic reluctance to update the curriculum.

There was a further dimension to Baden Powell's isolation in Oxford. Only a few months before the publication of the lecture, the Scottish philosopher William Hamilton had launched a devastating attack against what he regarded as the corruption of the university by the colleges. The Savilian Professor of Geometry accepted Hamilton's thesis that the ancient statutes prescribed a wide-ranging curriculum. These statutes specifically mentioned the duty to impart a scientifically oriented education, and nineteenth-century educational practice at Oxford was seen by both authors as the result of an unauthorized restriction of statutory prescription.

The only reform needed was therefore the restoration of legality within the University. Hamilton's authoritative and well-documented thesis caused serious alarm at Oxford. It is thus understandable that at a moment of deep anxiety for the future of the Establishment and the Anglican monopoly of higher

---

[27] (R. Walker), *A Few Words in Favour of Professor Powell, and the Sciences* (1832), p. 23; for attribution, see Bodleian Library, Baden Powell 32 (6); 'A Master of Arts', *A Short Criticism of a Lecture Published by the Savilian Professor of Geometry* (1832), p. 6. See Bodleian Library, Baden Powell 32 (7).

education, the support Baden Powell publicly gave to the views put forward by Hamilton was seen by the conservative faction of University opinion as an act of treason and by many moderate reformers as an unwise provocation.[28]

Though frustrated in his reforming purposes and already convinced that only pressure from without, from Parliament in particular, could achieve a significant result at Oxford, Baden Powell made a last attempt to forward his plans. In November 1833 he circulated a petition on the *Examination Statutes*, to be signed by members of Convocation and addressed to the Heads of Houses, the Proctors, and the Vice-Chancellor. The main feature of the memorandum was its insistence on the idea that physical and mathematical studies were 'an essential branch of a liberal education'. A general acquaintance with the first principles of science was a 'necessary qualification for the degree of B.A.'. Students were to be invited to pay attention to a topic of their choice drawn from a wide range of scientific disciplines: algebra, arithmetic, geometry and natural philosophy.[29]

To ensure publicity for his memorandum, Baden Powell wrote a paper for the *Quarterly Journal of Education*, the magazine edited – and almost written – by Augustus De Morgan on behalf of the Society for the Diffusion of Useful Knowledge. Baden Powell was a member of the Society from 1830, the year in which he wrote to its secretary proposing to set up an Oxford committee. Baden Powell's first contribution was a paper published in January 1834. This anonymous essay was designed to exert pressure on the Hebdomadal Board, which was due to examine Baden Powell's memorandum in a few weeks' time. He also wanted to convince the public that the reform of the examination system at Oxford was a topic of national importance.[30]

The convention of anonymity allowed Baden Powell to express himself even more freely than in his 1832 lecture. De Morgan did in fact think that his younger colleague was going too far, and repeatedly intervened to soften the belligerent tone of the paper. For instance, Baden Powell attributed to an imaginary supporter of the Oxonian educational tradition the view that Oxford would never allow the reform of the curriculum to take place 'for the sake of introducing those low mechanical studies which are now filling the heads of unwashed mechanics with every kind of vain and dangerous delusions, through every dirty manufacturing district in the Kingdom'.[31]

---

28 (W. Hamilton), 'Universities of England – Oxford', *E.R.*, 53 (1831), 384–427 and 'English Universities – Oxford', *E.R.*, 54 (1831), 478–504. For some answers to Hamilton's attacks, see Oriel College, Hawkins Collection of Pamphlets.

29 (Baden Powell), *Examination Statutes* (Nov. 1833), pp. 1–3; copy in Bodleian Library, Baden Powell 31 (1).

30 London, University College Library, S.D.U.K. Papers, Baden Powell envelope, letters to Thomas Coates, Nov. 1830 – 14 March 1841. On the S.D.U.K. see A. Smith, *The Society for the Diffusion of Useful Knowledge 1826–1846* (1974). (Baden Powell), 'Physical Studies in Oxford', *Quarterly Journal of Education*, 7 (1834), 47–54.

31 (Baden Powell), 'Physical Studies in Oxford', p. 53.

De Morgan thought it advisable to introduce an emollient clause: 'these are curious confessions; but supposing them founded in fact . . .'. Baden Powell was not pleased by the editorial manipulation of his text. However, De Morgan's cautious insertions did not alter the aggressiveness of the paper. The closing paragraphs contained a veiled allusion to the possibility of Parliamentary intervention in the affairs of the universities: an allusion hardly capable of convincing or impressing the Oxford dons, especially the younger ones. The universities, Baden Powell argued, were supposed to serve the nation. The country was not prepared to tolerate that endowments and 'funds held in trust for the benefit of the public' were being diverted from their legitimate destination.[32]

On 24 February 1834 the Vice-Chancellor wrote to Baden Powell informing him that the Hebdomadal Board and the Proctors 'judge it inexpedient at present to propose any alteration of the Statute'. Baden Powell's reaction was a bitter denunciation of the 'oligarchy' which controlled the policy of the University. The veiled allusion of January 1834 to Parliamentary interference, became in the July paper commenting on the answer by the Board a reminder that 'the principle of Parliamentary interference has been now recognised in other points, and we do not despair of finding in it a remedy for the evils we now speak of, should others fail'.[33]

A year later, in July 1835, a paper on 'University Education' contained Baden Powell's reflections on the lesson to be learned from ten years of struggling for reform, and from the Parliamentary and University debate on the admission of dissenters: 'If . . . any great improvement is to be accomplished in the form and constitution of our Universities, it must be effected upon the recommendation of a commission for inquiring into the entire University system'.[34]

The radicalization of Baden Powell's attitude towards the university was not the result of mere frustration and disappointment. It would be more correct to say that frustration and disappointment made Baden Powell rethink many of his former convictions concerning the Anglican Church and the universities. It is important to evaluate his emancipation from the basically apologetic stand which characterized the early works. His change of attitude towards the Establishment and the universities followed a process of intellectual re-orientation which had at its centre the contemplation of contemporary political and theological debates.

As far as the universities were concerned, we have already noted Baden Powell's approval of Hamilton's historical and critical remarks. On the more

---

32 For De Morgan's editing, see copy of the articles, annotated by Baden Powell, in Bodleian Library, Baden Powell 19 (4).
33 Bodleian Library, Baden Powell 31 (2), Vice-Chancellor to Baden Powell, 24 Feb. 1834; (Baden Powell), 'Physical Studies in Oxford', p. 63.
34 (Baden Powell), 'University Education', *Quarterly Journal of Education*, 10 (1835), 8.

general question bearing on Church and State politics, in the early 1830s he
was clearly influenced by the teaching of Arnold, Whately's lifelong friend.
Baden Powell saw in the principles of political and religious tolerance advocated
by Arnold a logical development of the Noetic stand. Arnold's name was
never mentioned in the *Journal of Education* papers on university reform and
the admission of Dissenters. Nevertheless, a comparison between the line of
argument pursued by Baden Powell and the works published by Arnold at
the same period reveals marked similarities.[35]

In the *Principles of Church Reform*, a work Baden Powell read with great
attention, the national relevance of the Church and university establishments
was thoroughly discussed by Arnold. Echoing a recurrent theme in the Noetic
theological productions, Arnold repeated that dogmas were not the road to
salvation. Indeed, differences of opinion were to be expected on doctrinal and
exegetical issues. Such differences could never be eliminated except by reverting
to repression and persecution, two roads clearly impracticable in contemporary
British society.

The Church, which was and ought to be a national establishment, was
under the obligation to use every appropriate means to restore Christian unity,
to regain the support of the lost flock. Indeed, Arnold commented, 'Dissent...,
when it becomes general, makes the Establishment cease to be national'. The
Headmaster of Rugby pointed out that the evil of Dissent was not social and
religious only: it had cultural dimensions as well. Dissenting ministers exercised
a deep influence over the masses, Arnold argued, and in politically sensitive
areas of the country. Yet, their education was entirely left to chance: 'And
of what use is it to say that the *Church* does not suffer from his (the Dissenting
minister's) ignorance, and is innocent of encouraging it? the *nation* suffers
from it . . . .'[36]

In times of great national crisis, the nation could not tolerate the universities
remaining closed to a major section of the population. It was essential to
extend to the Dissenting ministry the benefit of higher education, of refining
contacts with the upper layer of society. It was clear that Arnold was developing
the Noetic theme of the assumption of hegemonic functions by the Anglican
universities.

Baden Powell fully agreed with Arnold's insistence on the *national* character
of the Church and the universities. In so far as differences of opinion in
doctrinal speculation were unavoidable, Baden Powell argued for tolerance

35 For an opinion of Arnold on Baden Powell, see annotation in a letter from Baden Powell to
    Coates, London, University College Library, S.D.U.K. Papers, 9 Nov. 1832: 'Baden Powell
    is a very sensible man, and a very liberal one...deeply interested in encouraging the study
    of physical science at Oxford'.
36 T. Arnold, *Principles of Church Reform* (1833), pp. 15–16, 18, 20, 25, 45, 75. E. L. Williamson,
    The Liberalism of Thomas Arnold (1964); D. Forbes, *The Liberal Anglican Idea of History*
    (1952); B. Knights, *The Idea of the Clerisy in the Nineteenth Century* (1978).

and Christian understanding. His concept of a Church adequately prepared to face the struggle of the day pivoted on the principle of free and candid discussion, which included an attitude of openmindedness towards lay culture. To his Oxford colleagues grouped around Keble and Newman, who advocated an integrated Anglican Christian world view, Baden Powell proposed a model for contemporary culture based on independent spheres of inquiry.

It was the duty of the Christian intellectual to pursue the inquiries on their own terms and according to their own methodologies. However, tolerance could not be extended to the intolerant. The nation was not to allow a few illiberal dons to enjoy the sinister power of jeopardizing its cultural advancement and social stability. In the July number of the *Journal of Education*, in the context of a review of the ultra-reactionary pamphlet on the admission of Dissenters by William Sewell (1804–74), Baden Powell pointed out that the universities were created at a time when there was no dissent. The religion contemplated by the fathers of the universities, he argued, 'was the religion of the *nation*'.[37]

It was difficult to maintain that in 1834 Anglicanism was the religion of the country. Thus, the University was bound to respect the intentions of the founders and open its gates to all students, of whatever religious denomination. Colleges, as private institutions of the Church of England, were free to retain their religious tests. Dissenters were therefore allowed to become members of the University, without necessarily belonging to a college or subscribing to the tests and discipline of the Anglican Church.

According to Baden Powell, the issue of the admission of Dissenters was the test case which proved the incapacity of the Anglican establishment to come to terms with the new situation. Furthermore, although the debate brought the Noetics and the University establishment into open opposition, it also pointed out the inability of the Noetics to formulate a coherent proposal and to agree among themselves on which policy to pursue.[38]

Hawkins, promoter of the declaration designed to supersede the subscription to the articles, emphasized that his proposal had no theological motivation, nor was it designed to provide a side door for the admission of Dissenters. A 'Senior Member of Convocation' – probably Hawkins himself – emphatically denied that the proposal was connected with the 'theological views of certain individuals'. It is noteworthy that one of the fiercest critics of Hampden's pamphlet on the admission of dissenters, actually accused his colleague of Socinianism, and pointed out the connection between the latter's nominalistic

---

[37] W. Sewell, *Thoughts on the Admission of Dissenters to the University of Oxford* (1834). (Baden Powell), 'On the Admission of Dissenters to the University of Oxford', *Quarterly Journal of Education*, 8 (1834), 78–92. Cf. (W. Hamilton), 'Admission of Dissenters to the Universities', *E.R.*, 61 (1834), 196–227, and 'The University and Dissenters', 422–45.

[38] (Baden Powell), 'On the Admission of Dissenters'.

theology and the attempt at changing the terms of admission to the Anglican universities.[39]

Baden Powell was opposed to Hawkins's interpretation of the measure in favour of abolishing subscription to the articles. He was convinced that the criticism of dogmatic theology elaborated by the Noetics was bound by logical consistency to provide the theoretical justification for the admission of Dissenters. For this reason too his stand was different from that of Hampden himself. Baden Powell approved the latter's *Observations on Religious Dissent*, yet he doubted 'whether his claim for the maintenance of the University as exclusively a Church of England institution is quite consistent with those opinions which he has expressed in previous publications'.[40]

Divided among themselves, the Noetics failed to throw the weight of their scholarship and polemical skills into the debate on the admission of Dissenters. Two major questions were at the centre of the discussion. One party, represented by Newman and his allies, believed that the universities were seminaries of the Church of England. They pressed for the reform of the tutorial system at Oriel, in order to increase the religious and spiritual content of academic education. Baden Powell and Whately on the other hand were convinced that the universities ought to be academies imparting a modern and comprehensive education, designed to train 'a body of well-educated men, competent to discharge the various and important administrative functions in the state'.[41]

The latter position failed to win support even within the Noetic circle. Hampden himself, the most outspoken of the Noetics on the admission of Dissenters issue, maintained that the universities were exclusively Church of England institutions. No legislative interference was to be allowed or tolerated. Hawkins, though he opposed the plan of the younger tutors for a closer spiritual supervision of the students, was equally opposed to 'illiberal' disciplines and the opening of the university to dissenters. Whately was ready to accept Baden Powell's solution of admitting the dissenters to the universities, provided that they were excluded from colleges which required religious tests. However, he chose to remain silent on the issue and limited his intervention to epistolary advice. More dramatic events in Ireland were absorbing his attention.[42]

39 'A Senior Member of Convocation', *A Letter to a Non-resident Friend upon Subscription to the Thirty Nine Articles at Matriculation* (1835), p. 7; 'A Resident Member of Convocation', *1835 and 1772. The Present Attack on Subscription Compared with the Last* (1835), pp. 3–9. 18. E. W. Grinfield, the earliest opponent of the Noetics, in 1836 refused to vote against Hampden, claiming that the principles advocated by the Professor of Divinity 'were originally advocated by Bishop Copleston and Archbishop Whately': he could not, therefore, support a motion of censure against the pupil, when no action was taken against his masters; see *Reflections, after a Visit to the University of Oxford* (1836), pp. 6–7.
40 (Baden Powell), 'University Education without Religious Distinctions', 9.
41 (Baden Powell), 'University Education without Religious Distinctions', 9.
42 Ward, *Victorian Oxford*, p. 92.

Thus, Baden Powell was the only member of the Noetic circle who proposed a well-defined and comprehensive solution to the question of the reform of the curriculum and the role and function of the universities in contemporary British society. His scheme was a sophisticated and original interpretation of the Noetic cultural and political strategy, updated with the substantial help of Arnold's controversial analysis of contemporary religious and secular institutions in Britain. As is by now clear, the debates on educational reform and the theological and political implications of the clash over the admission of dissenters were highly relevant to Baden Powell's intellectual development.

Yet, the battles over the reform of the statutes and the admission of dissenters were not the only ones in the early 1830s. To many of his colleagues the two issues were closely related and focused on the role of science in the modern world view: the cultivation of classical learning was the distinguishing feature of Anglican higher education, the cultivation of science was characteristic of the lower-level intellectual concerns pursued by dissenters.

The most outspoken representative of this view was William Sewell. He had no patience with scientific societies and 'those indefatigable philosophers who, every returning month...grind around the planets in an array, or electrify a dead frog for the advancement and the diffusion of science'. He proudly stated that a Christian university had nothing to do with such unchristian occupations: 'a nation of Newtons could no more produce a gentleman than a nation of infidels could create a Christian'.[43]

Within Anglican circles, the debate on the relationship between scientific and religious values became a crucial issue, closely related to the question of the role of the universities and of their educational priorities in modern society. The violent reaction to institutional change dominated the debate on the relationship between science and religion. As had been the case with the debate on the reform of the statutes and the admission of dissenters, Baden Powell discovered that his views were radically opposed by his old *British Critic* colleagues and failed to win approval from his Noetic teachers.

---

[43] William Sewell, *A Second Letter to a Dissenter* (1834), pp. 10, 37. See also Sewell's opposition to natural theology and the spread of scientific culture, in *The Attack upon the University of Oxford* (1834), pp. 21–2.

10

Science and revelation: 1826–1836

The decade from 1826 represented a period of deep intellectual and political re-orientation in the Anglican Church. The process of revision to which Baden Powell submitted his theological and political ideas also modified his early convictions on the subject of the relationship between science and religion. As we remarked when examining Baden Powell's early contribution to the science–religion debate, few of the certainties of the 1820s survived the political and intellectual storm of the late 1820s and the early 1830s.

The belief that modern geology triumphantly established the historical truth of the Mosaic deluge was found to be groundless. The conviction that it was always possible to point out elements of coincidence between geological discoveries and the word of scripture was progressively shaken by the outcome of geological debates. Leading British geologists abandoned important features of the diluvial doctrine and questioned the assumption that the earth's chronology as established by geology proved the literal truth of the Genesis account of creation.

Baden Powell became aware that his former hints concerning the antecedent moral corruption of those who opposed scientific findings to the scriptures could hardly apply to Buckland, John Fleming, George Poulett Scrope (1797–1876) or Sedgwick. He was also faced with the problem of repeated attacks by leading Anglican divines and members of the Hackney Phalanx against the alleged Christian unworthiness of scientific pursuits. Baden Powell made every effort to counteract a trend towards confrontation which hampered his endeavours at introducing scientific disciplines into the Oxford curriculum. Thus, when Rose published his Commencement Sermon lamenting the undue pre-eminence accorded to mathematical studies at Cambridge, Baden Powell wrote a conciliatory but firm letter to the *Christian Remembrancer*, denying Rose's allegations. He admired the *Discourses* against German theological rationalism published by Rose. Yet, he was also aware that the hard-line approach to theological and educational debates promoted by the Christian Advocate found a sympathetic audience at Hackney.

The *Tendency of Prevalent Opinions about Knowledge*, the sermon preached by Rose on 2 July 1826, made it clear that the Christian Advocate held philosophical and scientific studies responsible for the multifarious manifestations of contemporary infidelity. Rose expressed serious reservations about the role of scientific and philosophical studies in the curriculum of a Christian university. He also doubted their usefulness as auxiliaries of Christian apologetic. The cultural atmosphere of the time, he argued, was poisoned by the spirit of commercial gain which led to the cultivation of knowledge only in so far as it added to material wealth. The growth of utilitarian knowledge was followed by the growth of man's confidence in his powers. Men, blinded by the pride of reason, were now preparing a large-scale assault upon the word of revelation. It was the duty of the Anglican Church and of its universities to emphasize the role of liberal studies and of theology, the *regina scientiarum*, in the education of the future leaders of English society.[1]

Baden Powell saw in the sermon preached by Rose the signs of a dangerous retreat in the face of pressing cultural and social forces. In his letter to the *Christian Remembrancer* he reassured Rose that the pursuit of physical studies at an academic level had little to do with the solution of mechanical or industrial problems. He resented Rose's description of scientific abilities as implying nothing more than 'an expertise in handling the implements of the experimenter' and as being 'wholly of a low mechanical nature, applying only to temporal utility and profit, and absolutely useless and worthless in reference to the improvement of an intellectual nature'.[2]

Baden Powell was becoming increasingly conscious of the need to update the curriculum of the Anglican universities. Rose took the opposite line, deploring even the risible quantity of scientific teaching available at Cambridge and Oxford. The extreme position defended by the Christian Advocate was caused by what he regarded as provocation by the founders of University College London, who excluded religious teaching from their institution. Moreover, the success of the Mechanics' Institutes movement was regarded by Rose and other members of the High Church party as a further insidious attempt at creating non-religious sources of cultural authority among the masses. It was therefore imperative to make the best use of Anglican educational agencies in order to put a stronger emphasis on religious education.

The stand taken by Rose failed to win the support of the whole spectrum of the High Church party. The *British Critic* reviewer of Rose's sermon argued that the solution proposed was perhaps extreme and unrealistic. The reviewer acknowledged that physiologists, phrenologists, and geologists provided the sceptical party with 'its choicest and most numerous weapons' by attacking the concept of moral responsibility and the Mosaic narrative of creation. The reviewer could not agree with Rose, however, when the latter argued against

---

[1] H. J. Rose, *The Tendency of Prevalent Opinions about Knowledge Considered* (1826), pp. 1–3, 7, 17, 21.
[2] (Baden Powell), 'Observations on Rose's Commencement Sermon', *C.R.*, 8 (1826), 744–7.

all kinds of scientific pursuits, 'giving the unique privilege to moral and purer sciences'.[3]

It is nevertheless true that the most conservative members of the High Church party, and Rose with them, were convinced that the pace of scientific progress had resulted in a loss of control by the Anglican educational agencies and Christian scientists. The academic cultivators of geology, chemistry and mineralogy promised to exercise a positive control on the scientific movement in England, by giving impulse to scientific disciplines in the universities. The result was far from satisfactory. The scientific movement, its popularity and authority, were spreading far beyond what were regarded as the safe channels of upper-class *divertissement* or mere utilitarian applications; they were increasingly taking a key role in lay society.

The antagonistic attitude towards scientific debates and educational policies was endorsed by the Hackney Phalanx and the *British Critic* editorial board. Editors who disagreed were dismissed. Opposition to the secular values of the times also prevailed at Oxford and Cambridge and was the chief factor in the defeat of the effort by the educational reformers to update the curriculum or improve the educational efficiency of the two universities. It was therefore inevitable that Baden Powell's attempts to come to terms with contemporary science met with strong and determined hostility within Church circles.[4]

Baden Powell analysed the emerging novelties of the English intellectual scene in a sermon, *The Advance of Knowledge*, preached from St Mary's pulpit on Easter Day 1826. He invited his Anglican colleagues at Oxford and in the country manfully to face the cultural challenge of the day, thus avoiding the dangerous retreat into cultural and political isolationism. As the title of the sermon suggests, the theme of scientific and general educational progress was singled out for detailed discussion.

The sermon opened with the prophetic motto 'Many shall run to and fro, and knowledge shall be increased.' Of all prophecies, Baden Powell argued, Daniel xxi, 4 was the closest to fulfilment in modern times. He was little concerned, however, with prophecies or the millenarian chronology of technical and scientific discoveries. He reminded his audience that the advance of scientific knowledge was bound to have a significant impact on contemporary culture. This consequence was to be viewed not only as the accretion in knowledge of natural phenomena: it was rather 'the acquisition of new mental powers, leading (man) to new and more enlarged views, which constitutes the grand amelioration'.[5]

The rigorous procedures of scientific research were affecting the methodological standards of inquiries into every department of intellectual and social

---

3 (Anon.), 'On Systems of Instruction', *B.C.*, 1 (1827), 199, 205.
4 Marshall, 'Theology of Church and State', 500–8.
5 Baden Powell, *The Advance of Knowledge* (1826), pp. 1–2. For the tradition of Daniel xxi, 4 in British scientific apologetic, see C. Webster, *The Great Instauration*.

concern. Ideas as well as institutions were subjected to severe scrutiny. The basis of the authority of theological doctrines was being inspected with the degree of logical rigour applicable to scientific theories. Yet, Baden Powell did not see much cause for alarm in contemporary cultural developments. In 1826 his approach to the phenomenon of 'the universal progress of inquiry in all subjects and among all classes' was characterized by the Noetic and Hackney confidence in the possibility of directing the spread of information through the supervision of cautiously reformed Church educational agencies. However, the central argument implicit in his sermon was far from acceptable to many of his Oxford and Anglican colleagues.

It was clear that Baden Powell was prepared to recognize the prestige of scientific methodologies and discoveries. The rapid success of the Mechanics' Institutes and of the Society for the Diffusion of Useful Knowledge, the reforming ferments within the Royal Society, the diffusion of a taste for popular and scholarly scientific publications, the rise of specialized scientific societies, made Baden Powell aware of the growing strength and popularity of the scientific movement. Scientific debates, and in particular the discussion relating scientific doctrines and passages of scripture, could not be dismissed with scorn without endangering the credibility of Christian apologetic.[6]

Rose's attitude was completely different. Moreover, his hostility to the diffusion of science and of scientific education was shared by Anglican divines, who identified scientific interests with the dissenting cultural strategy, Unitarian rationalism, and class threats to the stability of the British social order. The fervour of scientific pursuits was increasingly censured as yet another instance of the intellectual plague of the times, the pride of reason. A subtler form of opposition to the solution that Baden Powell put forward came from his Noetic friends, notably Whately. Baden Powell's approach to the relationship between science and religion took full advantage of the theological and philosophical critical tools elaborated by his Oriel colleagues. Nevertheless he failed to convince his allies and teachers that science was to be taken that seriously.

The increasing difficulty of reconciling modern geological findings with the Genesis narrative persuaded Baden Powell to inquire into the theological foundation and logical consequence of the methodological guideline 'revelation does not teach natural sciences'. Whately's reflections on this often-repeated thesis provided the occasion to re-examine the whole question of the relationship between science and revelation. In his 1828 review of Senior's *Introductory Lectures on Political Economy* Whately admitted the possibility that an inquiry into natural or social phenomena – he was actually defending political economy from the charge of being inimical to religion – could produce doctrines apparently contradicting the scriptural narrative. Whately warned against impulsive reactions to the alleged danger. He suggested that the friend of religion should

[6] Baden Powell, *The Advance of Knowledge*, pp. 1, 32, 37–8.

examine the controversial scientific or social doctrine on its own terms 'from such data as our natural powers supply'. The Bible, Whately explained, was not designed to teach astronomy or geology, but religion: 'nor was it intended to preclude enquiry, or to supersede the exercise of our natural faculties...on subjects within their reach'.[7]

Whately's sincere claim that the Bible did not preclude independent scientific research did not prevent him from believing that those theories which contradicted the word of scripture on points of crucial doctrinal relevance could not survive the scrutiny of a competent Christian critic. For this reason too he was convinced that sensitive branches of intellectual inquiry, like geology, political economy, or even logic, should find a place within the body of academic disciplines. A clergy professionally equipped to meet the adversary on his own terms ensured a close and effective supervision of contemporary lay and scientific culture. A few months after the publication of Whately's review, Baden Powell was asked to preach the sermon for Easter Day 1829. Recent geological debates and polemics made him aware of the insufficiency of his earlier ideas on the relationship between scientific advance and the scriptures. He also felt that Whately's solution, which was based on a fundamental reluctance about accepting embarrassing scientific doctrines, was inadequate to face the new situation.

It may be noted that a number of British geological authorities warned about the hazards of claiming a strict coincidence between the Genesis narrative and modern geology. In 1826 John Fleming, an author admired by Baden Powell, published a paper in which he attacked the diluvial terminology and stratigraphy elaborated by Buckland. The Fleming–Buckland debate, almost forgotten by historians, was something of an affair at the time. Academic and national rivalry – Fleming was a Scot – was coupled with a personal competitiveness and a certain degree of invective. The ponderous epithets Fleming and Buckland exchanged on the occasion were repeated with good humour in geological and academic circles.[8]

The anecdotal aspect of this polemic between two picturesque figures should not divert attention from the substance of the debate. British geologists and the public at large were becoming aware that the Mosaic interpretation of geological phenomena was thrown in doubt by recently undertaken research. In France, still the leading country in the natural sciences, Constant Prévost (1781–1856), Marcel de Serres (1782–1862), d'Audebard de Férussac (1786–1836) and Cuvier himself denied the geological credibility of world-wide

[7] (R. Whately), 'Oxford Lectures on Political Economy', *E.R.*, 48 (1828), 171–2.
[8] (J. Fleming), 'The geological deluge, as interpreted by Baron Cuvier and Professor Buckland, inconsistent with the testimony of Moses and the phenomena of nature', *Edinburgh Philosophical Journal*, 14 (1826), 205–39; K. Lyell (ed.), *Life, Letters and Journals of Sir Charles Lyell*, 2 vols. (1881), vol. i, pp. 285–90, Lyell to Fleming, 3 Feb. 1830; J. Fleming, *The Lithology of Edinburgh* (1859), pp. xxxvi–xxxviii, xl.vi. For a recent assessment of this debate, see S. J. Frankel, 'British geology and the universal flood' (B.A. thesis, Harvard University, 1986).

catastrophes such as a universal deluge. Baden Powell could not ignore that the probable defeat of the diluvial theory that he himself had earlier helped to publicize, discredited Buckland's Christian geology and geology in general in the eyes of many Anglican apologists. It was easy to foretell that the doubts recently expressed as to the reliability of Buckland's geology would give renewed vigour to the hostility felt by many Oxford dons towards the sciences.[9]

It will be remembered that 1829 was the year in which Baden Powell hoped to win his battle for giving a fresh impulse to scientific disciplines in his university. It is not surprising, therefore, that he preached a sermon entitled 'Revelation and Science'. The sermon was designed to tranquillize his colleagues by showing them that there was nothing to fear from recent geological debates, since no conflict was really possible between scientific advance and scripture.

It may be argued that Baden Powell implicitly addressed himself to his Noetic friends and especially Whately. He wanted to convince his Oriel colleagues that the use of their sophisticated theological tools could solve once and for all the endless controversy on the relationship between science and revelation. It is unfortunate that the original text of the Easter 1829 sermon has not been preserved. However, there is little doubt that the 1833 printed version contained, as the author claimed in the prefatory note, 'the substance' of the lecture delivered from St Mary's pulpit. Even the 'substance' of the sermon represented a marked departure from the traditional approach to the science–religion issue that Baden Powell himself had endorsed in the early 1820s.

The preacher maintained that the truth of scripture was not called in question by any geological or scientific doctrine seeming to contradict particular scriptural passages. Taking the concrete instance provided by recent geological debates on the universal deluge, Baden Powell argued that those who doubted the reliability of geological findings or the inspiration of the scriptures severely misjudged the function of the Old Testament in the divine strategy for the salvation of man.

Baden Powell added to the 'revelation does not teach natural sciences' thesis, Davison's remarks on the difference between the Old Testament and the new alliance preached by Christ, which was characterized by the abolition of the law and the establishment of the reign of the spirit. Baden Powell

---

9 For the authority of French science in the early decades of the nineteenth century, and the diffusion of French geological and biological ideas in England, see P. Corsi, 'The importance of French transformist ideas', *B.J.H.S.*, 11 (1978), 221–44. For the impact of French critiques of the diluvial doctrine, see J. W. Clark and T. Hughes, *The Life and Letters of the Rev. Adam Sedgwick*, 2 vols. (1890), vol. i, p. 376, Sedgwick to Murchison, 17 Nov. 1831: 'Humboldt ridiculed [the diluvial doctrine] beyond measure when I met him in Paris. Prévost lectured against it'. L. E. Page, 'Diluvialism and its Critics in Great Britain in the Early Nineteenth Century', in C. J. Schneer (ed.), *Toward a History of Geology* (1969), 257–71; Gillispie, *Genesis and Geology* (1951); Millhauser, 'The Scriptural Geologists. An Episode in the History of Opinion', 65–86; W. Coleman, *Georges Cuvier, Zoologist* (1964).

urged that the inspired writers employed a language adapted to the cultural
level of their audience. Thus, references to natural phenomena derived from
traditional cosmogonies well known to the early Jews. The chief object of the
old dispensation was the intellectual and moral elevation of the Jewish people,
an indispensable preparatory step to the coming of the Saviour.[10]

The thesis that no scientific doctrine ever questioned the truth of revealed
doctrine contradicted the view maintained by Whately in his 1828 paper on
Senior's *Introductory Lectures*. For the second time after the debate on the
ground of authority of the Christian sabbath, Whately felt it necessary to
differentiate between his approach to the science–religion issue and the one
put forward by his former pupil. The leader of the Noetic school devoted a
long paragraph of his 1831 *Introductory Lectures on Political Economy* to
discussing the relationship between science and revelation. He substantially
repeated the points made in his 1828 contribution to the *Edinburgh Review*,
though he was now more explicit. He unambiguously advocated the principle
that the text of scripture was not to be taken as a test by which to try the
conclusions of science. Yet, in opposition to what Baden Powell preached in
his Easter Sermon, Whately firmly argued that 'doctrines may be maintained
on subjects distinct from religion, but which nevertheless would, if admitted,
go to invalidate scripture'.[11]

The concrete example he chose to illustrate his case, was the polygenetic
theory of the origin of the races of man. Whately greatly admired the anthropological work of Prichard, the main source of his information on this subject.
In the preface to the second edition of his *Researches* Prichard summarized
the arguments of naturalists who maintained that the numerous races of man
could not be viewed as varieties of a primitive type, but as different species.
'Such a conclusion, no doubt, would go far to shake the foundation of our
religion', Whately commented. He also made explicit an idea only to be
inferred from his 1828 paper: a true Christian had in any case a strong
antecedent persuasion that scientific doctrines inconsistent with the scripture
'never will be established'.[12]

It would be wrong to interpret Whately's pronouncement simply in terms

---

[10] Baden Powell, *Revelation and Science*, pp. 8–9, 13–14. The thesis put forward by Davison
      had recently been authoritatively endorsed by P. N. Shuttleworth in his *Sermons on Some of
      the Leading Principles of Christianity* (1827), p. 253.

[11] Whately, *Introductory Lectures*, pp. 31–2.

[12] Whately, *Introductory Lectures*. Polygenist doctrines were very common in France during the
      first half of the nineteenth century. For a recent, masterly discussion of this issue, see
      Blanckaert, 'Monogénisme et polygénisme en France'; the *Bulletin des sciences naturelles et
      de géologie* edited by Férussac, a journal extremely popular in Europe and England in the
      1820s for its exhaustive coverage of contemporary scientific debates and novelties, carried
      several contributions by supporters of the polygenist thesis, such as Bory de Saint-Vincent,
      Julien-Joseph Virey and Antoine Desmoulins. When the Ashmolean Society was established
      at Oxford in 1830, the *Bulletin* was the only foreign scientific journal the library subscribed
      to.

of the fundamentally conservative aims of his approach to contemporary culture. His conviction that no scientific doctrine would ever contradict the word of the scripture stemmed from his ideas on the weak epistemological status of inductive investigations into physical and biological phenomena. The set of arbitrary assumptions implicit in all scientific doctrine made it impossible to consider any theory as the final word on the subject under investigation. Conversely, Whately had no epistemological doubt that revelation was the last word on spiritual matters, and he clearly believed that there were scientific hypotheses which could – or pretended to – contradict God's message.

The boldness of Baden Powell's solution to the problem of the relationship between science and religion failed to satisfy Whately and positively displeased Newman, who made clear his disappointment to his colleague. For tactical reasons relating to his academic manoeuvres, Baden Powell did not print his controversial sermon of 1829, nor did he answer his critics. Newman's opposition to his approach and Whately's settled disagreement made Baden Powell aware of the difficulty of convincing his colleagues and friends that they needed to adapt the cultural stance so validly advanced in the 1820s to the controversies of the early 1830s.

The defeat suffered by his educational proposals forced Baden Powell to renounce his projects for reform from within the university. The 1832 lecture on the state of mathematical studies at Oxford was designed to gain support for his educational plans by directly appealing to the British liberal intelligentsia. He now applied the same tactic to the debate on the relationship between science and revelation. He was aware that his solution to the science–religion debate failed to win support at Oxford. Moreover, the unfavourable reception given by the university authorities to the Oxford meeting of the British Association for the Advancement of Science in 1832, the comments on this meeting by Frederick Nolan in his 1833 Bampton Lectures, and the repeated attacks against scientific pursuits by leading Anglican divines, convinced Baden Powell it was time to publicize his views on the relationship between science and the scriptures.[13]

The choice of Nolan, a rather eccentric High Church intellectual, as Bampton lecturer for 1833 was in itself a symptom of the cultural and political atmosphere prevailing at Oxford in the early 1830s. In the early 1800s Nolan had been an opponent of the reforming plans by Copleston and Davison. He defended the antiquated and inadequate textbooks then used to help students pass their examination, in the teeth of the Oriel campaign for higher standards of academic proficiency. Nolan also joined the campaign against the British

---

[13] On the B.A.A.S. see L. Pearce-Williams, 'The Royal Society and the founding of the B.A.A.S.', *Notes and Records of the Royal Society*, 16 (1961), 221–33; for a different interpretation, see S. F. Cannon, *Science in Culture* (1978), chs. 6 and 7; for an exhaustive and thoroughly documented study of the foundation and early meetings of the B.A.A.S. see Morrell and Thackray, *Gentlemen of Science*. On the reaction of Oxford dons and authorities to the 1832 meeting, see Yule, 'The impact of science', 142–8.

and Foreign Bible Society, denouncing any compromise with Dissenters and popular preachers as a subversive tendency. For his skill in prophetical investigation and his opposition to the Test and Corporation Acts he acquired much merit in the eyes of the Hackney leaders and the most conservative circles at Oxford.[14]

Nolan was a man of some learning, though better acquainted with late eighteenth-century scientific polemics and the prophetical literature of the seventeenth century, than with current intellectual and scientific affairs. As Dr Yule aptly remarks, 'his was a learned, if a selective and completely ineffective science'. Of his Bampton Lectures, it is sufficient to say that the author collected all sorts of objections to the epistemological reliability of modern science, as well as to scientific societies and gatherings. Nolan was clearly convinced that the scenes of unrest which surrounded the passing of the Reform Bill were a rehearsal of the revolutionary threats of the 1790s. Naturalists protesting against the cultural immobility of the Royal Society, forwarding the plans of the Society for the Diffusion of Useful Knowledge, or declaiming against the decline of science in Britain were part of the eternal conspiracy of the *Illuminati* to overthrow Christianity.[15]

In 1831, commenting on the probable date of the millennium, Nolan 'predicted' the foundation of the British Association by warning his readers that the 'march of the intellect' in itself was not sufficient to disestablish the Christian kingdom: 'the fatal blow...will be struck by...Antichristian associations which are banded together under the semblance and title of masons'. Thus, when in 1833 he was called upon to make seasonable commments on the Oxford meeting and the general question of the advance of knowledge, Nolan thought it was his duty to denounce the conspiracy. Overtaken by the fervour of his prophetic insights he hinted that the British Association cultivated obscure subversive aims. It was somewhat unfortunate for his thesis that his name appeared in the list of participants in the Oxford meeting, as Baden Powell ironically pointed out.[16]

Nolan's strictures were not Baden Powell's major preoccupation. He was deeply worried by what he regarded as the incapacity of many of his colleagues to understand the terms of current geological debates. In the eyes of many *British Critic* reviewers the discussion on the diluvial theory was taking a disquieting turn. In his presidential address to the Geological Society, delivered in 1831, Adam Sedgwick had admitted that geologists 'have not yet found

---

[14] F. Nolan, *A Letter to Phileleutheros Orieliensis* (1804); 'Phileleutheros' was John Davison, who in 1803 attacked a university textbook by H. Kett, a friend of Nolan and of the Hackney leaders; Nolan, *Objections of a Churchman to Uniting with the Bible Society* (1812).

[15] Yule, 'The impact of science', 100.

[16] Nolan, *The Time of the Millennium Investigated, and its Nature Determined on Scriptural Grounds* (1831), pp. 81–3. Oliver, in the otherwise excellent *Prophets and Millennialists* fails to mention Nolan, one of the most prolific and learned contributors to prophetic literature in the early nineteenth century. Baden Powell, *Revelation and Science*, p. 38.

certain traces of any great diluvial catastrophe', and had publicly abandoned the thesis that the diluvial doctrine proved the historical truth of the universality and uniqueness of the Mosaic deluge.[17]

In private correspondence and conversation, several distinguished Oxford dons expressed their bitter disillusionment at the 'unexpected' outcome of geological and apologetic debates of the 1820s. Dean Gaisford felt relieved by Buckland's departure for a trip to Europe: 'we shall hear no more, thank God, of his geology', he exclaimed. In view of his known connection with Buckland's exercises in biblical exegesis, Pusey was particularly embarrassed by the dramatic revision of geological opinion on the Mosaic deluge. Answering negative comments by his friend Newman, he wrote 'I quite feel what you say about Buckland's *Reliquiae*. It has made me distrust every theory of geology ever since.'[18]

Irritated by Sedgwick's public announcement, the *British Critic* reviewer of Whately's *Errors of Romanism* asked the rhetorical question whether it was really the duty of a Christian naturalist to convince the people, with Buckland and Cuvier and Sedgwick, that shells on the top of mountains were not the remnant of the deluge. In January 1833 a reviewer of Arnold's *Sermons* remarked disapprovingly that many were now seeing geology as 'a formidable aggressor on the regions of revealed truth'. John Bowden, author of the *British Critic* review of Baden Powell's sermon, commented that 'geology has come as a fresh and unexpected card into the hands of the infidels'.[19]

The printed version of Baden Powell's sermon was designed to resolve the worries expressed by many Anglican divines and *British Critic* reviewers. It was also intended to make clear that the extreme opinions voiced by Nolan, Sewell or the *British Critic* were viewed with disfavour by such a well-qualified member of the Anglican establishment as the Savilian Professor of Geometry at Oxford. Baden Powell strongly disagreed with those who, like the *British Critic* reviewer of Whately's work, hinted that it was better to avoid public acknowledgment of the discrepancy between geology and the book of Genesis. He reminded his colleagues that 'Physical knowledge is rapidly spreading among the lower classes': 'there are not wanting teachers, who know how to accommodate their lessons to the prevalent appetite of the popular mind'.[20]

---

[17] A. Sedgwick, 'Address to the Geological Society delivered on the Evening of the 18th of February 1831', *Proceedings of the Geological Society of London*, 1 (1831), 312–13, 314.

[18] E. O. Gordon, *Life and Correspondence of Buckland* (1894), p. viii; H. P. Liddon, *Life of Pusey*, vol. iv, p. 78. See also Ellis, *Seven against Christ* (1980), p. 75. Dean Gaisford had personal reason of animosity against Buckland: see Ward, *Victorian Oxford*, p. 51.

[19] (Anon.), 'Whately's *Romish Errors*', *B.C.*, 12 (1833), 175; (J. Bowden), 'Nolan and Powell', *B.C.*, 15 (1834), 421. It is noted that the passages quoted above, and further evidence which will be discussed below, do not substantiate Dr Yule's thesis that Churchmen were not worried by geological advance. It is more appropriate to conclude that the failure of Buckland's Christian geology convinced many to abandon the apologetic line defended during the late 1810s and the 1820s, and to avoid direct discussion of relevant issues.

[20] Baden Powell, *Revelation and Science*, p. 43.

Furthermore, Baden Powell argued, it was extremely unwise in an age characterized by scientific advance to make the truth of revelation stand or fall upon the agreement or disagreement between scientific discoveries and passages of scripture describing natural phenomena. Those who maintained this opinion failed to pay due attention to the allegorical, poetical and impressionistic features of the language employed by Old Testament writers. Many contemporary Christian apologists, he concluded, were fighting a futile and dangerous rearguard battle. The recent geological debates made it impossible to deny the contradiction between the creation narrative and the results of modern stratigraphical inquiries. Yet, Baden Powell maintained that: 'Neither is the existence of those absolute contradictions any argument against the truth of revelation in general, or Christian religion in particular: nor are the accordances which may be made out necessary to its support'.[21]

It has been argued above that Whately's comments on the relationship between science and revelation represented his reply to the thesis put forward by Baden Powell in the Easter sermon of 1829. It is therefore not surprising that the first objection to his solution he considered in the printed version of the sermon was that formulated by Whately in the 1831 *Introductory Lectures*. Though no explicit reference to Whately's work was made, the detailed discussion of the polygenetic theory of the origin of the human races was clearly designed to resolve the difficulty pointed out by his Oriel teacher.

It might be that future physiological research would establish the scientific accuracy of the polygenetic theory; in Baden Powell's view, such scientific tenets could never be used to undermine the unambiguous divine revelation of original sin and the promise of salvation through Christ. God revealed those truths to which man could never have attained by his own unaided intellectual powers. Any difficulty in explaining original sin, if it were proved that mankind originated in different geographical regions and times, simply demonstrated the complex and mysterious ways of God in his dealings with man and nature. It should be noted that Baden Powell expressed his views in hypothetical form, since in 1833 he still believed in the monogenetic theory, as formulated by Prichard. It was his intention simply to prove the capacity of his solution to deal with future difficulties, even one as improbable as that instanced by Whately.[22]

Baden Powell tactfully omitted to mention Whately's name when dissenting from his teacher's views. However, he made amends for their disagreement on the religious import of the polygenetic theory by emphasizing his theological allegiances. The theological themes touched upon in *Revelation and Science* faithfully endorsed the Noetic teaching. Baden Powell devoted a long note to

[21] *Revelation and Science*, pp. 10–11.
[22] *Revelation and Science*, pp. 16–18, 19–21. Baden Powell's solution was closely resembling Senior's attempt to find an agreement between psychological materialism and the revealed doctrine of the immortality of the soul: see Levy, *Nassau Senior* (1970), Appendix.

defending Whately's works and ideas. He also extolled the analysis of the grounds of authority of the Christian sabbath his former teacher had provided in order to correct the mistake of the pupil. The closing paragraphs of the published version of the sermon summed up the themes which characterized recent Noetic productions, Hampden's critique of dogmatic theology in particular.[23]

The Noetic imprint of Baden Powell's approach to the question of the relationship between science and revelation could not have evaded the attention of Bowden, who was severely critical of the sermon. It has, however, escaped the attention of recent commentators that the tone and substance of Bowden's strictures betrayed the reviewer's design of using the critique of *Revelation and Science* as an excuse to reprimand the heretical teaching of the Noetic school. Thus, when explicitly referring to the Oriel Noetics Bowden explained that the charge of heresy was 'particularly applicable to the exclusive and self-complacent lawgivers of a college common room'. He also introduced Baden Powell to his readers as 'the representative of a new class of liberal and philosophical divines', who distinguished himself by using 'a plainer and bolder language than any other champion of the same school has yet ventured to use'.[24]

Bowden insisted on criticizing the theological side of Baden Powell's sermon precisely because he wanted to represent the ideas put forward by the Savilian Professor as the logical outcome of Noetic theological teaching. However, it would be wrong to stress the reviewer's theological and polemical aims to the point of suggesting that Bowden did not genuinely think that geology constituted a threat to the credibility of revelation. It would be equally mistaken to take at its face value Bowden's profession of tolerant indifference towards modern scientific pursuits.

It is true that Bowden repeatedly stressed he had no intention of conditioning scientific research by demanding that naturalists take their cue entirely from scripture. On the other hand, neither had he any intention of acknowledging that geology or science might credibly contradict the word of the scriptures. He clarified his view on this point by asking whether sincere Christians could possibly accept the 'story of the deluge (as) a chimera' or whether St Peter was wrong in believing in it, simply because geologists told them they were unable to prove the coincidence of their theories with the Genesis creation narrative.[25]

---

[23] Baden Powell, *Revelation and Science*, pp. 42–3, 47–8.
[24] (J. Bowden), 'Nolan and Powell', 414.
[25] 'Nolan and Powell', 421–2, 426; Yule, 'The impact of science', 124: 'the charge against Powell was a theological and not a geological question'; see also p. 140, 'Bowden meant no disparagement of science'. On Bowden's scientific interests see Ker and Gornall, *Letters and Diaries of Newman*, vol. ii, p. 241, and vol. iv, pp. 103, 108–10. Bowden had nothing against geology as collection of evidence relating to the history of the earth, but could not accept that geological findings could be construed as offering a theory of the earth independent of

It is notable that Bowden's standpoint had much in common with the comments made by Whately in 1828 and 1831 on the relationship between science and revelation. Whately might have judged as hasty and naive Bowden's explicit reference to St Peter's belief in the deluge, but there is little doubt that he shared Bowden's conviction that Christians found it difficult to accept the fundamental discrepancy between scriptural passages describing natural phenomena and modern scientific findings as preached by Baden Powell. It is equally interesting that Bowden's point of view was shared by Newman, Bowden's life-long friend and religious mentor.

It is not necessary here to embark upon a detailed examination of the approach adopted by the Oxford Movement leaders towards contemporary science. A superficial survey of statements by leading Tractarians would apparently substantiate the thesis that the Oxford Movement leaders were indifferent towards science, if not positively tolerant. Indeed, it could be pointed out that Newman, Pusey, Froude and Sewell attended lectures by Daubeny and Buckland. The biographies of leading Tractarians testify to their scientific curiosity and interests. Such testimony should, however, be considered in conjunction with evidence of an opposite tenor, such as Bowden's remark that 'so unworthy an employment' as scientific inquiries could not be taken as seriously as Baden Powell was doing.[26]

To Newman, Froude or Bowden, it was simply unthinkable that scientific culture, which they regarded as synonymous with illiberal utilitarianism or at best as an innocuous pastime, could be made to play a leading and authoritative role in the shaping of the modern world view. In Tract LXXXIX John Keble explained that 'such knowledge...(is)...but very remotely connected with the proper duty and happiness of mankind'. Keble, Bowden and Newman felt they had more important matters to attend to, such as raising the spiritual awareness of the Anglican clergy and laity, or fighting the Whig government: the pretences of geologists were dismissed, which did not imply they were not worried by the success of geological doctrines they regarded as dangerous.[27]

Bowden and the Tractarians were equally opposed to the Mosaic geologists. They acknowledged that the latter were animated by the pious wish to reconcile science with revelation, yet they were guilty of the same mistake as lay behind Baden Powell's approach. They too granted a high status of credibility to geological and inductive investigations in general. In this respect, it was Bowden who, via Newman, was the disciple of Whately, and Baden Powell took an independent road. It is however clear that agreement on the evaluation

the Mosaic narrative. To take an extreme case, William Sewell too claimed he had 'no fear for Christianity or mankind from science in itself': there is no doubt, however, that he abhorred the idea of a lay, science-based interpretation of nature. See his *A Second Letter* (1834), p. 5.

26 (J. Bowden), 'Nolan and Powell', 429.
27 (J. Keble), *On the Mysticism Attributed to the Early Fathers of the Church*, Tract LXXXIX (1841), p. 138.

of the epistemological limits of scientific inquiries was not sufficient to fill the gap between Whately's overall strategy of cautious supervision of contemporary secular culture, and the defiant stand *against* contemporary intellectual values taken up by Bowden and his Tractarian friends.

Despite the fundamental agreement between Whately and the Tractarians on the subject of the relationship between science and revelation, Bowden was in some sense right in claiming that the proposal put forward by Baden Powell was thoroughly Noetic. Whatever personal opinion Whately entertained of the actual consequences to be drawn from his tenets, there was little doubt that Baden Powell offered his solution as a logically consistent development of the Noetic theology, and Bowden made the best possible use of this claim.[28]

Thoroughly Noetic was also Baden Powell's answer to the charge of latitudinarianism and heresy brought by Bowden. In a severe letter to the editor of the *British Critic*, Baden Powell denounced the authoritarianism of Bowden's theology. The latter had attacked his proposals as heretical because, in his judgement, they contradicted the 'express letter' of scripture and were opposed to traditional interpretations of the Bible. Baden Powell pointed out that no divine authority was attached to commentaries framed by individual theologians or the formularies of the Church. He claimed that the principle of authoritative tradition advocated by Bowden implied 'the whole system of Romish infallibility'.[29]

It would be false to claim that Baden Powell foresaw the Romewards development of Tractarian theology, but he undoubtedly pointed out the possible consequences of resorting to dogmatic theology and Church authority. On the whole, the Savilian Professor appeared little impressed by the arguments advanced by his adversary. Years of discussion with the Noetics and the recent difference of opinion with such a master of polemics as Whately taught him mercilessly to pick out the logical and theological weaknesses of Bowden's criticism.

There was however a point upon which he found it difficult to convince his reviewer and his reader. To Bowden's reproach of a recent change of mind on the relationship between science and revelation, Baden Powell replied that it was no fault to modify one's views. But he added, Bowden was wrong: he had always maintained the thesis put forward in his sermon. This was of course not true, as Baden Powell was perfectly aware. It is significant that the Savilian Professor, who often indulged in laudatory quoting of his own works, never mentioned his earlier anonymous contributions to the *British Critic*, not even the letters to the *Christian Remembrancer* and the essays published under his name. He probably realized that on the relationship between science and revelation, he had modified his former ideas to the point

[28] (J. Bowden), 'Nolan and Powell', 416.
[29] Baden Powell, *A Letter to the Editor of the British Critic* (1834), p. 10.

of adopting an approach diametrically opposed to the one elaborated in his contributions to the *British Critic*.

It may be recalled that young Baden Powell was particularly severe against the Unitarian intellectuals whom he accused of mishandling the text of the scriptures and of adapting the biblical narrative to their philosophical and scientific preconceptions. It is therefore interesting that Baden Powell's solution to the Genesis–geology debate was strikingly similar to the one put forward by Belsham in his lecture of 1821. Belsham too maintained that Moses super-imposed the revealed doctrine of monotheism upon ancient Jewish cosmologies and cosmogonies. Belsham too preached the irrelevance of the scriptural narra-tive of natural phenomena with respect to the credibility of revelation. He was convinced that the superior moral truth of Christ's preaching was sufficient to inspire mankind to believe. It was the power of the spirit which converted humanity, not the misleading images of Genesis derived from primitive scien-tific or philosophical speculations.

Baden Powell could have ignored the content of Belsham's lecture. He did not however ignore Lawrence's *Lectures on Physiology*, where analogous views were expressed. Lawrence pointed out that distinguished oriental and biblical scholars doubted 'the entire or partial inspiration' of the Old Testament. The Genesis account of creation 'has the allegorical figurative character common to eastern compositions'. There was also a further similarity between Lawrence's lectures and Baden Powell's sermon. Lawrence approached the question as to whether the various races of man derived from a single or different species. He inclined to side with Prichard on this as on many other issues, yet he warned that the polygenetic theory was to be opposed on physiological grounds alone; no scriptural authority or religious principle could be enlisted to decide the issue.[30]

In 1833 Baden Powell was likewise convinced that theologians should avoid interfering with debates concerning scientific doctrines, whereas in 1825 he had argued that Lawrence's approach to natural and psychological science was unsound and dangerous from the Christian point of view. It is even more difficult to believe that Baden Powell forgot that in 1823 he considered the coincidence between the 'geological' deluge and the 'scriptural' one as a further, unexpected confirmation of Moses's claim to divine inspiration. Thus, in 1823 he had endorsed the same 'puritanical' view of the plenary inspiration with which he reproached Bowden in 1834.

In 1823 he also claimed that it was always possible to identify elements of coincidence between the Genesis creation narrative and modern geological findings. In 1834 he upheld the view that no such coincidence existed, nor was it necessary to establish the truth of revelation. Moreover, the epistemology sketched by Baden Powell in his 1826 essay on rational religion was closely

---

[30] Lawrence, *Lectures on Physiology*, p. 248. See ch. 4 above.

related to the views of Whately and Bowden on the low credibility of inductive natural investigations, whereas in 1833 he credited contemporary geological developments with a high credibility, amounting to certainty.[31]

It was not surprising therefore that Baden Powell found little support for his views. Arnold was the only Oriel colleague to accept in part the solution put forward by his younger colleague. Arnold's revision of the concept of biblical inspiration was primarily concerned with solving ethical and historical difficulties. Having revised his view on inspiration to meet these difficulties, it was relatively easy for Arnold to accept Baden Powell's point of view on the relationship between science and revelation. Thus, in his sermon on 'Creation' preached at Rugby chapel in February 1835, Arnold argued that the only 'inspired' element of Genesis was the revelation of God the Creator and of his moral plans for man. Arnold too came to the conclusion that Belsham was after all right. Christians could not take the account of creation as a piece of natural history, Arnold warned, without involving themselves in major difficulties. Arnold's support was obviously insufficient to gain credibility for Baden Powell's solution to the conflict between science and religion: if anything, it reinforced the fears of the ultra-conservatives as to the theological views of the 'new school of divinity'.[32]

By 1835 Baden Powell had completed his first major intellectual revolution. His early, wholehearted defence of the Anglican establishment and the universities against the 'northern calumniators' turned into severe criticism of the 'oligarchy' which blindly opposed all improvement and change. Baden Powell's theological views underwent considerable modification. The debate on the Genesis–geology issue showed that he came to accept views severely censured by him only a few years earlier. In 1826 Baden Powell commented that the 'folly' of modern rationalism was to believe

that the Gospel is a religion of reason; that it originated in an age of ignorance, and was fostered in centuries of barbarism and darkness, that it required the advance of intellectual illumination to purify its original doctrines from...corrupt additions...that in the present times the general diffusion of science is calculated to give men more worthy and rational notions of the pure and genuine forms of Christianity.[33]

The last of these 'follies' he openly professed in *Revelation and Science*. The former he fully endorsed in his later works, after a painful struggle to provide a solid foundation to his Christian apologetic.

From 1826 to 1835 Baden Powell completed his emancipation from the Hackney theological and political standpoint. He became convinced that the survival of the Church and of Christianity in England required deep institutional and intellectual change. He was confident that the theological and philosophical doctrines elaborated by the Noetics provided the right approach

---

[31] Baden Powell, *A Letter to the Editor of the British Critic*, pp. 4–5.
[32] T. Arnold, *Sermons, Chiefly on the Interpretation of Scripture* (1845), p. 2; see also p. 343.
[33] Baden Powell, *The Advance of Knowledge*, pp. 26–7.

to the intellectual and institutional crisis of the time. It was however clear that his Noetic friends were not satisfied that Baden Powell's conclusions represented a logical and acceptable development of their views. Yet, in the late 1830s there was no time for detailed criticism and reassessment: the Tractarian revolt of 1836 produced a radicalization of the conflict between the Noetics and the ultra-conservative party.

The need to unite against direct attack by the Tractarians prevented a discussion of the differences which had emerged between Baden Powell and Whately during the debate on the admission of dissenters and on the relationship between science and religion. Yet, fundamental differences clearly existed. In 1838 Baden Powell published his new synthesis of Christian apologetic, *The Connexion of Natural and Divine Truth*. He confidently asserted that he had succeeded in providing a conciliation between his views of the role of science in the modern world view and the Noetic brand of Christian apologetic. Baden Powell was also convinced that his synthesis achieved more ambitious goals: it solved the problem of the eternal conflict between the advance of knowledge and traditional Christian beliefs. During the following two decades the advance of knowledge convinced him that Whately's approach to Christian belief was outdated and ineffectual. The differences of the 1830s had created an insurmountable barrier between Baden Powell and the Noetics.

PART III

THE NEW SYNTHESIS AND ITS
DEVELOPMENTS

In the opening paragraphs of his essay on *Rational Religion* published in 1826, Baden Powell assumed that revelation was accepted by the British population at large. The controversial question was then how to interpret the scriptures. Baden Powell concluded that the theory of the reasonableness of Christianity endorsed by the Anglican Church provided the only approach capable of reconciling the advance of knowledge with a sound adherence to the Christian religion. During the following decade he became aware that the Christian religion failed to appeal to extensive sectors of the British population. He also came to appreciate that his 1826 synthesis of philosophy and Anglican apologetics was regarded as defective by growing numbers of his Oxford and Anglican colleagues.

Furthermore, in the context of the political, institutional and intellectual developments of the 1830s, his Noetic friends became increasingly hesitant to apply their coherent strategy of timely concession and cautious receptiveness to new intellectual trends. Baden Powell's appraisal of the contemporary social and political situation, the solution he proposed for the admission of Dissenters to the English universities, and his interpretation of the relationship between science and religion met with open hostility at Oxford, and failed to convince his Noetic allies.

Reflecting on his defeat, Baden Powell realized that his mistake had been to fight on individual and isolated issues. He had temporarily ceased to draw upon the main strength of the Noetic approach: the capability of providing a thorough critical analysis of the theological and philosophical presuppositions involved in the discussion of political, educational or ecclesiastical issues. In his last paper devoted to summing up the debate on the reform of the statutes and the admission of Dissenters at Oxford, Baden Powell vigorously stressed the need for duly considering the philosophical and political 'principles' involved. The unyielding conflict of the early 1830s between conservatives and reformers provoked deep division. Although it was now difficult to see the way to achieve a compromise, a viable solution capable of reuniting the phalanx of the Christian apologists was urgently needed. The time was ripe for a major effort to find a meaningful compromise between the various struggling factions.

143

The late 1820s and the early 1830s were characterized by a succession of dramatic events which had significant influence on the intellectual and, more specifically, theological debates of the time. The explosion of the Tractarian revolt at Oxford provoked in its turn a partial revision of opinion within the Noetic circle on many political and intellectual issues. Thus, for instance, after the persecution he suffered at the hands of the Tractarians in 1836 Hampden came to accept the principle of Parliamentary interference in academic affairs, a point which one year earlier had divided him from his friend Baden Powell.

The Tractarian movement also helped to relegate to private correspondence and conversation some theological and philosophical differences which had emerged in the early 1830s within the Noetic circle. Points of substantial difference nonetheless remained. Hawkins never accepted Arnold's ecumenical proposals. He consented to side with Arnold against the Oxford Movement, though he found Arnold's paper on the 'Oxford malignants' excessively polemical. Hinds failed to convince Baden Powell that the doctrines of the Church, though not directly instituted by divine command, were binding upon believers. Baden Powell held that dogmas admitted of latitude of interpretation and did not represent a rigid test of adhesion to a church.[1]

Family links, personal friendship and a tradition of intellectual co-operation helped the Noetics to overcome the difficulties of the early 1830s. One biographical event strengthened the personal relationship and intellectual understanding between Baden Powell and Whately. In March 1836 Baden Powell's first wife died. In September the following year he married Charlotte Pope, sister of Whately's wife Elizabeth. Baden Powell was thus welcomed into the family circle of the Archbishop of Dublin. By the late 1830s the Noetics of Whately's school were united in denouncing the danger from what they regarded as the attempt by the Tractarians substantially to modify the theological and apologetic tradition of the Anglican Church. Baden Powell, Whately and their friends were less worried by the alleged Romewards tendency of Tractarian theology, than by the long-term consequences of the Tractarian bias towards authority as the only safe means to counteract irreligion and social subversion.

The political and social disturbances of the late 1830s, and the Chartist movement in particular, made Baden Powell reflect on the extent and depth

[1] On the divergence of opinion between Whately and Hawkins, see Oriel College, Hawkins Papers, Whately to Hawkins, 2.177: 17 Aug. 1829; 2.180: 23 Nov. 1830; 2.182: 11 Oct. 1831; 2.193: 15 Aug. 1832; 2.199: 17 Apr. 1833; between Arnold and Hawkins, Hawkins Papers, 3.210: 6 Oct. 1833, Whately to Hawkins; 5.412: 11 Mar. 1835, Hawkins to Whately. Hawkins did not approve of Arnold's pamphlet on Church reform; rumours spread that 'the Provost has given him [Arnold] up': see Ker and Gornall, *Letters and Diaries*, vol. iii, p. 266, J. H. Newman to Jemima, 20 Mar. 1833. Baden Powell Papers, Letter from Baden Powell to Samuel Hinds, 13 June 1840: 'If a Church offer fair arguments as proofs of its infallibility, which yet are to me unsatisfactory, it has no right to condemn me for rejecting them'.

of the changes undergone by British society during the preceding decade. Thus, by 1837 he assessed his 1826 assumption that England was by and large a Christian country as a dangerous anachronism. The Tractarian failure to appreciate the spread of atheism and rationalism was making the task of politically and socially alert Anglican apologists more arduous. The growth of the trade union movement and a free-thinking or openly sceptical popular press were viewed by Baden Powell and his Anglican colleagues as symptomatic of the diffusion of active infidelity among the masses.

Social and political phenomena had already preoccupied the attention of the Hackney Phalanx leaders and the early Noetics. Yet, in the eyes of many churchmen the Chartist outbreak undoubtedly appeared far more dangerous than the sporadic and easily suppressed popular movements of the 1810s and the 1820s. The popular movements of the late 1830s made pressing demands upon the apologetic approach elaborated by the Noetics in the first quarter of the century. The approach of the 1820s, for instance, was designed to fight sophisticated theological and philosophical proposals like those put forward by Unitarians and Calvinists. Baden Powell appreciated that substantial readjustment was now required.

In 1826 he had stressed the early Noetic view that natural theology was a useful apologetic device in times of growing atheism, but almost useless if not positively harmful in those characterized by popular adherence to Christianity. This negative attitude was increasingly out of touch with current apologetic priorities, and was accordingly subjected by Baden Powell to close critical scrutiny. He aimed to elaborate a revision of the old Noetic position on this branch of the Christian apologetic.

Baden Powell and Whately believed that the Tractarian distaste for the rational evidence of Christianity represented the most serious threat to the preservation of revealed religion amongst the British masses and sections of the British intelligentsia. In a penetrating analysis of the social dimension of infidelity published in 1838, Whately condemned the attempt by the Tractarians to widen the gap between Christian culture and intellectual advance. Ecclesiastical authoritarianism was not the proper response to growing democratic demands and the proliferation of sources of intellectual authority independent of both State and Church. The study of the historical and philosophical evidence of Christianity, Whately argued, undoubtedly presented difficulties which the infidel was exploiting to his own advantage. It was nevertheless a poor tactic to say that arguments from the evidence of Christianity were to be discarded because the 'unlearned cannot comprehend it'.[2]

Whately warned that there was no way of preventing the 'unlearned' from

---

[2] R. Whately, *Remarks on Some Causes of Hostility to the Christian Religion* (1838), p. 21. Rose himself felt that the Tractarians were excessively obstinate in their rejection of natural theology, and extolled the virtues of the design argument for the salvation of unbelievers: see Burgon, *Lives of Twelve Good Men* (1891), p. 135

listening to the propaganda of unscrupulous agitators; the demagogues considered Christianity as the only barrier against their subversive social plans and accordingly used all sorts of philosophical, scientific, and historical argument to undermine its credibility. Those who doubted that the situation had deteriorated so much were invited to make appropriate inquiries 'and would ascertain, *as I have done*, the existence among the labouring classes of Infidel Clubs, reckoning members by hundreds'.[3]

Whately insisted on the basic unity of purpose between Chartists and socialists on the one hand and Tractarians on the other. The agitators were convincing the masses that Christianity was a tale churchmen told them to preserve their own privileges; the Tractarians did their best to substantiate this charge by claiming that it was impossible to lay down in a coherent form the titles to credibility of Christianity. Christian doctrine had to be accepted and obeyed on the word of the Church. As Whately vividly wrote to Hawkins 'there is a third party [the Tractarians] aiding the mystics and the socialists, who, like partners at cards, are sitting opposite, but playing into each other's hands: both contending that no man can have any better reason for being a Christian than the Parson tells him'.[4]

Whately made few changes in his apologetic strategy. Fully taken up by the onerous duties of the Irish primacy, but also unwilling to modify conclusions painfully reached on the subject of his religious beliefs, he paid little attention to intellectual and theological developments during the 1840s and the 1850s. He had no patience with the pro-German sympathies of the transcendental school. The transcendentalists increasingly relied upon ethical and philosophical or psychological categories to support their apologetic programmes. Baden Powell's intellectual activity on the other hand was characterized by a sustained attempt at understanding the position of his religious and philosophical opponents, among whom he now reckoned friends like Blanco White or Francis Newman, who had abandoned Anglicanism in the pursuit of intellectually more rewarding theological and philosophical ventures.

Baden Powell too was reluctant to change the conclusions reached in 1833. He devoted a series of publications to summarizing and publicizing his apologetic devices. Nevertheless, his strong conviction that the Anglican apologist had to come to terms with the culture of the day made him relax his opposition to the 'mystical' school to the point of accepting some of its tenets. In his last works Baden Powell came to rely on faith as the cornerstone of the modern Christian apologetic, and submitted to devastating criticism the apologetic tradition which emphasized the scientific or philosophical evidence of Christianity.

---

[3] Whately, *Remarks on Some Causes of Hostility*, p. 21.
[4] Oriel College, Hawkins Papers, 3.241: 4 Mar. 1840, Whately to Hawkins. There is no comprehensive study dealing with Whately's activities in Ireland, nor indeed any significant assessment of his work.

Biographical details help explain the personal reasons which reinforced Baden Powell's tolerant attitude towards contemporary theological and philosophical developments. Charlotte Pope, his second wife, was a close friend of Blanco White. When the latter left Dublin for Liverpool, Whately expressed his conviction that White's fascination with the transcendental theology of the new Unitarian leaders of the Martineau school was due to a state of mental derangement, caused by bodily suffering and the abuse of opium. Charlotte Pope thought differently. She kept up a correspondence on religious subjects with White and found in his deep mystical beliefs a reinforcement of her own faith. Baden Powell was not convinced that White's conversion to Unitarianism was justified on strictly theological and philosophical grounds, but he did not question the basic soundness and intellectual honesty of his friend.[5]

In 1837 he invited Blanco White to stay with him at Oxford, undoubtedly a courageous gesture at a time of Tractarian supremacy in the university. Baden Powell rightly appreciated that White's conversion was the symptom of a wider and deeper intellectual change which it was unwise to define in the individual psychological and pathological terms chosen by Whately. To understand the theological and philosophical motivations of the decision taken by White was essential, if conviction by force of argument was to prevail over condemnation by personal invective. Whately appeared to forget that in the 1820s he had invited the more conservative faction of the Anglican Church to debate with their opponents. He had then pointed out that ostracism and invective could avail little against historical processes or deeply rooted intellectual traditions.

Baden Powell took full advantage of the re-valuation of the evidence of Christianity and natural theology within Whately's school. He insisted on the necessity of enlisting contemporary epistemological debates in support of Christian apologetic. In his work on the *Connexion of Natural and Divine Truth* (1838) Baden Powell made explicit the epistemological foundation of his belief in the reliability of modern geological doctrines. He also justified on philosophical and exegetical grounds his conviction that there was an unbridgeable gap between the Old Testament cosmogony and the preaching of Christ. His philosophy of science made ample albeit original use of Whately's analysis of induction, as well as of themes taken from the epistemological reflections of Stewart, Herschel and Whewell.

The evaluation of the ground of evidence of scientific investigations became central to Baden Powell's 1838 synthesis. Nevertheless, it is important to stress that his comments on the methodology of scientific investigation were subservient to the apologetic task of providing natural theology with a strong

---

5 For a critical assessment of Whately's and Baden Powell's views on White's defection, see J. H. Thom, 'Archbishop Whately and the Life of Blanco White', *Theological Review*, 4 (1867), 88–120; see also (Baden Powell), 'Life of the Rev. Joseph Blanco White', *W.R.*, 44 (1845), 275–325.

epistemological foundation. It was Baden Powell's conviction that the philosophical dignity of scientific procedures could provide the required authoritative basis for a modern natural theology.

Baden Powell's insistence on natural theology rather than on the evidence for Christianity marked a further point of difference between his apologetic approach and Whately's. The latter chose to expand upon the evidence of biblical inspiration afforded by miracles. He was convinced that God intervened in the historical development of the human race. Civilization itself was a gift of God. Primitive populations, he argued, could never of themselves have crossed the gap between the savage, animal-like stage and civilization. The use of the boomerang by the Australian aborigines, for instance, was to Whately a notable instance of God's miraculous dispensation to man. As Baden Powell confirmed to Whately, the boomerang was a weapon based on sophisticated dynamic principles, far above the presumed poor intellectual capabilities of the Australian indigenous population, and was clearly God's gift to the aborigines.[6]

By contrast, Baden Powell became increasingly sceptical of the evidential value of miracles in an age characterized by rapid scientific advance. He also questioned the theories of the origin of civilization put forward by his former teacher, and ultimately sympathized with the polygenic theory of the origin of the human races. Baden Powell ended his intellectual journey by denying that miracles could be a *proof* of revelation. He accepted them only *because* narrated in the scriptures. The only external evidence of the existence of God he relied upon, was the inductive proof of the unchangeable order of nature, bespeaking infinite power. As far as the evidence of Christianity was concerned, in 1857 and 1859 Baden Powell had little to say, but that science did not oppose the belief in Christianity. Everyman's faith provided the needed confirmation of the truth of revealed religion.

The conclusion of Baden Powell's career as Christian apologist deeply shocked his friends. Whately reacted immediately to this last development of Baden Powell's thought. The campaign against Baden Powell's rejection of miracles was opened by a review inspired and partly written by Whately and published a few months before the appearance of the *Essays and Reviews*. It is interesting to note that Baden Powell's contribution to the *Essays* was in fact an irritated tirade against Whately's criticism. The elements of disagreement which had been relegated to a secondary role in the 1840s and 1850s, had time to work and widen the gap between the two thinkers, culminating in the eventual break-up of their friendship in 1860, a few months before Baden Powell's death.

Whately found Baden Powell's sympathy for transformist ideas in biological sciences a weak and dangerous point in his pupil's system. Conversely, Baden

---

[6] R. Whately, *Introductory Lectures*, p. 122; Baden Powell Papers, letter from Whately to Baden Powell, 13 Sept. 1837. R. Whately, *On the Origin of Civilization* (1854).

Powell's methodology of science fully justified a research project based on a transformist conjecture. His natural theology increasingly required that a transformist solution of some kind should be found for the species puzzle. A theory explaining in naturalistic terms the 'mystery of mysteries' would have extended the dominion of natural laws, thereby reinforcing man's belief in a supreme mind who planned the evolution of the world in a single creative thought.

The following chapters will be devoted to analysing the central features of Baden Powell's 1838 synthesis. The elements of continuity with respect to his previous standpoint will be stressed. Particular attention will be paid to the development of his ideas on the methodology of science and natural theology. Passing reference will also be made to the major intellectual developments which favoured Baden Powell's transition from the apologetic solution put forward in 1838, to the controversial statements in *Essays and Reviews*.

The critical assessment of Baden Powell's intellectual and religious certainties, of his frequent inconsistencies and in particular of his capacity for reversing conclusions previously reached, will add considerable interest when examining his later writings. It is indeed worthy of careful consideration that the essays Baden Powell published in the late 1850s were in fact a reprint of works published in the late 1830s and early 1840s, with the notable and surprising difference that the apologetic apparatus elaborated in 1838 was in later years employed to establish opposite conclusions. Whately publicly and privately challenged Baden Powell to provide an explanation for this extraordinary *volte-face*.

Baden Powell's answer to Whately's invitation offered many justifications for his change of mind on the subject of the Christian apologetic, but few or no reasons. It will therefore be our task to follow Baden Powell's intellectual development and to provide an explanation for the surprising conclusion of his career as a Christian apologist.

11

The methodology of science

The new synthesis of 'Natural and Divine Truth' put forward by Baden Powell in 1838 represented his attempt to provide a comprehensive answer to the many philosophical and theological issues debated in the early 1830s. The polemical exchange with John Bowden and the implicit conflict with Whately over the interpretation of the relationship between science and religion, convinced him that fundamental epistemological objections prevented many Anglican intellectuals from accepting the findings of modern science and current geological research in particular.

More than two-thirds of the examples chosen by Baden Powell to substantiate his account of scientific procedures were taken from geology. The reflections on the methodology of science put forward in the *Connexion of Natural and Divine Truth* were designed to prove that the conclusions reached by geologists on the history of the earth were entitled to the same degree of assent accorded to results of inquiries pursued in other departments of science.

In his answer to John Bowden's criticism of his sermon, Baden Powell warned his colleague that the opposition between the letter of the Mosaic account of creation and modern geology was not an opposition between '*revelation* and *any speculation, theories, or inferences of human reason*; but a discordance between matters of fact'. As he repeated in his 1838 essay, the stratagem of objecting to geological theories by declaring that the science was still in its infancy represented a serious mistake. Baden Powell was also aware that his failure to convince his Oxford colleagues of the need for academic scientific education was partly caused by their refusal to acknowledge that scientific pursuits were suitable topics for a liberal education. Issues like the relationship between science and religion or educational reform therefore could not be approached without taking into account wider theological and philosophical dimensions. It was thus a matter of urgency to lay down systematically the claims to philosophical dignity of the contemporary debate on scientific procedures.[1]

[1] Baden Powell, *The Connexion of Natural and Divine Truth* (1838) and *A Letter to the Editor of the British Critic*, pp. 5–6.

(i) Baden Powell and William Whewell: the 'a priori' in science

Baden Powell's early reflections on science were influenced by the philosophy of Stewart. Mathematics and geometry constituted the model of perfect science. Definitions constituted the key element of mathematical discourse and theorizing. The deductions from the definitions followed the implicit indications of a few fundamental axioms, which were rarely expressed by researchers and men in general, and yet were the pre-conditions of all reasoning acts. The unconscious application of axioms to the definitions allowed the deployment of deductive procedures; it was thus possible to show that the objects described in the definitions enjoyed a given set of properties. Conclusions could be deductively reached which were necessary and universal truths.

The case with the natural sciences was very different. No assurance could be given that our definition of the objects under investigation included all their connotations. Indeed, this was very rarely the case. In the analysis of induction put forward in the fourth book of his *Logic* Whately significantly opposed the kind of 'reasoning' which characterized mathematics or geometry to procedures followed in geology: 'the most extensive information is requisite; and though sound reasoning is called for in making use of the knowledge acquired, it is well known what erroneous systems have been devised, by powerful reasoners, who have satisfied themselves too soon with observations not sufficiently accurate and extensive.'[2]

Whately did not expand upon the discussion of the inductive method. He was himself, in his own way, more concerned with the 'philosophy of mind' than with the philosophy of inductive inquiry. He distinguished between 'induction' as the collection of facts and data, and 'induction' as inference. The first use of the term, he argued, referred to extra-logical – and extra-philosophical – operations which called for the skill of the observer, his past experience, and his personal capability to grasp the essential features of the phenomena or class of phenomena under investigation. This feature of inductive procedures scarcely concerned Whately. His central aim was to show that 'induction as inference' was under the dominion of logic and was inevitably expressed in syllogistic form.

Baden Powell was deeply indebted to Whately's discussion of induction. Nevertheless, he felt that something more should be said on the first of the two meanings of the word 'induction' identified by Whately. It was important to examine the procedures adopted in collecting data for the premises of inductive inferences. Furthermore, notwithstanding his basic agreement with the epistemology of the Scottish philosophical school, Baden Powell felt that Stewart's sophisticated account of inductive procedures disregarded important

---

[2] R. Whately, *Elements of Logic* (Ninth edn., 1852), p. 166; see also pp. 151–6.

departments of modern scientific research, the natural sciences in particular. He agreed with Stewart that the inductive inference had weaker epistemological status than the mathematico-deductive one. He was nevertheless convinced that the philosophical problem involved in inquiries into the natural world was the question of ascertaining the grounds of evidence of conclusions reached through induction.

The dissatisfaction with traditional accounts of the methods followed in the natural and physical sciences, and with the explanation put forward by the Scottish philosophers in particular, was authoritatively expressed by William Whewell. In his appreciative review of Herschel's *Preliminary Discourse* Whewell remarked that too many volumes had been written on the nature of human knowledge and the laws of human thought. Yet, he added, the mental processes embodied in and exemplified by the progress of modern science were scarcely noticed or analysed by the northern philosophers. In a further, implicit reference to the Scottish tradition and to Whately's *Logic* Whewell remarked that

the day will come when...the received 'philosophy of mind' shall have its leading chapters devoted to the most successful employments of the intellect: when the received 'art of reasoning' shall contain something more than the rules for deriving the consequences of assumed principles; and when 'definitions' shall no longer be considered as the fountains of what we can know with regard to things altogether independent of the operations of human thought.[3]

In his review of Richard Jones's *Essay on the Distribution of Wealth*, published in the same month (July 1831), Whewell again emphasized his opposition to the deductive approach privileged by his opponents, and censured their attaching 'an extravagant and false importance to *definitions*'. Moreover, a paper in the *Philological Museum* fully expressed Whewell's dissatisfaction with Whately's stress on deductive procedures. The heat of the polemic against Ricardian political economy, and what he considered to be the epistemological support it received at Oxford, made Whewell insist on the neglected virtues of induction, and of the laborious but sure process of ascending from observation to successive levels of abstraction and generalization.[4]

---

[3] (W. Whewell), 'Modern Science – Inductive Philosophy', 377; J. F. W. Herschel, *A Preliminary Discourse on the Study of Natural Philosophy* (1830, quotations from 1833 edn.). For comments on Herschel, and exhaustive bibliographical information, see S. S. Schweber (ed.), *Aspects of the Life and Thoughts of Sir John Frederick Herschel* (1981). See also M. Ruse, 'Darwin's Debt to Philosophy', *Studies in the History and Philosophy of Science*, 6 (1975), 159–81. When Whewell wrote his review of Herschel's *Discourse*, he was already engaged in a violent polemic against Whately and the remarks on the method of political economy put forward by Nassau Senior. See Cambridge, Trinity College, Whewell Papers, Whewell–Jones correspondence, Add. Mss. c 51 and c 52 and P. Corsi, 'The heritage of Dugald Stewart'; see also J. Losee, 'Whewell and Mill on the Relations between Philosophy of Science and History of Science', *Studies in the History and Philosophy of Science*, 14 (1983), 113–26.

[4] (W. Whewell), 'Jones – *On the Distribution of Wealth and the Sources of Taxation*', B.C., 19 (1831), 54 and 'On the Use of Definitions', *The Philological Museum*, 2 (1832), 263–72; on the exchange of polemical arrows between Whately and Whewell, see P. Corsi, 'The heritage

The years 1829–33 marked the period of Whewell's most determined attempt
t building a 'logic of induction', as he called it. In a passage rarely quoted
•y students of Whewell, the Trinity man, still in search of his own philosophy,
:xpressed views very different from, if not exactly opposed to the ones he
vas to support only a few months later. In his *Introduction to Dynamics* (1832),
Vhewell examined the epistemological foundation of the laws of motion, a
:lassic topic in contemporary British philosophy of science. He allowed that
he laws of motion represented such a luminous example of perfect mature
cience, that 'we often feel disposed to believe that truths so clear and compre-
ensive are necessary conditions, rather than empirical attributes, of their
:ubjects: that they are legible by their own axiomatic light, like the first truths
›f geometry, rather than discovered by the blind gropings of experience.' The
rocess of deduction, Whewell commented, 'fills the mind at every step with
confidence in its own workings, a consciousness of certainty', so that men
:asily tended to rely on it, rather than to pursue the more difficult path of
nduction, 'by which we arrive at principles'. His task, he declared, was to
ttempt a clarification of induction, and the establishment of the logical processes
vhich turned inductive generalizations into necessary truths.[5]

Whewell's project for a new and comprehensive 'philosophy of science'
nd Herschel's sophisticated and authoritative defence of induction were novel-
ies that Baden Powell was ready to enlist in support of his apologetic approach.
\s late as 1837 he could still inform his readers that there were Oxford dons
vho believed that 'mechanics may teach a man to construct a roof, and
:hemistry to dye a coat'. He thus welcomed the starting of a serious debate
›n the philosophical foundations of modern science, which was likely to add
›restige to scientific undertakings. It is however important to stress that in
he book he published in 1838, as well as in the essay on induction of 1855,
3aden Powell did not aim at producing his own philosophy of science. He
ncreasingly viewed himself as a philosopher commenting upon the works of
›thers. In typical Noetic fashion, he employed current philosophical, scientific
nd theological research for building a comprehensive and updated Christian
pologetic, rather than offering new theories.[6]

Baden Powell's reflections on scientific procedures were characterized by
n attempt at offering a compromise between the various components of his

of Dugald Stewart'. On Whewell's critique of Whately and his school, see Cambridge, Trinity
College, Whewell Papers, Add Ms c 51 (64–110) and Todhunter, *William Whewell* (1876),
vol. i, pp. 115–18 and 120–4. See also Losee, 'Whewell and Mill', pp. 131–3, and N. B. De
Marchi and R. P. Sturges, 'Malthus and Ricardo's Inductivist Critics', *Economica* (1973),
379–93. On the short-lived *Philological Museum*, see N. M. Distad, *Guessing at Truth* (1979),
pp. 74, 78.
5 W. Whewell, *An Introduction to Dynamics* (1832), pp. x-xi. On Whewell and the problem of
induction in the early 1830s, see also L. Goldman, 'The origins of British "Social Science":
political economy, natural science, and statistics, 1830–1835', *The Historical Journal*, 26 (1983),
587–616, and R. Yeo, 'An idol of the market place', *History of Science*, 23 (1985), 251–98.
6 Baden Powell, 'Introduction', *Magazine of Popular Science*, 1 (1837), 6.

philosophical background and the new developments introduced in the debate on science by the Oxford and Cambridge philosophical schools. Instead of widening the gap between the two standpoints, and of following Whately in counter-attacking the Cambridge men, Baden Powell aimed at harmonizing the accounts of induction offered by his teacher, by Herschel and Whewell with the traditional doctrine taught by the 'philosophy of mind' school.

He stressed that all the Scottish and English authorities he referred to agreed, albeit on different theoretical grounds, that induction implied a process of inference different from the mere accumulation of data. A fundamental difference, according to Baden Powell, distinguished the task of the 'collector' from that performed by the 'philosopher': no one indeed could deny – Baden Powell repeated with Herschel and with Stewart – that in inductive procedure 'we infer more than we can see'. When the naturalist considered several instances of a phenomenon, he was inevitably led to conclude that the properties observed in the cases under observation belonged to all the phenomena of the same class. At the very outset of the inductive inference the natural philosopher implicitly assumed the principle of the uniformity of nature, or in other words, that the same phenomena enjoyed the same properties every time and everywhere they were produced. This belief, according to Whately and to Baden Powell, represented the major implicit premiss of the inductive syllogism.[7]

The belief in the uniformity of nature was justified by an appeal to the laws of human thought. This principle, Baden Powell argued in typical Scottish fashion, was founded 'on the natural constitution of the human mind'. He also remarked that the daily confirmation of uniformity in the succession of natural events reinforced and extended our conviction regarding the uniformity of nature much beyond the limits of actual experience. He did nevertheless insist that the foundation of this principle was to be sought in the cognitive instruments inherent in the human mind. In his essay on the primary laws of motion, published in 1837, Baden Powell actually referred with approval to a passage in Stewart's *Elements*, in which the Scottish authority claimed the superiority of the 'philosophy of mind' approach over the account of scientific procedures offered by practitioners not versed in philosophical analysis.[8]

[7] Baden Powell, *Connexion* (1838), p. 16. On the contraposition between the 'collector' and the 'philosopher', see D. Stewart, *Elements* (1814, Hamilton edn., 1877), vol. ii, p. 327; in view of its popularity, this classic topic of Stewart's philosophy was often referred to by early nineteenth-century commentators, albeit without indication of the source see P. Corsi, 'The heritage of Dugald Stewart'. On the tendency of the human mind to 'leap forward' from a few observations to theories and hypotheses, see Herschel, *A Preliminary Discourse*, pp. 164-5, and comments by (Whewell) in 'Modern Science – Inductive Philosophy', 399. Herschel made ample use of themes and concepts of the 'philosophy of mind': 'the propensity of the human mind', and 'the disposition of the mind' were expressions frequently employed in the *Preliminary Discourse*.

[8] Baden Powell, *On the Nature and Evidence of the Primary Laws of Motion* (1837), pp. 63-4 and *Connexion* (1838), pp. 18-21.

Baden Powell was eager to stress that the individuation of the basic intellectual element of induction required a thorough acquaintance with the most sophisticated analytical tools provided by current philosophy and logic. Following Stewart and Whately, he too implicitly argued for the superiority of the philosopher over the practitioner; far from being superseded by the advance of technological and scientific progress, the role of the philosopher appeared to remain central for the clarification and solution of man's intellectual problematics. Yet, he was not prepared to follow Whewell in his colleague's attempt at establishing the necessity and universality of scientific truth through a sophisticated philosophical defence of the role of *a priori* categories in science.

In the years 1833–5, Whewell's views underwent a process of maturation and clarification. The long internal debate, and the discussion with such friends as Jones and Rose on the foundation of scientific knowledge led to the implementation of a philosophical programme which deeply revised the declarations of intent professed during the previous years, stressing the role of induction in science. Whewell's diaries, various letters to his friends, as well as manuscript essays and reading notes attest his persistent toying with the idea that necessity and universality of scientific truths depended on *a priori* elements provided by the intellect. In view of recent scholarly discussion of Whewell's debt to Kant and to German transcendental philosophy, it is interesting to mention that Whewell's earliest statements concerning the *a priori* nature of space and time as categories of the understanding occurred at a time when the young scientist had not yet read Kant. In the late spring of 1817, it was the reading of Stewart's *Philosophical Essays* which prompted Whewell to reflect on the part played by the intellect and the part played by experience in the acquisition of knowledge, and in scientific knowledge in particular.[9]

The earliest appreciative reference to Kant, following a highly critical if not ironic assessment of the cosmological theories put forward by the German philosopher, occurred when Whewell read in Madame de Staël's *De l'Allemagne* that Kant was strongly opposed to utilitarian reductionism in ethics, and sought to establish morality on necessary and universal grounds. In 1821 Whewell read summaries of the *Kritik der Reinen Vernunft* in de Gerando and other secondary works. It was only in 1827 that he carefully read Kant's

[9] For a recent, thorough discussion of this issue, see Fisch, 'Necessary and contingent truth in William Whewell's antithetical theory of knowledge', *Studies in the History and Philosophy of Science*, 16 (1985), 275–314. For Whewell's early, scattered reference to philosophical issues, and his reading notes, see Cambridge, Trinity College, Whewell Papers, Diaries, and in particular R.18.9 (2) [1817], R.18.9 (3) [1817], R.18.9 (4) [1818], R.18.9 (8) [1820]. On Whewell's early reflections on space and time, prompted by the reading of Stewart's *Essays*, see R.18.9 (3), fols. 39v–40v: 27 Aug. 1817; and fol. 41v: 28 Aug. 1817. See also R. Wellek, *Immanuel Kant in England* (1931); R. Yeo, 'William Whewell, natural theology and the philosophy of science', *A.S.*, 36 (1979), 493–516, see p. 494 in particular; M. Ruse, 'The Scientific Methodology of William Whewell', *Centaurus*, 20 (1976), 227–57; S. Marcucci, *L'idealismo scientifico di William Whewell* (1963); on the development of Whewell's thought, see M. R. Stoll, *Whewell's Philosophy of Induction* (1929).

work, and took extensive notes. Yet, as we have noted above, the polemic against Ricardian political economy and Oxford philosophy made him stress the inductive note, to an extent which perhaps did not reflect his inner struggle with the problem of the *a priori* epistemological foundation of scientific truth.[1]

Contemporaries who, like Baden Powell, had welcomed Whewell's announcement of his research programme focusing on induction, were not pleased by the eventual outcome of his reflections. In the pages of *The Mechanical Euclid* (1837) devoted to a systematic critique of Stewart and Oxford philosophy, Whewell argued that 'in each inductive process, there is some general idea introduced, which is given, not by the phenomena, but by the mind'. In 1832 Whewell had maintained that the laws of mature physico-mathematical sciences were understandably but wrongly regarded as 'necessary conditions', rather than as 'empirical attributes' of their subject-matter. In 1837, he firmly stated that these laws were based on axioms 'self-evidently true', 'not to be learnt from without, but from within'.[11]

Baden Powell was familiar with the development of Whewell's epistemology and was fully aware that his Cambridge colleague based on philosophical grounds his opposition to widening the Cambridge curriculum to natural sciences. One year before the publication of the *Connexion of Natural and Divine Truth*, Baden Powell joined battle with Whewell on the subject of the *a priori* elements involved in scientific knowledge. In a paper published in the *Transactions of the Cambridge Philosophical Society* Whewell argued that the axioms of dynamics referred to the fundamental idea of cause, and could be stated as follows: (a) every change is produced by a cause; (b) causes are measured by effects; (c) action is accompanied by reaction. Whewell further argued that axioms (a) and (b) were truths absolutely and independently self-evident. Axiom (c) was involved in our idea of body or matter. From these

[10] See Cambridge, Trinity College, Whewell Papers, Diary, R.18.9 (8), fol. 7v: [1820]: 'Odd tendency of this sect to abuse inductive philosophy. In Coleridge it is natural from the elevated imagination and in most of the rest from the smallness of their reasoning powers Kant has proved *a priori* in 1754 that there *must* be a planet beyond Saturn *because* there must be a gradation from planets to comets all the orbits becoming more excentric as they are further from the sun! This is demonstration'. But see fols. 16v–17v for the earliest reference to Kant's 'notions of time, space, possibility, reality, etc.', and his theory of moral which 'makes the principle of duty' a necessary feeling. Whewell was then reading Mme de Staël's *De l'Allemagne* (1810); only four copies of the first edition survived the search by Napoleon's police. The book, immensely successful, was translated into English in 1813 (London, J. Murray). R.18.9 (9), fol. 41v: [1821?] reveals Whewell's interest in Kant. He quoted de Gerando's *Histoire comparée des systèmes de philosophie* (1804), the *Encyclopaedia Londinensis* (1797–1829), and mentioned the *Kritik der Reinen Vernunft*. On 25 July 1827 Whewell started a series of notes summing up and translating passages from the *Kritik*: see R.18.9 (14). A comprehensive assessment of Whewell's early philosophical standpoint is still a desideratum of studies on early nineteenth-century British philosophy. In particular, attention should be paid to his concern for the foundation of a new, anti-utilitarian moral philosophy

[11] W. Whewell, *The Mechanical Euclid* (1837), pp. 173, 159; and *An Introduction to Dynamics* (1832), pp. x–xi.

axioms he deduced the laws of motion, which he claimed were necessary and universal truths.[12]

Whewell challenged the account of scientific procedures given by Stewart and Whately, denying that the laws deduced with the help of axioms were only consistent deductions from given propositions: they were laws of nature. Whately and Stewart restricted the analysis of scientific procedures to the examination of the logical consistency of reasoning. Basic to their epistemological approach was the conviction that disciplines dealing with natural objects could never produce statements which were necessary and universal truths. As Whately put it in his most determined attack against Jones and Whewell, definitions were real only in mathematical disciplines: thus, only deductions from mathematical definitions deserved the title of truths.[13]

Taking as an instance the laws of motion, Whewell pointed out that these products of the human intellect could not have been applied to phenomena without the aid of experience. The case of the laws of motion, according to Whewell, exemplified the combination of *a priori* and experimental elements in science. The mind provided self-evident truths, the contradiction of which was felt to be logically impossible. These truths could not be understood, as Stewart and Whately argued, as mere forms of functioning of the human mind, deprived of all cognitive power. In their own way, Whewell explained, axioms spoke about the world, without having, as such, any concrete content. Thus, the axiom that every change is produced by a cause, Whewell stated, was a self-evident truth. This 'form of the intuition', or 'regulative idea' was capable of guiding the organization of experimental data, and of leading the natural philosopher to the formulation of universal scientific truths. Universality and necessity, according to Whewell, were conditions which no sum of single observations could have provided nor guaranteed, whereas the self-evident necessity of ideal conceptions needed reference to experience in order to lead to scientific truth.[14]

---

[12] W. Whewell, 'On the Nature of the Truth of the Laws of Motion', *Transactions of the Cambridge Philosophical Society*, 5 (1834), 149–72 and *Thoughts on the Study of Mathematics as Part of a Liberal Education* (1835), *On the Principles of English University Education* (1837). See also Whewell's polemic against Stewart and Whately, in *The Mechanical Euclid* (1837), pp. 143–76, and the answer by F. Ellis, 'Whewell's *Mechanical Euclid*', *E.R.*, 67 (1838), 81–102. For a recent discussion of necessity and contingency in Whewell and the relevant bibliographical information, see M. Fisch, 'Necessary and contingent truth in William Whewell's antithetical theory of knowledge', *Studies in the History and Philosophy of Science*, 16 (1985), 275–314.

[13] R. Whately, *Introductory Lectures on Political Economy* (1832), p. 243. The quotation is from the 'Ninth Lecture', which appeared as a separate pamphlet early in 1832, and was then added to the original eight: see P. Corsi, 'The heritage of Dugald Stewart'. It is important to note that Whately explicitly referred to the second volume of Stewart's *Elements*.

[14] W. Whewell, 'On the Nature of the Truth of the Laws of Motion', *Transactions of the Cambridge Philosophical Society*, 5 (1834), 149–72; Baden Powell, *On the Nature and Evidence of the Primary Laws of Motion* (1837), pp. 11–14, 59–61;

Baden Powell found Whewell's 'metaphysical refinements' fallacious and denied that the axioms indicated by Whewell were to be seen as *a priori* truths independent of experience. The real philosophical problem, according to Baden Powell, was represented by the analysis of the '*simplest* and *fewest* physical assumptions to which it is necessary to refer' when formulating the premises of our research into the realm of motion. Baden Powell could not see why Whewell needed to have recourse to experience to provide the experimental element of the laws of motion established through *a priori* axioms, when the *a priori* elements themselves were highly sophisticated abstractions from the data of experience. Thus, Baden Powell was unable to accept that the guiding principles which made the inductive inference something more than the mere accumulation of data, needed to be *a priori* categories of the human mind.[15]

At a more general level, Baden Powell stressed that the process through which science expanded its boundaries involved further reference to *a priori* conceptions, which guided new observations and experiments, and provided the first working hypothesis. Yet, in this case too there was no place for the axioms and forms of the understanding which constituted the core of Whewell's philosophy of science. No natural philosopher, Baden Powell explained, nor man in general, ever put himself in front of nature without bringing with him the bulk of his previous experience. Thus, the *a priori* elements in the inductive inference were provided by the acquaintance with principles or laws which already proved good explanations of phenomena, however different or removed from the ones under observation. ANALOGY, as Baden Powell wrote in capital letters, provided the conceptual guidelines for man's investigation into new departments of scientific investigation. He remained faithful to Stewart's belief that 'axioms' were only the implicit, always present but rarely formulated principles of functioning of the human mind: every perception is apprehended in spatial and temporal terms; we always face experience with the firm presupposition that nature is governed by the principle of uniformity. These were the only 'axioms' philosophers could legitimately assume. The axioms Whewell referred to, Baden Powell concluded, were in themselves a form of acquired knowledge.[16]

---

[15] Baden Powell, *Primary Laws of Motion*, p. 12. Without quoting Herschel, Baden Powell was clearly siding with his colleague in regarding axioms as extremely sophisticated abstractions from observation and sensory experience in general. Cf. Herschel, *A Preliminary Discourse*, p. 95: 'The axioms of geometry themselves may be regarded as in some sort an appeal to experience, not corporeal, but mental'. In his review of Whewell's *History*, Herschel openly criticized the *a priori* interpretation of the axioms of mechanics put forward by his friend: 'As we admit no such propositions, other than as truths inductively collected from observation, even in geometry itself, it can hardly be expected that, in a science of obviously contingent relations, we should acquiesce in a contrary view', reprinted in *Essays* (1857), p. 216.

[16] Baden Powell, *Primary Laws of Motion*, p. 12; see also *Connexion*, p. 25. Cf. Herschel, *A Preliminary Discourse*, p. 149: 'If the analogy of two phenomena be very close and striking, while, at the same time, the cause of one is very obvious, it becomes scarcely possible to refuse to admit the action of an analogous cause in the other, though not so obvious in itself'; see also pp. 94, 174, 219.

Baden Powell conceded that there was no recipe for seizing upon the right analogy to connect various sets of phenomena. In his textbook on logic Whately remarked that the choice of premisses for the inductive inference depended on the skill and professional ability of the observer. He thus implied that the establishment of a correct premiss involved elements of chance of a purely personal and occasional nature. Baden Powell's aim was on the contrary to stress that scientific advance depended upon a developing scientific culture. The more naturalists met and discussed, and the further scientific education and literature spread, the higher the chances that a discovery in a given field of physical investigation might stimulate a scientist to adopt analogous methods of inquiry for the solution of problems in a totally different field of research.[17]

Reference to the analogical use of established physical laws in approaching new problems explained the apparently puzzling fact that hypotheses often preceded observation. It often happened that discoverers simply verified by an appeal to experiment or observation a theory that they had formulated independently of observation. This fact, according to Baden Powell, could not be taken as a substantiation of Whewell's *a priori* ideas, but simply showed that it was possible to apply analogy to scientific investigation.[18]

Baden Powell was convinced that the successful application of analogies in science powerfully reinforced man's belief in the uniformity and simplicity of natural arrangements. Thus, the assumption of the uniformity of nature as the psychological category, the law of human belief which played a fundamental role at the very outset of the inductive inference, was proved by a growing series of unexpected substantiations to correspond to the actual state of things in the external order of nature.

Baden Powell agreed with Stewart that the ground of evidence provided by successful analogies did not amount to demonstrative certainty. He still accepted the distinction between mathematical demonstration and inductive inference. Nevertheless, he also argued that the growing evidence afforded by modern science to prove the principle of uniformity of nature allowed the naturalist 'to proceed with a confidence equal to that inspired by demonstration'. In other words, even though the premisses of an inductive inference were based on analogy and did not enjoy the epistemological status of geometrical or mathematical definitions, the *a posteriori* confirmation of the principle of uniformity on the one hand and the concrete results obtained in modern scientific investigations on the other, increased the reliability and the status of the analogical procedures adopted, and of inductive procedures in general.[19]

[17] Whately, *Elements of Logic*, pp. 164–5.
[18] Baden Powell, *Connexion*, pp. 26–35.
[19] Baden Powell, *Connexion*, pp. 70–2.

(ii) Cause and effect: the limits of Baden Powell's philosophy

Consideration of the inductive procedures and of the grounds of evidence for their conclusions prepared the way for approaching the much debated question of the relationship between cause and effect. In the early 1800s the discussion of this issue was at the centre of a conflict between the Scottish philosopher Thomas Brown, who supported a basically Humean concept of causation, and those Scottish and English intellectuals who saw Brown's move as an attempt at reviving atheistical philosophical tendencies. Brown's *Inquiry into the Relation of Cause and Effect* went through several editions and enjoyed much popularity up to the 1830s and 1840s. Discussion of the theory of causation was a compulsory topic in all philosophical treatises dealing with the methodology of science.[20]

The analysis of causation loomed large in Herschel's and Whewell's treatises. Baden Powell too touched upon the subject, though he avoided examining in detail the solutions put forward by his colleagues. In his 1838 work, his standpoint was characterized by an attempt at mediating two opposed positions. Some authorities, he explained, maintained that 'cause and effect' merely indicated the invariable succession of two events or sets of events. Other philosophers held an opposite view: that the expression 'the phenomenon A is the cause of the phenomenon B' implied more than mere sequence. Baden Powell conceded that inductive procedures as such only proved invariable sequence. He nevertheless argued that when naturalists said 'the pulsations of air are the cause of sound' they did not assert a mere sequence, but 'the dependence of a particular effect upon a very general principle'. 'Cause' thus became synonymous with 'general principle'.[21]

The relationship between cause and effect was seen by Baden Powell as established *a posteriori*, as a consequence of the individuation of a general law expressing a complex set of phenomena. He felt justified in concluding that causation thus implied more than mere sequence: 'we rationally extend our notion of physical causation beyond the bare instance of two consecutive phenomena, to the conviction of an intimate union between them.' This conviction, however, admitted of degrees. It was dependent upon the degree of generality and comprehensiveness of the natural law discovered by induction.[22]

---

[20] T. Brown, *Inquiry into the Relation of Cause and Effect* (Fourth edn., 1835); see J. G. Burke, 'Kirk and Causality in Edinburgh, 1805', *Isis*, 61 (1970), 340–54; The *B.C.* took an active part in the debate, deprecating the tendency of contemporary philosophy to form unwanted alliances with infidelity.

[21] Baden Powell, *Connexion*, pp. 80–2, 88–91. Herschel, *A Preliminary Discourse*, pp. 144, 151; W. Whewell, *History of Inductive Sciences* (1837, 1847 edn.), and *Philosophy of the Inductive Sciences* (1840, 1847 edn.). On contemporary debates on causation, see V. K. Kavaloski, 'The *vera causa* principle: an historico-philosophical study of a meta-theoretical concept from Newton through Darwin' (Ph.D. thesis, Chicago University, 1974).

[22] Baden Powell, *Connexion*, p. 104.

The kind of intimate connection Baden Powell established between cause and effect was thus carefully distinguished from the idea of 'efficient causation', a concept which, he argued, was wholly foreign to inductive procedures. The distinction between physical and efficient, and between moral and physical causation, found appropriate employment when Baden Powell considered the question of the relevance of induction to the proof of the existence of God. He argued that to assume moral and efficient causation in inductive procedures in order to prove that the world had a moral and efficient cause represented an unacceptable mode of circular argument. He warned that those who denied the presence of a rational plan in the universe were little impressed by an apologetic thesis which contained as premiss the very point to be established. Baden Powell's insistence on avoiding concepts like 'moral cause' or 'efficient cause' in natural and physical sciences was designed to prepare the way for a consistent Christian apologetic capable of fighting the philosophical sophistication of rationalistic infidelity.

Baden Powell's discussion of causation, and the application of his interpretation to concrete physical examples, revealed an unsolved ambiguity. He stated that the correct concept of physical causation excluded belief in the efficient connection between events, and simply referred to the relation established *a posteriori* between them. He then moved on to discuss the concept of *vera causa*. His sketchy account of this epistemological category followed Herschel's interpretation of the Newtonian rules for establishing *verae causae*. Scientifically legitimate causes, Baden Powell argued with Newton and Herschel, had to be *true*, that is had to be inferred from events actually observed, and *sufficient*, that is had to provide an adequate explanation of the phenomena under investigation. Significantly, the concrete examples of *verae causae* were taken from current geological doctrines, from Lyell's geological dynamics in particular.[23]

Baden Powell listed as *verae causae* of geological change the action of rivers, volcanoes, earthquakes, etc. He was clearly unable to avoid contradicting his theoretical investigation of the concept of cause and effect. Indeed, he argued at theoretical level for the *a posteriori*, non-efficient relationship between phenomena, but referred to actual physical agents as true and efficient causes of geological change. Furthermore, he did not appear to realize that this difficulty was providing arguments for Whewell's diffidence about the claims of modern geological doctrines. Baden Powell's example of a logically consistent causal proposition, quoted above, was taken from acoustics, a science which according to Whewell had reached the stage of maturity. Conversely, the

---

[23] Baden Powell, *Connexion*, pp. 93–103; Herschel, *A Preliminary Discourse*, pp. 151–7; Herschel too singled out the search for *verae causae* in geology as indication of the progress of the science: see p. 285. For an extremely competent summary of the debate on the theory of causation in the 1820s and the 1830s see O. A. Kubitz, 'Development of John Stuart Mill's *System of Logic*', *Illinois Studies in the Social Sciences*, 18 (1932), 151–87.

examples Baden Powell offered of geological causes proved that the science was still confined to the stage of postulating efficient causal links between phenomena and could not, as yet, prove 'the dependence of a particular effect upon a very general principle'.[24]

The unsatisfactory account of causation was not the only philosophical weakness of Baden Powell's discussion of inductive procedures. The complex philosophical and scientific issues analysed by Herschel or Whewell were only partially referred to by Baden Powell; we shall therefore limit our discussion to a critical analysis of his interpretation of contemporary philosophical debates. Baden Powell never attempted to formulate a systematic account of scientific procedures except for the purpose of supporting general points relating to the role of scientific investigation and conclusions in contemporary thought. Thus, he appeared little concerned with problems like verification, experimentation, or the increasing mathematical sophistication which characterized the physical sciences in the 1840s and 1850s. He was not concerned with providing solutions more refined than an appeal to the empirical, non-metaphysical foundation of man's knowledge of natural events. He argued that all the authorities he referred to, agreed in supporting the high reliability of inductive conclusions: this was the fact the Christian apologist had to take into careful account.

The limited goal of Baden Powell's excursus into epistemological debates was fully consistent with the Noetic cultural style. Copleston wrote on economic and political issues, though he never was or pretended to be a philosopher or an economist. Whately wrote on logic, theology and political economy, but never pursued those interests in a systematic way. Baden Powell was clearly more committed than his teachers to pursuing scientific investigations. Nevertheless, he was unwilling to come to terms with the rapid development of contemporary physical research. In typical Noetic – and Stewartian – fashion he increasingly regarded himself as the 'philosopher' who pointed out the 'general principles' involved in the pursuit of particular branches of scientific research. His chief objective was to emphasize the general relevance of scientific and philosophical advance for contemporary culture and religion.

It is important to stress that this attitude characterized his philosophical or apologetic approach, as well as his scientific contributions. From the late 1830s Baden Powell specialized in writing reports on current physical research. He also embarked on a successful role as popular lecturer on scientific subjects, on astronomy and physics in particular. As he confessed to John Lubbock in

---

[24] Baden Powell, *Connexion*, pp. 93–103. Herschel did not agree with Baden Powell that geological causes such as volcanoes or the action of rivers and the sea, were as yet proven to be sufficient to explain past changes on the surface of the earth: see *A Preliminary Discourse*, pp. 285–6. Discussing Lyell's theory of climate, Herschel argued that the 'cause' indicated by the geologist – the shifting distribution of land and sea over the centuries – was 'possessing the essential requisite of a *vera causa*...on which a philosopher may consent to reason'. Yet, he also warned that the matter was still 'undecided...till...more thoroughly investigated', pp. 146, 147.

1838, 'I have no pretension to original power of analysis myself, and am therefore the more anxious to get some of these points [the calculation of the wave surface of the undulations of light] well investigated by those who have, and whose labours I should then have the satisfaction of commenting upon, together with all due acknowledgement.'[25]

The correspondence with John Lubbock is particularly revealing of Baden Powell's standpoint with respect to current scientific research. Lubbock substantially helped him when the complexity of the mathematical apparatus required to approach contemporary physical research proved beyond Baden Powell's amateurish scope. When Lubbock pointed out a serious mathematical mistake in a paper on the theory of dispersion his colleague published in the *Transactions* of the Royal Society, Baden Powell was clearly unable to solve the problem by himself. In a letter thanking Lubbock for his help, the Savilian Professor of Geometry included a discomforted and revealing passage:

> I am thus clear of absolute error in the mathematical details. I shall be satisfied for the present, though fully aware there is much to be done in following up your various valuable suggestions...I...feel fairly relieved from the immediate annoyance. I have felt it to a degree which you will doubtless think foolish – but with me is constitutional – several times under similar circumstances I have felt determined at the moment never again to meddle with science.[26]

He did however go on meddling with science, though he was increasingly forced to adapt his interests to a different and less ambitious dimension. When in 1841 Baden Powell published his *General and Elementary View of the Undulatory Theory of Light* he lucidly described what he regarded as his task in current scientific investigation. He pointed out that scientific knowledge was increasing. Masses of new data were daily brought to light: he felt there was 'a constant necessity for a vigilant review and connected recapitulation of them from time to time'.[27]

Baden Powell's decision to act as a 'vigilant reviewer' of current cultural affairs applied to his contribution to scientific research as well as to his survey of contemporary epistemological debates. It is, however, a matter of historical interest to note that the choice of the epistemological topics he dwelt upon

[25] Royal Society, Lubbock Papers, Lub. P. 283–331, Letters from Baden Powell to Lubbock, fol. 287: 16 Jan. 1838.

[26] *Ibid.*, fol. 301: 5 Feb. 1839; see also fol. 294: 19 Jan. 1839, 'my want of command of analysis may have led to an error'. Baden Powell, 'Remarks on the Theory of the Dispersion of Light', *Philosophical Transactions*, 128 (1838), 253–64 and 'A Supplement to a Paper Entitled "Remarks..."', ibid., 130 (1840), 157–60.

[27] Baden Powell, *General and Elementary View* (1841), p. i; for an excellent introduction to contemporary researches and debates in optics, and Baden Powell's role in the discipline, see G. Cantor, 'The reception of the wave theory of light in Britain', *Historical Studies in the Physical Sciences*, 6 (1975), 109–32, 'The historiography of Georgian optics', *History of Science*, 16 (1978), 1–21 and *Optics after Newton. Theories of light in Britain and Ireland, 1704–1840* (1983). See also A. J. L. James, 'The physical interpretation of the wave theory of light', *B.J.H.S.*, xvii (1984), 47–60.

in the 1838 work related to his defence of the epistemological reliability of modern geological doctrine.

(iii) The foundations of geological knowledge

In the *Connexion of Natural and Divine Truth* Baden Powell devoted 32 out of 98 pages on scientific procedures, to supporting the reliability of geological findings. More than two-thirds of the examples chosen to illustrate the author's epistemological tenets were taken from geology. Geology was clearly the science Baden Powell had in mind when he summed up the features of the epistemological debate relevant to his approach. It is however to be observed that he carefully selected the epistemological tenets of the authorities he relied upon. He purposely avoided discussing concepts which could have weakened the credibility of inductive conclusions and of geology in particular.

Baden Powell referred to the principle of the uniformity of nature in terms borrowed from Whately's *Logic* and Stewart's *Elements*. He quoted with approval Whately's remarks on the 'logic' of scientific inference, but avoided expanding on the criteria distinguishing necessary from contingent truth which had been elaborated by his philosophical mentor. Furthermore, he chose not to notice that Whewell's philosophy of science was designed to confer universality and necessity upon the results of inductive investigation, because the criteria indicated by his colleague denied reliability to geological findings. In 1838 Baden Powell appeared convinced that to engage in debate over the criteria of necessity and universality amounted to acknowledging that on strict epistemological grounds he could hardly claim the title of 'truth' for geological findings.

It is interesting to point out that in 1849, when Baden Powell entered the debate between Whewell and John Stuart Mill, he characterized scientific knowledge in terms closely resembling the discussion of scientific procedures offered in his 1826 essay on *Rational Religion*. There he defined 'necessary truth' as the conclusions deduced from definitions of objects which were 'the creature of our faculties'. He also characterized as 'contingent' the conclusions reached with the help of logically consistent reasoning, but from premises 'which refer only to concrete objects and their properties discovered by observation'.[28]

The conclusions of the second kind, and inductive inferences in particular, were seen by Baden Powell as '*necessarily* true *relatively* to the premises, or first assumptions'. This central topic in Baden Powell's epistemological thought was completely omitted from his 1838 essay, which was devoted to proving that 'contingent' truths were entitled to full assent. It was therefore for tactical

---

[28] Baden Powell, *On Necessary and Contingent Truth* (1849), pp. 8–9.

reasons that in 1838 he chose not to take issue with Whewell on the criteria of contingency and necessity. On strict epistemological grounds, though on different theoretical assumptions, he had to agree with Whewell that the epistemological reliability of geological findings never attained demonstrative certainty.[29]

The debate on the epistemological status of geological inquiries in the early 1830s turned on Lyell's controversial approach to the discipline. Lyell, who significantly called his survey of the science *Principles of Geology*, claimed that geologists should attempt to explain the succession of geological changes in terms of causes or natural agents now in operation. By adopting this procedure of inquiry, he claimed, geological research avoided cosmological assumptions and acquired the status of a mature science. Whewell reviewed with approval the first and the second volume of the *Principles*, but did not accept Lyell's actualism or the geologist's belief that the history of the earth unfolded without sudden revolutions or catastrophes.[30]

Whewell praised Lyell's contribution to the establishment of what he defined as 'geological dynamics', but thought the projection of actual causes to explain changes in the past was unwarranted on epistemological grounds. Thus, in the *History of Inductive Sciences* Whewell concluded that 'several generations must elapse before ... geological dynamics can become an exact science'. Whewell did not question the reliability of geological findings with the avowed intent of weakening the case of those geological doctrines that contradicted the word of revelation. In other words, he was not a John Bowden. Yet, Baden Powell felt that those who at Oxford and elsewhere agreed with John Bowden would take full advantage of Whewell's criticism of recent geological developments and of Lyell's methodology.[31]

Baden Powell built his case on behalf of modern geology with the utmost care. He provided suitable geological examples of almost every epistemological issue he touched upon. When considering the role of analogical reasoning in science, he compared the methodological criteria of astronomical research with the procedures adopted in geological investigations. Whewell vigorously protested that no comparison could be made between astronomy and geology. Astronomy was a science based on dynamics, the purest of all physical sciences. The science of dynamics developed from a few necessary and universal truths.

29 *On Necessary and Contingent Truth*, pp. 8–9.
30 C. Lyell, *Principles of Geology*, 3 vols. (1830–3); for recent historiography on Lyell see M. J. S. Rudwick, 'The strategy of Lyell's *Principles of Geology*', *Isis*, 61 (1970), 5–33; 'Lyell centenary issue', *B.J.H.S.*, 9 (1976), 91–240; cf. L. G. Wilson, *Charles Lyell. The years to 1841* (1972); R. Laudan, 'The role of methodology in Lyell's science', *Studies in the History and Philosophy of Science*, 13 (1982), 215–49. (W. Whewell), 'Lyell's *Principles of Geology*', *B.C.*, 9 (1831), 180–206, and 'Lyell's *Geology*, Vol.2', *Q.R.*, 47 (1832), 103–33.
31 W. Whewell, *History*, vol. iii, pp. 603, 670, 674; (J. Bowden), 'Nolan and Powell', pp. 431–2.

Conversely, geology was based upon a mass of miscellaneous observations. Geological conclusions, according to Whewell, were at best 'doubtful speculations', whereas dynamical theories attained mathematical certainty.[32]

Baden Powell could not see why his colleague admitted the principle of uniformity as far as astronomical or dynamical theories were concerned, but refused to acknowledge its value for geology. Undeterred by Whewell's censure and openly polemical about the tenets so vigorously expounded by the Trinity man, Baden Powell argued that when geologists extended the action of geological causes active in the present to explain phenomena of the past, their procedure was no different from that adopted by astronomers. Geologists were fully entitled to conclude that huge deposits of pebbles were accumulated by the constant and uniform action of the sea over thousands of years. This procedure was strictly analogous to that adopted by astronomers who extended the action of the law of gravitation from the fall of a stone in our world to the motions of the most distant planets.[33]

Baden Powell's discussion of controversial geological doctrines constantly referred to Lyell's *Principles of Geology*. It should, however, be noted that his approval of Lyell's theories did not amount to an uncritical endorsement of all the tenets defended by the geologist. Implicitly combative towards Whewell, Baden Powell observed that the majority of contemporary geologists abandoned the belief in sudden universal destructions and creations. The practitioners of geology agreed that the 'causes' now in operation – volcanoes, earthquakes, the action of water, etc. – were capable of explaining changes occurring in the past. Nevertheless, Baden Powell conceded, there was a certain degree of dissension as to the former intensity of these natural agents. In discussing this delicate issue, Baden Powell appeared to follow Herschel's remarks on the question. In his *Preliminary Discourse* Herschel described the debate on actualism as an unsettled issue, though he did not conceal his personal sympathy for Lyell's attempt at explaining geological change 'by having recourse to causes now in action'.[34]

As was noted above, Baden Powell's aim was to criticize Whewell's views, as expressed in the *History of the Inductive Sciences*. A comparison between the texts of Baden Powell and Whewell reveals that the former was providing an almost *verbatim* commentary on the paragraphs the latter wrote against geological actualism. In a lucid passage criticizing Lyell's uniformitarianism, Whewell pinpointed one of the many epistemological shortcomings he saw in

[32] W. Whewell, *On the Principles of English University Education* (1837), pp. 42, 7, 9, 15, and *History*, vol. iii, p. 670; on Whewell's critique of the epistemological analogy between astronomy and geology, see J. H. Brooke, 'Natural theology and the plurality of worlds', *A.S.*, 34 (1977), 273–7. Herschel, *A Preliminary Discourse*, p. 287, argued that 'geology, in the magnitude of the objects of which it treats, undoubtedly ranks, in the scale of the sciences, next to astronomy'. Yet, he was also convinced that geology had just started its slow progress towards the status of a mature science.

[33] Baden Powell, *Connexion*, p. 31.

[34] Herschel, *A Preliminary Discourse*, p. 285; Baden Powell, *Connexion*, pp. 100–1.

Lyell's work. He could not accept Lyell's stress on the category of time as the crucial element of geological explanation, or Lyell's refusal to admit the possibility that the intensity of natural agents varied in the course of the earth's history. As Whewell put it,

Time, inexhaustible and ever accumulating his efficacy, can undoubtedly do much for the theorist in geology; but *Force*, whose limits we cannot measure, and whose nature we cannot fathom, is also a power never to be slighted; and to call in the one to protect us from the other, is equally presumptuous, to whichever of the two our superstition leans.[35]

Baden Powell strongly objected to Whewell's assessment of the strategy deployed by Lyell. He was convinced that there was a fundamental epistemological difference between extending *in time* the known operations of a cause, and hypothetically assuming an extension of its intensity. A volcano of markedly higher energy, which no one ever observed, was not a true cause, that is, a cause found to exist in nature. Thus, according to Baden Powell, the multiplication of time instead of force was 'the method which alone seems to bring us within the dominion of known causes'.[36]

Baden Powell did not conceal his conviction that, thanks to Lyell's work, modern geologists had freed themselves from cosmological assumptions, and geology was now legitimately taking its place among the most advanced sciences of the time. The diluvial theory, the last vestige of the cosmological spirit, had recently been abandoned. The defectiveness of the theory was not due to the intellectual timidity of those who supported it, but to the fact that geologists – and *British Critic* reviewers like himself – accepted '*some other authority*' than that of simple induction. The need to relate the results of geological investigations to the scriptural narrative of creation retarded the development of science.

Religious concerns were probably the reason why commentators on science showed a 'singular partiality' towards geology. It was commonly accepted that Halley's comet had an elliptic orbit of billions of miles or that the numerical evaluation of the atomic structure of chemical elements stretched the human imagination. When, however, geologists adopted the same methods of investigation which proved successful in astronomy and physics, and modestly concluded that millions of years ago the earth 'was governed by the same physical laws which prevail now', those who accepted the marvellous conclusions of physical research decried the arrogance of geologists and 'the pride of science'.

The methodology of inductive procedures, Baden Powell stressed, was one

---

35 Whewell, *History*, vol. iii, p. 669.
36 Baden Powell, *Connexion*, pp. 100–1. In his *Philosophy*, vol. i, p. 670, Whewell probably had Baden Powell in mind, when he submitted that 'if a volcano may repose for a thousand years, and then break out and destroy a city; why may not another volcano repose for ten thousand years, and then destroy a continent, why not the whole habitable surface of the earth'.

and applied equally to all branches of scientific investigation. He admitted that the force of inductive conclusions did not amount to demonstrative certainty. However, he did feel confident that his survey of inductive procedures proved that geological conclusions 'legitimately demanded the abandonment of preconceived notions and the surrender of long-cherished prejudices'. It was however clear that many people were reluctant to abandon such prejudices, especially when these were part of the scriptural narrative.[37]

(iv) Baden Powell and John Stuart Mill

The epistemological tenets developed by Baden Powell underwent little change during the 1840s and 1850s. On the whole he remained faithful to the approach elaborated by Stewart and Whately. It is nevertheless appropriate to consider his reaction to the main philosophical debates of these decades. Firstly, it is notable that between 1838 and 1849 Baden Powell abstained from discussing epistemological issues. In 1838 the discussion of the degree of evidence of inductive conclusions provided the basis for Baden Powell's demonstration of the existence of a universal mind, a moral first cause of natural phenomena. On the certainty of scientific conclusions rested the reliability of a modern natural theology. Analysis of the essays and articles he wrote during the 1840s reveals that Baden Powell was mainly concerned with current theological and ecclesiastical affairs.

He concentrated his apologetic effort to defending the Noetic brand of Anglicanism from attacks by Tractarians and by intuitionist theologians who increasingly relied upon psychological arguments of various kinds to support belief in Christianity. The only reference Baden Powell made in the early 1840s to the epistemological issues discussed in 1838 was in advising his readers to consider the philosophical dimension of scientific procedures and his own essay *The Connexion of Natural and Divine Truth* in particular.

The publication of John Stuart Mill's *System of Logic* in 1843 represented the major philosophical novelty of that decade. The work attracted immediate and favourable comment in specialized philosophical circles. It was nevertheless indicative of the intellectual climate of the time that Mill's work was slow to become established with the educated public. Mill's *Logic* failed to attract the attention of professional scientists, who probably regarded it as a re-publication of Herschel or Auguste Comte. As Whewell perceptively pointed out, Mill's remarks on induction were substantiated by examples taken from his own *History* and from Herschel's *Preliminary Discourse*: 'though acute and able, he is ignorant in science', Whewell wrote to Herschel.[38]

---

37 Baden Powell, *Connexion*, pp. 63–70.
38 Todhunter, *William Whewell* (1876), vol. ii, p. 315, Whewell to Herschel, 8 Apr. 1843. On Mill's debt to Herschel and his struggle with the concept of induction, see Kubitz, 'Development of Mill's *System*', ch. 4. See also F. Restaino, *John Stuart Mill e la cultura filosofica britannica* (1968).

Baden Powell, faithful to his policy of taking into account cultural events only when they became objects of public debate or were discussed within the circle of his friends and colleagues, waited a few years before carefully reading his copy of the *System of Logic*. Notwithstanding Whewell's comments, Mill's work was slowly but securely making its mark in British philosophy. Baden Powell admired Mill's empiricism, and the anti-metaphysical stand of the *System of Logic*. The philosophy of Stewart was the starting point for many of Mill's philosophical discussions, thus creating a shared background of problematics between the *System* and the Oxford professor. Baden Powell was also pleased by Mill's respectful criticism of Whately's contribution to logic. Mill had been one of the earliest reviewers of Whately's *Elements of Logic*, and had commented upon it in approving terms. At the time of the polemics on the method of political economy which opposed Whately and Senior to Whewell and Richard Jones, Mill sided with Oxford against Cambridge. It is not surprising, therefore, that Whewell labelled the *System* as the product of a follower of Whately. As he wrote to Richard Jones, 'I agree with you that the *Logic* is fairly logical; also, that it is deadly dull. The Whatelian logicians are to me far more oppressive than the Aristotelians; far more immersed in verbal trifling and useless subtility.'[39]

Baden Powell understandably found the defect of Mill's work that Whewell pointed out the most attractive feature of the *System of Logic*. Indeed, he found Mill's work more satisfactory than Whately's. Mill was capable of combining the logico–deductive structure of the discussion of induction by Stewart and Whately, with the profession of empiricism by Herschel and Comte. In the long controversy which opposed Mill to Whewell, Baden Powell obviously sided with the former, though he still relied upon central features of the philosophy of Stewart and Whately in surveying the most controversial issues of contemporary philosophical debates. His continued allegiance to the Stewart–Whately tradition was clearly perceptible in the discussion of the concepts of contingency and necessity, a central question with both Whewell and Mill.[40]

---

39 Todhunter, *William Whewell*, vol. ii, p. 314, Whewell to Jones, 7 Apr. 1843; (J.S. Mill), 'Whately's *Elements of Logic*', *W.R.*, 9 (1828), 137–72. The only systematic discussion of Mill's debts to Stewart can be found in Kubitz, 'The Development of Mill's *System*'; see also Corsi, 'The heritage of Dugald Stewart', for Mill's epistemological dialogue with Stewart on the subject of the method of political economy.

40 On the debate between Whewell and Mill, see: W. S. Jackson, *An Examination of the Deductive Logic of John Stuart Mill* (1941); F. Restaino, *J. S. Mill e la cultura filosofica britannica* (1968); H. T. Walsh, 'Whewell and Mill on induction', *Philosophy of Science*, 29 (1962), 279–84; G. Buchdal, 'Inductivist *Versus* deductivist approaches', *Monist*, 60 (1971), 343–67; D. Wilson, 'Herschel and Whewell's version of Newtonianism', *Journal of the History of Ideas*, 35 (1974), 79–97; M. Ruse, 'The scientific methodology of William Whewell', *Centaurus*, 20 (1976), 227–57; S. Hollander, 'William Whewell and John Stuart Mill on the methodology of political economy', *Studies in the History and Philosophy of Science*, 14 (1983), 127–68; S. Collini, 'The tendency of things: John Stuart Mill and the philosophical method', in S. Collini et al., *That Noble Science of Politics* (1983), pp. 127–39.

Baden Powell was critical of Whewell's claim that 'necessity' was a category applicable to 'fundamental ideas' only. Yet, he did not agree with Mill's remark that the distinction between contingent and necessary truth was a mere 'illusion'. Baden Powell sided with Mill – and with Herschel – in considering mathematical and geometrical objects as derived from experience by a process of abstraction. Nevertheless, he also argued that the abstract concept of time, length, space, number, etc., became objects of pure reasoning in so far as they were expressed by appropriate and unambiguous definitions. Being very simple, 'elementary' concepts, these abstractions were capable of being expressed by definitions exhausting the existential connotation of the object under investigation. Geometrical and mathematical definitions thus became '*the produce of thinking, or a creation* of the mind'.[41]

In 1849 Baden Powell opposed the discussion of necessity and contingency by Stewart and Whately, to what he regarded as Mill's empiricist reductionism. He felt that Mill's excessive reliance on empiricism was depriving scientific results of their title to philosophical dignity. On the other hand, Whewell's criterion of necessity excluded geology and the natural sciences in general from the number of the most developed sciences, thereby invalidating the title to credibility of geological doctrines. The analysis of the categories of necessity and contingency Baden Powell expanded upon in the Ashmolean paper of 1849 was reproduced almost verbatim in the 1855 *Essays on the Spirit of the Inductive Philosophy*, where he also revised his standpoint on causation.[42]

The concept of causation was a further point of division between Whewell and Mill. Whewell maintained that the idea of cause, interpreted as active efficiency, was an axiom inherent in the human mind. The idea that 'every event must have a cause' was the fundamental conception with which men approached all successions of phenomena. Experience, according to Whewell, provided the phenomenal occurrence of a succession of events, but it was the 'fundamental idea' of cause which introduced the indispensable clarifying element in the otherwise chaotic succession of events. Mill on the contrary argued that the correct philosophical concept of causation excluded the idea of efficient causation or power. Mill accepted the Humean account of causation as mere succession of phenomena. He was however impressed by Herschel's analysis of the concept of cause as deduced from a consideration of the physical sciences. Mill was clearly indebted to Herschel for the description of the methods to be followed in ascertaining the *verae causae* of phenomena. In the *System of Logic* Mill argued that a phenomenon A was the cause of the

[41] Baden Powell, *Necessary and Contingent Truth*, pp. 5–16; J. S. Mill, *System of Logic* (1843, *Collected Works* 1973), vol. i, p. 224.

[42] Baden Powell, *Essays on the Spirit of Inductive Philosophy* (1855), henceforth *Essays*. Whewell, *Philosophy* , vol. i, book I, ch. 2, sect. 2, 'Necessary and Experimental Truths', pp. 19–21. See also R. E. Butts, 'Necessary truth in Whewell's theory of science', *American Philosophical Quarterly*, 2 (1965), 161–81, and M. Fisch, 'Necessary and contingent truth' (1985).

phenomenon B, when A could be proved to be the 'unconditional invariable antecedent' of B, where by 'unconditional' he meant that there was no other phenomenon A proved by experience to be a condition of B.[43]

The discussion of Mill's and Whewell's views of causation offers a typical instance of Baden Powell's attempt to provide conciliatory solutions of opposing epistemological tenets. It could however be argued that his examination of contemporary epistemological debates offered eclectic rather than incisive solutions. It is nevertheless interesting to point out that Baden Powell's own views of causation underwent certain modification under the influence of the doctrines put forward by Mill. In 1838 Baden Powell oscillated between a concept of cause as relationship between phenomena within the context of a natural law, and a concept of cause – such as geological causes – as natural agents performing observable operations. In the 1855 essay on the spirit of inductive philosophy Baden Powell appeared decidedly to opt for the first of the two accounts of causation. The concept of cause, he argued, implied 'a connexion, not in the *events* in the way of physical agents, but in the *reason* and *logical dependence* of the two ideas ... The cause is a more *general and better understood class* or *genus* of phenomena to which we can refer the effect, as a particular *species*'.[44]

The major development which occurred in Baden Powell's philosophy was the abandonment of the psychological categories of the philosophy of mind, and his acceptance of Mill's empiricist explanation of the conceptual presuppositions assumed in the inductive syllogism. In 1838 Baden Powell agreed with Whately and Stewart that inductive inference always presupposed the belief in the uniformity of nature. Such a conviction was justified by referring to the principles of belief intrinsic to the human mind. In 1855 Baden Powell drew a firm line between the commonsense belief that the sun will rise tomorrow and the *a posteriori* philosophical conviction of the uniformity and constancy of the natural order.

In 1838 the principle of uniformity was introduced by Baden Powell with explicit democratic connotations: every man was naturally endowed with laws of belief and with the principle of the uniformity of nature in particular. Every man was therefore capable of conceiving the idea of a rational principle responsible for the order and the harmony of the universe. In his 1838 apologetic synthesis, the principle of the uniformity of nature was designed to guarantee the universality of a scientific and philosophical natural theology, grounded on the 'laws of human belief' and on the advance of scientific

---

[43] Whewell, *Philosophy*, vol. ii, pp. 451–2. J. S. Mill, *System* (1843, *Collected Works* 1973), vol. i, p. 338. On Mill, Herschel and causation see note 40 above. On the subject of causation, Baden Powell was also influenced by W. R. Grove (1811–96), *On the Correlation of Physical Forces* (1846); Grove had been a pupil of Baden Powell at Oxford. See also G. N. Cantor, 'William Robert Grove, the Correlation of Forces, and the Conservation of Energy', *Centaurus*, 19 (1976), 273–90.

[44] Baden Powell, *Essays*, p. 123, and pp. 118–39.

knowledge. In 1855 Baden Powell argued that the 'philosophical belief' in
the uniformity of nature was 'utterly beyond the attainments of the many'
It was 'preeminently an acquired idea', a philosophical *a posteriori* conviction
of the uniformity and constancy of the natural order.[45]

In 1855 Baden Powell was however little concerned with the theological
and apologetic consequences of his claim that the belief in the uniformity of
nature was the exclusive property of the intellectual élites. This important
change of emphasis in his apologetic will be discussed in detail below. It is
however appropriate briefly to consider the political and social changes which
reassured Baden Powell that the exclusion of the masses from an appreciation
of a philosophical natural theology was without social and political consequences.

In 1838 the danger of the inception of a democratic society required
according to Baden Powell, a Christian apologetic grounded on the cultural
priorities of the social groups which demanded reform and change. He was
convinced that the alternative culture put forward by dissatisfied Dissenting
and radical élites was scientifically oriented. It was important to seek for an
approach capable of convincing the honest mechanic of the scientific demonstration of the existence of God. In 1855 the social and political fears had
vanished or were considerably weakened. The major crisis represented by the
Chartist movement had been overcome and the government appeared aware
of the need for positive policies to relieve social tensions and for upgrading
cultural agencies to meet contemporary requirements.

Baden Powell increasingly referred to scientific and philosophical culture
as the prerogative of social and cultural élites. Representatives of the lower
echelons of society, he came to think, eagerly debated issues like materialism
biblical criticism or transformist hypotheses in biological sciences, convinced
that the destiny of Christianity depended on victory or defeat over a single
issue. The philosopher, the Christian philosopher in particular, knew that
scientific or religious discourses followed highly complex patterns. It was
therefore the duty of the Christian apologist to stress the wider orders of
consideration bearing upon any single issue under debate, in order to prove
his capability to adapt to any development of science or philosophy. Single
scientific doctrines, in other words, were not to affect an apologetic approach
grounded on the philosophy of science as understood by authoritative contemporary epistemologists. Baden Powell also argued that the faith of the masses
required little speculation or reflection in its support, since the doctrines of
Christianity were often believed on mere traditional or psychological grounds
It was only the more cultivated who felt they had to inquire into the grounds
of belief, or that they had to include scientific and philosophical advance in

---

45 Baden Powell, *Necessary and Contingent Truth*, pp. 34–6 and *Essays*, pp. 90–102; cf. J. S. Mill
    System (1843, *Collected Works* 1974), vol. ii, pp. 306–14.

a comprehensive and harmonious Christian apologetic. It was to them that the Christian apologist addressed himself.

Baden Powell's reflections on the methodology of scientific investigation underwent limited change from his early contribution to the *British Critic* up to his 1855 essay on the spirit of inductive philosophy. The basically nominalistic account by Whately and Stewart of inductive procedures remained the central point of reference of Baden Powell's epistemological reflections. Allegiance to the philosophical authorities of his youth was reinforced by his reading of Mill's *System of Logic*. Mill was deeply indebted to Stewart and Whately, even though it was clear that he gave original reinterpretations, modifications or critiques of many of their tenets.

An acute critic like Whewell did not fail to perceive the same style of rationality and explanation emerging from the works of Stewart, Whately and Mill. The latter repeatedly stressed that the 'seminal minds' who greatly influenced his intellectual upbringing were Bentham, Coleridge and Comte. He failed to acknowledge that he learned much from Stewart and Whately as well, as shown by the footnotes to his early editions of the *System of Logic*, or by his paper on the method of political economy, which was in fact a commentary – albeit original – on the epistemology of political economy elaborated by Stewart and by the Noetics. It is not surprising, therefore, that the reading of Mill's logic reinforced the 'logical' leanings of Baden Powell's analysis of induction. He read Mill as a pupil of Whately and Stewart. He found much in the *System of Logic* to confirm the views of his teachers.[46]

In 1838 Baden Powell chose to emphasize the analysis of induction as the collection of data for the premises of the inductive syllogism, rather than the consideration of induction as inference. His ambition was to combine the deductive rigour of his teachers' approach to the methods of science with a strong emphasis on the dignity and reliability of conclusions reached in the natural sciences, a department of intellectual investigation characterized by the extreme difficulty of formulating clear definitions of the objects under investigation. Thus, if on the one hand Baden Powell stressed the inductive dimension of scientific procedures, he remained convinced that rigour and reliability were distinctive and exclusive features of axiomatically arranged deductive systems. It was not surprising therefore that he failed to convince Bowden and Whately of the epistemological reliability of geological doctrines. In the *Connexion of Natural and Divine Truth* Baden Powell acknowledged, albeit in a passing remark, that inductive conclusions failed to satisfy the requirements of demonstrative evidence. Contrary to what he hoped for, this admission was all Whately and Bowden needed to avoid altering their 'prejudices'.

---

[46] On Mill's debt to Stewart and Whately on the subject of the method of political economy, see P. Corsi, 'The heritage of Dugald Stewart'.

(v) Baden Powell, Auguste Comte and British positivism

The Comtean philosophy was a major influence on late nineteenth-century thought. The question of the impact of Comte on British philosophy earlier in the century has still to be critically assessed. Though till recently largely ignored by historians of nineteenth-century British cultural life, the debate on Stewart's philosophy and the impact of Herschel's *Discourse* and Whewell's *History* and *Philosophy of the Inductive Sciences* introduced contemporaries to sophisticated forms of philosophical analysis. A certain degree of reluctance in endorsing fully-blown philosophical systems did not prevent the diffusion of a taste for the discussion of methodological issues relating to the development of single scientific disciplines or science in general. As Baden Powell pointed out, a consideration of contemporary priorities made it impossible to forecast 'a very favourable reception of any extensive and new philosophical system' and to Comte's *Cours* in particular. There were however controversial features of the Comtean system which were bound eventually to attract strong reactions from the British intelligentsia, as there were Comtean ideas relating to the philosophy of history and knowledge which caused little surprise because they had already been debated in Britain.[47]

In 1839 Baden Powell contributed to the *Monthly Chronicle* an essay-review of the first three volumes of the *Cours de philosophie positive*. He praised Comte's theory of the progress of science through the theological, the metaphysical and the positive stages. He also admired Comte's determination to exclude reference to final causes from scientific discourse. He did however disagree with Comte on several issues. According to Comte, the undulatory theory of light exemplified the persistence of the metaphysical spirit in the most advanced fields of physical investigation. Baden Powell agreed that the theory was incomplete and only partially satisfactory, but stressed its heuristic value and its potential for suggesting new experiments and explanatory concepts.[48]

Baden Powell sympathized with Comte's systematic analysis of the development of various scientific disciplines and praised his colleague's attempt to provide a comprehensive view of contemporary science. He was however deeply

---

[47] The question of epistemological debates in early nineteenth-century Britain is increasingly attracting the attention of historians of science, of philosophy and of British intellectual life in general. Since the completion of the first version of this work in 1980, many important essays have been published on the subject. See in particular: L. Goldman, 'The origins of British "Social Science": political economy, natural science, and statistics, 1830–1835', The *Historical Journal*, 26 (1983), 587–616; S. Collini *et al.*, *That Noble Science of Politics. A study in nineteenth-century intellectual history* (1983); B. Fontana, *Rethinking the Politics of Commercial Society* (1985); R. Yeo, 'An idol of the market-place: Baconianism in nineteenth-century Britain', *History of Science*, 23 (1095), 251–98.

[48] (Baden Powell), 'M. Comte's System of Positive Philosophy', *Monthly Chronicle*, 3 (1839), 228, 230, 232. Baden Powell reviewed vol. i (1830), ii (1835), and iii (1838) of the *Cours*. See also Baden Powell, *General and Elementary View of the Undulatory Theory*, pp. ii–vii.

disappointed to find that the French philosopher failed to take geology into account. According to Baden Powell, no science had ever progressed more rapidly than geology. With the publication of Lyell's *Principles*, geology reached the positive stage and was entitled to the respect and consideration of contemporary epistemologists. Baden Powell also pointed out that Comte considered 'rational cosmology' as a legitimate field of inductive speculation. Comte expressed the conviction that the nebular hypothesis proposed by Laplace, and his own calculation supporting the theory, provided a sound foundation for modern cosmological doctrines. Baden Powell could not understand why Comte failed to realize that geological investigation provided important information relevant to cosmology.[49]

It is interesting to note Baden Powell's early conviction that a speculative, rational cosmology drawing upon the results of inductive disciplines was a legitimate field of philosophical and scientific discourse. In view of the debates on cosmology which characterized the next two decades, it is noteworthy that already in 1839 Baden Powell saw the nebular hypothesis proposed by astronomers and the theory of geological change put forward by Lyell as the key doctrines of a rational inductive cosmology.

Comte's epistemology failed to make a great impact upon Baden Powell. The author of the *Connexion of Natural and Divine Truth* had no difficulty in agreeing with Comte that hypotheses and hypothetical theories were essential components of the inductive method. He nevertheless felt compelled to remind the reader that the view of hypotheses proposed by Comte 'is in fact no other than that which has been recently contended for on quite different grounds' by two British philosophers, namely Whately and Baden Powell. The readers were referred to the *Connexion* and to the *Elements of Logic* for further information on the subject.

Baden Powell discussed at length the views on the relationship between science and religion put forward by Comte. He felt a justified sense of superiority when he reminded his French colleague that his criticism of theology only applied to a particular kind of theology. He opposed, as Comte did, the unphilosophical pretence of those who employed theological categories in scientific investigation or argued for a close theological supervision of science. The Baden Powell who fought and lost a hard battle to establish the independence of science from theology was little impressed by Comte's tirade against theological interference in science. Indeed, Baden Powell argued that the progress of science disclosed new and more sophisticated evidence of the existence of God. The primitive and limited view of God's direct action in nature was superseded by the concept of operation through law. If anything, it was the 'positive philosophy' which provided the intellectually most advanced argument in favour of the existence of God.

[49] (Baden Powell), 'M. Comte's System', 232–3.

From 1839 to 1855 Baden Powell did not consider the Comtean philosophy sufficiently important to deserve further detailed comment. He clearly considered the debate between Mill and Whewell more relevant than Comte's increasingly eccentric productions of the late 1840s. Towards the end of the 1840s the propaganda of George Henry Lewes (1817–78) and Harriet Martineau (1802–76) succeeded in attracting the attention of the reading public. Both writers were critical of the religious development of the positive system. They stressed the epistemological, anti-theological and anti-metaphysical features which characterized Comte's early works. In view however of the peculiar financial circumstances relating to the publication of Martineau's summary of the *Cours* in 1853 and the precarious condition of the *Westminster Review* during the 1850s, it is fair to say that the proselytizing effort of the British positivists relied on a small number of disciples rather than on public favour.[50]

Baden Powell was aware that positivism was the creed of a few intellectuals. He was nevertheless convinced that changes in the beliefs of the educated élites deserved the attention of the Christian apologist. In his later works he commented further upon the Comtean philosophy. Yet, significantly, he employed the term 'positive philosophy' in a broad sense. He defined as 'positive' the system of knowledge and the epistemological doctrine which avoided direct or indirect reference to theological or metaphysical categories. He never considered the system elaborated by Comte but as one of the many attempts to inquire into the philosophical foundation of modern science.

According to Baden Powell, the positivists were weakening their cause when they criticized old-fashioned theological doctrines. The polemic between the positivists and orthodox theologians was to some extent an anachronistic waste of energy. There were intellectual ferments abroad both in philosophy and theology which positivists and traditional theologians alike consistently failed to appreciate. Thus, in accordance with the approach he learned at Hackney and at Oriel Baden Powell set himself the task of evaluating the relationship between philosophic and scientific advance, and the defence of religious beliefs. As was typical of his approach, it was the wider theological and broadly cultural dimension of the philosophical debate which concerned him.

As has often been argued in the course of this study, there is a need for a comprehensive historical assessment of British philosophy in the early decades of the nineteenth century. The project should deeply revise accepted chronological boundaries, and consider the debate of the years 1829–33, or the discussion of Mill's work, as important episodes in a story which started with

50 G. H. Lewes, *A Biographical History of Philosophy*, 2 vols. (1845–6) and *Comte's Philosophy of the Sciences* (1847); see R. E. Ockenden, 'George Henry Lewes, 1817–1878', *Isis*, 32 (1947), 70–86. H. Martineau, *The Positive Philosophy of Auguste Comte* (1853); G. S. Haight, *George Eliot and John Chapman* (1940), p. 53. R. K. Webb, *Harriet Martineau, A Radical Victorian* (1960). W. M. Simon, *European Positivism in the Nineteenth Century* (1963). S. Shuttleworth, *George Eliot and Nineteenth-Century Science* (1983).

with Stewart's provocative philosophical assessment and criticism of what was regarded as the scientific revolution of the last decades of the eighteenth century.

Due consideration should also be paid to the social and, at times, directly political dimension of contemporary debates on the philosophy of science in general and the philosophy of disciplines like geology and political economy. Concentration on such towering figures as Samuel Taylor Coleridge or John Stuart Mill should give way to a sympathetic survey of the plurality of voices which entered the debate on philosophy, and on the philosophy of science in particular. In view of the almost general neglect of Stewart's influence on early nineteenth-century English philosophy, the complex issue of his legacy should be thoroughly assessed.

Within the limits of our present concern, it is important to stress the interest of Baden Powell as a privileged witness of the philosophical culture of his time. Indeed, the analysis of his early and mature epistemological reflections and the development of his ideas on the methodology of science emphasizes interesting features of the contemporary philosophical debate. The themes Baden Powell touched upon and the change of emphasis in his epistemological considerations reveal the deep correlation between the philosophical debate and wider dimensions of the social, political and religious scene.

The shortcomings and contradictions of Baden Powell's epistemology cannot be fully assessed except within the wider context of his apologetic commitments. It was his aim to build a cultural synthesis capable of embracing modern scientific, philosophical and theological trends in a comprehensive scheme of Christian apologetic. Thus, the critique of natural theology became the second major theme of his 1838 synthesis. Baden Powell was proud of the conclusions he reached in 1838 on the subject of natural theology. It was nevertheless this feature of his synthesis which most lacked coherence and consistency. The attempt at solving the ambiguities of his natural theology forced Baden Powell to revise completely his Christian apologetic. Indeed, many contemporaries, and Richard Whately in particular, thought he had abandoned the task altogether.

12

The Christian apologetic and the fallacies of natural theology

From the outset of his career Baden Powell insisted on the key role of science for the modern mind. The social and political events of the 1820s and early 1830s convinced him that science was bound to become the intellectual spearhead of social groups then attaining political and economic power. Baden Powell made this conviction explicit when he repeatedly warned the 'higher classes' of England that their role in society was increasingly being questioned on political and economic, as well as on scientific and intellectual grounds. He was also persuaded that the Anglican intelligentsia was unprepared and indeed unwilling to face the new challenges. The clergy fiercely resisted even moderate and indispensable reforms. The dons gathering around Newman and Pusey were also elaborating a theology designed, they hoped, to revive the fortunes of the Anglican Church by appealing to authority and tradition against the pride of the intellect.

It is important to emphasize that Oxford was not Britain, and that the scientific movement found within the ranks of the Anglican clergy many sincere friends and devoted supporters. Baden Powell was obviously influenced and embittered by his dealings with the ultra-conservative spirit in Oxford and by the struggle with the Tractarians. As can be easily perceived, the situation at Oxford headed the list of his concerns. He was a teacher in the university and a member of a group of intellectuals who aimed at making Oxford the leading cultural centre of the Anglican Church, and themselves the leaders of Oxford. It would however be wrong to interpret Baden Powell's 1838 synthesis of natural and divine truth as the mere product of Oxonian theological squabbles. The failure of his reforming plans convinced Baden Powell of the necessity of appealing to the British intelligentsia.

The decision was reinforced by the full explosion of the Tractarian revolt in 1836. Baden Powell's position at Oxford became almost unbearable. As Elizabeth Whately wrote to Blanco White in 1838, Baden Powell was living at Oxford 'as it were in a desert'. The British Association, the Royal Society Council, the Geological Society meetings and metropolitan life in general provided a welcome escape from the oppressive isolation at Oxford. By 1838, Baden Powell saw the British intelligentsia at large as his audience. *The*

Connexion of Natural and Divine Truth represented an interesting attempt at
focusing the Noetic intellectual style on an examination of philosophical and
theological themes and on natural theology in particular. The book was
addressed to a wide range of readers of different religious and philosophical
persuasions. In view of the scarce credit enjoyed at Oxford by the natural
theology tradition, Baden Powell's declared intention of reassessing the argument
from design is of particular interest.[1]

Baden Powell himself acknowledged that Paley's natural theology was never
popular in the university. From the early 1800s Van Mildert regarded natural
theology as a weak *a posteriori* argument. The early Noetics agreed in principle
with Van Mildert's assessment of the shortcomings of natural theology. Their
criticism undoubtedly was more refined than that put forward by Van Mildert
or Jones of Nayland, but reached similar conclusions: natural theology was
at best a pious exercise. Suspicion of natural theology was also expressed by
the leaders of the Tractarian movement. Like Coleridge, they were 'weary'
of natural theology. A man who needed evidence for his Christian belief, they
declared, had already abandoned the path of the true faith. As William Sewell
emphatically declared, 'We do not require to be taught, as science has been
lately teaching us, that there is a God, and that we are his creatures. We have
much better evidence for this, and for all the solemn truths of our Bible, than
can be gathered by all the art of men from the orbits of the stars or the
bowels of the earth'.[2]

A sophisticated theoretical criticism of natural theology expressing the
Tractarian point of view came from William Irons, who published in 1836 a
treatise on *The Whole Doctrine of Final Causes*. Natural theologians, Irons
argued, were fully aware that on strictly philosophical grounds their inference
from design to mind amounted to mere probability: they 'heap up fact upon
fact, thinking thereby to increase the force of their premises, and consequently
augment the probability of their conclusions'. Irons pointed out that the
probability that design implied a designing mind amounted to certainty only
for those who already believed in God 'on other grounds'; it could never
convince the sceptic or the atheist. He used the reflections on the existence
of evil in nature put forward by Copleston to deny that a sufficient knowledge
of the attributes of God could be gained by contemplating the works of
creation.[3]

[1] Lambeth Palace, Whately Papers, 2164, fol. 285: 19 Oct. 1838, E. Whately to Blanco White.
[2] Van Mildert, *Historical View of Infidelity*, vol. ii, pp. 63–7; S. T. Coleridge, *Aids to Reflection*,
2 vols. (1848 edn.), vol. i, p. 333. On Coleridge see Overton, *The English Church* (1894), p.
164, and T. H. Levere, *Poetry Realized in Nature* (1981). On the fortunes of natural theology
in the early nineteenth century, see Yule, 'The impact of science' (1976), 166–7, 174. The
Athenaeum reviewer of Buckland's *Bridgewater Treatise* confessed to feel 'somewhat *saturated*
with the subject', n. 484 (4 Feb. 1837), p. 79. For the quotation from Sewell, see *The Attack
upon the University of Oxford* (1834), p. 21; see also pp. 21–22, 33–4.
[3] W. J. Irons, *On the Whole Doctrine of Final Causes* (1836), pp. 117–8, 142–3.

Irons did not refer, as Copleston did, to evil in general, but listed in detail the instances of social injustice which made England hardly an example of benevolent adjustment of moral and social phenomena. It may be noted that the Tractarians combined the emphasis on Church authority with a basically charitable approach towards the social ills of the country, whereas the Noetics, and Baden Powell with them, relied for the solution of social problems on the application of the iron laws of political economy, tempered by appropriate educational intervention. Irons was worried by the growing popularity of natural theology. Natural theology weakened man's reliance on the scriptures as the only source of religious instruction, and undermined the 'Loyalty, the Faith and the Morals of the Nation'. Irons firmly concluded that natural theology was untenable on philosophical, political, and theological grounds.[4]

Despite the coherent, albeit differently motivated Oxford critique of the 1830s, natural theology enjoyed a considerable revival early in the decade. The eight *Bridgewater Treatises* were chiefly responsible for conferring the highest authority upon the topic. Several distinguished British intellectuals, Lord Brougham (1778–1868), Charles Babbage (1792–1871) and Thomas Turton (1780–1864) among others, felt that they too had to add a title to the bibliography of natural theology. Some sought to derive personal advantage from the popularity of the subject, others expressed their dissent from or approval of the brand – or brands – of natural theology put forward by the Bridgewater authors.[5]

Natural theology literature became in the early 1830s a major cultural event, a fact which Baden Powell did not fail to appreciate. He became convinced that the brand of natural theology he proposed was capable of providing 'a kind of evidence...(which)...can be appreciated by all men of all classes'. Despite efforts by Christian intellectuals to reconcile science with Christian beliefs, he was also persuaded that the question of the relationship between the modern scientific culture and Christian apologetic was still open. Baden

---

4 Irons, *On the Whole Doctrine*, p. 208. Similar sentiments were expressed by the reviewer of Chalmers's *Bridgewater Treatise* (probably Sewell), who asked his readers: 'why is our time to be wasted, or our attention scattered, and our hearts seduced from the words of eternal life, by a vast apparatus of laws and phenomena, and adaptations, and mysteries of corpuscular action?', *B.C.*, 14 (1833), 240.

5 On the eight *Bridgewater Treatises* see bibliography below, and W. H. Brock, 'The selection of the authors of the *Bridgewater Treatises*', *Notes and Records of the Royal Society*, 21 (1966), 162–79; R. Young, 'The historiographic and ideological context', in M. Teich and R. Young (eds.), *Changing Perspectives in the History of Science* (1973), pp. 344–438, and *idem*, 'Natural theology, Victorian periodicals and the fragmentation of a common context', paper circulated in typescript, published in *Darwin's Metaphor* (1985), 126–63. Doubts on the 'common context' have found substantiation in J. H. Brooke, 'The natural theology of the geologists: some theological strata', in L. J. Jordanova and R. S. Porter (eds.), *Images of the Earth* (1979), pp. 39–64; I have also consulted a much expanded version of this paper, and have discussed these issues at length with Dr Brooke. On the deep disagreement between the Bridgewater authors on what natural theology was, and on what was atheism or Christian science, see ch. 15 below.

Powell felt that natural theologians were merely concerned with defending religion from science, rather than with using science to defend religion. Thus, having established the reliability and philosophical dignity of inductive procedures and of geological doctrines in particular, he moved on to consider how far current natural theology was capable of solving the most crucial question of contemporary Christian apologetic: how to harmonize natural with divine truth.[6]

Baden Powell opened *The Connexion of Natural and Divine Truth* with repeated expressions of esteem for current contributions to natural theology. Works by Whewell, Turton, Babbage and Lord Brougham were singled out for special mention. Yet, a careful analysis of the work and an understanding of Baden Powell's standpoint on the science–religion debate reveal that he had underlying tactical reasons for his preliminary ingratiating remarks. He chose not to criticize any work in particular, or at least not to do so explicitly. In fact, his thorough discussion of the shortcomings of contemporary natural theology revealed that he was far from satisfied with the works he praised.

During the 1830s Baden Powell repeatedly warned his Anglican colleagues that the advance of popular scientific education was bound to provide for the masses sophisticated critical tools with which to approach traditional religious teaching and the Christian apologetic. Moreover, notwithstanding the arguments put forward by the Mosaic geologists it was increasingly clear that the scriptural cosmogony was insufficient to explain even the simplest observable succession of geological strata. A major initiative was therefore required in order to reassure the worried and convince the doubtful that such a discrepancy between the revealed account of natural phenomena and the discoveries of modern science in no way undermined the truth of Christianity.

Baden Powell was persuaded that contemporary natural theologians were keeping silent on the real dimensions of the conflict between the traditional concept of religion and modern science. Endorsing the critique of natural theology put forward by Irons, Baden Powell argued that natural theologians limited their effort to listing instances of design and of allegedly providential arrangement of the natural and the moral world. Indeed, natural theologians appeared to agree with Rose, Sewell and several commentators in the *British Critic*, that science was distracting men from the contemplation of the first cause by exclusively engaging their attention upon the material second causes of natural events. The only task natural theology was thus asked to perform was to provide the student of the sciences with evidence of the action of a providential mind in the succession of 'second causes'. Baden Powell pointed out that this rearguard action on behalf of natural theology was conducted with little philosophical consistency. Natural theologians concentrated exclu-

---

[6] Baden Powell, *Connexion*, p. 2.

sively on alleged instances of benevolent natural arrangement. Only too often they disregarded elementary rules of logic in their reasoning.

Several natural theologians, including the most eminent of them, assumed the concept of final causes as the category that provided the link between the natural sciences and natural theology. It is interesting to note that the ideas elaborated by Whewell were the target of Baden Powell's strictures. The instances of final causes Baden Powell listed and his discussion of the famous debate of 1830 between Georges Cuvier and Etienne Geoffroy Saint-Hilaire on the unity of anatomical composition were clearly designed to oppose the teleological conclusions reached by Whewell. The examination of the latter's remarks on teleology had also a deeper polemical intention. Baden Powell wanted to point out that Whewell had changed his mind on the subject of final causes. He thus approvingly quoted earlier works produced by his Cambridge colleague but avoided mentioning the recent developments of Whewell's thought.[7]

It did not escape Baden Powell's attention that during the 1830s Whewell's philosophical ideas underwent considerable modification. In 1833 the Cambridge polymath concluded the chapter on 'Final causes' of his contribution to the Bridgewater series by expressing his conviction that teleological considerations were to be excluded from 'physical inquiry'. Baden Powell was pleased with the theological application of Whewell's tenet: 'It is precisely because he [the naturalist] has thus established his theories independently of any assumption of an end, that the end, when, after all, it returns upon him and cannot be evaded, becomes an irresistible evidence of an intelligent legislator.'[8]

Yet, when in 1837 he discussed the Cuvier–Geoffroy debate on the doctrine of the unity of composition, Whewell advocated the view that teleological considerations had a large and direct share in physiological and anatomical investigation. According to Whewell, it was impossible to approach anatomical or physiological phenomena without taking into account the *a priori* conviction of a creative purpose in the arrangement of organs and functions. The more Whewell relied on ideal conceptions as the key factors of the advance of science, the more he tended to include the scientific doctrines and concepts he approved of in the growing universe of *a priori* necessary conditions of experience. Thus, in *The Philosophy of the Inductive Sciences* the concept of final causes advanced from the status of 'invincible conviction' to the rank of 'Fundamental Idea', 'not *deduced* from the phenomena by reasoning, but *assumed* as the only condition under which we can reason on such subjects at all'.[9]

---

[7] Whewell, *History*, vol. iii, Book xvii, Ch. 8 'The doctrine of final causes in physiology'.

[8] Whewell, *Bridgewater Treatise* III *(Astronomy and General Physics)* (1833), Book iii, Ch. 7 'Of final causes', pp. 352–3.

[9] Whewell, *History*, vol. iii, pp. 507–15 and *Philosophy* vol. i, Book ix, Ch. 6 'Of the idea of final causes', pp. 620, 630–1, and vol. ii, Axiom cv, p. 464. See M. R. Stoll, *Whewell's Philosophy of Induction* (1929), pp. 8–10; for a recent discussion of the development of

It is true that Whewell distinguished the use of the teleological argument in the physical sciences from the reference to final causes in physiological and anatomical disciplines. He repeated that the concept of final causes found no legitimate application in physical science. Baden Powell was nevertheless convinced that this specification was of little value, when considered from the point of view of the logic of the natural theology argument. The rules of scientific investigation and the principles of induction applied equally to all departments of science. Baden Powell could not accept that it was legitimate to exclude final causes from physical investigation, only to reintroduce them into natural sciences in order to justify natural theology. Moreover, he argued that the concept of final causes defended by Whewell in his *History* represented a serious blow to the consistency of natural theology. Thus, endorsing the approach defended by Whewell in 1833, he pointed out that 'it is essential that we do not *assume* the operation of Divine will in the process of reasoning by which we seek to *prove* the operation of the Divine will'.[10]

Baden Powell was convinced that the discussion of teleological categories represented a typical instance of the confusion of thought induced by a loose metaphorical use of terms. The correct philosophical use of 'final causes' or 'adjustment' as he preferred, simply indicated that a given natural arrangement had a relation to another natural arrangement. No *a priori* reasoning was capable of establishing the modality and indeed the very occurrence of such adjustments. 'Final causes' were only observed instances of adjustment, which led the naturalist 'to the further idea and belief of design and intention'. The strength of natural theology, he argued, was its capability to prove design: its weakness, or rather the weakness of Whewell's natural theology, was to assume God's creative intention at the outset of anatomical investigations.

Baden Powell could not allow the remarks by Whewell on teleology and natural theology to pass unnoticed: the popularity of the *History* and the authority of the naturalists Whewell quoted in support of his stand were too great. Baden Powell was convinced that the censure Whewell passed on Geoffroy Saint-Hilaire's tenets was motivated by the rejection of final causes advocated by the French naturalist. As he put it, the debate between Cuvier and Geoffroy Saint-Hilaire had been 'obscured' by the 'tendency' ascribed to the tenets of the two naturalists.[11]

Baden Powell was particularly pleased with Geoffroy's claim to be 'the Historian of *what* IS'. The assumption of final causes as *a priori* conditions of physiological and anatomical investigation, he argued with Geoffroy amounted to the presumption of knowing God's creative intentions. Baden Powell did not question the crucial importance of the discoveries in natural sciences made

Whewell's theory of Fundamental Ideas, see M. Fisch, 'Necessary and contingent truth', *Studies in the History and Philosophy of Science*, 16 (1985), 275–314.
[10] Baden Powell, *Connexion*, pp. 176, 128–37.
[11] *Connexion*, p. 129.

by Cuvier. Yet, he argued for the methodological superiority of Geoffroy's attempt to describe the most general anatomical and physiological plan common to all organic beings. Baden Powell pointed out that Cuvier himself acknowledged the existence of 'plans' in the organic world. Cuvier concluded that the multitude of organic beings could be reduced to four basic types of organization. Nevertheless, Cuvier also maintained that further generalization was epistemologically untenable and unsupported by observable facts.

According to Baden Powell, Cuvier wrongly pretended to define and establish once and for all the criteria of legitimacy for physiological and anatomical investigations. The concept of 'final causes' put forward by Cuvier and Whewell imposed a restriction upon God's plans, whereas modern physiologists and anatomists were able to point out the regularity of the apparently most curious and obscure natural phenomena, like the existence of abortive organs in the phases of foetal development. Cuvier and Whewell were satisfied that comparative anatomy and physiology had reached the utmost degree of generality ever to be achieved. From the scientific doctrines they thought substantiated by current research, they deduced considerations supposedly proving the existence of a creative mind. They were thus forced to censure Geoffroy Saint-Hilaire's attempt to extend the boundaries of natural knowledge. Indeed, the theory put forward by their colleague was jeopardizing the validity of their scientific doctrines and their natural theology. By seeking immediate apologetic results from their theories, both Cuvier and Whewell condemned the natural theology argument to representing scientific conservatism.[12]

Baden Powell was convinced that the shortcomings of the methodology privileged by Cuvier and Whewell were unfortunately common. Natural theologians in general paid little attention to the question of whether the existence of a creative power was better inferred from known natural laws or from classes of phenomena still unexplained. Baden Powell believed that failure fully to appreciate the relevance of this basic question caused serious and recurrent problems to the friends of religion. Natural theologians failed to realize that a cosmic arrangement based on the uniform action of unvarying laws represented the highest evidence of an omnipotent creative mind. Instead they considered the failure to provide a scientific explanation of phenomena or class of extraordinary events, as an indication of the action of a supernatural agent. Taking an opposite line, Baden Powell argued that phenomena still unexplained and alleged exceptions to the uniformity of nature represented the real obstacle to the natural theology argument. Baden Powell emphasized that events interrupting the order of nature were facts to be explained by naturalists and a problem for the natural theologian.

The natural theologians who looked at unexplained events as the proof of

[12] *Connexion*, pp. 130–1; on Cuvier and Geoffroy Saint-Hilaire, the English debate on philosophical anatomy and the doctrine of the unity of organic composition, and the relative bibliography, see ch. 15 below.

God's intervention in nature were forced to censure as impious, hypotheses providing a provisional explanation of newly discovered phenomena. Baden Powell increasingly came to regard conjectural hypotheses as auxiliary proofs of the philosophical natural theology he developed. It is not surprising, therefore, that he took part in the debate on species with a strong presumption in favour of a natural explanation of the succession of organic forms throughout the history of the earth. It is also interesting to point out that Baden Powell developed the apologetic scheme he deployed in later years to deal with transformist hypotheses, before the debate on species became a major feature of the fourth and fifth decade of the century. In 1838 he referred to the transformist hypothesis of Lamarck or Geoffroy Saint-Hilaire as legitimate conjectures. He also opposed the attempt by Whewell to proscribe the debate on the origin of species from natural history.[13]

The critique of natural theology and the examples Baden Powell gave of its logical and scientific weakness marked the distance between his brand of natural theology and that proposed by the leading contributors to the Bridgewater series. Nevertheless, the muted echo of his work proved that he failed to convince, and there is evidence to suggest that he positively irritated some of his friends. Babbage, for instance, took offence at what he regarded as Baden Powell's mistaken account of his interpretation of the scriptural passages relating to natural events. Babbage had hinted that it was difficult to understand exactly the meaning of poetical or inspired expressions of any ancient writings. Baden Powell interpreted this remark by Babbage as a positive assertion of the impossibility of understanding the true meaning of large sections of the Old Testament. Babbage did not like his *Ninth Bridgewater Treatise* being attacked by his theological and scientific opponents and misrepresented by incautious admirers. The friendly relationship between the two men underwent a period of cool formality.[14]

Baden Powell's strictures on traditional natural theology and its contemporary revival emphasized his aim of systematically approaching contemporary cultural debates. He thus stressed the need to clarify the epistemology of natural theology. He also insisted that natural theology could not be viewed as a topic in itself, but presupposed a philosophy and required a theological application. Yet, whether his synthesis of natural and divine truth succeeded in providing the comprehensive and satisfactory natural theology and Christian apologetic for which Baden Powell argued, is a question that needs to be carefully considered.

[13] Baden Powell, *Connexion*, pp. 155–76, 148–54; see ch. 15 below.

[14] C. Babbage, *The Ninth Bridgewater Treatise* (1837), ch. 5, pp. 78–81; British Library, Babbage Correspondence, Add Ms 37.190, fol. 337, Baden Powell to Babbage, 1 Jan. 1838. Baden Powell was deeply impressed by the apologetic potentiality of Babbage's calculating machine: cf. *Ninth Bridgewater Treatise*, ch. 2, 'Argument in favour of design from the changing laws in natural events', pp. 31–49, and *Connexion*, p. 157.

The aim of Baden Powell's analysis of current writings on natural theology and the apologetic programme he set out to develop were clearly stated on the first page of *The Connexion of Natural and Divine Truth*: 'The stability of natural theology rests upon the demonstration of physical truth; and upon the assurance of the great doctrines of natural theology must all proof, and even all notions of a Revelation be essentially founded.'[15]

The first claim Baden Powell made on behalf of his new synthesis was that the proposed scheme was thoroughly consistent. He proudly pointed out that the philosophy of science sketched in the first part of *The Connexion of Natural and Divine Truth* was free from anthropomorphic and teleological assumptions. The concept of moral and efficient causation found no place in his account of inductive procedures. Thus, the conclusion that the natural world was regulated by fixed and uniform laws was reached independently of direct or implicit reference to teleological and theological considerations. It was then the task of the natural theologian to reflect upon the disclosures of science reached independently of religious preconceptions.

Baden Powell maintained that the effects produced by an intelligent creature were marked by clear indications of rational arrangement and purpose. The natural inquirer demonstrated that the world was organized according to general rational principles. Thus, Baden Powell concluded,

unless miserably blinded by prejudice, or incapacitated by moral perversion, the most untaught mind instantly recognises the evidence of the Divine existence and attributes and unhesitatingly regards the visible order and adaptations of the natural world, as no other than the created manifestations of the Divine perfections.[16]

The firm rational conviction of the existence of God guided man's approach to the scriptures and the evidence of their inspiration. Baden Powell claimed that the very notion of a revelation depended on the previous assumption of the truth of the 'primary doctrines' of the existence of God and his attributes. The same assumption was also at the basis of man's belief in miracles, the mark which conferred divine authority upon revealed doctrines. Baden Powell contended that men were ready to acknowledge the evidential value of miracles, only in so far as they possessed the antecedent belief in the existence of an omnipotent being.[17]

It is interesting to observe that the summary of the 1838 synthesis of natural and divine truth outlined above is in fact an almost *verbatim* account of the substantiation Baden Powell offered of his apologetic programme. By far the greater part of the *Connexion* was devoted to establishing an *ad hoc* epistemology supporting the reliability of geological doctrines and to criticizing current natural theology. The solution to the science–religion conflict he actually proposed was in fact limited to the emphatic assertion of the truths

[15] Baden Powell, *Connexion*, p. 1.   [16] *Connexion*, pp. 118.
[17] *Connexion*, pp. 216–20.

of natural theology and of their value as the solid foundation on which to build a new philosophical Christian apologetic. A recent commentator probably had in mind Baden Powell's claim to philosophical consistency when he described the *Connexion* as 'the best argued and most intelligent contemporary statement of the nomic-uniformitarian natural theology...the texture of the analogical reasoning involved betrayed a subtlety and philosophical rigour not to be found in the variously deficient productions of, for instance, Babbage or Brougham'.[18]

Baden Powell would have been pleased by this account of his work. It was indeed his ambition to introduce a philosophical dimension into contemporary scientific debate and natural theology, in order to stress the sophistication of the solution he put forward. Yet, a close analysis of the argument of the *Connexion* and a comparison with the apologetic proposals put forward in 1826 reveals a surprising discrepancy between his declaration of intent and the actual philosophical or theological substantiation of his tenets he was capable of offering. The discussion of the inference from natural order to the idea of God – undoubtedly the key point of the 1838 apologetic scheme – revealed that Baden Powell found it difficult to substantiate fully his assertion that the contemplation of nature unquestionably proved the existence and attributes of God.

Irons devoted a long section of his essay on the concept of final causes to examining and refuting the legitimacy of the transition from the order of nature to God. He argued that the scientific contemplation of natural phenomena at best provided the idea of a '"Cause" (or Causes) for all things in Nature'. It was however impossible to prove that the 'Cause' or 'Causes' were *one*, or that the 'Cause' was a person, or to form a clear idea of the attributes of the mind alleged to be the organizing principle of nature. Baden Powell found it extremely difficult to oppose the claim by Irons that the attributes of the alleged moral cause of nature were not open to man's intellectual apprehension. Irons skilfully endorsed Copleston's thesis that the existence of evil nullified the reliability of the idea of God as perfect good, as deduced by natural theologians. Irons contended that on purely logical grounds the striking combination of good and evil in nature authorized one conclusion only: that there were two organizing principles in nature, the one responsible for the good, the other for the evil. Thus, Irons concluded, man was incapable of forming the simplest idea of God's existence and perfections.[19]

Baden Powell felt the weight of the argument deployed by Irons, and could not forget that in 1826 he himself had argued on similar lines. It is furthermore

[18] Yule, 'The impact of science', 248–9; similar views were expressed by Young, 'Natural theology, Victorian periodicals', in *Darwin's Metaphor* (1985), p. 146: 'Powell was the most clear-sighted of the interpreters of the uniformitarian point of view.... Powell's position throughout his writings was consistent'.

[19] Irons, *Final Causes*, p. 143; for interesting comments on Kant by Irons, and the Coleridgean inspiration of the book, see pp. 159, 182, 193–4.

surprising to note that Baden Powell's discussion of the criticism of natural theology put forward by Irons revealed that he still endorsed the approach he had defended in 1826: in other words, that he agreed with his opponent Moreover, the terminology he employed to qualify the idea of God derived from natural theology betrayed a marked shift from the overconfident tone of the opening statement of the *Connexion*. Baden Powell thus argued that the powers of the human mind were clearly inadequate for investigating the attributes of God. The plain and humble method of inductive inference, he pointed out, provided the understanding with 'sublime but insufficient deduc tions...and prepare [it] to advance towards the higher attainments of religiou illumination'.[20]

What Baden Powell contended and was able to account for on philosophica grounds was that, despite their constitutional weakness, man's intellectua powers were capable of forming a partial idea of God's existence and attributes Thus in 1838, as in 1826, he emphasized the insufficiency of natural theology though in 1838 he argued that the vague, partial and limited conclusions of natural theology offered 'at least *some* first rudiments of belief in a Deity' The only feature of the Noetic criticism of natural theology Baden Powell set out very cautiously to correct was the admission of the existence of absolute evil in nature. He conceded that '*bare reasoning...*can conduct us no furthe than to the inference of good mixed with evil'. He did however maintain that it was indeed possible that the human concept of evil derived from incapacity to understand fully the complex relationship between phenomena. An even judged as evil by man could be proved to answer an ultimately good purpose Yet, Baden Powell felt he could not push this line of defence too far. As he immediately pointed out, he simply wanted to stress that the existence of evil in nature did not invalidate the idea (albeit imperfect) of God's benevolence.[2]

It could be argued that Baden Powell's caution in proposing a solution for the existence of evil was motivated by his desire not to refute a crucial feature of the Christian apologetic devised by Copleston and endorsed by the Noetics It is also possible that Baden Powell was aware that the solution he put forward involved his argument in further and deeper difficulty. Indeed, the thesis that human understanding of the class of phenomena defined as evil was intrinsically imperfect, would have weakened the contention that the human intellect was capable of forming a reliable concept of the order of nature. More particularly, it would have been difficult to maintain that the objections against the existence of evil did not apply to the belief in the existence of good. If evil was a relative concept, so too was good.

Baden Powell did not fail to realize that his detailed discussion and justi fication of the idea of God derived from natural theology, contradicted the

---

[20] Baden Powell, *Connexion*, p. 216.
[21] *Connexion*, pp. 210–13; a footnote at p. 210 referred to Whately's discussion of the existence of evil in nature in *The Right Method*, p. 119.

claim that 'even the most untaught mind instantly recognises the evidence of the Divine Existence'. He thus felt it appropriate to add that an acknowledgement of the deficiencies of natural theology did not invalidate the general conclusion that 'reason may supply some first rudiments of religious knowledge'. It is, however, impossible not to emphasize that the kind of justification of the natural theology argument put forward by Baden Powell revealed and indeed widened the gap between the author's initial overconfident statements and the results actually achieved. The 'great doctrines of natural theology' were shown to be mere 'insufficient deductions'. The 'truth of those primary doctrines' amounted to the recognition of man's capability of acquiring the 'first rudiments of religious knowledge'.[22]

The evaluation of Baden Powell's 1838 essay cannot be limited to drawing attention to the weakness of his apologetic thesis or the gap between his declaration of intent and the result actually achieved. It is essential to stress that the shortcomings of his new synthesis were the symptom of a deeper problem facing his apologetic. In the course of the 1830s Baden Powell became convinced that the scheme of Christian apologetic he propounded in his early theological works was considerably weakened by the theological and scientific inquiry of the past ten years.

The 1826 essay opened with the declaration that the existence of God and of revelation were truths questioned by few in contemporary England. In 1838 Baden Powell agreed with Whately that popular atheism was becoming a serious threat to the preservation of the social and religious establishment. Chartist agitators and trade-union leaders rebelled against God and even questioned the existence of a supreme source of authority in the social and the natural world. Unquestionably, the analysis of contemporary social and political threats persuaded Baden Powell to stress the rational evidence of God's existence provided by natural theology. He clearly aimed at convincing the atheist by offering a kind of Christian evidence accessible 'to all men of all classes'.

It would however be wrong to explain Baden Powell's 1838 emphasis on natural theology as exclusively determined by social and political motivations. The natural religion theory at the basis of the apologetic strategy put forward in the *Connexion* also revealed his failing confidence in the internal evidence the scriptures offered of their divine inspiration. In 1826 Baden Powell accepted that scriptural miracles and prophecies attested the divine inspiration of the Bible. In the 1838 essay the word 'prophecy' never occurs. Moreover, the credibility of miracles as evidence of a superior intervention in the natural order, attesting the truth of the revealed doctrines, now depended on the natural theology proof of the existence of God.

As far as prophecies were concerned, the further decline of the Anglican

²² Baden Powell, *Connexion*, pp. 118, 216.

prophetic literature, already well under way in the 1820s, made reference to this class of evidence obsolete and to some extent counterproductive. Whatever the fortunes of the prophetic argument in the 1830s, Baden Powell's silence on this point was in itself a symptom of the decreased confidence in the evidential value of the scriptural prophecies. As far as miracles were concerned, it may be mentioned that Arnold, an author looked upon by Baden Powell with increasing admiration during the 1830s, proposed significant limitations to their value as test of divine inspiration.[23]

In his controversial sermon on the inspiration of the scriptures, Arnold proposed to interpret miracles as adaptation of extraordinary natural phenomena to the time and place where they were needed to support the authority of crucial doctrinal revelations. The miracle was therefore the foreseen coincidence of an unusual natural phenomenon with the disclosure of a religious doctrine, not the natural event itself. Arnold did however believe in the evidential value of miracles. He was also convinced that the miracle of the resurrection of Christ was sufficient to attest the divine origin of revelation. The subject of miracles was discussed on various grounds in the late 1820s and early 1830s. The Humean argument against miracles was a topic widely debated. Moreover, many Anglicans felt they had to qualify the limits of human assent to miracles on account of famous contemporary instances of alleged miracles, such as the gift of tongues displayed by the Irvingites, or the increased theological belligerence of Irish and English Catholics.[24]

Baden Powell was convinced that the modern Christian apologist was faced with a difficult and crucial problem. The scriptures claimed to derive from God and preached his existence, attributes, and doctrines. Yet, the modern mind and sincere Christians had many objections against the evidence that the scriptures offered of their origin. It was thus essential to establish the credibility of the existence of God and his attributes independently of the revealed doctrines themselves. As soon as the idea of God was established on

[23] Harrison, *The Second Coming*; W. D. Conybeare, *Inaugural Address* (1831), p. 68: 'prophecy...must...be esteemed subsidiary to miracle'. Stanley, *Life of Arnold* (1890 edn.) p. 43: 'I have never seen a single commentator who has not perverted the truth of history to fit the prophecy'. W. J. Irons, *On Miracles and Prophecy* (1867), p. 66.

[24] T. Arnold, *Sermons, with an Essay on the Right Interpretation of the Scriptures* (1833), pp. 416, 470–3; on Arnold, see Williamson, *The Liberalism of Thomas Arnold* (1964), p. 82. P. N. Shuttleworth, *The Consistency of Revelation with Itself and with Human Reason* (1832), p. 136: 'none but the wildest fanatics will...believe...in every deviation from the...laws of nature'; on the many 'wildest fanatics' see C. M. Davies, *Unorthodox London* (1876). (W. Empson) argued against the Irvingites that 'the history of Protestantism is a uniform disclaim of the existence of any promise in the Scripture that miraculous powers should be continued in the Church', 'On Pretended Miracles', *E.R.*, 53 (1831), 302. A contrary view was defended by J. H. Newman, *An Essay on the Miracles Recorded in the Ecclesiastical History of the Early Ages* (1843). See also Babbage, *Ninth Bridgewater*, pp. 118–42. W. Cannon, 'The problem of miracles in the 1830s', *Victorian Studies*, 4 (1960), 5–32; M. Ruse, 'The relationship between science and religion in Britain, 1830–1870', *Church History*, 45 (1975), 505–22.

sufficient ground, then the historical, ethical and scientific difficulties of the sacred writings could be acknowledged without impairing belief in the Christian doctrines. Baden Powell was also persuaded that the inability of the Christian apologist and the natural theologian to account for the manifest contradictions between the scriptures and modern science provided the enemies of religion with very effective weapons.

The modern mind was a scientific mind. Modern man considered that the standards and procedures so successfully employed by the scientific investigator were the most powerful intellectual tools humanity had forged. Thus, the project of linking the 'external', non-scriptural demonstration of the existence of God and of his attributes, to the intellectual values of the most popular cultural phenomenon of the time represented a very telling apologetic move. It was clearly Baden Powell's ambition to unify the religious and the scientific dimensions of contemporary culture, though stressing the independence of scientific research from theological considerations and preoccupations. Only in so far as the naturalist was free from theological assumptions was he able to provide a solid and independent basis for the development of scientific natural theology.

Viewed from the perspective of the ambitious plan Baden Powell sketched in the opening paragraphs of the *Connexion of Natural and Divine Truth* the apologetic strategy he actually devised was inconsistent and undermined by fundamental weaknesses. Notwithstanding his claim, his synthesis was not a system of Christian apologetic, but an argument for theism. The transition from the rational principle in creation to the God of the scriptures was acknowledged as the crucial point of the evidential argument. Thus, Baden Powell repeatedly claimed that the idea of God that could be derived from the contemplation of the natural order provided an indispensable precondition for the acceptance of the revealed doctrines. He did not, however, expand upon the theme of the evidence of Christianity, though he was aware he had to prove not only that there was a god but that Christianity was the true religion. The theme of the evidence of Christianity was indirectly approached in a few passing remarks. It is of great relevance to the understanding of later developments that the topic he touched upon in this context was the question of the evidential value of miracles.

The polemic against the thesis put forward by Irons on behalf of the Tractarian anti-evidential stand provided the occasion for considering the limits and the condition of the miraculous evidence of Christianity. Irons, Baden Powell explained, denied that natural theology constituted 'the indispensable basis' of the belief in revelation. Irons was convinced that men were bound to question on rational grounds the evidence for the existence of God and his attributes afforded by the contemplation of nature. It was however impossible to refuse assent to doctrines revealed by a being performing miracles.

Irons maintained that a man who accepted the revealed doctrines on the strength of miracles was prepared to acknowledge the corroboration of the revealed message offered by the natural theologian.[25]

Baden Powell found this argument unconvincing. He denied that a witness who did not believe in God would '*logically* infer from the performance of a miracle the teacher's commission from *some* superior being'. In order to believe that an extraordinary event was a miracle, it was necessary to acknowledge the existence of a being with the power of suspending the laws of nature: a belief, Baden Powell significantly added, 'which, to any one versed in physical inquiries, would be the most difficult point of all'. A man who denied or ignored the conclusions of natural theology was rationally inclined to consider a miracle as an event he was at present unable to explain, but which was open to scientific investigation. Thus, already in 1838 Baden Powell clearly believed that miracles in themselves failed to provide adequate evidence of the existence of God or of the divine origin of a doctrine.[26]

It is fair to argue that the step Baden Powell took in 1859 when he denied the credibility of miracles on scientific or philosophical grounds was theoretically less dramatic than the one he took in 1838 with respect to his former opinion on the subject. In the 1826 work on rational religion Baden Powell accepted scriptural miracles as the undisputed internal evidence of the truth of revealed doctrines. In 1838 he maintained that the kind of evidence they provided presupposed the antecedent credibility of the existence of God. Rationally and scientifically considered, miracles were only extraordinary events, open to further inquiry and possibly to future scientific explanation.[27]

Baden Powell felt strongly that the evidential value of miracles needed thorough reassessment. As he wrote to Babbage, he had intended to write a long section or sequel on miracles for the *Connexion* but at the last moment he decided to avoid the subject. The few passages he devoted to miracles did however reveal the deep change undergone by his apologetic. An analysis of the crucial features of the 1838 synthesis emphasizes the distance between the approach followed in his 1826 essay on rational religion and the one proposed in the *Connexion of Natural and Divine Truth*.[28]

Natural theology, criticized as an insufficient and to some extent dangerous exercise in 1826, became the pivot of the 1838 apologetic scheme, though it is somewhat disturbing to note that in 1838 the same arguments used in *Rational Religion Examined* to criticize the topic were actually deployed to support its conclusions. Indeed, in the *Connexion* he considered sufficient the

25 Irons, *Final Causes*, pp. 162–4.
26 Baden Powell, *Connexion*, pp. 162–4.
27 Irons, *Final Causes*, pp. 162–4; Baden Powell, *Connexion*, pp. 219–20.
28 British Library, Babbage Correspondence, Add Ms 37.190, fol. 337, Baden Powell to Babbage, 1 Jan. 1838. Cf. Yule, 'The impact of science', p. 291: 'in the antitractarian essays of 1836–48 geology and miracles were minor concerns'.

conclusions condemned as insufficient in 1826. The evidential value of miracles was lowered from the primary role played in 1826 to the still important function of proof of Christianity, though dependent on the establishment of the primary truths of natural theology. Having abandoned miracles and prophecies as the axiomatic foundation of Christian apologetic, Baden Powell was forced to extol the validity of natural theological conclusions he was in fact unable to ground on a firm demonstrative basis.

It could however be argued that the new synthesis was designed to fulfil the same apologetic function as the one put forward in 1826. Then, as in 1838, Baden Powell wanted to stress that the contents of faith had no point of contact with reason. The office of the rational inquiry into religious matters was an ancillary one. It was the duty of the Christian apologist to demonstrate that men's intellectual powers proved the reasonableness of faith. The cultural developments of the past ten years prompted Baden Powell to modify the arguments supporting his Christian apologetic. Nevertheless, it was still his goal to argue for full assent to the revealed message. Thus, the central theological aim of the 1838 synthesis was to prove that the existence of God justified the assent to miracles and the consequent spiritual acceptance of revealed doctrines in their literal expression. Reason had nothing to do with faith, but to prove its title to rational assent. It is not surprising, therefore, that Baden Powell felt entitled to repeat the old accusations against Dissenters, Roman Catholics and rationalists.

The apologetic commitment of *The Connexion of Natural and Divine Truth* and the task of pointing out the many factual and methodological fallacies of other people's work prevented Baden Powell from carefully considering the consistency of his own proposals. His 1838 system rested on two fundamental theses. The first, responsible for the proof of theism, was dependent on the philosophical legitimacy of the inferential chain, natural order – moral cause – personal God. The second thesis, responsible for securing the belief that Christianity was the true religion, rested on the evidential value of miracles. The discussion of the evidence of Christianity upon which he embarked in the next two decades convinced Baden Powell that both theses were untenable and forced him to a further drastic revision of his apologetic.

13

Christian tolerance

(i) The psychological foundations of faith

During the 1840s Baden Powell's writings became characterized by the discussion of current theological doctrines. As the Noetics had warned since the early 1820s, the danger facing contemporary Anglican apologetic was that of over-reacting to the social and intellectual challenges of the day. The alleged failure by rational and evidential apologists to preserve the faith of the nation was taken by many to indicate the failure of all kinds of rational discourse on religious subjects. Alternative strategies were avidly sought for. Many of the solutions put forward were however opposed to what Baden Powell and Whately regarded as the dominant spirit of the age.

The Tractarians invoked the millenarian tradition of assent to Christianity and its doctrines. They answered difficulties by demanding submission to the teaching of the Anglican Church. At the opposite side of the theological spectrum, the 'mystics' – a term employed by Baden Powell to indicate the followers of the American transcendental school, or individual thinkers like Blanco White, Francis Newman, John Daniel Morell (1816–91) or John Sterling (1806–44) – made religious ideas and feelings the basis of their philosophy of religion.

In numerous essays and tracts devoted to theological polemic Whately and Baden Powell pointed out that both groups of theologians wrongly believed that the 'external' rational evidence of Christianity was untenable, ineffective or dangerously weak. Joining hands with the infidels, these groups proclaimed 'the dissociation of religion and reason, of Christianity and its evidences'. In the papers he contributed to various quarterlies during the 1840s Baden Powell insisted on the validity and security of his demonstration of the rational evidence of Christianity. He also referred to Whately's work and approved his brother-in-law's campaign in support of the evidential approach. It was however clear that Baden Powell's confidence in the validity of his solution was inversely proportional to the vehemence of his denunciation of the doctrines of his theological opponents. Whenever he attempted to substantiate his tenets, he was forced to admit that his certainties were mere polemical assertions.

In *Tradition Unveiled* Baden Powell emphatically maintained the thesis that miracles were the crucial evidence of the divine inspiration of the sacred writings. When faith was reduced to an act of obedience, he argued against the Tractarians, the appeal to the rational conviction of the believer was lost, and religion became a matter of mere feelings, common to all religions true or false. The establishment of the evidential value of miracles was therefore essential to the claim that Christianity was the true religion. It is interesting to note in this context that of the two theses which characterized the 1838 apologetic synthesis – the inference from the order of nature to God, and the credibility of the Christian miracles – it was the latter which was first submitted to a fundamental reassessment. Indeed, the polemic against the Tractarians developed in *Tradition Unveiled* represented the only explicit defence of the traditional concept of miracles upon which Baden Powell ventured after 1838.[1]

In his 1859 critical review of Baden Powell's intellectual career Whately quoted at great length the discussion in *Tradition Unveiled*, and denounced the change of mind by his former pupil on the subject of miracles. A close analysis of the very passages Whately quoted in support of his charge, itself reveals the discrepancy between Baden Powell's firm declaration of belief in the evidential value of miracles, and his attempt to substantiate his position. He endorsed the Paleyan argument that miracles were the sole attestation of the divine origin of Christianity. Yet, he also made it clear that the question of the credibility of miracles presented serious difficulties.[2]

Baden Powell did not deny the validity of the Christian evidence, but expressed the conviction that the modern Christian apologist had to search for a more convincing reformulation of the traditional argument. He was not prepared, however, to give any hint as to his actual solution. It was nonetheless clear that the problem was much in his mind. When in 1847 he devoted a paper to discussing the evidence of Christianity, his analysis significantly concentrated on the definition of miracles and the grounds of their credibility. The authorities Baden Powell quoted in support of his view, or the ones whose tenets he opposed, prove that the question of Christian miracles was subjected to serious public discussion.

The current critique of miracles derived from a complex intellectual approach to religion increasingly popular in British intellectual circles. Theodore Parker (1810–50) and Blanco White, two theologians sympathetically regarded by the cultivated élite of the time, denied the essential connexion between the credibility of Christianity and the evidential value of miracles. At the extreme left of the theological spectrum, in his controversial *Leben Jesu* the German theologian David F. Strauss argued for the *a priori* impossibility of miracles. The translations of Strauss by Hetherington and George Eliot caused heated discussion and deep anxiety, on account of their successful attempt to put

---

[1] Baden Powell, *Tradition Unveiled* (1839, 1841 edn.) pp. 49, 38.
[2] (R. Whately, W. Fitzgerald, W. Elwin), 'Order of Nature', *Q.R.*, 106 (1859), 424–7; (Baden Powell), 'The Study of the Christian Evidences', *E.R.*, 86 (1847), 397–418.

into mass circulation the critique of contemporary exegetical thought developed by Strauss. It was symptomatic of his intellectual development that Baden Powell did not appear to share the views of those who saw recent theological writings as dangerous attacks on the religion of the country. He warned his Anglican colleagues not to credit Strauss with the subversive design the German theologian altogether disclaimed.[3]

Baden Powell was particularly impressed by the fact that Blanco White, Sterling and many British intellectuals with them sincerely believed in the existence of God, but showed a variously motivated reluctance to endorse the evidential value of miracles. They actively questioned the need for such a primitive and material proof of the revelation of a superior moral truth. It is therefore understandable that the contemporary debate on miracles forced Baden Powell to expand upon their role in his apologetic scheme. The solution he offered in 1847 represented a marked shift with respect to the interpretation elaborated in 1838. For the first time in his intellectual career Baden Powell explicitly advocated the principle that miracles were not to be regarded as 'real breaches of the great laws of uniformity'.

He was not unaware that this declaration contradicted the doctrine put forward in his earlier works. Furthermore, Baden Powell firmly believed that to the popular mind miracles represented the chief evidence of the divine origin of revealed doctrines. On the other hand, he also wanted to convey the impression that an enlightened Christian apologetic and his own version of Anglicanism in particular dispensed with invoking the subversion of the natural order and reconciled the apologetic requirements of both the evidential and internal schools. In other words, it was possible to please the masses as well as the élite. Baden Powell made the best use of Arnold's solution to the question of miracles and Babbage's accommodating calculating machine, and declared that 'in coincidence with the pre-established order of events, appealed to as concurring with the disclosure of a moral and a religious revelation... we trace design and thence the evidence of a common origin; and we are led to

---

3 Blanco White, 'On inspiration and miracles', *Christian Teacher*, 4 (1842), 333–53 and 'The argument from design', ibid., 5 (1843), 137–55; on Blanco White's popularity in the 1840s, see Lyell, *Life*, vol. ii, p.154. T. Parker, *A Discourse of Matters Pertaining to Religion* (1842): Baden Powell reviewed the first English edition of this work, published by John Chapman in 1846; see also (J. Martineau), 'Theodore Parker's *Discourse of Religion*', *Prospective Review*, 2 (1846), 83–118. On the *Prospective Review* and the *Christian Teacher* see *Wellesley Index*, vol. iii, pp. 337–46, and Sellers, 'Political and social attitudes of English Unitarians'. D. F. Strauss, *The Life of Jesus*, 3 vols. (1846); on the translation by Miss Brabant and M. A. Evans (G. Eliot) see G. W. Cooke, *George Eliot* (1883), pp. 21–5; on the cheap weekly edition of Strauss by Hetherington, see J. M. Robertson, *A History of Freethought* (1929), pp. 148–59, and J. R. Beard (ed.), *Voices of the Church in Reply to Dr D. F. Strauss* (1845). On Julius Hare's 'bitter opposition' to Strauss, see Distad, *Guessing at Truth* (1979), pp. 166–7. On the reception of Strauss by Unitarians, see V. Dodd, 'Strauss's English Propagandists and the Politics of Unitarianism, 1841–1845', *Church History*, 1 (1981), 415–35. (Baden Powell), 'The Study of the Christian Evidences', 401, 407–8, 414.

acknowledge the divine manifestations, accrediting the divine word, to those to whom it is addressed, according to their moral capability'.[4]

For the first time in Baden Powell's work, his discussion of the Christian evidence, and of miracles in particular, took full notice of the contemporary emphasis on the spiritual and moral dimension of revelation. Though convinced that it was important to stress the rational grounds of the claim that Christianity was the true religion, Baden Powell made significant concessions to the 'mystics' and to the apologetic school that relied on the psychological evidence of Christianity. As he implied in the passage quoted above, there were various kinds of evidence, suited to different minds. Thus, some of the witnesses to Christ's preaching needed miracles, others were satisfied with acknowledging the moral superiority of the revealed doctrine.

It could be argued that the crucial point of the 1847 paper was not the hard-pressed and barely convincing attempt at preserving the evidential value of miracles when actually denying their occurrence, but the acknowledgement that the 1838 programme of providing evidence 'for all men of all classes' could not be fulfilled. Notwithstanding its intrinsic weakness, the doctrine of miracles put forward in 1847 satisfied Baden Powell. He was convinced that his interpretation constituted a viable compromise capable of accommodating the diverging interpretations produced by contemporary schools of Christian apologetic. It was only in 1859 that he publicly announced the final development of his ideas on the evidential argument, particularly regarding miracles. In the papers devoted to theological subjects Baden Powell avoided discussing natural theology or miracles and concentrated on the defence of freedom of inquiry in religious matters.

The theme of Christian tolerance had already made its appearance in Baden Powell's works. When discussing the tenets of the Tractarians, he strongly emphasized that he was not questioning the right of the Oxford Movement leaders to put forward their ideas, but rather their claim to be the authoritative voice of the Church. Following the development of the debate on the historical and philosophical credibility of Christian revelation and on the foundation of a modern Christian apologetic, Baden Powell became increasingly convinced that no unity of doctrine was possible in an age characterized by intellectual advance and a free intercourse of ideas. It could be argued that Baden Powell's plea for tolerance represented a logical development of the anti-dogmatic standpoint elaborated by the Noetics. Doctrines were human accounts of the revealed message. Doctrines appealed in different ways to different minds, as the Christian evidence did. Obviously a great variety of interpretations of the Christian message was to be expected.

It is interesting to note that Baden Powell never mentioned the term 'Broad

Church', a loose expression employed in the 1850s to indicate those theologians who did not press for dogmatic unity of doctrine, but preached the paramount importance of the common belief in Christ and salvation. A thorough discussion of the Broad Church movement – if indeed it makes historical sense to use this term for trends emerging in the 1830s and 1840s – lies beyond the scope of the present study. It is however important to point out that the term has recently been applied to groups of theologians, philosophers and scientists who had little in common but the fact of living in the same college or university, or taking part in the British Association for the Advancement of Science.[5]

It is indeed surprising that, for instance, Whewell has been credited with being one of the seminal minds of the Broad Church movement, together with a group of his Cambridge colleagues and friends who widely differed from his approach to contemporary philosophical, theological and educational policies. It is undoubtedly true, for instance, that a common Coleridgean and pro-German argumentative style both in theology and philosophy united thinkers like Julius Hare and Whewell, though a close study of the Trinity College manuscripts will not fail to introduce important elements of intellectual division between two men who did nevertheless remain friends all their lives. It is however difficult to isolate significant or lasting elements of common belief between Whewell, Augustus De Morgan and Adam Sedgwick, or Baden Powell himself, undoubtedly the most outspoken Anglican advocate of religious and scientific tolerance in the 1830s and 1840s.[6]

The late Susan F. Cannon, author of major studies on the relationship between the Broad Church movement and the natural sciences, failed to appreciate the minor and major differences within her own definition of the Broad Church movement. It could indeed be argued that at times she has taken friendship and collegial intercourse as indicators of deep intellectual sympathy. Moreover, her concentrated attention to Cambridge intellectual

---

[5] On the early use of the term, preceding its 'official' introduction into theological polemics by W. J. Conybeare, see C. R. Sanders, *Coleridge and the Broad Church Movement* (1942), pp. 7–15 and S. F. Cannon, *Science in Culture* (1978), pp. 52–3. For representative and contrasting assessments of the Broad Church issues see: (W. J. Conybeare), 'Church parties', *E.R.*, 98 (1853), 273–342 – who actually limited the scope of his avowedly loose definition to the small group of Oxford dons and former pupils of Arnold gathering around A. P. Stanley and B. Jowett; J. H. Rigg, *Modern Anglican Theology* (1857), pp. 25–33; (F. Newman), 'Jowett and the Broad Church', *W.R.*, 16 (1859), 41–67; Tulloch, *Movements of Religious Thought*, pp. 26–62; D. G. Wigmore-Beddoes, 'A Study of the affinity between Unitarianism and Broad Church Anglicanism' (1963), ch. i; O. Chadwick, *The Victorian Church* (1966), p. 545. J. Morrell and A. Thackray, *The Gentlemen of Science* (1981) claim that in the early 1830s the theology of the leaders of the British Association 'was that of a distinct party within the Church of England, the 'Liberal Anglicans' or 'Broad Church Party'', p. 25. See also pp. 21, 38 and *passim*.

[6] It is noted that very reasonably historians of theology never included intellectuals active in the 1830s and the 1840s into the category Broad Church without due qualification and appropriate distinctions. Ellis, *Seven against Christ*, has emphasized the complexity of the issue, and rightly warned against taking a polemical term like Broad Church as an historical interpretative tool.

affairs has produced a lack of understanding for the positions developed by Baden Powell, and has obscured the real standpoints defended by Stanley and Jowett, the theologians who actually inspired Conybeare to create the term. As we have shown, our author clearly reached what, according to Cannon, are Broad Church positions following an intellectual path opposite to the one pursued by many of his Cambridge colleagues and certainly opposed to the strategy deployed by Whewell.[7]

It is difficult to believe that Baden Powell and Whewell were both Broad Churchmen, when the first regarded the second as one chief representative of theological and philosophical conservatism, and Whewell publicly denounced the dangerous and subversive tendencies of the philosophy taught at Oxford by the Noetics. It has also to be pointed out that the ideas of many of the alleged founders or members of the Broad Church movement underwent considerable change during the 1840s and 1850s, a period characterized by deep personal and collective reorientation. The entire question of Broad-churchmanship before 1850 clearly requires fundamental reassessment and further detailed investigation.[8]

Baden Powell's plea for tolerance and doctrinal pluralism represented an original development of the Noetic theological tradition. It should however be stressed that he was the only Oriel man who fully exploited the liberal potentiality of the criticism of dogmatic theology which characterized Noetic teaching. Hampden increasingly emphasized the dogmatic authority of official Anglican doctrine and became one chief instigator of the prosecution against *Essays and Reviews*. Whately was reluctant even to read the works of philosophers and theologians who differed from his own views. Baden Powell did however deny that the Christian tolerance he was preaching implied latitudinarianism. He was convinced that latitudinarianism derived from a basic indifference towards the particular 'truth' advocated by various religious sects or churches. The concept of theological liberalism he defended required on the contrary that each theological inquirer was convinced of the truth of his own doctrine. According to Baden Powell, faith in one's own belief did not imply intolerance. The plurality of truths and of sincere Christians willing to discuss the foundation of their doctrine was bound to deepen the understanding of the revealed message and to clarify the essential Catholic features of Christianity.[9]

---

7 Cannon, *Science in Culture*, pp. 29–71.
8 On Whewell's opinion on the tendency of Noetic teaching, and for reference to the relative manuscript and printed evidence see Corsi, 'The heritage of Dugald Stewart'.
9 On Hampden's 'most determined' effort to seek the prosecution of *Essays and Reviews*, see Ellis, *Seven against Christ*, pp. 163–4. For Whately's typical attitude concerning contemporary intellectual developments, see Baden Powell Papers, 10 Mar. 1855, Whately to Baden Powell: 'I have not read Dr Whewell's book. I have purchased sundry of his works, but I *cannot* get on in any of them beyond a few pages; his style is, to me, so stiff and obscure'.

Baden Powell's emphasis on Christian tolerance and understanding was connected with important biographical events. His second wife, Charlotte Pope, died in October 1844. In March 1846 Baden Powell married Henrietta Grace Smyth, daughter of Captain William Henry Smyth, an amateur astronomer and leading figure in metropolitan intellectual and social life. The new family connections and the life in London progressively severed Baden Powell's ties with Whately. He became acquainted with the leading representatives of the metropolitan liberal intelligentsia, as well as with distinguished visitors like the Baron von Bunsen. Baden Powell's manuscript journal provides evidence of his frequent contacts with Francis Newman, William Benjamin Carpenter (1813–85), Julius Hare and radical intellectuals like H. T. Buckle. He became increasingly aware of the changing cultural priorities; he grew to realize that the appeal to religious feelings and ideas made by his new friends was grounded on authoritative philosophical traditions. The choice of the 'internal' apologetic was the consequence of contemporary increasing interest in post-Kantian philosophy and German theology.[10]

Baden Powell was aware of the basic principles advocated by the internal school. In 1838 he briefly expanded upon the proposal to regard religious feelings and ideas as ontological categories and firmly denied the relevance of this kind of evidential argument for the credibility of the Christian religion. He did however concede that the subject was open to further investigation. A thorough inquiry into the philosophy of the human mind was possibly capable of disclosing constitutional categories of religious knowledge, and providing the Christian apologist with relevant subsidiary argument. The speculations of James Martineau (1805–90), John Daniel Morell (1816–91), Francis Newman, Parker, Ralph Waldo Emerson, or William Ellery Channing, represented an authoritative answer to Baden Powell's request for sound and convincing research in religious philosophy and psychology.[11]

Baden Powell's appraisal of the social, intellectual, and religious situation of the 1840s and 1850s also favoured a more conciliatory approach to the apologetic strategy of different schools and tendencies. The Church had not

[10] Baden Powell Papers: from the late 1830s Baden Powell corresponded with F. Newman, who had been his pupil at Oxford, and W. B. Carpenter. On the specific features of their intellectual co-operation, see ch. 16 below. On Blanco White's debts to German theology and philosophy, see Oxford, Manchester College, Blanco White's notebook and journal entries on Eichorn, Immanuel Hermann von Fichte (1796–1879), and Neander; on F. Newman's early interest in German theology see J. R. Bennett, 'F. W. Newman and Religious Liberalism' (1960), ch. 4, and W. Robbins, *The Newman brothers* (1966), p. 91. F. Bunsen, *A Memoir of Baron Bunsen*, 2 vols. (1868), vol. ii.

[11] J. D. Morell, *An Historical and Critical View of the Speculative Philosophy of Europe*, 2 vols. (1848), and *The Philosophy of Religion* (1849), ch. 2 , 'On the distinction between the logical and the intuitional consciousness', pp. 27–61: Morell, like Blanco White, was a disciple of Fichte the younger. J. Martineau, *The Rationale of Religious Inquiry* (1836), and papers in *Prospective Review*, see *Wellesley Index*, vol. iii. On Channing's relationship with Blanco White, see W. E. Channing, *Memoir of William Ellery Channing* (1851), pp. 279–312.

made theological concessions and indeed proved incapable of formulating a unified theology, as the Gorham case abundantly proved. It did however take full advantage of the administrative reforms of the 1830s and was making appreciable progress among the once neglected urban population. The advance of Dissent had been stopped. The Unitarian leadership took positive steps towards establishing good relations with the Anglican intelligentsia, proposing a united front against Roman Catholics and radical Dissenters. They also and vehemently opposed the Christian Socialists and any concession to pressure from below, thereby finding points of contact with the more conservative factions within the Anglican Church.

The acceptance of a basically Coleridgean and pro-German religious philosophy by influential groups of Anglican intellectuals helped establish a current of cultural sympathy between the Unitarian 'transcendentalists' and the Coleridgeans. This was not, however, the only feature of the Unitarian outlook which attracted the sympathy of intellectuals like Lyell, De Morgan or Baden Powell. There was indeed a substantial and marked difference between conversion to the radical Unitarianism of the 1800s, and adhesion to the philosophy of Unitarian thinkers active in the 1840s and the 1850s. The Unitarian preachers of the later period spoke to the social élites and made clear their opposition to the dangerous demagogic teaching of the evangelicals and the Christian Socialists, or the fervent apostolate among the poor of the pro-Catholic and the evangelical factions within the Anglican Church. Unitarian thought now relied upon the religious philosophy elaborated by James Martineau and, in its more radical expression, on the anti-Providential philosophy of William Rathbone Greg (1809–81).[12]

Leading Unitarian representatives felt that the Christian concept of providence, and the Christian practice of charity were the remnants of a primitive and anthropomorphic religion. 'Iron laws' governed the natural and the social world. True charity was to teach men this universal truth, not to give them the illusion of ministering to their condition with the utopian schemes of a Christian co-operative society. Francis Newman, who in the 1840s and 1850s allied himself to the Liverpool Unitarians, resented the invitation by Christ to the apostles to abandon their work and follow him: this was to him the starting point of social subversion. Newman's combination of a basic evangelical and emotional religious philosophy with a deep dislike for any form of social equality and Christian brotherhood made him rather popular with many factions of the intellectual élite.[13]

Baden Powell was aware that his apologetic, based on the natural theology

---

12 Wigmore-Beddoes, 'Affinity between Unitarianism and Broad Church'; on the interpretation of Christian charity by Unitarians, see A. Holt, *A Ministry to the Poor* (1936). W. R. Greg, *The Creed of Christendom* (1851), pp. 251–76.

13 Oxford, Manchester College, Newman Correspondence, 58 letters to J. Martineau, letter 14: 5 Dec. 1847: Christ 'was a carpenter, he left his trade, and wandered about, living on the substance of others...he fiercely attacked the rulers of his land'.

argument, did not please a class of thinkers preoccupied with establishing clearly marked divisions in both this and the other world. To those who expressed concern that biblical criticism and the sophisticated transcendental apologetic were shaking the belief of the masses, William Rathbone Greg replied that the masses always believed what they were told by their betters. The British population had to be educated to the new truth. Notwithstanding the deep difference between his interpretation of the natural theology argument, and that put forward by the Bridgewater authors and their epigones, Baden Powell realized that he had to justify his apologetic solution to his new audience. He was aware that the great majority within the London theological and philosophical élites considered natural theology inadequate as a meaningful contribution to the study of religious experience.[14]

Conservative philosophers and theologians like William Hamilton or Henry Longueville Mansel conceded that inquiry into the classic natural theology proof of the existence of God failed to satisfy the requirements of a philosophically consistent Christian apologetic. A paragraph on 'Final Causes and Natural Theology' in the *Essays on the Spirit of the Inductive Philosophy* published in 1855 represented Baden Powell's last attempt at reconciling the evidential argument defended in 1838 with the new philosophical and theological trends. As far as natural theology was concerned, Baden Powell fully conceded that 'those arguments, when correctly understood, lead only to a *very limited* conclusion; and one which falls infinitely *short* of those high moral and spiritual intuitions on which Mr. F. Newman grounds his religious views'.[15]

The concept of divine personality derived from natural theology was insufficient to prove the existence of the divine attributes, in particular of God's infinite omnipotence and benevolence. Baden Powell's 1855 critique of these attributes was clearly designed to deny the existence of miracles and the concept of providence. The God disclosed by the contemplation of nature never altered his course. In 1855 Baden Powell felt he was free to reply again to the remarks made by Copleston on the existence of evil in nature. In the *Connexion* he attempted a justification of the existence of evil in the moral and the natural world. In 1855 he had no hesitation in endorsing Copleston's views and drew the conclusion that the existence of evil in nature proved the insufficiency and philosophical weakness of the human concept of benevolence and providence. 'Providence' was never to be understood as a benevolent intervention in the arrangement of natural phenomena, but as 'the preservation of pre-ordained causes for the general good, not the individual one'.[16]

Baden Powell agreed with the intuitionists that the results of physical

[14] Greg, *The Creed of Christendom*, p. 241. Whately approved Greg's ultra-conservative political stand, but deprecated his 'anti-religious enthusiasm', see E. Whately, *Life and Correspondence of Richard Whately*, 2 vols. (1866), vol. ii, pp. 231–2 and 209.
[15] Baden Powell, *Essays*, p. 146. The reference is to F. Newman, *The Soul* (1849).
[16] Baden Powell, *Essays*, pp. 162–3.

investigation 'prove nothing but a physical cause' and announced that he had no objection to raise against the new 'internal' school of Christian apologetic. Those Christian philosophers who felt they found a resting place in the 'sole consciousness of internal emotions or the intuitive impressions of individual experience' were reassured that the 'external' evidence of Christianity – indeed the little of it Baden Powell offered in 1855 – 'offers no disparagement' to the psychological argument. The shortcomings of the 1838 synthesis, pointed out above, were fully acknowledged by Baden Powell in 1855. He expressed the conviction that the argumentative chain he devised in 1838 was incapable of performing any meaningful apologetic function. The conclusions reached with the help of the natural theology argument were at most of a negative kind. The inductive conclusions on the succession of natural phenomena did not oppose the claims of faith, but did not provide a foundation for them either.[17]

Emphasis on the contemplation of the order of nature did not exclude, however, the possibility of drawing an analogical inference from the existence of a plan in nature, to the existence of a designer of the natural harmony. Whately's edition of Archbishop King's sermon was referred to as the authoritative assessment of the origin and limits of analogical reasoning in religious matters. It is interesting that Baden Powell, as had been the case with the natural theology argument of 1838, was converting into positive the negative judgement he passed in 1826 upon the role of analogical reasoning in religion. In 1826 he repeated with Copleston and Whately that there was no sound cognitive element in the analogical inference from man to God. In 1855 he did however explain the transition from design to designer in analogical terms. Yet, there was little doubt that the criticism of traditional natural theology which he put forward was in fact undermining the external evidence of theism and of Christianity. Contrary to the argument deployed in 1838, Baden Powell clearly believed in 1855 that natural theology could no longer be regarded as the cornerstone of a convincing Christian apologetic.[18]

(ii) New alliances

The 1855 *Essays* represented the peak of Baden Powell's popularity. In less than a year a new edition of the work was called for. The publishers, Longmans, immediately committed themselves to publishing two series of essays by Baden Powell, *Christianity Without Judaism*, which appeared in 1856, and the *Order of Nature*, published in June 1859. The success of the *Essays* had various causes. Baden Powell succeeded in condensing the philosophical and theological reflections of the past twenty years into a series of essays touching upon the most controversial issues debated in contemporary England.

---

[17] *Essays*, p. 163; see also p. 143 for a quotation from J. Sterling, *Essays and Tales*, ed. with a memoir by J. C. Hare (1848), pp. 121–3.

[18] Baden Powell, *Essays*, p.166.

His epistemological theory of the philosophy of conjecture allowed Baden Powell to review with calm superiority such delicate topics as the plurality of worlds or the debate on the *Vestiges of the Natural History of Creation*. The coverage of a variety of philosophical and scientific topics forced him to clarify many of his ideas and to acknowledge the insufficiency of his 1838 synthesis. He did, however, fail to provide satisfactory solutions for the many problems left unsolved by his abandoning the natural theology approach of 1838.

In view of later pronouncements on his work by Francis Newman and contributors to the *Westminster Review*, it is fair to argue that Baden Powell discussed with his radical theological friends the merits and limits of his approach to religious philosophy. Hints in the George Eliot correspondence prove that Baden Powell's 1855 essays pleased the group of London intellectuals attempting to provide theological radicalism with a unified strategy and an appropriate editorial platform. From the late 1840s, a group including authors like Robert William Mackay (1803–82), Charles (1809–50) and Sara Hennell, Francis Newman and Charles Bray (1811–84) aimed at bringing together what they regarded as the vital elements of current British philosophy and theology. Their project was ecumenical. Strong emphasis was placed on tolerance and free debate. The *Westminster Review* group was also supported by several distinguished philosophical and theological radicals of different schools, including John Stuart Mill, James and Harriet Martineau, Emerson, Parker and George Combe.[19]

Baden Powell undoubtedly felt he was witnessing the birth of a new powerful school of thought, capable of attracting the sympathy of the social and intellectual élite. He was convinced that the London theological and philosophical radicals represented, as they claimed, the most vital cultural ferments of the time. They were probably destined to exercise authoritative leadership over the cultural developments of the next decades. The 'mystics' of the 1840s were now a group of sophisticated liberal intellectuals drawing upon a philosophical and historical scholarship largely ignored or opposed by the great majority of the Anglican clergy.

Baden Powell's tolerance and critical fairness, as well as his ambition to appear informed on the most recent developments in theological and

---

[19] G. S. Haight (ed.), *The George Eliot Letters*, 9 vols. (1954–78), vol. ii, pp. 205, 264, 279, 382, and *George Eliot and John Chapman*. Evidence quoted by Haight suggests that the anatomist Richard Owen was a frequent guest at Chapman's. Recent work by Adrian Desmond, based on the systematic study of the important and much neglected Owen papers collection preserved in the British Museum (Natural History), throws much needed light on this group of radical intellectuals, and their contacts with the scientific milieu: see Desmond, *Archetypes and Ancestors* (1982). In his journal, Baden Powell never mentioned John Chapman or George Eliot, though he had frequent contacts with George Henry Lewes, Richard Owen, Edward Forbes, William Benjamin Carpenter and Robert Chambers, all active guests at the soirées organized by Chapman. Herbert Spencer too is never mentioned in the journal: see ch. 18 below. On the *W.R.*, see *Wellesley Index*, vol. iii, pp. 528–58.

philosophical thought made his 1855 *Essays* a book widely read and discussed. To many readers, the plain style of the narrative made the book a useful summary and guide to the cultural debates of the day. Baden Powell was regarded by a man like Lewes as one of the few Anglican divines with whom it was possible to have a constructive discussion. The 1855 *Essays* was highly appreciated by Henry Thomas Buckle, an author whose great popularity in the late 1850s was soon followed by an equally unjustified obscurity.

It is interesting that Baden Powell's journal shows Buckle to be the London intellectual most frequently visited during the 1850s. Yet, no biographer of Buckle has ever expanded upon this relationship. It is significant that when Buckle was asked to name two reliable and authoritative referees capable of advising the publisher John Parker on the merits of his manuscript *History of Civilization* he mentioned Baden Powell as a friend and intellectual of undisputed authority. As we shall emphasize below, Baden Powell, Henry Thomas Buckle, William Benjamin Carpenter, Francis Newman and Robert Chambers constituted a group animated by well-defined social and intellectual aims, interacting with intellectuals such as George Eliot, John Stuart Mill and George Henry Lewes who are better remembered today.[20]

The success of the *Essays* attracted favourable attention from the highest quarters and helped Baden Powell to solve to his advantage a conflict with the Bishop of London. In January and February 1855 he preached a series of sermons from the pulpit of Trinity Church, Paddington. A distinguished member of the congregation, the archaeologist and orientalist Reginald Stuart Poole, wrote to the Bishop of London complaining about the allegedly heretical views put forward by the preacher. The Bishop's secretary warned Baden Powell by letter of the possible disciplinary consequences he could face, were he to persist in preaching unsafe doctrines. Baden Powell's answer failed to satisfy the Bishop, who wrote personally to Baden Powell forbidding him to preach again in the diocese. On 1 April 1855 the *Essays* was published. On 15 April Baden Powell preached at Kensington Palace Chapel before the royal family. During 1855 and 1856 he was repeatedly invited to put forward his views at Kensington Palace. The invitations included the important Easter sermon of 1856. The Bishop of London was thus forced to lift his ban and Baden Powell resumed his preaching in London.[21]

---

[20] A. H. Huth, *The Life of Henry Thomas Buckle*, 2 vols. (1880), vol. ii, pp. 113–14; Buckle was also influenced by Carpenter and G. Combe, cf. G. St. Aubyn, *A Victorian Eminence. The life and works of Thomas Buckle* (1958).

[21] Baden Powell Papers: R. S. Poole to the Bishop of London (C. J. Blomfield, 1786–1857), 5 Feb. 1855; C. D. Dalton, secretary to Blomfield, to Baden Powell, 8 Feb. 1855; draft of letter from Baden Powell to Blomfield, 10 Feb. 1855; Blomfield to Baden Powell, 13 Feb. 1855: Blomfield retired in 1856. In a charge delivered in 1854 Blomfield launched a powerful attack against the Broad Church, which made religion 'subservient to temporal and earthly purposes of social progress' and 'deny the inspiration of the scripture'. In the life of his father, Alfred Blomfield printed excerpts from the charge, immediately followed by the Bishop's letter to Baden Powell, though the name of the Savilian Professor was not printed. See *A Memoir of*

The success of the book does not absolve the commentator from critically examining the actual standpoint defended by Baden Powell nor did it settle the problems the author left open. The 1855 *Essays* did not deal systematically with natural theology. Baden Powell did, however, make clear his change of mind on the apologetic value and limitations of natural theology. No reference was made to the evidential value of miracles or to the theological implications of the concept of the invariable nomic uniformity of nature defended in the essays. Yet, the question of miracles and the evaluation of the various Christian apologetic or theistic strategies were topics central to the cultural policy of the *Westminster Review* group, which represented the chief dialectical target of the *Essays*.

It is therefore fair to argue that Francis Newman or other members of the radical *Westminster Review* circle stimulated Baden Powell to explain in positive and direct terms his actual stand on these topics. Moreover, the 1855 *Essays* proved Baden Powell's difficulty in establishing an epistemologically reliable proof of the existence of the Christian God. Thus, in view of the key position held by the inference from natural theology in Baden Powell's theological contributions from 1838 to 1855, it is understandable that the apologetic category he decided to examine in the light of recent philosophical and theological developments was the question of the relationship between the scientific description of nature and the foundation of the idea of God.[22]

It is appropriate to mention in this context that in 1854 Baden Powell was invited to sit on the board of scholars to examine the theological essays submitted for the Burnett Prize. Two hundred and eight essays on the evidence of Christianity were entered in the competition. In January 1855 the first prize was awarded to Robert Anchor Thompson for a work on *Christian Theism*. The second prize was given to John Tulloch, a theologian destined for great fame as historian of religious thought. Both Thompson and Tulloch relied heavily on contemporary German theology for their apologetic. Thompson was a follower of William Hamilton and, faithful to the philosophical guidelines elaborated by the Scottish master, criticised Kantian and post-Kantian schools of thought. Tulloch, too, was a disciple of Hamilton. He deployed Kantian concepts in criticizing recent philosophical and theological developments in Germany and England.[23]

The reference to Hamilton's brand of transcendental philosophy by authors like Tulloch, Thompson, and Mansel alerted Baden Powell to the danger of

Bishop Blomfield, 2 vols. (1863), vol. ii, pp. 172–3 and 174; see also G. E. Biber, *Bishop Blomfield and His Times* (1857), pp. 367–71.

[22] On the debate on miracles among the *W.R.* group, see: Greg, *Creed of Christendom*, ch. 13, pp. 191–207; C. Hennell, *An Inquiry Concerning the Origin of Christianity* (1838), chs. vii–xi, pp. 113–215, and *Christian Theism* (1839), pp. 1–9; R. W. Mackay, *The Progress of the Intellect*, 2 vols. (1850), vol. i, pp. 6–8, 19–22. On F. Newman and miracles, see p. 213 below.

[23] R. A. Thompson, *Christian Theism*, 2 vols. (1855), vol. i, pp. 38, 92 and vol. ii, p. 230. J. Tulloch, *Theism: The witness of reason and nature to an all wise and beneficent creator* (1855), pp. 252, 288–95.

a sharp reaction by moderate and conservative factions against the spiritual theism of Francis Newman, the higher criticism of Hennell and Mackay, or the followers of Strauss and Feuerbach. There were also signs of a strong reaction against the positivist school represented in England by vociferous apostles like Lewes or Harriet Martineau. Representatives of conservative religious standpoints looked at their anti-metaphysical propaganda with considerable apprehension.[24]

It was however the reaction from Anglican philosophers which preoccupied Baden Powell. Hamilton and Mansel saw their philosophies as specifically directed against the dangerous materialistic tendencies of John Stuart Mill and the contemporary scientific movement on the one hand, and the pantheistic transcendental philosophy of religion on the other. Hamilton put forward his sophisticated criticism of the limitation of Kantian and post-Kantian philosophy as a classical metaphysical argument in defence of Christianity. Hamilton insisted that the concept of infinity was not accessible to man's understanding. Obedience to scriptural revelation was therefore but a logical step. His pupil Mansel expanded upon the apologetic side of Hamilton's philosophy. He examined the limits of human understanding when applied to matters pertaining to religion and morality. Mansel developed a brand of Christian agnosticism heavily indebted to German philosophy.[25]

It has escaped the attention of commentators that Mansel was also indebted to early Noetic thought. Mansel's discussion of the limits of man's intellectual powers in religious matters was supported by appropriate quotations from Whately's edition of the sermon on the existence of evil by Archbishop King. Irons's extreme development of the criticism of analogical reasoning put forward by Copleston was also referred to. Hamilton and Mansel equally opposed the philosophy of John Stuart Mill and positivism in general. To these authors, Mill's philosophy excluded the metaphysical dimension of human knowledge, and made the relative results achieved through inductive procedures the only reality accessible to man. Though not opposed to science *per se*, both authors opposed the attempt at making science the exclusive yardstick of philosophical evaluation.[26]

Representatives of various philosophical and theological schools active in

---

[24] R. A. Thompson, *Christian Theism*, attacked F. Newman, Parker and Hennell: vol. i, pp. 200–340, and the *Vestiges*: vol. i, pp. 111–28; J. Tulloch, *Theism* (1855), see pp. 72–7 on *Vestiges*. It is significant, however, that both authors criticized the sceptical and materialistic application of the doctrine of organic development, but emphasized the theistic spirit of the *Vestiges*. Thompson acknowledged to follow 'some valuable hints from Professor Baden Powell' when discussing the contemporary debate on species, vol. ii, p. 111. See also ch. 13 above. The most determined and violent attack against the new intuitionist philosophy of religion and the inroads made by German biblical scholarship in England and within the Anglican Church came from (W. Palmer), 'On tendencies towards the subversion of faith', *English Review*, 10 (1848), 399–444 and 11 (1849), 181–94.

[25] W. Hamilton, *Discussions on Philosophy and Literature* (Second edn. 1853).

[26] H. L. Mansel, *Prolegomena Logica* (1851), pp. vii, 74, and *The Limits of Religious Thought* (1858), pp. 260, 265, 363, 429.

the 1850s put forward a wide range of ideas and earnestly discussed a plurality of cultural options. The task of describing in detail the philosophical and theological proposals debated during this period has never been attempted. Indeed, relatively few and partial reconstructions of this lively phase of modern English culture are available. Thus, for instance, critics and admirers of Mansel have exclusively focused on the relationship between his Christian agnosticism and the philosophy of Kant and Hamilton. Little attention has been paid to the fact that Mansel's work represented his response to contemporary cultural developments. His reference to German philosophy was mediated and conditioned by English religious philosophy and the discussions which characterized it in the 1840s and 1850s. A reading of his *Bampton Lectures* and of the numerous notes appended to the volume makes it clear that Mansel deployed an authoritative philosophical tradition to counteract the growth of pro-German British transcendentalism and spiritualism. Works by Francis Newman, Morell and Greg, as well as by Hegel, Strauss and Feuerbach were criticized at length in the notes.[27]

It was against this context of debates, intellectual developments and challenges that Baden Powell submitted his ideas to the final revision.

[27] Mansel, *Limits of Religious Thought*, pp. 286, 293, 297–8, 316, 355, 361, 398, 404, 411–2, 421–3, etc.; Mansel (pp. 189, 287) also criticized Baden Powell's *Christianity without Judaism*. K. D. Freeman, *The Role of Reason in Religion: a Study of H. L. Mansel* (1969), mentions F. Newman once, p. 14; cf. also W. R. Matthews, *The Religious Philosophy of Dean Mansel* (1956), and S. Marcucci, *H. L. Mansel. filosofia della coscienza ed epistemologia della religione* (1969).

14

The parting of the ways: Baden Powell versus Richard Whately

(i) The last mediation

In 1857 Baden Powell published an essay surveying the works submitted to the Burnett Prize Commission, and commented upon current philosophical and theological tendencies in Britain. His attempt at mediating various apologetic proposals put forward by his contemporaries made Baden Powell's reading of their works extremely selective and at times misleading. The difficulty and occasional inconsistency of his later output, as contemporary commentators noticed, mainly derived from his attempt at reconciling intellectual traditions that often reflected opposing philosophical and theological approaches.

Baden Powell's chief goal in 1857 was to show that there was no case for a conflict between science and theology, because there was no common ground between them. This intellectual choice and the actual implementation of it in the 1857 essay were clearly at variance with the thesis put forward in *The Connexion of Natural and Divine Truth*. The 1838 synthesis presupposed a common ground between science and theology, represented by the natural theology argument. Indeed, since the scriptural evidence of Christianity was increasingly questioned on historical and philosophical grounds, the external evidence provided by the inductive philosopher became the key link of the apologetic exercise. Yet, though desperately needed, the link was clearly a weak one.

The anti-evidential stand taken by representatives of various schools investigating the philosophy of consciousness, as well as the Millean criticism of the inference from nature to volition, confirmed the general dissatisfaction with natural theology. At the same time, the development of various brands of philosophy of consciousness and religious intuitionism convinced Baden Powell that the fall of natural theology left the fabric of Christian apologetic solidly grounded on the most advanced philosophical principles of the time.

It was nevertheless clear that Baden Powell felt he had to justify his change of policy. Indeed, he called upon Jones of Nayland, Van Mildert, Coleridge, Irons, Archbishop King, Whately, Copleston and even Hamilton to support his conclusion that the traditional natural theology argument was unphilosophical and void of cognitive content. The various kinds of natural theology advanced during the 1830s were described as 'the desultory disquisitions of the Bridgewater Treatises'. The only deduction legitimately to be drawn from the contemplation of the order of nature was the conclusion that the regularity of natural events betokened the existence of a rational principle. The concept of cause Baden Powell developed in 1849 and 1855, as a sequence in reason and not as efficient power ('the order of physical causes is a dependence of ideas in reason') reinforced at the epistemological level the belief in the rationality of the natural arrangement.

Baden Powell stressed in 1854 that the inference from the rationality of the natural order to the concept of a personal god was philosophically and logically unwarranted. He argued that the religious conceptions outside the reach of scientific or philosophical deductions were not necessarily excluded from the field of human experience. At the level of popular mentality, the 'universal nature of feeling' of awe, veneration and the spontaneous need of an object of worship transformed the concept of a supreme rational principle into the idea of a personal god. Popular natural theology and psychological natural religion prepared the untaught masses for the reception of revelation. The universal consent to religious feelings, Baden Powell concluded, needed no demonstration and was sufficient for all practical purposes.[1]

It was however clear that the philosopher and the cultivated gentleman familiar with the philosophical and ethical thought of the preceding decades was dissatisfied with popular religious beliefs. Thus, Baden Powell allowed that the views of ordinary people differed considerably from those of the philosopher. With the help of strict inductive procedures the philosopher deduced a conception of the world as unvarying rationality and unchangeable regularity. Philosophical deductions and scientific inference were unable to provide an idea of God capable of satisfying the religious needs of man in general. Indeed, the natural theological conclusion of the existence of a rational principle hardly spanned the gap between deism and theism, let alone between deism and Christianity.

Baden Powell did therefore embark upon a survey of accounts of the genesis of religious ideas and paid particular attention to the theory formulated by Ludwig Feuerbach in his *Essence of Christianity*, a book translated in 1854 by George Eliot (who used her own name, Mary Ann Evans, to sign the translation). Baden Powell had no difficulty in conceding that different moral, social, and physical circumstances of different races and ages, and of different individuals in the same age, produced different ideas of God. Ignorance, superstition, and naïve anthropomorphism produced a wide range of religious conceptions representing the religious needs of man. He did however disagree

---

[1] Baden Powell, 'The Burnett Prizes. The Study of the Evidences of Natural Theology', in *Oxford Essays*, vol. iii (1857), pp. 178–81, 193, 197–8.

with Feuerbach's contention that such religious conceptions were 'nothing more than subjective creations'.[2]

Baden Powell's criticism of Feuerbach was designed to question the tenets of the subjectivist and intuitionist school. He did not deny the spontaneous generation of religious ideas and feeling in man, but opposed the thesis that these conceptions lacked reference to an objective reality. Popular religion was indeed, to some extent at least, a subjective creation. It was however essential not to forget that the scientific and philosophical proof of the existence of a rational principle in nature proved, according to Baden Powell, that the subjective creation had an objective foundation.

At first sight, the apologetic scheme put forward in 1857 seems to preserve traces of the 1838 solution. Science and philosophy proved the order of nature. The concept of a mind in nature provided the antecedent credibility of the personal God, revealed in the scriptures. It is not difficult to perceive, however, that the resemblance was superficial. In 1838 Baden Powell maintained that the 'doctrines' of natural theology disclosed a god endowed with personal attributes, imperfectly, albeit positively, apprehended. In 1857 Baden Powell's overtly deistic natural theology only provided the concept of a universal rational principle which corrected the concept of god spontaneously generated by the human consciousness. '*It is the peculiar function, then, of the PHYSICAL argument to correct, to regulate, to confirm the internal impressions by the appeal to external fact.* The *subjective* ideas are thus rendered objective also: the vague and undefined emotions are reduced to a definite standard.'[3]

The existence of a supreme rational principle in nature was 'the conviction of improved knowledge and scientific research'. Baden Powell was confident that the analysis of the various levels and kinds of apologetic arguments – based on the acknowledgement of a plurality of intellectual and spiritual constitutions – provided an articulated conciliatory approach to contemporary theological debates.

In the last paragraph of the 1857 essay Baden Powell reassured the reader that his brand of philosophical apologetic confirmed that revelation was the only source of instruction in religious matters. The study of the religious consciousness proved the constitutional truth of the idea of God. The study of nature proved its ontological truth. Both lines of inquiry, he reassuringly claimed, established the truth of Christianity. Moreover, Baden Powell declared that his Christian apologetic was 'equally adapted to the wants and desires of the humblest, and satisfactory to the aspirations of the highest stages of human enlightenment'.[4]

It was not difficult to perceive that the reconciliation between inductive philosophy and theological metaphysics proposed by Baden Powell failed to

[2] 'The Burnett Prizes', p. 201, reference to Feuerbach, *The Essence of Christianity* (1854), p. 125.
[3] Baden Powell, 'The Burnett Prizes', p. 203.   [4] 'The Burnett Prizes', p. 203.

provide adequate substantiation of the claim that Christianity was the only true religion. Furthermore, the impossibility of miracles on philosophical and scientific grounds precluded any meaningful appeal to miracles as evidence of Christianity. In both 1855 and 1857 Baden Powell provided hints as to the possible solution of the crucial problem facing his apologetic. He increasingly came to rely on the theory of the progressive historical development of religious consciousness, according to which Christianity was acknowledged as the highest stage of mankind's spiritual progress.

It is interesting to note that Baden Powell did not endorse the Comtean theory of the three stages of philosophical development – theological, metaphysical and positive – or Theodore Parker's interpretation of the positivist philosophy of history in terms of religious psychology. It is appropriate to recall that already in the early 1820s Baden Powell viewed Christianity as a marked improvement on Judaism. The reign of the spirit superseded the reign of the law. God's dispensations were suited to the cultural level of the chosen people and represented a powerful means of education and civilization. Baden Powell approached the various French, German, and American theories of development with the calm superiority of the intellectual who had held analogous views since the days of his early contributions to theology. He was also convinced that the fierce opposition to the theory of development voiced by Mansel represented an excessive reaction to the theoretical and historiographical excesses of the positivists and of the German school. It was indeed possible to use the theory of religious development as a basis for arguing that the truth of Christianity was proved by the immediate apprehension of the moral superiority of Christ's preaching.[5]

Baden Powell's implicit denial that there was unequivocal rational evidence of the truth of Christianity and of the existence of the Christian God constituted the final blow to the Noetic evidential argument which he himself had endorsed during three decades. As events proved, his final and open admission that miracles were to be rejected on scientific grounds for the sake of keeping pace with the march of the intellect, was a step that few Anglicans and Christians in general were ready to take. There is no direct evidence as to why Baden Powell decided to put forward his criticism of the evidential value of miracles. It is possible he decided to complete the revision of the 1838 apologetic scheme by correcting the second weak point of the argument, that is, the contradiction between the proof of God derived from the order of nature and the proof of Christianity derived from the miraculous subversion of that order.

It is also possible that Baden Powell took very seriously the challenge his friend Francis Newman addressed to him in the *Westminster Review* of January 1858, in a paper on 'The Religious Weakness of Protestantism'. Newman appreciated his former teacher's endeavour to update Anglican apologetic. He did, however, stress that a religion relying on miracles as the chief evidence of its truth was bound to fall victim to scientific and intellectual advance. 'We submit to him that we are right in insisting, that a theory which places the strength of religion in the miraculous is naturally of atheistic tendency. It entraps into Atheism those students of science who, having no religious philosophy of their own, borrow its fundamental principles from the Church.'[6]

Moreover, in his *History of Civilization* Buckle expanded upon a concept which had become a commonplace of British radical theology. He described the religion of an ignorant and primitive people as characterized by the belief in extraordinary interventions by the gods or god in natural and human affairs. The historian sketched the progress of religion from Judaism to Christianity and the Reformation. The Christianity of the English Reformation was a religion favourable to free inquiry, 'a religion less full of miracles, saints, legends and idols'.[7]

Baden Powell clearly felt he had to prove that the Anglican apologetic was ready to come to terms with the theological and philosophical views of the élite. From early 1859 he made considerable efforts to fit the writing of the *Order of Nature* into a timetable which included canvassing for membership of the Athenaeum, weekly dinner parties and conversations with Leonard Horner, Newman, Buckle, Richard Owen, Carpenter and Roderick Murchison. The style and argumentative consistency of the book clearly suffered from the author's many and diverse commitments. The result of Baden Powell's basically compilatory exercise was a list of quotations with commentary and an unimaginative repetition of themes and solutions already discussed in the 1855 and 1856 essays.

The novelty of the *Order of Nature* consisted of the third essay, 'The Rationalistic and other Theories of Miracles'. Baden Powell rejected the view put forward by F. Newman that the progress of scientific inquiry led men of science to abandon Christianity. He pointed out that modern scepticism and infidelity derived essentially from metaphysical and ethical speculations. It was equally untrue that, as Mansel, Tulloch and other Anglican divines argued, positivism and the inductive philosophy were opposed to religion. Baden Powell acknowledged that orthodox and unorthodox theologians in both England and Germany debated the question of miracles as if the destiny of Christianity and of religion depended on the issue. He reviewed the interpretation of the evidential value of miracles by authorities ranging from Francis and John Henry Newman to Strauss, Feuerbach, Georg Heinnish von Ewald (1803–75), and Johann August Wilhelm Neander (1789–1850). The preponderance

---

[6] (F. Newman), 'The Religious Weakness', *W.R.*, 12 (1858), p. 152 and pp. 140–50, 151.

[7] H. T. Buckle, *History of Civilization*, 2 vols. (second edn., 1858), vol. i, p. 237. In *Order of Nature* Baden Powell quoted Buckle, pp. 83, 204, 279; Mackay, p. 484; F. Newman, pp. 441, 476; Charles Bray, p. 264.

of continental theologians referred to was revealing of the impact of German speculation and scholarship in the 1850s.[8]

The solution put forward by Baden Powell questioned the legitimacy of conclusions reached by the authorities he quoted. He criticized the explanatory contortions of the school which resorted to a complex hypothetical machinery in order to save both miracles and the stability of the natural order. He also opposed the more radical positivist or spiritualist claim that there were no miracles in any conceivable meaning of the term. Baden Powell deployed the conciliatory guideline sketched in 1857 and argued that the acknowledgement of two distinct and at times opposed spheres of human intellectual experience suggested a viable compromise between the supporters and the opponents of miracles: 'It is the general appeal to a primary distinction in nature and function between *reason* and *faith*, – intellect and religious sense – and the admission that what is legitimate object of the one, may not even be recognisible by the other which seems to afford the most satisfactory solution'.[9]

Miracles were therefore defined as 'facts' of faith, and impossibilities of science and philosophy. Interestingly there was a certain similarity between Baden Powell's account of miracles and the solution proposed by Feuerbach in the *Essence of Christianity*. The German theologian argued that miracles were as absurd and inconceivable to reason as 'a circle without periphery'. He nevertheless acknowledged the reality of miracles as objects of faith and indeed as direct creations of faith: 'Faith has reference only to things which, in contradiction with the limits or laws of nature and reason, give objective reality to human feelings and human desires.'[10]

Baden Powell agreed with Feuerbach that miracles were objects of faith. He however did not believe they were purely subjective creations. His intention was clearly to exploit the admission of the reality of miracles at the level of faith made by Feuerbach, in order to argue on behalf of the miracles described in the Gospels. The faith of the believer gave concrete existence to the scriptural miracles, even though science and philosophy rejected miracles from the field of legitimate intellectual conceptions.

To some extent, Baden Powell's defence of miracles on religious and philosophical grounds represented an effective move with respect to the theistic ploys defended by Parker or Francis Newman. Transcendentalists and spiritual theists rejected the historical features of Christianity, but professed their admiration for the superior moral truth revealed in the Gospels. They stressed the spiritual and aesthetic appeal of Christ's preaching and life. Baden Powell invited them to consider miracles as part of the same narrative and of the same spiritual revelation: an impossibility to reason, an object of faith. The

[8] Baden Powell, *The Order of Nature* (1859), pp. 381–460. See H. R. Murphy, 'The ethical revolt against Christian orthodoxy', *American Historical Journal*, 60 (1955), 800–17.

[9] *The Order of Nature*, p. 429.

[10] L. Feuerbach, *Essence of Christianity*, p. 125.

revelation of a superior moral truth was in itself radically opposed to the ethical and rational priorities prevalent at the time of the dispensation. The preaching of Christ addressed itself to the spiritual dimension of man. Baden Powell argued that the ethical and religious development stimulated by Christianity made the believer accept the miracles narrated in the scriptures 'as a part of the Gospel, not as the antecedent or preliminary proof of it'.[11]

Baden Powell's attempt to convince his readers that he was keeping a middle road between the intuitionist and the evidential school was largely unsuccessful. It was clear that his concessions to the intuitionists amounted to a full acknowledgement of the insufficiency of all external proof of Christianity. Judged by the yardstick of the apologetic defended by Whately and indeed by the great majority of contemporary Christians, the solution put forward by Baden Powell amounted to the total rejection of miracles as evidence of Christianity. The only vestige of the 1838 synthesis left in 1859 was the claim that the study of nature and of the procedures of science proved the rationality of the natural arrangement. Contrary to what he declared in 1838, his epistemological and cosmological lucubrations only established, at best, the legitimacy of deism.

There is ground for arguing that the occasional inconsistency displayed in the *Order of Nature* reflected the author's implicit acknowledgement that his apologetic sophistication involved him in perplexing negative results. He thus stressed that his natural theology was an argument for theism and emphatically pointed out that the study of physical causes represented 'the sole real clue to the conception of a moral cause'. Yet, a few pages further on he acknowledged that 'to attempt to reason from law to volition, from order to active power [...was] to adopt grounds of argument and speculation entirely beyond those of strict philosophical inference'. It was thus clear that the acceptance of miracles on grounds of faith amounted to acknowledging the title of 'true religion' to any religion. The counter-argument that Christianity was immediately apprehended as a superior moral doctrine was already questioned by Francis Newman and the secularist movement on ethical grounds. The doctrine of the atonement was for instance regarded as ethically unacceptable. Baden Powell had clearly no reason to offer for preferring Christianity to deism or to humanitarian agnosticism and spiritualism.[12]

(ii) 'Essays and Reviews'

Baden Powell's 1859 essays, like those published in 1855, pleased a class of readers ranging from George Eliot to Francis Newman and George Henry Lewes. His later works were also admired by such authoritative figures as Sir William Grove, Charles Darwin, John Stuart Mill and Robert Stevenson.

---

[11]　Baden Powell, *The Order of Nature*, p. 436.
[12]　*The Order of Nature*, pp. 235, 244.

They did not please Whately, Baden Powell's old teacher and friend. The growth of the transcendental school reinforced Whately's suspicion of all kinds of internal evidence and intuitionist philosophy. He confessed his inability to read the philosophical and ethical writings produced by Whewell, which he regarded as instances of German metaphysical obscurity. He could not understand why Mrs Arnold advised him to read a book like Greg's *The Creed of Christendom*. He did however take Baden Powell's later works very seriously indeed. The *Order of Nature* appeared in June 1859. In August Whately wrote to Baden Powell powerfully summing up his views on the latest apologetic theses put forward by his former pupil:

It is undeniable that most people do, and some do not believe in God (in the ordinary acception of the word, – as a personal intelligent agent) and that some hold Jesus Christ to be the founder of a true religion, while others condemn or deride it as imposture or delusion. Now, it is evident which class a Minister of our Church is presumed (suppose him an honest man) to belong to – for, no one in his sense will reckon among the *open questions* left by our church, the question whether Christianity is true or false. And if he is a rational being, he must have *some* reason for believing whatever he believes. Indeed, you have yourself held up to just censure and derision, those who make 'religion a mere matter of feeling', and who make faith rest not 'on evidence but on faith, i.e. on itself'. And as, in a former work, you have sought to remove belief in Christianity from the foundation of 'Tradition' and 'Church Authority'; so in your last work, you have sought to remove it from the foundation of a belief in sensible miracles. I do think therefore that you are clearly and strongly bound to set forth what you regard as the right foundation; set before you, in imagination, the opponents of Christianity, and the doubters; and bring forward the reasons which you think ought to silence the one, and to convince the other: and put forth these reasons publicly, and clearly and speedily. If such a work should not be approved by all, as superseding all former treatises of Christian Evidence, it will at least guard against dangerous misrepresentations of what you have published: dangerous both to some of your readers, and to your own character for probity. And I trust therefore you will receive this suggestion in the same friendly spirit in which it is offered.[13]

Baden Powell did not inform Whately that he had just written a new essay on the evidence of Christianity, which he sent on 10 February 1859 to Henry Bristow Wilson as a contribution to the *Essays and Reviews*. On the other hand, Whately failed to warn his former pupil that he, his friend and pupil Bishop Fitzgerald and Whitwell Elwin (1816–1900) (the editor of the *Quarterly Review*) had decided not to wait for a retraction or explanation. The October 1859 number of the *Quarterly* contained a paper written by the three authors and clearly inspired by Whately, attacking in the most determined way Baden Powell's work and personality.[14]

---

[13] Tuckwell, *Pre-Tractarian Oxford* (1909), pp. 213–14. E. Whately, *Life and Correspondence of R. Whately*, (1866), vol. ii, pp. 152–6; on Greg, vol. ii, pp. 209, 231; on Coleridge and philosophy, vol. ii, p. 316. Baden Powell Papers, Whately to Baden Powell, 11 Aug. 1859.

[14] On *Essays and Reviews*, and Baden Powell's contribution to the series, see Ellis, *Seven against Christ* (1980).

The reviewers charged the Savilian Professor with having joined 'the infidel party'. They accused him of holding views at variance with the doctrine of the Anglican Church and with his academic and clerical status. They also pointed out his unexplained and unjustified change of mind on the subject of miracles. Long extracts from Baden Powell's earlier works were quoted to prove the inconsistency of the doctrines propounded in the *Order of Nature* with the ones defended during twenty years of theological polemic against the Tractarians and the 'mystics'.[15]

As might be expected, the theory of miracles proposed by Baden Powell was the target of the most venomous darts. The reviewers pointed out that the choice was not 'between physical and moral miracles, but between physical miracles and the abandonment of Christianity as a revelation from God'. They stressed the social and theological implications of Baden Powell's rejection of miracles. They recounted the tale of a worker who questioning the credibility of Christianity with arguments taken from Holyoake's *Reasoner*, had been driven out of the factory by a devout mechanic skilfully handling Paley's evidences. The picturesque side of the review should not divert attention from the seriousness of the charges and the violence of the attack. The review came as a total surprise to Baden Powell, who did not expect such a severe public rebuke from Whately. Forty years' friendship and strong family ties were not sufficient to disarm Baden Powell's anger.[16]

In January 1860 Baden Powell received the proof of his contribution to the *Essays and Reviews*, 'On the Study of the Evidences of Christianity'. It is fair to conjecture that he had no time to re-write the entire essay. It is however reasonable to maintain that the most direct and sarcastic references to Whately's work and evidential standpoint were not in the original text, and were added after the publication of the *Quarterly Review* paper. Baden Powell was not concerned with justifying his change of mind on the subject of Christian apologetic, in particular the evidential value of miracles. His answer to Whately's charges was instead centred on a theory of the natural progress of the evidential argument.

He argued that his apologetic solution followed the development of contemporary British culture. Whately and his friends, on the contrary, severely endangered the credibility of Christianity by appealing to a cultural tradition rejected by the new generations. The 'prevalent mode of thought' and the 'dominant philosophy' conditioned the debate on the evidence of Christianity

---

[15] (R. Whately *et al.*), '*Order of Nature*', pp. 421, 423–9, see p. 429: 'Of this change of opinion and feeling there is not the slightest hint in the volume before us.... It has been conjectured, indeed, that his object has been to supply the Theory of the Transformation of Species with (what is sadly lacked) an actual instance of the sort of transmutations it supposes. Certainly, a fish changing into an ape would hardly be a more astonishing metamorphosis'; W. Elwin, *Some Eighteenth Century Men of Letters*, ed. with a memoir by Whitwell Elwin, 2 vols. (1902), vol. i, pp. 222–3.

[16] Baden Powell, *Order of Nature*, pp. 448, 450.

throughout the centuries. As far as miracles were concerned, Baden Powell invited his opponents to consider the development of the interpretation of miraculous evidence in the apologetic literature. Miracles were assumed as obvious signs of divine power in the early periods of Christianity. Following Buckle, Baden Powell maintained that after the Reformation the apologists of Christianity stressed the exceptional nature of miracles. God's intervention in the natural arrangement was an extraordinary event, designed to impress a visible sign of superior authority upon the revelation of a momentous spiritual doctrine.

Baden Powell pointed out that the transition from the first to the second mode of interpreting miracles implied the assumption of two different conceptions of God and of his dealings with the material and the spiritual world. The God of the early miracles of the Church was the supreme autocratic ruler of the universe. The God of the Reformation was instead conceived as the creator of a system of laws, reluctant to subvert the harmony of the natural arrangement.[17]

A third major phase of development of the evidential argument was of recent origin. The boundaries of knowledge were daily advanced. The belief in the mysterious, animistic nature of physical events was superseded by the conviction that phenomena admitted of a rational explanation, and followed a nomic path. Whately's insistence that the apostles and crowds of contemporary Jews were witness of miracles, failed to grasp the question at issue. At the time of the preaching of Christ, it was common to interpret various classes of phenomena as manifestations of supernatural power. By contrast, an English audience of the 1850s was bound to react to alleged miraculous performances by inquiring into the probable natural causes of the events. The modern mind had developed a strong antecedent disbelief in miracles. The Christian apologist had the duty of taking this fact into careful consideration. Those who refused to acknowledge the deep change that British culture had undergone in the past three decades were blindly opposing the ineluctable fact of historical intellectual progress.[18]

Baden Powell was convinced that the second major apologetic development of the past decades was a direct consequence of the growth of science and philosophy. The more physical knowledge advanced, the more it became clear that Christianity was not connected with physical truth. The Christian apologists were forced to inquire into the essential spiritual dimension of the Christian religion. It was the fault of Anglican theologians that the task of investigating the dimension of the internal evidence was left to Parker, Blanco White, Emerson and Francis Newman. Baden Powell stressed he was far from agreeing with all the tenets of the spiritual theists. Yet, he also insisted on

---

[17] Baden Powell, 'On the Study of the Evidences of Christianity', in *Essays and Reviews* (1860, quotations from the first American edn., 1860), 106–62; see pp. 106–7, 114–23, 127.
[18] 'On the Study', p. 124.

the opportunity of 'giving a full and patient discussion to this entire class of arguments which now command so many adherents'.[19]

According to Baden Powell, the two major strategies debated by contemporary apologists relied upon either natural theology and the miraculous evidence of religion, or the rejection of all appeal to physical arguments by the intuitionists. Baden Powell had critical remarks to make on both schools. It was however clear that he was more sympathetic towards spiritual theism than towards Whately's evidential argument. The difference between his approach and theirs relied on the different emphasis placed on the role of revealed doctrines. Francis Newman submitted all revealed doctrines to the critical evaluation of his concept of spontaneous spiritual humanism. Baden Powell appeared instead convinced that the spontaneous idea of moral duty and religion investigated by intuitionist theists was bound to lead to an acknowledgement of the superiority of revelation, and to the acceptance of Christianity as the true religion.

The combination of the concept of the rational principle of nature with the inborn idea of God and the direct perception of the moral superiority of revealed doctrines guaranteed faith in the entire body of the Christian doctrine. It should however be observed that this reconstruction of Baden Powell's 1859 and 1860 apologetic scheme is only an inference from his latest writings. The preoccupation with defending his standpoint and the difficulty of putting forward a new consistent and comprehensive apologetic strategy made him reluctant to expand upon the actual details of his approach.[20]

His moderate and sympathetic criticism of the intuitionist school sharply contrasted with his irritated denunciation of the anachronism of the evidential school, and of the theses long defended by Whately. The evidential school assumed the belief in miracles as 'the primary axiom' of Christian apologetic. The traditional evidential apologist failed to realize that to the modern mind 'a revelation is...most credible, when it appeals least to violations of natural causes'. Baden Powell concentrated his attack on Whately's work and ideas. It was his intention to discredit the apologetic devised by his former teacher, by stressing that it belonged to the past and was based on priorities rejected by the contemporary intelligentsia. It was thus significant that he commented upon the *Historic Doubts relative to Napoleon Buonaparte* (1819), one of the earliest of Whately's works. According to Baden Powell, works like the *Historic Doubts* had little apologetic value and were to be regarded as mere exercises in parody, witty but ineffectual: 'These delightful parodies of scripture (if they prove anything) would simply prove that the Bible narrative is no more properly miraculous than the marvellous exploits of Napoleon I, or the paradoxical events of recent history'.[21]

[19] 'On the Study', pp. 128–9.   [20] 'On the Study', pp. 130–8, 141–2.
[21] 'On the Study', p. 158.

Baden Powell did not spare the evidential argument most cherished by
Whately, the thesis that civilization originated in and developed through God'
intervention in human affairs. He now found totally unconvincing the instance
listed by Whately of the alleged miracles performed by God to emancipat
man from barbarism. As he ironically pointed out, 'if the use of fire, th.
cultivation of the soil and the like, were divine revelations, the most obviou
inference would be that so likewise are printing and steam. If the boomeran;
was divinely communicated to savages ignorant of its principle, then surel;
the disclosure of that principle in our time by the gyroscope was equally so'.[22]

Baden Powell had no doubt that Whately and the remnant of the evidentia
school still active in producing natural theology literature were 'altogethe
behind the age'. Many of his readers conceded that Baden Powell was on th
contrary a man of his time, though his Christian brethren doubted he was .
Christian of his age. The reaction to Baden Powell's contribution and to *Essay*
and Reviews in general was immediate and violent. Events of the past tw•
decades, such as the defection to Rome of leading Tractarians, the Chartis
crises, and the papal aggression of the early 1850s kept the attention of Anglica;
opinion focused on basically defensive policies, about which it was not difficul
to hold a common ground.

The new ferments within the Anglican Church, represented by the religiou•
experiences of Hare and Sterling, the theological and philosophical investi
gations of Maurice, the scholarly research of Benjamin Jowett, Frederic;
Temple and Henry Bristow Wilson, or the plans of intellectual reform draw;
by Arthur P. Stanley passed almost unnoticed during the 1840s and attracte•
growing popular attention only during the 1850s. The attacks on Maurice an•
other theologians who attempted to update the traditional Anglican doctrin•
became a feature of the latter decade.[23]

The publication of the *Essays and Reviews* catalysed the energies of thos•
within the Anglican Church who opposed innovation. Several Anglican divine
of different schools, ranging from Evangelicals to Puseyites and High churchme;
like Whately and Mansel, thought it was time to put an end to theologica
investigations which they regarded as dangerously similar to the ones pursue•
by the most determined enemies of Christianity. There is evidence suggestin;
that the growing influence of the *Westminster Review* group, the impact o
the secularist campaign led by Holyoake and the popularity of authors lik•
Francis Newman, Emerson and Parker caused considerable apprehension. I

[22] 'On the Study', pp. 156, 157.
[23] A. P. Stanley's contributions to contemporary quarterlies, and W. J. Conybeare's 1853 *Edinburg*
Review paper on 'Church parties' discussed above, gave prominence to the various trend
of innovation within the Anglican Church, as well as the (wrong) impression that a well
defined and more or less organized party of theological reform was already at work. See th
excellent discussion of this issue in Ellis, *Seven against Christ* (1980). See also (W. Palmer
'On Tendencies towards the subversion of faith', *English Review*, 10 (1848), 399–444.

is against this intellectual background that the reaction to *Essays and Reviews* is to be understood.[24]

The first edition of the controversial essays appeared on 23 March 1860. In April Baden Powell felt the first symptoms of the bronchial infection from which he died on 11 June. It is impossible not to suppose that the sudden and untimely death deprived him of the national popularity he clearly aspired to and never enjoyed. It also saved him from an almost certain prosecution. Indeed, a reading of the polemical literature originated by the debate over the essays shows that his denial of the physical possibility of miracles was the target of the most determined attacks.

Baden Powell's 'heresy' was clearly the most notorious and one on which country parsons found it easy to exercise their rhetorical abilities. His death on the eve of the two great debates of the next decade, on the *Essays and Reviews* and *On the Origin of Species* thus deprived Baden Powell of the honour of entering the official histories of science and of theology as the first Anglican divine who enthusiastically greeted the publication of Charles Darwin's work. Indeed, it is not far-fetched to guess that Baden Powell would not have missed the chance of re-editing his survey of the debate on the philosophy of creation, appropriately enlarged by the discussion of the theories put forward by Darwin. Evidence discussed below (chapter 17) shows that by the end of 1859 he had already distinguished himself in metropolitan scientific and cultural circles as a vociferous and enthusiastic supporter of Darwin.

The Order of Nature and the essay 'On the Study of the Evidences of Christianity' represented the end of a long journey through the culture of early nineteenth-century Britain, from the days of the discussion of the apologetic implication of the philosophy of Stewart, to the new era dominated by evolutionary debates, the philosophy of John Stuart Mill and the agnosticism of the cultivated élite. Concentration on the relationship between the cultural priorities of his time and Christian apologetic emerged as the central feature of Baden Powell's intellectual career. The policy he learnt at Hackney and at Oriel, of carefully watching the move of the adversary, he followed with almost naïve determination. It could indeed be argued, as Whately did, that his apologetic sophistication and his desire to prove that the Christian apologist was always at the forefront of contemporary culture made him renounce the claim that there was any rational evidence of Christianity.

It is difficult to formulate a comprehensive critical assessment of Baden

---

[24] For representative replies to *Essays and Reviews* see: *Replies to the Essays and Reviews*, with a preface by Samuel Wilberforce (1862); W. J. Jelf (ed.), *Faith and Peace* (1862); J. N. Griffin, *Seven Answers to Seven Essays and Reviews* (1862); W. Thomson (ed.), *Aids to Faith* (1861); see also Oxford, Bodleian Library, collections of pamphlets on the *Essays and Reviews*, 100 a 21, 100 a 22, 100 f 6, 100 i 1. Favourable replies must not be overlooked; see the excellent R. B. Kennard, *Essays and Reviews* (1863). W. H. Brock and R. MacLeod, 'The Scientists' Declaration', *B.J.H.S.*, 9 (1976), 39–66. For the most comprehensive survey of reactions to the *Essays and Reviews* see Ellis, *Seven against Christ*.

Powell's work as a Christian apologist. It is clear that a careful internal analysis of his entire apologetic output reveals the extent to which repeated contradictions and inconsistencies characterized its development. It is nevertheless possible to emphasize a few constant features underlying Baden Powell's approach throughout the endless correction and revision of major and minor features of his apologetic. Firstly, it is undeniable that he never questioned the truth of Christianity, even though he ended his search for a rational foundation of the belief in revelation by stressing the intuitional primacy of faith.

It could however be argued that the contradictions he was unable to solve in 1857 and 1859 paradoxically depended on his persistent confidence in the evidential strategy, even when it became clear to him that there was no rational evidence of the kind he and Whately hoped for. As he often repeated, the tenet which divided him from the intuitionists and the spiritual theists was the conviction that it was possible to identify the rational foundation of the submission to the dictates of revelation. He thus stubbornly repeated that there was an objective foundation to the idea of God, even though he found it increasingly difficult to identify the rationality of nature with Jesus of Nazareth.

The second constant feature of Baden Powell's apologetic was represented by the concept of the independence of faith and of the basically non-rational nature of revealed doctrines. A rational foundation was required only for the act of abandoning the pretence of rationally judging the doctrines of revelation. Thus, the more he became convinced that scientific and philosophical developments failed to provide arguments for the submission to revelation, the more he needed faith to justify faith. He consoled himself by believing that the modern philosopher relied upon the contemplation of the order of nature to become or to remain a Christian. It is nevertheless true, as Whately pointed out, that the final summary of the alleged apologetic results he was capable of offering sounded like a parody of the axiomatic apologetic Baden Powell put forward in 1826 and 1838:

The philosophic thinker, whatever view he takes of any, or all, of the rationalistic speculations, will perceive that the grand inductive principle of the immutable uniformity of natural causes – the sole substantial ground for belief in a supreme moral cause – must ever remain unassailed, and firmly grasping this broad principle on the one hand, and perceiving the essential spirituality of Christianity on the other, – he will repose on these convictions, and admit that the miraculous narratives of the Gospel may be received for the divine instructions they were designed to convey, without prejudice to the invariable laws of physiology, of gravitation, or of the constitution of matter.[25]

As far as the masses were concerned, Baden Powell abandoned the dream of a Christian apologetic for all men of all classes, which had represented his

25 Baden Powell, *The Order of Nature*, p. 377.

answer to the democratic threat of the late 1830s. The 1850s were characterized by relative social stability. The British ruling classes survived major revolutionary threats by making concessions which did not subvert the basic elements – education, wealth, and political power – of the social hierarchy. In 1838 Baden Powell expressed his conviction that the higher classes of society were bound to lose their social authority should they fail to produce adequate cultural answers to the new radical trends. He believed that in the next decades the battle for cultural hegemony would have to be fought on scientific and philosophical grounds.

In the late 1850s, it became increasingly clear that no single factor was to be singled out as chiefly responsible for the stability of the system. Evangelicals and ritualists, Dissenters and parish priests installed by the Church Commission, helped alike to recreate the bonds of social cohesion within the unruly masses that had been politically active in the previous decades. The riotous element of the urban population was held at a level of constant statistical minority, increasingly identified with Irish immigrants and the lunatic fringe. There was no visible working-class leadership equipped to challenge the established order. Radical leaders of the 1820s and the 1830s often turned into middle-class reformers or even conservatives when faced with the threat of Chartist or socialist demands. Richard Carlile, who suffered prison for the freedom of the press, was not ready to fight for the freedom of the masses. In the aftermath of the first Chartist agitation, several radical leaders abandoned mass struggle for a paper and ink battle to gain respectability for secularist or atheist views, and managed to become the heroes of the historians of the freethinking movement.[26]

The impact of the changed political and social atmosphere of the 1850s upon intellectual priorities and cultural strategies is a question well deserving detailed investigation. As far as Baden Powell was concerned, his reflections on the changed political mood of the time appeased his preoccupation with democracy. Thus, in the last of his works he emphasized that the masses believed for a variety of reasons; the popular mind could never have grasped the principles of sophisticated deism that he proposed or the spiritual theism of Francis Newman, though it had to be told that such sophisticated demonstrations of Christianity did exist. The idea of a plurality of apologetic arguments suited to different levels of intellectual sophistication betrayed the major change in Baden Powell's thought.

During his life he looked for evidence accessible to the average intellect of the average man. The belief in a rational evidence of faith asserted the basic democratic nature of the Christian evidential argument: the truth of a true religion had to be apparent to every candid inquirer. At the end of his career,

[26] J. Robertson, *History of Freethought* (1929); A. W. Benn, *The History of English Rationalism in the Nineteenth Century*, 2 vols. (1906); for recent scholarly work on freethinkers and atheists in early Victorian England, see E. Royle, *Victorian Infidels* (1974).

he had no evidence to point out, except for the fact of historical religion. From the search for the *evidence* of Christianity he moved to the search for a convincing *justification* of existing religious beliefs and practices. He thus concluded his last apologetic essay by remarking that 'the reason of the hope that is in us is not restricted to external signs, nor to any one kind of evidence but consists of such assurances as may be most satisfactory to each earnest individual inquirer's own mind: and the true acceptance of the entire revealed manifestations of Christianity will be most worthily and satisfactorily based on...the...assurance of faith'.[27]

One merit with which Baden Powell must be credited was that of an acknowledged intellectual honesty and an unusual determination to pursue his line of investigation to its logical extreme. The very fact that he constantly revised the conceptual cornerstones of his apologetic signified his dissatisfaction with the solution put forward in 1838 and his determination to provide an adequate answer to the objections of his adversaries. When he reached the conclusion that no satisfactory evidence of the truth of Christianity was possible, at least of the kind he and Whately had insisted upon during three decades, he fairly admitted the unprofitability of the line of inquiry formerly pursued. It is however understandable that Whately and many contemporary Christians could not forgive a renowned champion of the evidence of Christianity for his public admission that faith was based on faith and that every man had his own reasons for believing what he believed.

To the cultural historian Baden Powell's intellectual biography and his career as Anglican Christian apologist offer a unique insight into the changing intellectual priorities of early nineteenth-century Britain. His open-mindedness and flexibility of outlook enable him to be used as a barometer of intellectual change within an important sector of the contemporary intelligentsia. Detailed analysis of his writings reveals the centrality of broad theological considerations in his intellectual development. Baden Powell repeatedly claimed that his apologetic scheme was capable of avoiding major clashes with the culture of his time and with scientific advance in particular. During the 1840s and 1850s, when the debate on species and the philosophy of creation became a central issue, he had a chance of providing a concrete instance of the possibility of reconciling Christian apologetic with scientific advance. It is therefore of great interest to inquire into the relationship between Baden Powell's apologetic stand and his detailed discussion of the species question. In this case too, concentration on his career and his intellectual strategy helps to throw new light on the cultural context of biological debates which led to the publication of Charles Darwin's *On the Origin of Species*.

[27] Baden Powell, 'On the Study of the Evidences of Christianity', 162.

PART IV

THE QUESTION OF SPECIES

The analysis of Baden Powell's contribution to theological and philosophical debates from the early 1820s to the late 1850s emphasizes the need to approach major intellectual phenomena with a full awareness of their wider historical context. Baden Powell was convinced that developments in theoretical disciplines were relevant to the modification of broader attitudes towards society and traditional religious beliefs. A sincere Christian and an active member of the clergy and the university professoriate Baden Powell believed that the Christian apologist had major tasks to accomplish on the social and intellectual scene. It was unquestionable that the progress of knowledge had increased its pace during the last decades. At organizational and literary levels the scientific movement represented the most vital intellectual phenomenon of the recent past. During the 1830s Baden Powell argued that scientific standards of inquiry were bound to influence traditional representations of the natural and the moral world.

His early contributions to the *British Critic* on the relationship between science and revelation reflected the confidence that the results of geological investigation never contradicted the scriptural narrative of creation. Physiological and psychological materialism originated from the political and ethical preconceptions of their supporters. Such doctrines were rendered unwarrantable by modern philosophical analysis and physiological investigations. The collapse of this certainty forced Baden Powell deeply to revise his approach to the sacred writings and natural sciences. He therefore argued that the contradiction between geological findings and the Genesis narrative warned men not to mistake the purport of revelation. The book of nature was open to man's rational inquiry. The book of revelation was designed to disclose those superior moral truths which taught man his eternal destiny in the plan of creation. The truth of nature and the truth of scripture belonged to two different systems.

Baden Powell believed that there existed at least one point of contact between the realm of faith and the realm of natural knowledge. The advance of inductive investigations and reflection on the philosophical foundation of modern science unfolded a view of the universe dominated by rational laws and characterized by the perfect arrangement and harmony of all its parts. The concept of the regularity of nature became the key feature of Baden Powell's philosophical natural theology. The idea of a moral cause inferred from the intelligent arrangement of the works of nature provided man with the idea of the antecedent credibility of the existence of God. The evidence of religion and Christianity relied upon the rational proof of the existence of God.

Confidence in the comprehensiveness and consistency of his apologetic scheme allowed Baden Powell to review the most controversial scientific hypotheses and doctrines debated by his contemporaries. During the 1830s the debate on the succession of species throughout the ages of the earth became a central feature of the natural sciences. Awareness of French developments in natural history created great anxiety among British intellectuals, in particular the Christian apologists. It could indeed be argued that the first phase of the debate on species in Britain represented the reaction to new trends in French science. It is therefore important briefly to sketch the most important features of the transmission of ideas from France to England during the 1820s and early 1830s and to describe the attitude of eminent British naturalists and natural theologians towards French scientific doctrines.

15

The French threat

(i) France and England: hopes and fears

It is well known that the second volume of Charles Lyell's *Principles of Geology* contained a long refutation of the transmutation hypothesis proposed by the French naturalist Jean-Baptiste de Lamarck. Historians have often claimed that Lamarck had no followers and his ideas attracted no attention or elicited totally negative comment. Lyell was, on the contrary, convinced that Lamarckism was dangerously alive and popular among French and European naturalists and geologists. I have dwelt elsewhere upon the question of the extent to which Lamarck's ideas were known and discussed in Britain. Subsequent detailed investigation has substantiated the view that Lamarck's ideas were widely discussed in France and elsewhere in Europe, in Italy – a country Lyell often visited – in particular.[1]

From the early 1800s an extremely popular edition of Buffon's works, edited by Sonnini de Manoncourt, or successful collective enterprises like the *Nouveau dictionnaire d'histoire naturelle* edited by Julien-Joseph Virey and the *Dictionnaire classique d'histoire naturelle* edited by Bory de Saint-Vincent criticized or approved of many of Lamarck's ideas. Even those naturalists who, like Cuvier, strongly opposed Lamarck's philosophical approach to natural history, did not ignore his substantial contribution to conchology and the study of the invertebrata. Authorities ranging from Ducrotoy de Blainville (1777–1850) and Paul Deshayes (1797–1875) to Etienne Geoffroy Saint-Hilaire (1772–1844)

---

[1] P. Corsi, 'The importance of French transformist ideas' *B.J.H.S.*, 11 (1978), 221–44. On the spread of, and discussion about Lamarck's ideas in France and Italy see P. Corsi, '"Lamarckiens" et "Darwiniens" à Tourin (1812–1914)', in Y. Conry (ed.), *De Darwin au Darwinisme* (1983), pp. 49–66 and 'Lamarckiens italiens', *Revue d'histoire des sciences* 37 (1984), 47–64. On often neglected continuities between the pre- and the post-Darwinian debates in European countries, see also my 'Recent Studies on the French Reactions to Darwin' and 'Recent Studies on the Italian Reactions to Darwin', in D. Kohn (ed.), *The Darwinian Heritage* (1985), pp. 698–711 and 711–29. Professor M. Vachon is completing a list of pupils who attended Lamarck's lectures at the Muséum, which is likely to indicate new paths of historical investigation; see his 'Lamarck Professeur', in Y. Conry (ed.), *De Darwin au Darwinisme*, pp. 233–47. See also the excellent dissertation by G. Laurent, 'Paléontologie et évolution en France de Lamarck à Darwin', 2 vols. (Thèse de Doctorat d'Etat, Université de Paris I, Sorbonne, 1984).

and Audebard de Férussac (1786–1836), including several contributors to various scientific journals, mentioned Lamarck as a leading and respected figure among natural scientists.[2]

Lamarck's high reputation as a taxonomist was established in both France and Britain throughout the first three decades of the nineteenth century. There were also several distinguished naturalists who, while rejecting the actual transformist model put forward by Lamarck, nevertheless agreed that it was possible to represent the history of life on earth as a series of successive developments and transformations.[3]

Bory de Saint-Vincent elaborated a materialistic interpretation of life. His view was that the fauna and flora peculiar to islands placed at great distance from the nearest continent proved the continuous production of organic forms. Organic life developed from monads to man according to the physical and chemical characteristics of a given locality. Furthermore, contrary to Lamarck's declared beliefs, he attempted to include the new theory of the unity of composition elaborated by Geoffroy Saint-Hilaire and the transcendental anatomy of the German *naturphilosophen* into the body of a reformed transformist research programme.[4]

Bory was an extremely popular figure of European natural history of the first four decades of the nineteenth century. His *Dictionnaire classique d'histoire naturelle* where he collected the contributions of several distinguished members of the anti-Cuvier party, enjoyed great popularity. It was translated into Italian, and found its way into Captain Fitzroy's cabin aboard the Beagle. The leading articles, all written by Bory, extolled the scientific and philosophic virtues of polygenism and transmutationism. Bory was highly respected on account of his work on infusoria and invertebrates. Darwin often used the articles of the *Dictionnaire classique* as a quick reference work for the identification of the species he collected on his voyage. The 1820s represented the peak of Bory's

---

[2] P. Corsi, *Oltre il mito. Lamarck e le scienze naturali del suo tempo* (1983), forthcoming English language edn., *The Age of Lamarck*, University of California Press, 1988. Sonnini de Manoncourt (ed.), *Histoire naturelle, générale et particulière par Leclerc de Buffon*, 127 vols. (1797–1807), cf. vol. lxv, p. 27, and vol. xciii, pp. 318, 331, 350–5 for comments on Lamarck by P. A. Latreille. The *Nouveau dictionnaire d'histoire naturelle*, 24 vols. (1803–4), successfully competed against the rival *Dictionnaire des sciences naturelles* edited by Fréderic Cuvier, and inspired by Georges Cuvier. The latter publication failed at vol. 3 (1804–5). The competition continued with the second edition of the two works: *Nouveau dictionnaire*, 36 vols. (1816–19) and *Dictionnaire des sciences naturelles*, 64 vols. (1816–45). A comprehensive study of early nineteenth-century French scientific 'dictionnaires' and their European diffusion is still a desideratum in historical investigation. H. D. de Blainville, 'Resumé des principaux travaux dans les différentes sciences physiques', *Journal de physique*, 86 (1818), 88–9.

[3] P. Corsi, *Oltre il mito*, chs. 5 and 7, and 'The importance of French transformist ideas', pp. 222–3. On early English admirers of Lamarck's taxonomical work, see also A. Desmond, 'The making of institutional zoology in London, 1822–36: Part I', *History of Science*, 23 (1985), 163–5, 181.

[4] A. Role, *Un destin hors de série* (1973). I have discussed at length the ideas of Bory de Saint-Vincent in *Oltre il mito*, ch. 7.

European popularity. His *Dictionnaire classique* was completed in 1832, when he had just returned from an important naturalistic expedition in Greece.[5]

During the 1820s Etienne Geoffroy Saint-Hilaire intensified his struggle against Cuvier. He accused his colleague of opposing the development of science and of transcendental comparative anatomy in particular. Geoffroy Saint-Hilaire's defence of the concept of 'unity of organic composition' displayed by all living forms attracted favourable attention. The anatomist repeatedly advised young naturalists to read Lamarck, and indicated that the latter's discussion of the concept of use and disuse of organs was one of the best chapters ever written in natural history. Strictly speaking, Geoffroy Saint-Hilaire was not a Lamarckian. He elaborated his own model explaining the succession of beings throughout the ages of the earth. Changes occurred at an embryonic level similar to the ones which occurred in monstrosities. Some of these abnormal forms, generated in a changing environment during past ages, constituted the prototypes of new species of beings. Geoffroy Saint-Hilaire regarded his mechanism of embryonic mutation as inductively demonstrated by his experimental studies on the incubation of chicken's eggs. His ideas were widely known in Europe and in England.[6]

Tension between Cuvier and Geoffroy Saint-Hilaire mounted towards the late 1820s. Contrary to classic accounts of this famous confrontation, it was the latter who first provoked the more powerful colleague. In a series of memoirs and reviews Geoffroy Saint-Hilaire surveyed his own transcendental anatomical philosophy and doctrine of transmutation in order to embarrass and attack what he considered the scientific and philosophic conservatism of his former friend. Cuvier decided to put an end to the provocation by counter-attacking on a ground he was well familiar with – comparative anatomy.

Even though the famous 1830–2 controversy between Cuvier and Geoffroy Saint-Hilaire never touched the question of species, few contemporaries and the actors of the drama had any doubt that the fate of fixism or transformism was also at stake. Geoffroy Saint-Hilaire took care to tell his readers this, and Cuvier was considering a survey of the entire issue of the species question when in 1832 death put an end to his intellectual and social career. The European fame of the debate helped to propagate the ideas of Geoffroy Saint-

---

[5] On Darwin's early interest in invertebrate biology, and the relevant complex historiographical issues, see P. Sloan, 'Darwin's invertebrate program, 1826–1836', in D. Kohn (ed.), *The Darwinian Heritage* (1985), pp. 71–120. It is to be stressed that Bory's anthropological theories were very popular in Europe. For representative critiques of Bory's polygenism, see N. Wiseman, *Twelve Lectures on the Connexion between Science and Revealed Religion* (1836, 1842 edn.), pp. 118–19, and E. Hitchcock, *The Religion of Geology and its Connected Sciences* (1851, 1861 edn.), p. 237. See also A. Desmond, 'The making of institutional zoology in London, 1822–1836: Part II', *History of Science*, 23 (1985), 236–7.

[6] I. Geoffroy Saint-Hilaire, *Vie, travaux et doctrine scientifique d'Etienne Geoffroy Saint-Hilaire* (1847); T. Cahn, *La vie et l'oeuvre d'Etienne Geoffroy Saint-Hilaire* (1962); Corsi, *Oltre il mito*, ch. 8.

Hilaire. The death of Cuvier convinced many that it was the latter who was bound, rightly or wrongly, to influence the next generations of naturalists.[7]

It is important to stress that Lamarck, Geoffroy Saint-Hilaire, and Bory were not alone in arguing for an evolutionary explanation of the succession of organic forms. Several naturalists throughout Europe were convinced that species succeeded each other through the agency of some unknown mechanism which adapted them to changed environmental conditions. D'Omalius d'Halloy, a leading Belgian geologist and politician, endorsed the belief in transmutation and provided a conciliation between this scientific hypothesis and his own Catholic faith. Constant Prévost, a promising young French geologist, destined to a distinguished career, did not endorse Lamarckism in any form, but emphasized the legitimacy of hypotheses attempting to explain one of the most fascinating problems in natural history.[8]

Towards the late 1820s, and in the early 1830s, the success of Lamarck's *Histoire naturelle des animaux sans vertèbres*, and the importance of the work for geologists working on fossil shells of the quaternary terrains in Europe, increased the interest for the ideas of the French naturalist in general. The *Philosophie zoologique*, Lamarck's fundamental theoretical text, was sought for in Europe and in England. The publisher Baillière, who had offices in London as well as in Paris and the major European capitals, bought all the remaining copies of the work at the auction of Lamarck's properties, printed a new title page, and offered the work as the second edition of the masterpiece by the recently deceased naturalist. The personal isolation which surrounded Lamarck on his death-bed did not extend to his ideas, and European naturalists were well aware of this.[9]

Several British naturalists and medical students knew at first hand what kind of debates were current in French natural history of the late 1810s and the early 1820s. David Brewster, for instance, visited Paris in 1814, attended lectures at the *Muséum*, and met Lamarck. More important for the fate of the debate on species was the visit Robert Edmund Grant paid to the *Muséum*

[7] T. A. Appel, 'The Cuvier-Geoffroy debate', forthcoming, Oxford University Press; for a detailed discussion of the thesis that the issue of transformism was not far from the surface of the Cuvier–Geoffroy debate, see my *Oltre il mito*, ch. 8. On Georges Cuvier as a public man, see the recent innovative biography by D. Outram, *Georges Cuvier. Vocation, science and authority in post-revolutionary France* (1984). For a contemporary comment on the debate, see L. Jenyns, 'Report on the recent progress and present state of zoology', *Report of the Fourth Meeting of the B.A.A.S.* (1835), p. 219.

[8] On representative features of European Lamarckism, see note 1 above. In my *Oltre il mito* I have discussed at length the controversial issue of the fortune of Lamarck's ideas in early nineteenth-century France and Europe. C. Prévost, 'Essai sur la constitution physique', *Journal de physique*, 91 (1820), 347–67; J.-J. d'Omalius d'Halloy, *Elements de géologie* (1831), pp. 523–31. On the influence exercised by d'Omalius d'Halloy on pre- and post-Darwinian French evolutionism, see P. Corsi, 'Recent studies on French reactions to Darwin', p. 707.

[9] P. Corsi, *Oltre il Mito*, p. 363. In March 1827 Lyell borrowed the *Philosophie zoologique* from his friend G. Mantell, and 'devoured [it] *en voyage*', see K. Lyell (ed.), *Life* (1881),vol. i, p. 168.

d'histoire naturelle in the winter of 1816–17, the first of several journeys to Paris. Robert Knox, the controversial Edinburgh anatomical teacher, spent the year 1821 in Paris, and returned to Scotland a convinced supporter of Geoffroy Saint-Hilaire's philosophical anatomy and of Lamarck's transformism. Grant and Knox made no mystery of their leanings in the lectures they delivered to crowded classrooms during the mid and late 1820s.[10]

During the 1820s, several hundred British and Scottish medical students attended zoological, anatomical and botanical lectures in Paris. The growing popularity of the teaching of Etienne Geoffroy Saint-Hilaire, and the spreading myth of the blind, heroic Lamarck – the dramatic, romantic symbol of philosophical natural history opposed to the powerful and dry academic coterie – were attracting the attention of students, as well as of prominent foreign visitors. 'An extreme admiration of the French school of anatomy and physiology has for some time prevailed in England', John Conolly lamented in 1828, inviting students and teachers alike to pay more attention to the works and research of the British school, of Charles Bell in particular.[11]

Information on recent trends in French natural history was also available in British teaching institutions, the medical establishments in particular. We have already referred to the stir caused by William Lawrence's pro-French anatomical lectures of 1816 and 1819. J. H. Green, the medical man better known for his friendship with the poet and philosopher Samuel Taylor Coleridge, delivered in 1824 a series of lectures at the College of Physicians, in which he discussed the taxonomical and philosophical views put forward by Lamarck. In 1830, Jones Quain delivered *Two Lectures on the Study of Anatomy and Physiology* where he confronted the doctrines of Lamarck with the ones defended by Cuvier.[12]

Summaries of Lamarck's ideas were not infrequent in scientific texts and the periodical literature in general, often preceded or followed by harsh comments on the atheistical tendency of his doctrines. John MacCulloch, writing in the then subversive *Westminster Review*, agreed with Conybeare and Phillips that Lamarck's geological speculations deserved 'to be ranked among the ravings of insanity'. The two authors of the *Geology of England and Wales* did however approve the merits of Lamarck's *Histoire naturelle des animaux sans vertèbres*, but questioned the soundness of the first, theoretical

[10] E. O. Gordon, *The Home Life of Sir David Brewster* (1881), p. 41; A. Desmond, 'R. E. Grant: the social predicament of a pre-Darwinian transmutationist', *J.H.B.*, 17 (1984), 197–8; P. F. Rehbock, *The philosophical naturalists* (1983), 31–7.

[11] R. Maulitz, 'Channel crossing: the lure of French pathology for English medical students, 1816–1836', *Bulletin of the History of Medicine*, 55 (1981), 476, 491. (J. Conolly), 'Nervous System', *E.R.*, 47 (1828), p. 475.

[12] For information on J. H. Green's and J. Quain's lectures, see T. H. Levere, *Poetry realized in nature. Samuel Taylor Coleridge and Early Nineteenth-Century Science* (1981), p. 263, n. 41, and P. M. H. Mazumdar, 'Anatomical physiology and the reform of medical education: London, 1825–1835', *Bulletin of the History of Medicine*, 57 (1983), 230–46.

volume of the work, to which they conferred the new title of *De credulitate infidelium*.[13]

The debate over the quinary taxonomical system elaborated by William S. MacLeay, and the exchange of polemical writings which accompanied it, did contribute to the dissemination and better understanding of Lamarck's work. John Fleming, who well knew the ideas of Lamarck, provided a detailed and concise summary of the main theses put forward by his French colleague. He did not abstain from suitable ironic comments on the 'dream of imagination' which produced doctrines like the one defended by Lamarck. Yet, Fleming warned that Lamarck 'has succeeded in making some converts'. It is appropriate to mention in this context that Fleming knew Robert E. Grant well, and had probably discussed with his friend the virtues and shortcomings of Lamarck's theses. It is also interesting to point out that in his discussion Fleming linked the theory of Lamarck to the progressionist interpretation of the fossil record embraced by several British geologists, though with professedly anti-transformist intent.[14]

It would be wrong to claim that conservative naturalists and natural theologians were worried only by the transmutationist hypothesis of Lamarck or materialistic accounts of the origin of life. Indeed, Lyell's denunciation of Lamarck touched upon a far wider range of issues. Lyell clearly considered the possibility that recent developments in French and German natural sciences, ranging from new doctrines on geographic distribution and embryonic development, to philosophical comparative anatomy and inquiries into the development of the nervous system, could be used as complementary evidence by supporters of the evolutionary theory. He therefore surveyed and criticized theories and trends which could have been used to build a comprehensive evolutionary synthesis: Bory de Saint-Vincent was already inviting his colleagues to do so.[15]

Lyell's 1832 discussion of Lamarck and of transformism in general represented the crucial starting point of the British debate on species. Yet, before examining the role played by the *Principles of Geology* in the development of British natural sciences it is relevant to point out that Lyell's work was not

[13] (J. MacCulloch), 'Penn's *Mineral and Mosaical Geology*', *W.R.*, 4 (1825), 462, and W. D. Conybeare and W. Phillips, *Outlines of the Geology of England and Wales* (1822), p. 1.

[14] On the debate over the quinarian system, and the accusation against MacLeay of having borrowed from Lamarck without due acknowledgement, see Corsi, 'The importance of French transformist ideas', pp. 223–4; D. Ospovat, *The Development of Darwin's Theory* (1981), pp. 102–3. (J. Fleming), 'Systems and Methods in Natural History', *Q.R.*, 41 (1829), 320. See also Rehbock, *The Philosophical Naturalists*, pp. 26–30. Fleming, an anti-progressionist, linked Lamarckism and progressionism to score a polemical point against his opponents. Moreover, he well knew that Edinburgh students were discussing in materialistic terms the doctrine of the progressive development of the nervous system put forward by Tiedemann: see H. Gruber and P. H. Barrett, *Darwin on Man* (1974). Fleming succeeded in convincing Lyell of the faults and dangers of progressionism, a doctrine many French colleagues often associated with transformism, Corsi, 'The importance of French transformist ideas', p. 224.

[15] Corsi, 'The importance of French transformist ideas', and *Oltre il mito*, ch. 7.

the only channel through which the British reading public was allowed to appreciate the breadth and depth of the issues debated in French and European natural history.

Robert Edmund Grant published in 1826 an anonymous paper praising Lamarck's theories. In 1829 he printed his inaugural lecture in the course delivered at University College London. He expanded approvingly upon the doctrines of Friedrich Tiedemann (1781–1861), Antoine Etienne Serres (1786–1868) and Lamarck on the progressive development of the nervous system throughout the animal kingdom, though he did not mention their names.

The conclusions reached by Tiedemann and Serres were however publicly commended by William Charles Henry (1774–1836) in the 'Report on the Physiology of the Nervous System' which he contributed to the 1833 meeting of the British Association at Cambridge. Henry relied almost exclusively on French authorities. He devoted the last page of the *Report* to summing up the results of modern physiological researches on the nervous system. He endorsed the recapitulation theory and argued that the development of the intellectual faculties throughout the animal kingdom was a function of the development of the nervous system. He also stated that 'the brain is the material organ of all intellectual states and operations'.[16]

A further detailed account of French natural science was printed in the report of the Edinburgh meeting of the British Association. The Reverend Leonard Jenyns contributed 'The Progress and Present State of Zoology', and commented upon taxonomical developments from the publication of Cuvier's *Le règne animal* to recent publications by Geoffroy Saint-Hilaire. Jenyns expanded upon the latter's theory of the unity of composition, which he described as a modification of the doctrine of four 'embranchements' elaborated by Cuvier; he also observed that the theory of the unity of composition 'I believe, has been adopted by many German and French naturalists, as well as by some in other countries'. British intellectuals were thus aware that the doctrines propounded by Cuvier represented only one aspect of developments in comparative anatomy, physiology and geology. Those who, like Baden Powell in his early papers, forced the theories of Cuvier to serve Christian apologetic purposes were now faced with new generations of scientific authorities maintaining opposite views.[17]

[16] (R. E. Grant), 'Observations on the nature and importance of geology', *Edinburgh New Philosophical Journal*, 1 (1826), 297, and *An Essay on the Study of the Animal Kingdom* (1829), pp. 1–3, 15; Grant eventually accepted the ideas of E. Geoffroy Saint-Hilaire, cf. British Library, Babbage Correspondence, 37.196, fols. 489–90. Important new information on Grant's personality and work is provided by A. Desmond, 'R. E. Grant' (1984), and 'R. E. Grant's later views on organic development', *Archives of Natural History*, 11 (1984), 395–413. W. C. Henry, 'Report on the physiology of the nervous system', in *Report of the Third Meeting of the B.A.A.S.* (1835), pp. 59–91. On the anti-transformism of Serres, see Corsi, 'The importance of French transformist ideas', p. 235.

[17] L. Jenyns, 'Report on recent progress and present state of zoology', 143–251: on Geoffroy Saint-Hilaire, 51, on Virey, 156. F. Tiedemann, *Anatomie und Bildungsgeschichte des Gehirns* (1816); E. A. Serres, *Anatomie comparée du cerveau*, 2 vols. (1824–6).

As had been the case with the earliest comments on Lamarck, the reaction to the transformist and transmutationist doctrines propounded by Geoffroy Saint-Hilaire, Bory de Saint-Vincent, d'Omalius d'Halloy, and to Virey's polygenist views was not always favourable or moderate. In his posthumous and influential *Consolations in Travel* Sir Humphrey Davy denounced the atheism of the sophistic school 'which supposes that living nature has undergone gradual change by the effect of its irritability and appetencies; that the fish has in millions of generations ripened into man'. The *Consolations* are interesting to the historian also in view of the testimony they offer of the spread of development doctrines within medical circles. Though no culprit was named, it is clear that Sir Humphrey had someone in mind when he declared:

When I heard with disgust, in the dissecting room, the plan of the physiologist, of the gradual accretion of matter and its becoming endowed with irritability, ripening into sensibility and acquiring such organs as were necessary, by its own inherent power and at last rising into intellectual existence, a walk into the green fields or woods on the banks of rivers brought back my feelings from nature to God.[18]

In his 1834 *Discourse on the Study of Natural History* William Swainson (1789–1855) praised the labours of his French colleagues, but did not approve of their 'ill-concealed spirit of materialism'. In a later contribution to the *Cabinet Cyclopaedia* Swainson applauded Lamarck's 'admirable arrangement of the testacea, mollusca and shells', but reprobated 'those atheistical theories no less impious than absurd, which he introduced in his writings'. Swainson did however support the doctrine of the unity of the anatomical plan, though he avoided mentioning Geoffroy Saint-Hilaire in this context. Swainson declared himself a pupil of Stewart and of Hampden; he appreciated the philosophical import of the use of analogy in science, and ignored the criticism of those who considered the doctrine of unity of anatomical plan a veiled form of atheism. His quotations from philosophical and theological literature reinforce the thesis of wide-ranging implications of contemporary naturalistic debates.[19]

Several contributors to the *Bridgewater Treatises* commented upon French science. Historians have arbitrarily assumed that there existed a uniform body of natural theology based on the design argument re-deployed by Paley on behalf of nineteenth-century audiences. Scholars have recently questioned this assumption and have pointed out the variety of interpretations to which the design argument was submitted. We have emphasized in previous chapters

[18] Sir H. Davy, *Consolations in Travel* (1830), pp. 150, 219.
[19] W. Swainson, *Preliminary Discourse on the Study of Natural History* (1834), p. 88; on Swainson's debts to Stewart and Hampden, see pp. 116–17, 282–4, 286, 290, 293–4 and *A Treatise on the Geography and Classification of Animals* (1835), pp. 200–1. On Swainson's support of the theory of the unity of composition, and on his career, see A. Desmond, 'The making of institutional zoology: Part I', 175–8. Desmond has pointed out the importance of the friendship with Broderip for the development of Swainson's ideas: the fact that Broderip had been educated at Oriel College, may well explain Swainson's philosophical and theological allegiances

the spectrum of approaches to natural theology among theologians active in the first decades of the century. Intellectual and political developments prompted members of the Noetic group to revise their attitude towards natural theology. The reaction to French natural science by some Bridgewater authors revealed further and serious elements of disagreement within the very group of authors who have been supposed to represent the official Anglican 'orthodoxy' on natural theology.[20]

William Kirby, the veteran entomologist and Hutchinsonian member of the Hackney Phalanx, strongly objected to the attempt at explaining natural phenomena in terms of natural laws or secondary causes. This attitude was also shared by Thomas Chalmers, who, in a passage implicitly critical of Lyell's *Principles of Geology*, condemned those geologists who proceeded on the assumption of the sufficiency of natural laws 'for building up the present economy of things'. It was his view that modern geologists explained the succession of formations 'by laws and laws alone', thus excluding the agency of God from nature. Kirby was even more explicit in denouncing dangerous developments in natural science. He submitted to detailed criticism the attempt by Laplace and Lamarck to ascribe the works of creation to the action of secondary causes. He denounced the atheistic implications of the nebular hypothesis and the transmutation doctrine. Laplace and Lamarck were allied in putting forward a naturalistic cosmology which excluded the repeated intervention of God in nature.[21]

Kirby criticized Lamarck's works in detail, and quoted the latter's lesser-known contributions to the *Nouveau dictionnaire d'histoire naturelle* edited by Virey. He praised Lyell's refutation of Lamarck from the point of view of natural science, and took upon himself the task of expanding upon the theological implications of the doctrine put forward by the French naturalist. It is however significant of the changed atmosphere of the time that Kirby acknowledged the 'variety' of Lamarck's 'talents and attainments', the 'acuteness of his intellect' and 'the clearness of his conceptions'. Only a few years earlier, Kirby would have employed a different language to discuss scientific theories allegedly leading to atheism and materialism.

Sir Charles Bell too was aware of recent French developments in natural history. He avoided names, but the targets of his strictures were immediately

[20] D. Ospovat, 'Perfect adaptation and teleological explanation', *Studies in the History of Biology*, 3 (1978), 33–56; Corsi, 'Natural theology, the methodology of science and the question of species in the works of the Reverend Baden Powell' (1980); J. H. Brooke, 'The natural theology of the geologists', in L. J. Jordanova and R. S. Porter, *Images of the Earth* (1979), pp. 39–74; G. Grinnell, 'The rise and fall of Darwin's second theory', *J.H.B.*, 18 (1985), 51–70.

[21] T. Chalmers, *Bridgewater Treatise I*, 2 vols. (1833), vol. i, pp. 27–9; W. Kirby, *Bridgewater Treatise VII*, 2 vols. (1835), vol. i, pp. xxiv–xlii. Yule, 'The impact of science'. On Kirby and Lamarck, see a recent discussion by G. Gale, 'Darwin and the concept of a struggle for existence', *Isis*, 63 (1972), 321–440.

clear to contemporary readers. Bell was aware of basic features of the recapitulation theory of Tiedemann and Serres. He also appeared familiar with the doctrine propounded by Virey that man's superiority was chiefly and only due to the superior development of his brain and his intellectual faculties. Man, Virey argued, was an animal easier to kill than a worm. Bell strongly opposed this view. He emphasized that man was the most perfect being, the last to be created by God.[22]

Bell well knew that the doctrine of the progressive organic elaboration of living beings was looked upon by transmutationist naturalists as providing evidence for their views. He therefore stressed that man was superior to brutes, though he took care to specify that he was 'not arguing to support the gradual development and improvement of organization'. Bell also attacked Geoffroy Saint-Hilaire and Lamarck. He made ample use of the arguments against Lamarck deployed by Lyell, and concluded that 'everything declares that species have its origin in a distinct creation, not in a gradual variation from some original type'.[23]

Surprisingly, a moderate and sympathetic defence of Lamarck and E. Geoffroy Saint-Hilaire came from Frederick Nolan, the scholar and divine whose 1833 Bampton Lectures have been discussed above. Nolan was faced with the difficult problem of providing a naturalistic defence of monogenism against growing polygenist pronouncements from France. Yet, nearer to his key fundamentalist concern was the problem of reconciling the size of Noah's ark with the numberless number of known animals. He thus formulated a theory of limited variation from a relatively small number of originally created, pre-deluge pairs of animals and plants. Appropriate reference to recent naturalistic debates supported the thesis:

The distinction and permanence of species, from the time of their creation, has been maintained by Buffon, Linnaeus and Cuvier, and the great body of naturalists; but has been rejected by Lamarck, Geoffroy Saint-Hilaire and others, who passing into the opposite extreme, have maintained, that the agency of the animals themselves has been exclusively employed, in constructing the animal kingdom. As is generally the case in theories which thus stand directly opposed, there is partial truth on both sides of the question: the aggregate number of species having been probably limited at first, until by gradual development, in the process of nature, they assumed the various and settled forms, which at present possess, and from which there is scarcely any known variation.[24]

[22] C. Bell, *Bridgewater Treatise IV* (1833), pp. 147–9, 136–8.
[23] *Bridgewater Treatise IV*, pp. 38, 144–5; cf. Virey, 'Nature', *Nouveau dictionnaire*, second edn., vol. xii (1817), 79–81. The question of Virey's influence on British and European biological and anthropological debates still awaits assessment. It is argued that Virey's works, his contributions to the *Nouveau dictionnaire* and to the *Dictionnaire des sciences médicales* exercised considerable influence on the cultivated public and the medical profession. On Virey and polygenism, see C. Blanckaert, 'Monogénisme et polygénisme en France de Buffon à Broca' (1981).
[24] F. Nolan, *The Analogy of Revelation and Science Established* (1833), p. 486, note to p. 308; on the discussion of the size of Noah's ark, and the number of known species, see pp. 272–306.

A year after the publication of Bell's and Nolan's works, Peter Mark Roget (1779–1869) published his contribution to the Bridgewater series, *Animal and Vegetable Creation Considered with Reference to Natural Theology* (1834). Contrary to the conclusions reached by Bell, Roget maintained with Virey that man's superiority over the 'brute creation...which so frequently excels him in the perfection of subordinate powers' was due to the superior development of the intellectual faculties. Roget was also a follower of the theory of the unity of composition elaborated by Geoffroy Saint-Hilaire. He fully endorsed the Serres–Tiedemann theory of recapitulation. Again opposing the views of his Bridgewater colleague Bell, he argued that the contemplation of the analogies linking various organic forms substantiated the view that 'Nature appears to have kept in view a certain definite type or ideal standard, to which, amidst innumerable modifications, rendered necessary by the varying circumstances and different destinations of each species she always shows a decided tendency to conform'.[25]

Roget did however stress that species were immutable. He criticized Lamarck for maintaining the contrary and proposed his own model to explain the succession of beings throughout the ages of the earth. A textual analysis of the doctrine elaborated by Roget and a comparison with the summary of his views Virey offered in his *Histoire des moeurs des animaux* reveals the extent of Roget's debt to the latter's ideas. It is interesting to note that in the *Histoire* Virey frequently referred to the proof of the existence of God offered by his doctrine, and attacked the transmutationist hypothesis. Indeed, in almost every work he produced Virey extensively commented upon the ideas of Lamarck, and considered the transmutationist hypothesis a central issue in contemporary natural sciences.[26]

As far as he was concerned, Virey endorsed the theory of organic recapitulation and the unity of composition, and linked the history of life on earth to the progressive development of the earth's surface. Yet, he was also firmly convinced that God was directly responsible for the transition from one degree of organic development to the next one. Roget was clearly indebted to Virey, and to the latter's 'Christianized' interpretation of the theories put forward

---

[25] P. M. Roget, *Bridgewater Treatise V*, 2 vols. (1834), vol. ii, pp. 578–9. On the diffusion of the recapitulation theory in England see Rehbock, *The Philosophical Naturalists*; Rehbock fails to distinguish between Marcel de Serres (1782–1862) and A.-E.-R.-A. Serres; see also L. S. Jacyna, 'The romantic programme and the reception of cell theory in Britain', *J.H.B.*, 17 (1984), 13–48 and 'Principles of general physiology: the comparative dimension of British neuroscience in the 1830s and 1840s', *Studies in the History of Biology*, 7 (1984), 47–92. Meckel was personally known to several London physicians, and in 1827 an attempt was made to secure for him a teaching position at the newly established London University, see Mazumdar, 'Anatomical physiology and the reform of medical education', 236.

[26] Roget, *Bridgewater Treatise V*, vol. i, pp. 54–7 and vol. ii, pp. 627, 630–5, 635–7. Cf. Virey, *Histoire*, 3 vols. (1822), vol. i, pp. 70–112, 491–4, and vol. ii, pp. 95–9. There is no comprehensive study of Virey; see A. Berman, 'Romantic Hygeia', *Bulletin of the History of Medicine*, 29 (1965), 134–42. See also Corsi, 'J.-J. Virey, premier critique de Lamarck', in S. Atran et al., *Histoire du concept d'espèce dans les sciences de la vie (1987)*, pp. 176–7.

by Geoffroy Saint-Hilaire, Tiedemann and Serres. He was not convinced, as
many of his colleagues were, that the new trends in French natural sciences
necessarily led to atheism. He argued that the researches of the transcendental
anatomists and embryologists enlarged man's views of God's providential care
for his creatures.[27]

The debate on natural sciences and on their relevance to natural theology
was a prominent feature of English intellectual life of the early 1830s. A
plurality of approaches to, and of conclusions drawn from, recent developments
in natural history found expression in writings which enjoyed wide popularity.
The Bridgewater authors offered a variety of interpretations of the consequences to be expected from the impact of French natural history on
contemporary natural theology, reflecting the serious concern of representatives
of the apologetic standpoint. The debate focused on the opposition between
those who insisted that the regularity of natural phenomena was the chief
evidence of design, and those who were prepared to allow for various degrees
of divine interference in the natural arrangement.

Kirby and Chalmers differed in the emphasis placed on their conclusions,
but agreed that 'natural laws' were incapable of fully accounting for natural
phenomena. Roget did not express himself on the subject, but clearly believed
that the observed regularity of the succession of organic forms provided strong
evidence of the existence and benevolence of God. In his Bridgewater treatise,
Whewell argued along similar lines, though he concentrated on the evidence
of God's care for man provided by the contemplation of astronomical and
physical arrangements.

In his *Discourse on the Studies of the University* Adam Sedgwick praised
Whewell's comments on the role of natural laws in the fabric of the universe.
He fully expanded upon the apologetic use of the concept of the uniformity
of nature. Sedgwick strongly opposed the view of those who argued that the
emphasis on the explanatory powers of natural laws was leading to atheism.
Whewell and Sedgwick were equally certain that God did in fact intervene
in nature. However, their polemical opposition to theologians like Kirby and
their colleague Rose made them stress that the study of natural laws was not
excluding God from creation. In future years, Whewell and Sedgwick changed
the emphasis of their argument and vigorously stressed the exemplar of God's
intervention in nature provided by the creation of new forms of life.[28]

The present study has emphasized the discontinuities in British intellectual
debates during the early decades of the nineteenth century. Changes in the
political, social and intellectual scene induced changes in the apologetic policies

[27] On Virey's natural theology, see Corsi, *Oltre il mito*, pp. 140–4 and 'J.-J. Virey premier
critique de Lamarck'. Historians who have recently commented on Roget's *Bridgewater
Treatise* do not appear aware of the extent of his familiarity with contemporary French natural
sciences, and with the work of Virey in particular. A. Desmond has discussed Grant's allegation
that Roget had plagiarized his lectures, and suggests that this might well have been the case.

[28] W. Whewell, *Bridgewater Treatise III*, pp. 3–4, 7–8. Sedgwick, *A Discourse* (second edn.,
1834), pp. 19, 24, 29–30.

pursued by the Anglican intelligentsia. The debate on species offers the opportunity to focus upon a further instance of discontinuity. The anxiety aroused by trends emerging in French natural sciences of the 1820s proved unfounded. No French or German naturalist elaborated an authoritative transmutationist or materialistic synthesis upon the basis of recent embryological, anatomical or morphological investigations. It was in England that naturalists and intellectuals in general were going to explore the scientific, philosophical and theological dimensions of the transformist hypothesis.

The 1830 debate between Cuvier and Geoffroy Saint-Hilaire was put to a sudden end by the death of Cuvier in 1832. The increasingly metaphysical leaning of Geoffroy Saint-Hilaire's works contributed to weaken the impact of his late evolutionary writings. More sophisticated and politically safer anatomical and embryological researches undertaken in both France and Germany relegated his work to a secondary role, though his basic ideas were still influential. Moreover, the broad-based popularity which characterized French natural science during the early decades of the century rapidly declined. Literary, philosophical and political developments now attracted French popular attention. Naturalists concentrated on morphological and especially physiological investigations. The 'positive philosophy' found many supporters and disciples among naturalists. Slowly, Paris lost its title of capital of the natural sciences. German universities were taking the lead, and German was becoming the language of anatomy, embryology and science in general, followed by the slow but secure growth of the English language in the physical and biological disciplines.[29]

This sketchy survey of the first phase of the debate on species in Britain leads to an interesting conclusion. French transmutationist ideas were known and commented upon in Britain during the 1820s and the early 1830s. Concentration on the period only as a prologue to Charles Darwin's intellectual adventure has customarily prevented systematic investigation of the state of naturalistic debates independently from anachronistic preconceptions. The work of naturalists highly esteemed in the early decades of the century, or representatives of French science who promoted important and influential collective works, such as Bory de Saint-Vincent or Julien-Joseph Virey, still await critical assessment. It is unquestionable that the discussion of transmutation ideas by Bory and Virey exercised considerable influence in France,

[29] In view of the fact that transcendental anatomy was increasingly employed to check transformism, it is not surprising that the work of E. Geoffroy Saint-Hilaire was slowly forgotten; German anatomical philosophy was for a time seen as a safer alternative to the teaching of the French author, to the point that many thought Geoffroy Saint-Hilaire a follower of the Germans: the complex issue of the relationship between France and Germany in the early 1800s was thus obscured or extremely simplified. For an interesting, quasi-contemporary view of the situation, see (G. H. Lewes), 'Goethe as a man of science', *W.R.*, 2 (1852), 479–506, and 'Life and doctrine of Geoffroy Saint-Hilaire', *W.R.*, 5 (1854), 160–90. I have briefly discussed this issue in *Oltre il mito*, pp. 323–7.

England, Italy and Germany. The great majority of authors who in the 1820s commented upon the theories of Lamarck and Geoffroy Saint-Hilaire were familiar with Virey's and Bory's ideas and publications. The problem of the almost complete neglect by historians of their contribution to the debate on species thus poses interesting questions.

One explanation for this neglect is perhaps provided by the fact that the English debate developed along lines different from the ones which characterized the French debate. This was due to a great extent to the influence exercised by Lyell's critique of Lamarck. One of Lyell's claims on behalf of his geological theory was that his uniformitarian and actualistic approach to geological phenomena defeated the transmutationist hypothesis. The second phase of the debate on species in England was thus characterized by the discussion of the relevance of the species question to proving or disproving the validity of Lyell's uniformitarian geology. Geology became the privileged ground for commentaries on the species issue.

(ii) Geology, philosophy and the species problem: Whewell, Lyell and Baden Powell

In the first eleven chapters of the second volume of the *Principles of Geology* Lyell embarked upon a detailed examination of Lamarck's ideas and of doctrines used by supporters of new transmutationist hypotheses. Lyell was aware that it was possible to graft some of the tenets of the transcendental anatomists onto some modified form of transformism. The work of Tiedemann, Serres, and Geoffroy Saint-Hilaire could well have been used to support evolutionary models. He first criticized in some detail the transmutation mechanism elaborated by Lamarck, and concluded that the French naturalist was unable to cite a single positive fact on behalf of his doctrine. He also expanded upon Lamarck's opposition to the theory that species were destroyed in the course of geological change. Lamarck argued that species were capable of adapting themselves to uniform and gradual transformations of their environment. Lyell was on the contrary convinced that extinction of organic forms was part of the natural system and a positively observable fact.[30]

Like Lamarck, Lyell disliked catastrophes and regarded the question of extinction as a major problem which he had to solve in order to prove the validity of his own uniformitarian model of geological explanation. Lyell maintained that the action of natural agents currently shaping the surface of the earth – rivers, atmospheric phenomena, volcanoes, earthquakes, etc. – were sufficient to explain past geological events. The consideration of their action represented the only legitimate basis for inductive investigations of the history of the earth. He could not deny, however, that the sequence of fossil remains

30 For bibliographic references and a full discussion of Lyell's critique of Lamarck, see Corsi, 'The importance of French transformist ideas'.

showed that species suddenly disappeared. The phenomenon was held to substantiate the view that events of extraordinary magnitude were occasionally responsible for the destruction of entire populations.

Lyell approached the question of the extinction according to the methodology described in the first volume of the *Principles*. His detailed and documented survey of the 'balance of nature' argument and the ecological mechanism which altered and restored equilibrium among vegetable and animal populations led Lyell to conclude that the successive destruction of species was part of the regular and constant order of nature. Lamarck was therefore wrong when he claimed that living organisms adapted to new conditions by a slow process of modification. Observation of the actual workings of nature showed that a species weakened by environmental disadvantages was immediately destroyed by the pressure of other organic forms competing for the same station. Neither catastrophes nor transmutationist doctrines were required to account for the succession of organic forms displayed by geological findings. The regular operation of known natural agents produced environmental alterations responsible for the disappearance of some species.

Lyell was nevertheless aware that his mechanism was inadequate to explain the introduction of new species. His 'balance of nature' model rigorously excluded the possibility of adaptive variation. He was moreover convinced that individual variation was negligible and limited to the morphological level. No physiological or significant structural variation had ever been observed. It was furthermore well known that monstrosities had little or no chance of survival. Lyell appreciated that his failure to account for the introduction of new species represented a serious objection against the entire fabric of his uniformitarian geology. If indeed known causes were responsible for the destruction of species, which ones were responsible for the replacement of new forms? No natural cause was known to explain the introduction of new species. Lyell himself had acknowledged that species were introduced in pairs by God. Thus, if God intervened in the process of restoration of lost life, why should He not be also responsible for major intervention in the processes shaping the surface of the earth?

In the last chapter of the second volume of the *Principles* devoted to the species issue, Lyell announced that he was going to discuss the introduction of new species in nature, and he was going to prove that the process could be explained in natural terms analogous to the ones employed to explain the process of extinction. He did however fail to prove the point. He simply stated that the introduction of new forms of life followed a cycle man was not able to witness. In the third volume of his work, published in 1833, he simply asserted that the appearance of new species was as much part of the ordinary course of nature as extinction was. Critics were not satisfied that this was the case.

It could indeed be argued that Whewell, the most sophisticated critic of

the *Principles* was partly responsible for Lyell's attempt to apply his methodology to solve the question of the succession of the species throughout geological
time. In his *British Critic* review of the first volume of the *Principles*, published
in July 1831, he enumerated the three major weaknesses of the uniformitarian
doctrine. First, Lyell had not proved that known causes were adequate to
explain the magnitude of geological changes displayed by the arrangement of
strata. Second, an adequate theory of climatic change was lacking. Third,
uniformitarian doctrines failed to account for the discontinuity between one
set of fossil animal and vegetable species and another in successive strata. The
last proof was undoubtedly the most difficult to provide:

To frame even an hypothesis which will, with any plausibility, supply this defect in
his speculations is a harder task than that which Mr. Lyell has now executed. We
conceive it undeniable...that we see, in the transition from an earth peopled by one
set of animals, to the same earth swarming with entirely new forms of organic life, a
distinct manifestation of creative power, transcending the operation of known laws of
nature: and it appears to us, that geology has thus lighted a new lamp along the path
of natural theology.

According to Whewell, Lyell had no alternative: either he accepted a form
of transformism based on his uniformitarian and actualist methodology, thereby
condemning his work to social and theological reprobation, or he had to
acknowledge God's intervention in nature, thus avowing that his geological
system proved the insufficiency of science in reconstructing the history of the
earth.[31]

Whewell's review of the second volume of the *Principles* betrayed his concern
with the fact that transformist theories were dangerously popular among
French naturalists and geologists, and were attracting attention in England
too. Whewell was indeed aware that Lamarck was not an isolated case, and
expressed the view that the confutation of transformism by Lyell had come
at the right moment. Many geologists in France, he explained, 'entertain no
doubt that the theory of transformation being that by which the different
forms of animal life, at different periods of the earth's history, are rightly
explained'. Whewell mentioned the transformist conviction of d'Omalius
d'Halloy, and concluded that the doctrine 'requires to be fully considered by
geologists and naturalists alike'.[32]

The common front against transformism did not, however, prevent Whewell
from scoring his points against Lyell's pretence that uniformitarian geology
was entitled to be regarded as a mature science. Whewell shrewdly informed
his readers that Lyell's denial of the adequacy of Lamarckian actual causes

---

[31] (W. Whewell), 'Lyell's *Principles of Geology*', *B.C.*, 9 (1831), 194.
[32] (W. Whewell), 'Lyell's *Geology*, vol. 2 – *Changes in the Organic World now in Progress*', *Q.R.*,
47 (1832), 116. Cf. A. Brongniart, 'Notes sur la composition de l'atmosphère à diverses
époques de la formation de la terre, et sur l'opinion de M. Parrot à ce sujet', *Annales des
sciences naturelles*, 20 (1830), 427–41.

to explain the introduction of new species questioned the reliability of the extinction model itself. He conceded that '*some* species do become extinct by the operation of causes now in action', but challenged the legitimacy of Lyell's conclusion that *all* species perished as he described. Indeed, ignorance of the natural means responsible for new creations, made it impossible to claim that the means of extinction Lyell indicated were the only ones responsible for the disappearance of species.

Lyell argued that geological changes were to be explained by an appeal to actual *verae causae*. According to Whewell, Lyell himself provided the proof that his claim was unrealistic and unphilosophical. The transition from the inadequacy of actual causes to explain organic change to the general argument that actual causes were inadequate to explain all physical changes was an easy one. Whewell seized this opportunity to declare that 'when we find that such events as the first placing of man upon the earth, and the successive creation of vast numbers of genera and species are proved to have occurred within assignable geological epochs, it seems to us most natural to suppose, that mechanical operations also have taken place, as different from what goes on in the inorganic world, as the facts just mentioned are from what we trace in organic nature'.[33]

A few years later Lyell confessed to Herschel that commentators in both England and Germany were severely critical of his solution. The confutation of transmutationism and the failure to indicate alternative actual causes responsible for the introduction of new species 'left...nothing but the direct intervention of the First Cause'. Lyell was however consoled to find that Herschel agreed with him that 'the origination of new species...may be carried on through the intervention of intermediate causes'. Lyell also said that he left this conclusion to be inferred, in order not to offend a certain class of readers.[34]

As is well known, the famous letter from Herschel to Lyell referred to was discussed at the Geological Society, and printed by Babbage as an appendix to the second edition of his *Ninth Bridgewater Treatise* (1837). Commentators have recently argued that Herschel had no intention of endorsing the view that it was possible to formulate a naturalistic explanation of the introduction of new species. He simply meant that God did not intervene in the order of creation at random, but according to a regular plan. There were indeed passages in the *Principles* which could have suggested analogous interpretations. Thus, Lyell's statement that new species were introduced when required in single pairs or individuals could have been read as the admission that direct creative intervention was part of the dynamics of ecological systems. Whewell maintained that this was the only conclusion logically open to the reader who carefully

[33] (Whewell), 'Lyell's *Geology*, vol. 2', 121, 128.
[34] K. Lyell, *Life*, vol. i, p. 467.

followed Lyell's argument. As we shall point out below, several contemporary readers thought that the statement by Herschel was at least ambiguous. Indeed, many read it as an explicit endorsement of the legitimacy of investigations into the natural mechanism responsible for the introduction of new species.[35]

It is not necessary here to analyse further the various pronouncements on the succession of species put forward by Lyell, Herschel, Babbage and Whewell. The point to be emphasized is that the introduction of new species throughout geological time was a topic widely debated in naturalistic and intellectual circles. At Holland House in March 1837 the host asked Lyell to comment upon Buckland's *Bridgewater Treatise*, and 'this led to a talk on new species, and that mystery of mysteries, the creation of man'. The anthropological dimension of the debate over transformism was also calling for comments from Nicholas Wiseman, who discussed the issue in his lectures on the connexion between science and revealed religion (1836). The catholic author referred to the polygenist tenets of Antoine Desmoulins, Bory de Saint-Vincent and Virey. Contrary to Kirby, Wiseman had no sympathy for Virey, whose works he found 'even more revolting' than the ones produced by other French naturalists. As it might be expected, Lamarck's 'degrading theory' was the target of sharp criticism and sarcastic remarks.[36]

The amount of invective bestowed on Lamarck, on Geoffroy Saint-Hilaire and on French pro-transformist polygenists did not prevent, however, the discussion on how to explain the succession of beings throughout the history of the earth. Thus, for instance, the *Athenaeum* reviewer of Buckland's *Bridgewater Treatise* praised the geologist's refutation of Lamarck, but proceeded to give a fair account of the doctrine put forward by 'this eminent naturalist', the 'most able' advocate of 'gradual transmutation'. In his 'Life and works of Baron Cuvier' David Brewster criticized the 'more specious than solid' opinions on species Cuvier had to fight. Yet, he also added that these opinions had been asserted by 'naturalists of no mean names'. One year later, commenting on Lord Brougham's natural theology, Brewster again attacked the theory of 'successive transmutations'.[37]

Even though the threat of a new transmutationist synthesis from France appeared increasingly remote, Whewell was displeased by the curiosity and interest aroused by the debate on Lyell's actualism as applied to the organic world. In the *History of the Inductive Sciences* which appeared in 1837, he

---

[35] C. Babbage, *Ninth Bridgewater Treatise* (Second edn., 1837), pp. 202–27; cf. N. C. Gillespie, *Charles Darwin and the Problem of Creation* (1979), pp. 30–1. Cannon, *Science in Culture*, pp. 88–92.

[36] K. Lyell, *Life*, vol. ii, p. 8. Wiseman, *Twelve Lectures*, pp. 118–19, 120

[37] (Anon), 'Buckland's *Bridgewater Treatise*', *Athenaeum*, n. 484 (4 February 1837), p. 80; on Buckland's critique of Lamarck, see his *Bridgewater Treatise* (1836), vol. i, pp. 54, 239, 585–6, and Rupke, *The Great Chain of History* (1983), pp. 175–6. (D. Brewster), 'Life and works of Baron Cuvier', *E.R.*, 62 (1836), p. 280, and idem, 'Lord Brougham's *Discourse on Natural Theology*', *Q.R.*, 64 (1837), 263–302.

launched a systematic attack against uniformitarian geology and those who considered that the problem of a naturalistic solution to the species question was a legitimate issue of natural history. To some extent, Lyell's discussion of Lamarck had unwittingly sharpened the issue, and the 'victory' over transformism had not succeeded in silencing the controversy.

Whewell acknowledged the leading rôle played by Geoffroy Saint-Hilaire in reviving the transmutationist hypothesis. In 1837, however, he was less worried by his colleague's statement that the fixity of species was a concept rejected by naturalists. He did nonetheless believe that the debate on the succession of species had received a fresh impulse in England, and that this was due to recent geological debates and to Lyell's discussion of the issue. Geological researches, Whewell argued, 'again bring the question before us in a striking form, and on a gigantic scale'. Fully persuaded that Lyell had no solution to offer, Whewell forced the issue into a dilemma: either transmutationism or 'many successive acts of creation and extinction of species; acts which, therefore, we may properly call miraculous'.[38]

Whewell was nevertheless aware that a number of his colleagues were not ready to concede that this dilemma was the logical outcome of the discussion. There was widespread consensus that the Lamarckian model was severely defective, and Lyell's own criticism of Lamarck proved extremely telling. Many however concluded that the task now facing naturalists was to find a more convincing model. The mystery of the introduction of new species was not solved, but there was no reason to think it could not be solved. As we shall point out below, to many Lyell's second volume and Herschel's letter stressed the legitimacy of investigating the mechanism responsible for the historical succession of species.

The second task Whewell undertook in his *History* was thus to dispute the legitimacy of investigating the origin of species. Proving himself an experienced polemicist, Whewell used Lyell's own arguments to deny that the succession of species was open to scientific analysis. He reminded his readers that the inductive methodology was inadequate to inquire into the 'beginning' of things. Indeed, geology and astronomy failed to produce satisfactory accounts of the origin of the universe or of single species. Geologists confessed their inability to 'account by any natural means' for the production of new species. Whewell therefore concluded that 'the mystery of creation is not within the range of her [geology's] legitimate territory: she says nothing, she points upwards'.[39]

---

[38] E. Geoffroy Saint-Hilaire, 'Du Sivatherium de l'Himalaya', *Comptes Rendus de l'Académie des Sciences*, 4 (1837), 77–82: at p. 77 the author announced 'la clôture du siècle de Cuvier'. Whewell, *History*, vol. iii, pp. 630, 625, 631–9; cf. Baden Powell, *Connexion*, pp. 128–33. Baden Powell also quoted E. Geoffroy Saint-Hilaire's *Principes de philosophie zoologique* (1830).

[39] Whewell, *History*, vol. iii, p. 625. On Whewell's thoughts on natural theology, and his increasingly conservative stand, see R. Yeo, 'William Whewell, natural theology and the philosophy of science in mid-nineteenth century England', *A.S.*, 36 (1979), 493–516.

Baden Powell deeply disagreed with Whewell. He emphasized that the investigation of secondary causes responsible for the introduction of new species was perfectly legitimate and a crucial issue of contemporary natural history. He devoted long sections of his *Connexion of Natural and Divine Truth* systematically to refuting Whewell's criticism of Lyell's geology and of the transcendental anatomy elaborated by Geoffroy Saint-Hilaire. The reading of the Bridgewater treatises and of Whewell's *History* convinced Baden Powell that his colleagues had again failed to come to terms with the progressive nature of scientific knowledge. He concentrated on the *History* because it represented the best argued and most comprehensive attempt to deny the epistemological reliability of natural sciences, in particular of geology. Baden Powell was also worried that the attempt made by Whewell to define the legitimate limits of scientific investigation could provoke yet another confrontation between science and revelation, similar to the one which led to the abandonment of the diluvial theory.

Significantly, Baden Powell's discussion of the species question was characterized by the same degree of ambiguity noted with respect to statements by Herschel or even by Lyell. He explained that geology established the occurrence of extinctions brought about by the continued action of actual causes. The hypothesis of large-scale catastrophes responsible for the disappearance of entire systems of life was thus disproved. Geological investigations also indicated the gradual origination of new species but were silent on 'the particular method or process' responsible for the phenomenon.

Various explanatory models had been put forward. Baden Powell was however satisfied that transmutation hypotheses were not adequate to the task. He argued that there was 'preponderant evidence' against the doctrine of gradual adaptive transformation of organic beings and concluded that the sequence of successive creations disclosed by geology 'tend infinitely to exalt our ideas of the eternal and overruling Omnipotence by whose agency they were brought about'. It would however be highly misleading to take this statement as evidence that Baden Powell argued for divine intervention providentially adjusted to changes in the fauna and flora of a region.[40]

In a note on the issue of new creations Baden Powell explicitly questioned the thesis put forward by Thomas Thomson that the successive introduction of new species constituted proof of divine intervention in natural affairs. Baden Powell warned that 'we do not know what secondary means may have been employed to bring about those successive creations of species, or modifications of the forms of organized life'. According to Baden Powell, all creation emanated from God. Yet, he also argued that God as architect was more impressive a power than God as artificer. There was no reason to believe that God planned a system of natural causes which brought about the extinction of species but

---

[40] Baden Powell, *Connexion* (1838), pp. 145–54. Yule, 'The impact of science', 254.

failed to make provision to prevent the disappearance of life from a region. It was only reasonable to expect that new species were introduced by the usual agency of second causes.[41]

Baden Powell could not see the reason for the 'anxious debate' on the transmutation of species. Traditional Lamarckian hypotheses were disproved, but it was 'freely open to physical inquiry to trace the *secondary means* as far as the nature of the cause admits'. The influence of climate, domestication, or interbreeding of allied species was known to cause variation. Baden Powell stressed that the time-scale of natural operations made it legitimate to suppose that causes of variation ineffectual in the short term probably induced major changes over millions of years. The analogy between this argument and Baden Powell's defence of actualism was evident. The path to be followed for the solution of the 'mystery of mysteries' was the search for a mechanism responsible for variation in today's world; the redeployment of the same cause through a very long time-span would have ensured the production of new forms of life.[42]

Actualism was therefore the only legitimate assumption guiding the investigation of geological, as well as organic change. It should be pointed out that Lyell could not have been pleased by Baden Powell's defence. The latter solved the dilemma formulated by Whewell by endorsing the basic argument of the transmutationists. Lyell disliked the materialistic overtones of developmental theories and the idea that man descended from brutes. He was convinced there was no development, no progression, no directional change in the organic as well as the inorganic world. His geological chronometer required fixed species marking the age of strata or formations. Baden Powell endorsed Lyell's methodological approach to geology and the history of life on earth; yet, he also accepted the challenge formulated by Whewell, and believed that the uniformitarian and actualist approach was bound to solve the species puzzle.[43]

[41] Baden Powell, *Connexion* (1838), pp. 303–4; T. Thomson (ed.), 'Sketches of geology', in R. D. Thomson, *British Annual* (1838), p. 259.
[42] Baden Powell, *Connexion*, pp. 303–4.
[43] On Lyell's actualism, and on his reluctance to adopt transformism, see M. Bartholomew, 'Lyell and evolution', *B.J.H.S.*, 6 (1973), 261–303 and W. F. (later S. F.) Cannon, 'Charles Darwin, radical actualism and theory', *B.J.H.S.*, 9 (1976), 104–20.

16

Species without Darwin

(i) Cosmology and the history of life

Between the publication of Lyell's *Principles of Geology*, of Whewell's *History* (1837) and the appearance of Baden Powell's *Connexion* (1838), the debate on actualism dominated discussion. The Bridgewater authors and several commentators discussed, condemned or approved the cosmological and theological implications of French natural sciences. Lyell, Whewell and Baden Powell argued on the contrary that cosmological models offered no explanation at all. The debate concentrated on the question of the possible actual causes of organic change. The cosmological approach was stigmatized as unscientific, unphilosophical and unproductive. Those who believed in Lyell's actualistic uniformitarianism were invited by Whewell to cite observable *verae causae* to which the changes in the present living creation were to be ascribed.

It could be argued that when Charles Darwin opened his first notebook on species in July 1837, he was to a certain extent answering the public challenge by Whewell. Whatever Lyell might have thought of Darwin's attempt to discover the secondary means responsible for the introduction of new species, Darwin believed that he was doing a service to the epistemological and geological doctrines put forward by his friend. Baden Powell too was convinced that his defence of a naturalistic explanation of the question of species strengthened Lyell's case against Whewell.

The recent, vigorous production of studies on the development of Darwin's thought makes it possible to avoid discussing his reaction to the geological, epistemological and theological debate which absorbed the attention of his colleagues in the late 1830s. The only problem which is perhaps still to be investigated is the relationship between Darwin and the French evolutionary authorities he was constantly reading during his journey. Needless to say, I have no intention of claiming a 'debt' by Darwin to Geoffroy Saint-Hilaire, Bory de Saint-Vincent or Lamarck. During his journey, Darwin read some of their works, or, as was the case with Geoffroy Saint-Hilaire, summaries of their ideas; he was then fully convinced that Lyell was right in proscribing transmutationism of any sort from the realm of legitimate natural history investigation.[1]

It is possible that during the visit to Herschel at the Cape, in June 1836, he was informed of the wider context of the debate on Lyell's methodological proposals. Herschel knew that Darwin was probably the only known convert to uniformitarianism and actualism. He discussed with the younger colleague the problem of the origin of man and of languages. It is difficult not to speculate that Herschel showed Darwin the famous letter to Lyell, sent in February 1836. At any event, the personal acquaintance with Lyell in October 1836, the regular frequentation of the Geological Society meetings, of Babbage House and of the London scientific community made him aware that the question of species was very much on the agenda of contemporary geological, naturalistic, philosophical and natural theological debates.[2]

It is well known, however, that the thoughts Darwin developed on the subject of the species were not communicated to the public. To say the least, his role in the debate on species of the next two decades was extremely limited. This was not the case with Baden Powell. In 1855 he became the authoritative spokesman of a liberal approach towards a broadly evolutionary solution of the problem of species. From the early 1840s, he discussed the question of rational cosmology, and inspired favourable reactions to the *Vestiges of the Natural History of Creation*, a work considered below. It is therefore of some interest to examine the development of the debate on species from the point of view of Baden Powell and those among his colleagues and his friends who agreed with his approach.

The task of providing the cosmological and evolutionary synthesis which the French naturalists were increasingly unwilling to offer was left to their English colleagues, amateurs, and theologians. Already in 1833 William Kirby pointed out the impending danger when he emphasized the basic similarity of approach between Laplace and Lamarck. Both attempted a naturalistic synthesis to account for the history of the universe and of life. Kirby was

[1] It would be superfluous in this context to refer to the scores of recent contributions to Darwin studies. For a comprehensive and updated summary of Darwinian scholarship of the past fifteen years, see D. Kohn (ed.), *The Darwinian Heritage* (1985). Many of the essays appearing in the volume were completed in 1982–3. For a discussion of recent interpretations, see D. R. Oldroyd, 'How did Darwin arrive at his theory? The secondary literature to 1982', *History of Science*, 22 (1984), 325–74; A. La Vergata, 'Images of Darwin: a historiographical overview', in D. Kohn (ed.), *The Darwinian Heritage*, pp. 901–72. See also J. C. Greene, 'Reflections on the progress of Darwin studies', *J.H.B.*, 8 (1975), 243–73. My reflections on Darwin studies have greatly benefited from discussions with J. C. Greene, J. S. Hodge, D. Kohn, G. Pancaldi, S. S. Schweber and Frank Sulloway.

[2] Baden Powell's reference to the 'anxious debate' on transmutation provides authoritative evidence of contemporary discussions of the issue; A. Desmond has recently ascribed Richard Owen's ascent in zoological and anatomical circles, and the early success of his brand of transcendental anatomy, to the explicit anti-Lamarckian potential of Owen's philosophical natural history. On Richard Owen, see below.

outraged by the impious attempt of the two French thinkers. Others thought differently.

In 1838 the young William Benjamin Carpenter surveyed the scope and goals of 'Physiology as Inductive Science'. The physical sciences were rapidly reaching the highest stage of generalization. Before long 'one simple formula shall comprehend all the phenomena of the inorganic world'. Physiological science was not equally advanced. It was nevertheless possible that in future times a single law would account for the history of life on earth from its origin in inorganic matter to the succession of animal and vegetable populations. No materialistic assumption was involved in Carpenter's scientific vision. Should physical sciences progress to the point of the highest generalization, 'then we shall be led to a far higher and nobler conception of a Divine mind, than we have at present the means of forming'.[3]

It could be said that the views of one young Unitarian enthusiast do not support the claim that the possibility of a scientific cosmology was debated in intellectual and theological circles. It is therefore relevant to mention that a leading Dissenting theologian, the Hackney tutor and veteran anti-Unitarian polemicist John Pye Smith knew that the nebular hypothesis was criticized but nevertheless pointed out that 'some of the finest and most Christian minds' supported it; Whewell, Gideon Mantell and John Pringle Nichol were quoted as Christian authorities who endorsed this hypothesis. Smith's own view on the subject was that

I must profess it as the most reasonable supposition, and the correlate of the nebular theory, that God originally gave being to the primordial elements of things, the very small number of simple bodies, endowing each with its own wonderous properties Then, that the action of those properties, in the ways which his wisdom ordained, and which we call laws, produced, and is still producing, all the forms and changes of organic and inorganic natures.[4]

Various elements of a new 'rational cosmology', as Comte and Baden Powell called it, were therefore debated by growing numbers of naturalists and philosophers. The wide cosmological and theological implications of the nebular hypothesis or the mechanisms accounting for the succession of species were acknowledged by naturalists and natural theologians alike. A further development occurred in 1836 which hinted at the possible explanation of the origin of life on earth. At the 1836 Bristol meeting of the British Association Andrew

---

[3] W. B. Carpenter, 'The method and aim of the study of physiology', *British and Foreign Medical Review* (1838), reprinted as 'Physiology as inductive science', in W. B. Carpenter. *Nature and Man* (1888), pp. 156–8. Since the completion of this study, Carpenter's career and ideas have attracted considerable attention. See in particular the contributions by Desmond, Jacyna, Rehbock.

[4] J. P. Smith, *On the Relation between the Holy Scriptures and Some Parts of Geological Science* (1839), pp. 281–2. Smith criticized Baden Powell, pp. 198–204, but praised the latter's *Tradition Unveiled*, pp. 335–62. On Smith and Baden Powell, see Brooke, 'The natural theology of the geologists', 48–9.

Crosse, an amateur naturalist who had experimented on crystallization and electricity from the early 1800s, reported that he had been able to artificially to produce quartz crystals by galvanic action.[5]

The geologist Conybeare was so excited that he was unable to read his paper on the South Wales coal basins. John Dalton said he had never heard anything so exciting, and Adam Sedgwick 'passed a highly eloquent elogium'. Such an enthusiastic reception by leading naturalists has left no trace in the histories of science; Crosse was referred to in later years by opponents of Chambers's *Vestiges* as a scientific quack. The reason for the reversal in Crosse's fortunes was the subject of his British Association paper of 1837. Crosse announced, in the words of the lucid summary of a report read at the Parisian *Académie des Sciences*, 'd'avoir fait naître des acarus sur une pierre vésuvienne entretenue humide par du silicate de potasse étendu, sursaturé d'acide muriatique et constamment électrisé'. French scientists dismissed the matter without further notice. Only ten years earlier there were in Paris naturalists who would have taken full advantage of the 'discovery' made by Crosse.[6]

In Britain, the reaction was immediate. During the next twenty years, Crosse's experiments were referred to with praise by naturalists and theologians who supported the new progressionist cosmology, and ridiculed by the critics of the *Vestiges*. It is appropriate to recollect that the widely publicized discoveries by Christian Gottfried Ehrenberg (1795–1876) showed that infusoria and other minute forms of life were endowed with complex organic structures. There was no single monad-like form of life, as the supporters of various kinds of spontaneous generation maintained. Nevertheless, some thought that the *Acarus crossii* confirmed both the observations made by Ehrenberg and the doctrine of spontaneous generation. The organic forms spontaneously produced by combinations of mineral solutions and galvanic energy were in fact fully developed beings of high structural complexity. Even admitting that the ovum of the acarus was already present in the solution, it was the galvanic fluid which brought about its development. The hypothesis that there was a strong causal link between life and electricity was still valid.

It could be argued that the British Association for the Advancement of Science contributed to the development and spread of the taste for cosmologies

5 On Crosse, see *D.N.B.* and C. A. H. Crosse, *Memorials, Scientific and Literary, of Andrew Crosse* (1857); (W. S. Dallas), 'Andrew Crosse', *W.R.*, 12 (1857), 273–6.

6 On the excitement aroused by Crosse's memoirs on crystals see (Anon.), *Athenaeum*, no. 462 (1836), 632. Sedgwick paid a visit to Crosse's home in order to become better acquainted with the methods followed by his colleague, see J. W. Clark and T. H. Hughes, *The Life and Letters of the Reverend Adam Sedgwick* (1890), vol. i, p. 461. A. Crosse, 'On the production of insects by Voltaic electricity', *Annals of Electricity*, 1 (1836–7), 242–4, and 'Description of some experiments made with the Voltaic battery... in the process of which experiments certain insects constantly appeared', *Transactions and Proceedings of the London Electrical Society*, 1 (1837–40), 10–16; *Comptes rendus de l'Académie des Sciences*, 5 (1837), 640. See also Morrell and Thackray, *Gentlemen of Science*, pp. 457–8.

in England. Contrary to the aspiration of several founding fathers or foster-parents of the B.A.A.S., its meetings increased the authority of science, and fired the imagination of amateur and provincial naturalists. The case of Crosse represented a significant instance of the work of an isolated amateur publicized by the British Association. The faith expressed by Carpenter in the probable and imminent discovery of scientific principles providing unified explanations of complex sets of phenomena reflected the great expectations aroused by the Association. It appeared to many that the concentrated effort of the best minds of the country constituted a promise of boundless results. This is probably one of the reasons why such a gentleman of science as Whewell grew increasingly hostile towards the British Association. The plan of providing secure and enlightened supervision to British provincial science was suffering serious and counterproductive drawbacks.

For precisely the same reasons which caused worries to Whewell, Baden Powell felt justified in attempting to establish his Christian apologetic on the popularity and success of the scientific movement. His preoccupation with the possibility of a major clash between the scriptural view of nature and inductive rational cosmology derived from his familiarity with discussions within scientific circles, and his growing familiarity with young scientific enthusiasts such as Carpenter. Mosaic geologists and natural theologians were still endeavouring to reconcile a few verses of Genesis with elementary geological stratigraphy that contradicted them. The real question, as he saw it, was the confrontation between the whole account of creation provided by scripture and the inductive reconstruction of the history of the universe and life. *A Supplement to Tradition Unveiled* (1840) contains a clear summary of Baden Powell's view on the subject; those who maintained that the truth of Genesis was integral to the truth of scripture 'expose the whole cause of revelation to be involved in the rejection of this narrative. ... It therefore becomes immensely important that the matter should be taken up by the friends of Christian truth, and the ground pre-occupied; and from a hold for the adversary, converted (as it surely may be) into a most valuable vantage ground for the truth'.[7]

As has been noted above, Baden Powell's predictions of possible dangerous developments of current debates were often disproved. His warning in the supplement to *Tradition Unveiled* represented one of the instances in which he proved right. The debate on the possibility of a rational cosmology and the expectation of a scientific synthesis of the history of the universe and life

---

[7] Baden Powell, *A Supplement to Tradition Unveiled* (1840), pp. 36–7. Baden Powell Papers, W. B. Carpenter to Baden Powell, July 9, 1838: the young physiologist asked his colleague's help in getting permission from Herschel to inscribe the *Principles of Physiology, General and Comparative* to his name. The letter also implied that Baden Powell was well acquainted with Carpenter's father, the Unitarian Minister. On December 4, 1838 Carpenter sent Baden Powell a copy of the volume. In 1839 Francis Newman met Carpenter, and the two became friends for life: see Carpenter, *Nature and Man* (1888), p. 27.

persuaded some investigators to invest their energy in pursuit of the cosmological dream.

It was in 1840 that Robert Chambers conceived the idea of his *Vestiges*.
From 1840 to 1844 he abandoned his editorial engagements and lived in
isolation to complete his project. He voraciously read Comte (or 'Compte',
as he spelled it in his first edition), Laplace, Tiedemann, Carpenter, Quetelet,
and Prichard. The Bridgewater Treatise produced by Roget was a further
source of information. Indeed, it could be said that a critical examination of
the sources of inspiration for Chambers would provide highly fascinating
insights into British and European popular scientific culture. In October 1844
the *Vestiges of the Natural History of Creation* appeared.

It is significant that it was between 1842 and 1844 that Charles Darwin
wrote the pencil sketch and the first full draft of his theory. He gave instructions
to his wife for the publication of the manuscript in case of his death. Darwin
too clearly believed that the time was ripe for putting forward his mechanism
to explain the succession of beings. It is well known that his solution to the
question of species relied on the search of true actual causes rather than on
cosmological assumptions. His explanation of the introduction of new species
was to some extent based on the extinction model devised by Lyell rather
than upon the consideration of the progression of organic forms throughout
the strata, from early forms to more progressed beings. Yet, a close analysis
of Darwin's early notebooks reveals that he too was impressed by the possibility
of formulating a model unifying the nebular hypothesis with a mechanism
explaining the transition from one form of life to the next. The view of a
grandiose system of nature exclusively explained in natural terms certainly
appealed to him, though the 'castles in the air' were not to be mistaken for
the procedures of inductive investigation.[8]

It is however clear that Darwin was aware and part of a wider debate
discussing the possibility of models accounting for astronomical, geological,
anatomical, as well as psychological and social phenomena. Darwin was confident that metaphysics, ethics and religious psychology could be re-founded
on the light of such a model. Evolutionary cosmology provided the hypothetical, implicit structure which inspired the search of *verae causae*. A disciple
of Lyell, Darwin kept for himself his admiration for cosmological models. He
also considered the theological relevance of his solution and of the view of
nature it substantiated. His faith in traditional Christian beliefs was shaken
as a result of his reflections; in this too he was a member of an intellectual
community which experienced analogous anxieties and dilemmas. The more
daring anonymous author of the *Vestiges* maintained on the contrary that his ·
cosmological synthesis offered firm evidence of the existence of God. Carpenter,

8 H. Gruber and P. H. Barrett, *Darwin on Man* (1974); S. S. Schweber, 'The origin of the
Origin revisited', *J.H.B.*, 10 (1977), 229–316; D. Ospovat, *The Development of Darwin's Theory*
(1981).

Baden Powell, and Pye Smith had no doubt that a comprehensive synthesis of natural knowledge was bound to enlarge man's view of God's dealings with nature and his creatures.[9]

This view was not shared by all those who entered the debate on cosmology. The discussion of the succession of beings by William Chilton (1815–55) provides confirmation that the belief in a possible naturalistic explanation of the history of life on earth had reached popular level and was used to challenge Christian beliefs. From November 1841 to November 1843 the *Oracle of Reason* published a series of short articles by Chilton on 'The Theory of Regular Gradation'. Chilton argued for the origin of life out of the 'green matter' described by Priestley and for the progressive development of life caused by the self-evolving powers of nature. In the early articles Chilton's scientific information appeared as second-hand and outdated but extensive. Lord Monboddo, Charles White (1728–1813), Gottfried Reinhold Treviranus (1776–1836) and Pierre Boitard (1789–1859) were the sources for the author's defence of transmutationism. From the early numbers of 1842 Chilton showed increased devotion to his subject. The names of Lamarck, De la Beche, Ehrenberg and Mantell were frequently quoted.[10]

In May 1842 Chilton reviewed the debate on the experiments conducted by Crosse, and announced that from December 1840 to October 1841 'Mr. Weeks of Sandwich' had successfully repeated the observation. In October 1841 the first insect was seen and on 25 November of the same year five more living organisms were produced, all *Acari crossii*. Chilton severely criticized the timidity and reluctance of official scientific bodies and naturalists of high standing to tackle the issue of the origin and development of life with the powerful instruments at their disposal.[11]

In one of the last articles he published, Chilton apologized for mistakes and inaccuracies. He justified himself by explaining that his time was limited and he had no access to adequate sources. It was indeed a further proof of the 'cowardice and dishonesty of scientific men' that it was left to well-intentioned amateurs to draw together the results of scientific investigations. There were features of Chilton's digressions revealing the relative sophistication of the debate on species in popular culture and the radical press. From April 1842 Chilton started a polemic against the *Freethinker's Information of the People*, edited by Henry Hetherington (1811–1902). The scientific corre-

9 E. Manier, *Young Darwin* (1978), pp. 40–5. Cosmology had been one chief issue discussed by Brewster in his influential review of Comte's *Cours de philosophie positive*, see *E.R.*, 67 (1838), 271–308.

10 W. Chilton, 'The theory of gradation', *The Oracle of Reason*, n. 1 (1841), 5–6; n. 4 (1841), 29–30; n. 5 (1841), 37–9; n. 21 (1842), 173–5. On the *Oracle of Reason* see Royle, *Victorian infidels*.

11 W. H. Weekes, 'Details of an experiment', *Proceedings of the London Electrical Society*, 1 (1841–3), 240–57, and 'Extracts of notes describing the non-development of the *Acarus Galvanicus* without a Voltaic current', pp. 393–5.

spondent of this rival radical weekly endorsed Lyell's anti-transmutationist and anti-progressionist stand. Chilton did not 'have in hand' a copy of 'Mr. Lyell's book', but honestly quoted the summary of the latter's views published by the *Freethinker*.[12]

Chilton was at last able to get hold of Lyell's *Principles*, and realized that the second volume of the work contained much interesting material. From 12 August to 30 September 1843 Chilton reproduced the summary of Lamarck's theory provided by Lyell. By the end of his reading of Lyell, however, his confidence in progressionism was weakened but his faith unshaken. He reasserted the 'superior probability of the theory of regular gradation or of the transmutation of species, over the asserted *absolute creation* of all material substances and forms by an intelligent God'.[13]

Atheistical conclusions were deduced by Chilton from the theory of regular gradation. Matter was eternal and material laws were sufficient to produce the results 'attributed to intelligence'. 'The object of this series of articles', he explained in the last issue of the *Oracle of Reason*, 'was to show that matter can make men and women, and every other natural phenomenon, unassisted, undirected, and uncontrolled'. The *Oracle of Reason* was not an obscure radical journal. The first issue sold up to four thousand copies a week. The prosecution of the first editor, Charles Southwell (1814–60), and the even more famous court case against the second editor, George Jacob Holyoake (1817–1906), made the *Oracle* a test case of freedom of the press. Intellectuals and journalists who repudiated the atheism of the magazine nevertheless maintained the editors' right to put forward their views.[14]

It would be fair to claim that Chilton's materialism, and in general the profession of materialism and atheism by several outspoken 'martyrs' of the freedom of the press battle, made several Christian naturalists change their emphasis from 'natural law' to God's direct intervention in nature. Others, including Sedgwick and Whewell, did not need Chilton's crudities to draw their attention to the impending danger. In 1833 Sedgwick criticized those who denied the existence of 'natural laws' and ascribed all natural change to the direct intervention of God. He was however merciless against those who argued that natural phenomena were only explicable by known or hypothetical natural laws, and the theories of even his friends and colleagues were not spared from suspicion.[15]

On 20 January 1838 Lyell wrote to Sedgwick complaining about the latter's

[12] W. Chilton, 'The theory of gradation', n. 19 (1842), 157–60.
[13] 'The theory of gradation', nos. 87–94 (1843).
[14] 'The theory of gradation', n. 95 (1843), 340–1; n. 10 (1842), 83–5; n. 100 (1843), 378–80. Royle, *Victorian Infidels*, p. 81. There is no systematic study available of theological and scientific debates in the radical popular press. An important exception, limited to the investigation of phrenological debates, is R. Cooter, *The Cultural Meaning of Popular Science* (1984).
[15] Robertson, *History of Freethought*, pp. 173–5.

recent remarks on the second volume of the *Principles*. The *Norfolk Chronicle* of 13 January had reported that the Cambridge professor gave a lecture on 'various false theories' by 'infidel naturalists'. Lamarck's doctrines were an obvious target of his criticism. Yet, Sedgwick also opposed the view expressed by Lyell 'that the creation of new species is going on at the present day'. The speaker was of course aware of the debate on the succession of species among his colleagues and warned that he was not going to ignore their dangerous views. Lyell strongly protested against the implicit hint by Sedgwick that the doctrines propounded in the *Principles* led to infidelity.[16]

Towards the end of the 1830s Sedgwick and Whewell felt that it was time to check the dangerous enthusiasm for a naturalistic explanation of physical phenomena and the history of life. The policy of preventing materialistic and subversive uses of scientific doctrines by controlling and leading the scientific movement was showing signs of crisis. It was true that no 'infidel' dared to question openly the authority of geologists like Sedgwick or Buckland. Moreover, there were only a few isolated naturalists who overtly embraced materialistic doctrines. Yet, naturalists, scholars, and a section of the radical reading public were endorsing the view that men were near solving all mysteries in nature.[17]

Distinguished members of the educated élite reproached Sedgwick and Whewell for their unreasonable opposition to the debating of broad cosmological questions. Cosmology attracted popular curiosity and wide interest. The crisis of scientific lectures at the Mechanics' Institutes of the late 1830s and the 1840s never affected the popular demand for astronomical and cosmological classes. Furthermore, it became increasingly accepted that hypotheses and general views of nature played a stimulating role in inductive investigations. Though engaged in theological polemic Baden Powell found time to put forward his views on the subject. He surveyed the debate on cosmology in the entry 'Creation' he contributed to John Kitto's *Cyclopaedia of Biblical Literature*, a two-volume work published in 1845. Baden Powell's manuscript journal reveals that the paper was written and sent to the editor almost two years before the publication of the *Vestiges*, between December 1842 and January 1843.[18]

The article 'Creation' offered an interesting survey of the state of cosmological debates as seen by Baden Powell. Two questions significantly attracted his attention: the nebular hypothesis and the interpretation of the succession of living forms. Baden Powell agreed with Lyell and Whewell that inductive

[16] K. Lyell, *Life*, vol. ii, p. 36.
[17] Opposition against the 'imperialism of law' in the explanation of natural phenomena was also expressed by N. Wiseman, whose popular *Twelve Lectures* of 1836 were reprinted in 1842, and reached the sixth edition by 1859.
[18] Baden Powell, 'Creation', in J. Kitto (ed.), *Cyclopaedia of Biblical Literature*, 2 vols. (1845), vol. i, pp. 480–1. Kitto was a friend of F. Newman, see J. Eadie, *Life of John Kitto* (1857), pp. 232–47. B.P.J., 5 Dec. 1842, 6 Feb. 1843, July 1843.

science was only concerned with the succession of phenomena and not with their origin. Thus, the only secure result astronomy contributed to cosmology was the doctrine of the stability and regularity of the planetary system.

According to Baden Powell, the nebular hypothesis formulated by Laplace 'does not (as has been sometimes represented) account for the creation of the solar system': it simply offered a mechanical model explaining its possible formation. The religious implications of the constancy of celestial arrangements were the evidence it provided of a supreme mind. It was however legitimate to argue that the nebular hypothesis too offered material for theological application: 'by *probability* [it] carried a step further back into past time' the evidence of a mind which pre-ordained from eternity the development of the planetary system and endless worlds.[19]

As far as geology was concerned, Baden Powell vigorously stressed that it was not the task of the geologist to formulate hypotheses on the origin of the earth. Sound geology was not cosmogony. Geology became science precisely when geologists renounced cosmological dreams. The true causes of change investigated by geologists were those 'really proved to exist, and...proved by experience to be in operation'. Recent geological investigations did however provide 'incidental' material and arguments relevant to rational cosmology. Geology disclosed a time when no forms of life existed, and established the '*fact of their having in some way received a commencement of being*, and in truth the occurrence of many such events'. Yet, geology failed to provide adequate support for models explaining the succession of beings.[20]

Baden Powell appeared to endorse Whewell's thesis that the subject was not a legitimate issue of natural history. An act of creation, he argued, was a 'beginning' and therefore outside the reach of inductive inquiry. He clearly realized that Whewell had taken full advantage of a key methodological assumption of Lyell's geology. The cosmological approach was unproductive and geologists exclusively relied on *verae causae* now in operation to investigate the past.

The agreement with Whewell did not mean that Baden Powell accepted all the conclusions reached by his colleague. He paid homage to the sophistication of Whewell's argument but nevertheless felt free to insist that the investigation of 'secondary means' responsible for the succession of species was a perfectly legitimate issue in natural history and geology. The transmutation theory he now defined as 'more like the hallucinations of insanity than the sober deductions of science': 'Yet, the broad question respecting

[19] Baden Powell, 'Creation', pp. 480–1.

[20] 'Creation', p. 482. In the late 1830s Baden Powell became well acquainted with Richard Owen. He was probably influenced by Owen's detailed criticism of Lamarck in the British Association Report on *British Fossil Reptiles*, see *Edinburgh New Philosophical Journal*, 33 (1842), 65–88. Owen's Report also contained an attack on R. E. Grant, see p. 75. On Owen's anti-transformist, and anti-Grant campaign, see A. Desmond, 'Richard Owen's reactions to transmutation in the 1830s', *B.J.H.S.*, 18 (1985), 25–50.

the immutability of species, and the abstract possibility of a transition from one into another, and the modifications of intermediate races being perpetuated, of a new species thus eventually introduced, have fairly formed subject of debates among physiologists'.[21]

A further feature of Baden Powell's 1843 survey of current cosmological debates was his support for the doctrine of progressionism. The issue had been mentioned in the appendix to the *Connexion of Natural and Divine Truth* written by the geologist John Phillips. The latter rejected transmutationism and criticized the work on evolutionary palaeontology by Geoffroy Saint-Hilaire. Phillips did however endorse the progressionist view of the succession of beings throughout geological time. His appendix was reprinted almost verbatim by Baden Powell in the article 'Creation', albeit without acknowledgement. In 1843 Baden Powell was convinced that the fossil record offered sufficient evidence to conclude that the history of life on earth developed along a path of increasing organic complexity. Baden Powell still endorsed the methodological requirements of Lyell's geology. Contrary to the latter's view, however, he believed organic variation sufficient to explain the succession of species, and supported the evolutionist interpretation of the progressionist doctrine.[22]

Baden Powell also touched upon the question of the origin of man. He confirmed that the appearance of man upon the scene was a recent occurrence. He nevertheless emphasized that this hypothesis was open to possible confutation from future palaeontological investigation. He explained that '*as far as research has yet gone* (1843), *it detected* no human remains' of great antiquity. Moreover, he concluded his survey of the arguments supporting the gradual succession of species by pointing out that 'the human race (probably) did not come into existence till the period to which the present state of things belongs'.[23]

The goal of Baden Powell's survey of astronomical, geological, and cosmological doctrines was to stress that the scientific theories under debate offered a view of nature opposed to the one found in the Mosaic narrative. The Old Testament cosmogony had to be viewed as a mythical composition adapted to the fertile imagination and primitive scientific notions of the Jews. Mosaic cosmology was not part of revelation. It only represented the literary device chosen by the inspired writer to convey his religious message. If this was the case, then the discovery of fossil man or of a mechanism explaining the succession of beings could not constitute an objection against the credibility of revelation: it only proved that the Jewish cosmology was an inadequate representation of natural events.

[21] Baden Powell, 'Creation' (1845), p. 484.
[22] Baden Powell, 'Creation', pp. 483–4; *Connexion* 'Supplementary Note, on the Geological Evidence of the Former Condition of Organized Life and its Unbroken Succession', by J. Phillips, pp. 309–13. On John Phillips, see J. Morrell and A. Thackray, *Gentlemen of Science* (1981). See M. Bartholomew, 'The non-progress of non-progression', *B.J.H.S.* (Lyell centenary issue), 9 (1976), 166–74; P. J. Bowler, *Fossils and Progress* (1976), pp. 69–89.
[23] Baden Powell, 'Creation', p. 484.

In his review of the *Vestiges* David Brewster argued that the anonymous author broke the alliance between science and religion. Naturalists and Christians agreed that the book of nature was distinct from the book of revelation. Divine truth was then preserved from contamination by scientific hypotheses and speculations: 'we did not expect that this holy alliance would be disturbed either by the philosopher or the divine'. The survey of the debate on cosmology reveals that it was Brewster's error not to have perceived that many divines and naturalists did not share his view. From the early 1830s representatives of various streams of religious and radical thought discussed the effect of modern science upon the traditional Christian view of nature. The immediate impact of the *Vestiges* proved that large sections of the reading public were alerted to the problem and avidly read the most systematic summary of cosmological and development hypotheses to emerge during the past ten years.[24]

(ii) The reception of the 'Vestiges'

The *Vestiges of the Natural History of Creation* appeared in October 1844. Four editions of the work were called for in seven months. The tenth edition was printed in 1853. By 1860 the book had sold 23,750 copies. Other commentators have discussed in detail the theories put forward by Chambers. It would be difficult if not misleading to give a brief summary of Chambers's ideas, especially as the author considerably modified his views in every successive edition of the work. Chambers was ready to give up central features of his original theory of cosmic and organic evolution because he defended a vision of nature rather than individual scientific doctrines. His ambition was to explain the succession of cosmic and terrestrial phenomena in terms of natural laws. A detailed analysis of the earlier editions of the *Vestiges* would substantiate the claim that there was little which was new in the book from the point of view of the specific hypotheses put forward, the brand of natural theology and the philosophy of nature it endorsed.[25]

The fault to which friends and foes immediately drew attention was the dogmatism with which the author discussed scientific doctrines originally proposed by naturalists as hypotheses or speculations. Naturalists were taken by surprise by the boldness of many statements offered by Chambers. The

---

[24] (D. Brewster), '*Vestiges of the Natural History of Creation*', *North British Review*, 3 (1845), 471. See also R. M. Young, *Darwin's Metaphor* (1985).

[25] (R. Chambers), *Vestiges of the Natural History of Creation* (1844); see twelfth edn. (1884) with an introduction by A. Ireland, p. xxv. M. B. Ogilvie, 'Robert Chambers and the successive revisions of the *Vestiges*' (1973); M. J. S. Hodge, 'The universal gestation of nature', *J.H.B.*, 5 (1972), 127–51; J. H. Brooke, 'Precursors of Darwin', in J. H. Brooke and A. Richardson, *The Crisis of Evolution* (1974), pp. 38–43; P. J. Bowler, *Fossils and Progress* (1976), pp. 53–62; H. G. Gruber and P. H. Barrett, *Darwin on Man* (1974), pp. 207–8. P. J. Bowler, *Evolution. History of an idea* (1984).

nebular hypothesis was accepted by many. Others endorsed the recapitulation theory and the theory of the gradual progression of life towards higher levels of organic complexity. Few were prepared to support Chambers's view that the actual or hypothetical natural laws he indicated were sufficient to account for the progression from monad to man. Yet, the general approach to the relationship between philosophy, theology and science deployed by Chambers had many points in common with the synthesis defended by Baden Powell in 1838. The natural theology of the *Vestiges* stressed the higher concept of God derived from the contemplation of a natural system pre-ordained from eternity to fill the universe with endless successions of worlds and organic forms. These views were common to Chambers, Baden Powell, Carpenter, Pye Smith, Francis Newman and other critics of the book, as well as to those radical theologians who argued against miracles and special providence.

The hysterical reaction by Sedgwick and the severe criticism by Brewster have often been taken as typical answers to the *Vestiges*. It has also been maintained that there was a clear-cut distinction between the favourable reaction by large numbers of non-scientific readers, and the unanimous negative response by 'professional' naturalists and intellectuals in general. A survey of the debate on rational cosmology during the 1830s and the early 1840s shows complex cross-currents in the diversified answers to the *Vestiges*.[26]

The *Athenaeum* reviewer of *Vestiges* had no quarrel with the author's alleged 'heterodoxy', but rather with his 'unsupported conclusions'. He nevertheless acknowledged that the anonymous writer – 'a Scotchman, a large reader, but not an original observer' – had produced an interesting book. After reading *Explanations: A Sequel to 'Vestiges of Creation'*, a subsequent, apologetic publication by Chambers, the *Athenaeum* reviewer emphasized that the author had 'produced a book [*Vestiges*] which may in some manner serve as an outline to the vast range of the natural sciences'.[27]

William Henry Smith (1808–72) showed greater alertness than Brewster or Sedgwick about new trends within natural science. According to Smith, those who argued that inductive investigations only accounted for the preservation of natural equilibrium took 'but a limited view of science'. 'New phenomena, new arrangements, new objects are successively developed' according to natural laws. Smith stressed that cosmological doctrines were still at the stage of hypotheses, and criticized the author of the *Vestiges* for taking them for granted. It was nevertheless perfectly legitimate to study the laws of nature 'in their creative as well as reproductive function'.[28]

As far as the theory of the origin and development of life was concerned,

---

[26] M. B. Ogilvie, 'Robert Chambers and the Nebular Hypothesis', *B.J.H.S.*, 8 (1975), 214–32; M. Ruse, 'The relationship between science and religion', *Church History*, 44 (1975), 514.

[27] (Anon.), '*Vestiges*', *Athenaeum*, n. 897 (4 Jan. 1845), 12 and '*Explanations*', n. 946 (13 Dec. 1845), 1190–1.

[28] (W. H. Smith), '*Vestiges*', *B.M.*, 57 (1845), 448–9, 452–3.

Smith was satisfied that new species were produced by the direct intervention of God. He was however ready to listen 'with curiosity and attention' to any new theory explaining the secondary means responsible for the introduction of new species. The reviewer was deeply dissatisfied with the doctrine of the origin and development of life put forward by the anonymous author. He found the results of the experiments by Crosse and Weekes unreliable and the recapitulation theory imperfect, and made sarcastic remarks about the doctrine of the unity of composition. Yet, Smith was equally severe against those who accused the *Vestiges* of reviving scientific materialism and atheism. To explain nature in natural terms was not, as some pretended, to exclude God from nature. He was convinced that 'there is nothing atheistic, nothing irreligious, in the attempt to conceive creation, as well as reproduction, carried on by universal laws'.[29]

This was also the opinion of Carpenter, who wrote an interesting and detailed review of *Vestiges* for the *British and Foreign Medical Review*. Carpenter argued that the nebular hypothesis represented 'the greatest contribution which science has yet made to religion'. He however complained that Chambers ignored the difference between 'probable' and 'established' scientific theory. The scientific side of the *Vestiges* was undoubtedly weak. Many mistakes were to be corrected before the doctrine put forward in the book became an acceptable hypothesis. Carpenter did nevertheless assent to the 'fundamental ideas' of the *Vestiges*.

He reviewed with particular care the electrical experiments by Crosse and Weekes, and was clearly sympathetic towards the possibility of direct creation of animal forms out of inorganic elements. 'If fact it be' that the *Acarus crossii* was produced by electrical agency, then the origin of man could be explained in the same way. Carpenter felt that such a bold hypothesis required authoritative support. Contradicting former statements on the irrelevance of Genesis to science he now argued that

the Creator formed man out of the dust of the earth, we have scriptural authority for believing; and we must confess our own predilection for the idea that at a period however remotely antecedent, the Creator endowed...certain forms of inorganic matter with the properties requisite to enable them to combine...into the human organism, – over that which led us to regard the great-grand-father of our common progenitor as a chimpansee or an oran-outang.[30]

One month after the publication of Carpenter's paper, in February 1845, Francis Newman published his review of the *Vestiges*. Newman left the evaluation of the scientific reliability of the book to the experts of various disciplines. The reviewer suspected that the author was inaccurate in some details, but 'it is impossible that he should have gone wrong in any of the greater results

[29] (Smith), '*Vestiges*', 456, 450.
[30] (W. B. Carpenter), '*Vestiges*', *British and Foreign Medical Review*, 19 (1845), 155–81.

on which his whole argument turns'. Newman was particularly keen to discuss the theological implication of the transmutation hypothesis. God, he argued, acted by law, 'not by muscular force or special interference'. The by now famous statement by Herschel on the possibility that new species were introduced by the agency of natural laws, was quoted with understandable approval. Newman ridiculed Lamarck's 'speculations', though his summary of the latter's views revealed that he attributed to Lamarck the anti-Lamarckian hypothesis of adaptive change through monstrosity proposed by Geoffroy Saint-Hilaire.[31]

Baden Powell did not take part in the debate on the *Vestiges*. We will discuss below the reasons for this restraint. There is however little doubt that Newman was reviewing the *Vestiges* as a disciple of Baden Powell. Newman declared that the alleged atheism of physiologists and anatomists was in fact a 'verbal controversy' caused by ignorance of the epistemological foundation of inductive sciences. The theories Baden Powell put forward in the *Connexion* guided the approach to the *Vestiges* privileged by Newman. The reviewer argued that philosophical natural theology was based on the acknowledgement that God operated through laws: 'all increased acquaintance with those laws should be hailed by every intelligent worshipper'. His survey of the debate on the succession of species was also indebted to Baden Powell. Newman praised Geoffroy Saint-Hilaire's views on the unity of anatomical composition as having enlarged man's view of God. His praise of his Oxford friend was even more enthusiastic: 'Undaunted by the stigma of atheism which has rested on St. Hilaire, the intrepid Baden Powell in his excellent volume upon the *Connexion of Natural and Divine Truth* has calmly reviewed the whole controversy; and has in no ambiguous terms showed his conviction, that the old-fashioned idea of Creation must in certain important particulars be remodelled'.[32]

The second scientific authority Newman relied upon was Carpenter. He quoted the latter's passages on spontaneous generation of intestinal parasites as confirming the assertion by Chambers that creation through natural means was an ongoing process.

It is not irrelevant that Newman, Carpenter and Baden Powell were at the time in close contact. Carpenter was introduced to Newman in 1839 and they became friends for life. Both Newman and Carpenter were well acquainted with the new Unitarian leadership at Liverpool, James Martineau and Blanco White in particular. Carpenter recommended Newman to his brother Russell and to James Martineau as a suitable candidate for the classical tutorship at Manchester College. Blanco White and Newman expressed their admiration for Baden Powell's *Connexion*. They tended to follow the theses of their friend when approaching scientific issues. Newman had been a pupil of Baden Powell when a student at Oxford, had studied with profit Whately's *Logic*, and was

[31] (F. Newman), '*Vestiges*', *Prospective Review*, 1 (1845), 52, 54.
[32] (Newman), 62, 60, 70, quotation p. 63.

himself interested in the subject, as well as in broad philosophical issues relating to science. Baden Powell's works were approvingly referred to by the *Christian Teacher* and its successor, the *Prospective Review*, the new magazine sponsored by the Liverpool Unitarians and published by John Chapman, who in later years bought the *Westminster Review*, thereby providing a new platform for radical theologians and philosophers such as George Henry Lewes.[33]

It could therefore be argued that from the late 1830s and the early 1840s there were signs of rapprochement between Baden Powell and the new Unitarian intellectual leadership. Differences on theological subjects were clearly marked and emphasized, but reciprocal criticism was always fair and basically sympathetic. On scientific subjects, and in particular on the question of cosmological or transmutation theories and their relation to religion, the agreement was complete. Baden Powell and his Unitarian allies had solved the theological dimension of the issue, and looked with benevolent interest at the development of science. To Francis Newman, science had nothing to do with religious experience, and natural theology was irrelevant. To Baden Powell, the discovery of new natural laws provided evidence of the existence of a rational principle in nature.

Baden Powell's view was not shared by Sedgwick and Brewster. To them, the *Vestiges* was 'prophetic of infidel times' and a clear attempt to force science towards materialistic and atheistic conclusions. Sedgwick maintained that no man who had 'any name in science...has spoken well of the book, or regarded it with any feelings but those of deep aversion'. The reaction to the *Vestiges* was clearly more complex than Sedgwick suggested. Indeed, it is extremely revealing that all the reviews analysed above were published *before* the ones by Brewster and Sedgwick, which appeared in July and August 1845. There was unquestionably a section of the intelligentsia which did not speak well of the book, but felt no aversion to it either. The kind of questions Chambers asked seemed to be legitimate ones, even though his answers were wrong.[34]

Further detailed investigation on the immediate impact of the *Vestiges* would not fail to emphasize the complexity of the reaction by representatives of the scientific and theological communities. The case of Richard Owen deserves notice, for the new light it throws on the actual reaction to Chambers's work.

---

33 Baden Powell Papers, Correspondence. Letters from W. B. Carpenter and F. Newman. Carpenter, *Nature and Man*, pp. 27–42. (J. Blanco White), 'The argument from design', *Christian Teacher*, 5 (1843), 137–55. Charles Bray (1811–84), the early mentor of George Eliot, confessed that it was Baden Powell who convinced him to abandon scriptural literalism, see *Phases of Opinion* (1884), p. 12; see also p. 187. Bray married the sister of Charles Hennell; the Hennells were pupils of the Reverend Robert Aspland, the Hackney Unitarian. I have found no trace, as yet, of early contacts between Baden Powell and the young Unitarian intellectuals gathering around Aspland.

34 (Brewster), '*Vestiges*', p. 471; (Sedgwick), '*Vestiges*', *E.R.*, 82 (1845), p. 3

The anonymous author of *Vestiges* instructed his publisher to send two hundred copies of his work to naturalists and intellectuals of standing. A letter of acknowledgment to Chambers which has caused considerable debate among historians was the one sent by the palaeontologist and comparative anatomist Richard Owen. The letter has been interpreted by Owen's biographer and by several scholars as indicating approval of the doctrines of the *Vestiges*. Further inquiry has brought to light important manuscript material and emphasized the extent and nature of Owen's opposition to the doctrines of the *Vestiges*.[35]

Yet, Owen wrote to the anonymous author of the *Vestiges* and the letter was obviously civil. Few of the naturalists who received the book bothered to acknowledge the gift. Moreover, in a letter to Whewell dated 14 February 1845, Owen wrote to his Cambridge friend: 'I desire not to appear as having directly or personally aided in any thing that may be regarded as a refutation or antidote to the *Vestiges*.' Owen justified his desire not to appear thus by arguing that the public interest in the book was bound to fade away: to attack the *Vestiges*, Owen said, would serve only to publicize the book more widely. A few selected reviews of the *Vestiges* published between October 1844 and February 1845 shows that the response of critics was more mixed than has been previously acknowledged. Thus, since the *Vestiges* was anything but still-born, the justification offered by Owen is not perfectly convincing.[36]

Owen's personality has lacked appeal for historians as well as for his contemporaries. The idiosyncrasies of his character have contributed to obscure the fundamental importance of his palaeontological and anatomical studies. I would like to argue that Owen's reaction to the *Vestiges* brings certain features of his character into focus and provides further indirect evidence of the success of the book not only with the public at large, but also within limited but highly influential circles. It is well known that Owen was very reluctant to oppose authority, whether intellectual, political or aristocratic. This is not to say he was impressed by the success of the *Vestiges*. He could certainly have disregarded the favourable response by Carpenter or Francis Newman, even though documents recently brought to light by Adrian Desmond show that Owen himself was an active albeit ambiguous member of the group gathering around John Chapman and George Eliot. He had however to take into account the opinion of a circle of personalities with whom he was not prepared to differ.

A letter of William Benjamin Carpenter records some early reactions to the *Vestiges*. In 1844 the physiologist was employed as tutor to Lady Lovelace's

[35] R. Owen, *The Life of Richard Owen*, 2 vols. (1894), vol. i, p. 253.
[36] For the relevant bibliographical information, and a detailed discussion of the issue, see J. H. Brooke, 'Richard Owen, William Whewell and the *Vestiges*', *B.J.H.S.*, 10 (1977), 142, 139.

sons. In the fashionable aristocratic salon of his patroness Carpenter met Miss Murray, one of the Queen's maids of honour. Miss Murray's conversation was as interesting to Carpenter as it is to the historian: 'she was very amusing, especially as she was full of royal and noble opinions upon phrenology and mesmerism, and especially upon the *Vestiges* which is being very extensively read in the highest circles, and generally attributed to me. Prince Albert is reading it aloud to the Queen in an afternoon'.[37]

It is of course perfectly understandable that the name of Carpenter was mentioned as a guess at the identity of the anonymous writer. It is not surprising, however, that there was also gossip ascribing the book to Prince Albert or Lady Lovelace. Sedgwick expressed the conviction that the book was the product of a feminine hand. It would be interesting to know whether he was aware of the rumours attributing it to Lord Byron's daughter.[38]

Owen was perfectly aware of the various sophisticated models put forward to explain the succession of species. He himself had some views on the subject. It did not take him much time to realize that the first edition of the *Vestiges* was a dogmatic summary of crudities. Yet, he wrote the anonymous author a rather benign letter, in which he pointed out with kindness the defects of the book. Brooke has suggested that the letter printed by Owen's biographer could have been edited; the latter is indeed known to have taken liberties with the documents at his disposal. The evidence quoted above concerning the success of the *Vestiges* in the 'highest circles' could suggest however that Owen wrote the letter as reproduced by his biographer.

Owen knew of Prince Albert's passion for palaeontology and transcendental anatomy; he had often lectured the Prince on those subjects. The *Vestiges* might well have been, as many said, the work of a clever and enthusiastic amateur like Prince Albert. Owen compromised with a letter of thanks sufficiently kind not to offend and sufficiently critical to point out the major defects of the book. It is to be noted that he acknowledged in his letter that the 'discovery of the secondary causes concerned in the production of organized beings' was a crucial issue of natural history.

In the early months of 1845 Sedgwick and Whewell expressed anxiety and strong opposition regarding *Vestiges*. Owen found himself in a difficult position. He did not want to contradict the views of his Cambridge colleagues. In the first place, he agreed with them that the book was scientifically weak. Secondly he hoped to persuade them that the universities should give more space to comparative anatomy. He saw himself as the best candidate for a new chair. In 1848, when it had become clear that the reforming intents of his Cambridge

---

37 Carpenter, *Nature and Man* (1888), p. 34; *Vestiges*, twelfth edn., p. xviii; A. Desmond, *Archetypes and Ancestors* (1982). Philip Sloan is undertaking a major study of Owen's early anatomical lectures.   38 (Sedgwick), '*Vestiges*' (1845), p. 4.

colleague had come to a halt Owen sent Whewell one of the few blunt and self-respecting letters he wrote in his life:

> If the universities be unable of themselves, or unwilling to create and endow a Professorship of Zoology and Comparative Anatomy, will it do them no good to appeal to the Power that made them – directly or permissively to supply that among other defects? I can understand the hint that the fulfilment of the duty which my connection with those sciences imposes on me to join in such a prayer [the appeal for the University Commission] may be of no benefit to myself. But what of that![39]

In 1845 Owen had still some hope that his Cambridge colleagues might help him to a chair. He thus shrewdly decided at that time to offer his competent advice to his Cambridge friends, but specified that Whewell should not identify him as an opponent of a work enjoyed by royalty. His justification for this request was reasonable and to some extent sensible, though it is difficult to believe that he really considered the *Vestiges* a work destined to be still-born. He well knew that many of his London colleagues and friends thought otherwise.[40]

In July 1845 the review by Sedgwick appeared, followed in August by Brewster's one. Francis Newman's reaction to their criticism was revealing: he attacked their intolerance and expressed his belief that the questions discussed in the *Vestiges* were legitimate and required further investigation, but was forced to agree that the book contained crudities and inaccuracies. It is difficult to assess whether admirers of the *Vestiges* in the 'highest circles' were equally swayed by the criticism of the *Edinburgh Review* author. It is however probable that, like Newman and Carpenter, many remained convinced that the 'fundamental ideas' of the *Vestiges* were still acceptable, even though still unsubstantiated by scientific evidence.[41]

The discussion of the new view of nature proposed by the anonymous author, and the general problem of scientific cosmology emerged as the major feature of the debate on the *Vestiges*. As Newman wrote with satisfaction, 'a new spirit is already powerful among us'. Conversely, many Christian naturalists were as we have seen deeply critical of the opinion that every natural phenomenon was and could be explained by an appeal to natural laws. Herschel himself thought it appropriate to intervene in the debate. His name had been often quoted in support of the view that the introduction of new species was a natural, as opposed to a miraculous event.

---

[39] This letter has till now escaped the attention of historians, probably for its unlikely location: Oxford, Oriel College, Hawkins Papers, 2.142: Owen to Whewell, 12 Jan. 1848. Whewell clearly sent the letter to Hawkins, in order to inform him of Owen's deprecable – to his eyes – support of the University Commission.

[40] On Owen's difficulties with the Chapman group on the one side, and his Oxbridge colleagues on the other, on the subject of *Vestiges*, see A. Desmond, *Archetypes and Ancestors* (1982), pp. 31–3.

[41] (F. Newman), '*Explanations*', *Prospective Review*, 2 (1846), 33.

In his presidential address to the 1845 Cambridge meeting of the British Association Herschel made it clear that his 1836 statement had been misunderstood and misrepresented as a declaration in favour of a naturalistic explanation of life. He attacked *Vestiges* and the cosmological use of the nebular hypothesis. As far as the succession of species was concerned, Herschel warned against mistaking the 'Rule' for the 'Act'. The assumed regularity of the succession of beings did not mean that the introduction of new species was caused by the action of law. He therefore concluded, 'take these amazing facts of geology which way we will, we must resort elsewhere than to a mere speculative law of development for their explanation'.[42]

It could be argued that the hysteria of Sedgwick's review, the severity of the attack by Brewster, and Herschel's comments on the meaning of 'natural law' were directly proportional to their awareness that the machinery of natural laws which they had contributed to build was escaping the control of its Christian masters. Lyell's arguments against transmutationism and the cosmological approach to the history of life were used to criticize the transmutation model offered by the author of the *Vestiges*. It could therefore be said that the attack by Sedgwick had the merit of redirecting attention to the question of the true actual causes of variation presently acting in the organic creation. This, he asserted, was the only path towards the solution of the problem of the succession of beings. Sedgwick clearly believed that Lyell's arguments, as Whewell noted, proved that species were immutable, and that there was no mechanism available to explain the introduction of new forms of life. He nevertheless wrote, in terms to which Lyell and Baden Powell wholeheartedly subscribed, that 'as all our knowledge of the celestial mechanism is derived from our previous knowledge of the laws of matter studied on the earth; so all our exact knowledge of organic laws of the old world can only be learnt from a study of the organic phenomena of living nature. With such phenomena we must begin, as we have no philosophical starting point'.[43]

The reviews by Sedgwick and Brewster succeeded in the short term in achieving their purpose. The vehemence of their denunciation was nevertheless counterproductive in the long term. The basic issue at stake in the debate over the *Vestiges* was not the reliability of individual scientific doctrines but rather the question of whether the modern view of nature did or did not admit of explanations referring to extra natural processes and agencies. It is relevant to point out again Newman's reaction to the review by Sedgwick, as representing an honest and lucid testimony of contemporary views often ignored by historians of the period. Francis Newman denied the right of naturalists to criticize the *Vestiges* in the way Sedgwick and Brewster had done: 'The

---

[42] J. F. W. Herschel, 'Address', *Report of the Sixteenth Meeting of the B.A.A.S.* (1846), pp. xliii, xxxviii–xxxix; Schweber, 'Origin of the *Origin*' (1977), 312–3.

[43] (Sedgwick), '*Vestiges*' (1845), p. 50.

Author of the *Vestiges* is attacked as if he were responsible for the great ideas, to establish which the leading members of the British Association have been devoting their whole life'.

In his youth Newman had been an extreme evangelical and believed the literal truth of scripture. It was Sedgwick and his colleagues who convinced him that the six days of Genesis were not really six, nor days: 'it was very slowly and unwillingly that many of us, unscientific people, first received' the discoveries of modern geology. Newman explained that he had been taught by naturalists that it was more honourable for God to work by law than by direct action. Many adopted this higher view of creation and sought to explain the works of nature in terms of a system of sophisticated laws, similar to the ones displayed by Babbage's calculating machine.

Newman could not understand the vehemence of Sedgwick's denunciation. The animosity against the *Vestiges* clearly betrayed ulterior motives: 'Some are desirous to securing immunity to their own speculations, by a cheap display of eloquent zeal against all who dare to go against their measure'. The debate which geologists and naturalists had energetically launched in the early 1830s had become of great relevance to the layman and the religious philosopher. The question of how to interpret natural operations or the relationship between the view of nature disclosed by science and the religious representation of creation was a problem which concerned the believer and the philosopher as much as the geologist: 'geologists will not be allowed to assign the limits of human thought'.[44]

Baden Powell shared, if not actually inspired, the point of view so eloquently put forward by Francis Newman. His remarks on the relationship between science and religion constantly emphasized the danger of avoiding problems for fear of the religious consequences of scientific advance. It was however clear that representatives of the intelligentsia and a conspicuous sector of the educated public debated with great interest precisely the questions avoided or attacked by official culture. Crucial geological, and later, anatomical and physiological issues were to be taken into careful consideration by professional naturalists, philosophers and theologians.

Baden Powell did not take part, however, in the debate on the *Vestiges*; 1844 and 1845 were years of family tragedy and renewal. He was in the same years engaged in theological controversy against the Anglo-Catholic movement. It is also fair to argue that he did not want to face unnecessary adverse publicity. He was at Cambridge on 19 June 1845 when Herschel delivered his presidential address, and was perfectly aware of the anti-*Vestiges* mood prevailing among his colleagues. His friend Newman did however publicize Baden Powell's views on the subject of creation. The debt to Baden Powell

---

44 (F. Newman), '*Explanations*' (1845), pp. 36–7, 41. For a perceptive comment on the role of the B.A.A.S. in fostering a lay cosmology, see Morrell and Thackray, *Gentlemen of Science* (1981), p. 245.

was evident and indeed fully acknowledged. Moreover, the article on 'Creation' the latter wrote for Kitto's *Cyclopaedia of Biblical Literature* was published in the spring of 1845. Baden Powell's views on the subject of species and of rational cosmology were therefore known.

The survey of the debate on the *Vestiges* and on the second volume of Lyell's *Principles of Geology* reveals that during the 1830s and the 1840s the question of species was discussed with full awareness of the epistemological, cosmological and theological issues involved. Mainly thanks to the *Vestiges* and to the violent reaction by Sedgwick and Brewster, powerfully aided towards the end of the 1840s by Hugh Miller, the question of species became the highly publicized ground for the confrontation between those who believed that nature was governed by laws, and those who insisted on the continuous intervention of God in natural and human affairs. It is not surprising that it was this wider dimension of the debate which attracted Baden Powell's attention. One of the *Essays* he published in 1855 was devoted to discussing the progress of the debate on species after the publication of the *Vestiges* and to assessing the relevance of the species question to the modern view of nature.

17

Towards the Origin

The debate on species during the late 1840s and 1850s covered a wide range of topics. The discussion of the probable laws regulating the geographical distribution of organic forms, inquiries into the natural history of mankind, discoveries in embryology and physiology, the accumulation of palaeontological data and broad theological and natural theological considerations were issues acknowledged as relevant to the solution of the species puzzle. Few naturalists were known or suspected to hold transmutationist views. The great majority of participants in the debate acknowledged the inadequacy of available trans-mutationist mechanisms, though among anthropologists and medical authors both in England and in Europe, forms of transformism were actually upheld.[1]

Interpretation differed widely as to the consequences to be expected from explanations of the succession of beings in natural terms. Some were convinced that the very fact of asking this question implied support for a basically materialistic view of nature. Sedgwick and Hugh Miller were the most outspoken representatives of this opinion. Sedgwick turned successive editions of his 1834 *Discourse* into an interminable anti-transmutationist manifesto. The fifth edition published in 1850 had a preface of 442 pages containing a detailed criticism of all possible arguments used to support the naturalistic interpretation of the succession of species.

Sedgwick warned that the ideas put forward by the *Vestiges*, Geoffroy Saint-Hilaire, and 'other materialists of the same school' were bound to have disastrous effects on society: materialism, 'if current in society,... will under-

---

[1] For contemporary views on the high degree of specialization of the species issue, see (H. Holland), 'Natural history of man', *Q.R.*, 86 (1849), 1–40; (W. B. Carpenter), 'Natural history of man', *E.R.*, 88 (1848), 429–87; (J. Wilson), 'The Dodo and its kindred', *B.M.*, 65 (1849), 81–98. On developments within the biological debate on species, see W. Coleman, *Biology in the Nineteenth Century* (1971); D. Ospovat, *The Development of Darwin's Theory* (1981); A. Desmond, *Archetypes and Ancestors* (1982); P. J. Bowler, *Evolution. History of an idea* (1985). Note that systematic debate of the species issues in 'respectable' periodicals started with the articles on anthropological matters published in 1848–49. During the early 1850s, Robert Knox gave popular and well attended anthropological lectures in London, in which he upheld transformism and polygenism. In the 1850s Knox had a house in Hackney, and in 1860 he became keeper of the Museum of the Ethnological Society. Baden Powell attended the lectures given by Knox. See Rehbock, *The Philosophical Naturalists* (1983), pp. 54–6.

mine the whole moral and social fabric, and inevitably will bring discord and deadly mischief'. Miller was equally convinced that the development theory was not only wrong but dangerous. When intelligent mechanics became materialists, 'they become turbulent subjects and bad men'.[2]

Others preferred to look at the question from the point of view of the knowledge available. Joseph Dalton Hooker expressed the conviction that information collected by naturalists was insufficient to 'decide upon the general question of the origin and permanence of species'. He was not opposed, however, to any attempt to explain the distribution and chronological succession of beings, provided that the theory put forward was a scientifically sophisticated hypothesis. Edward Forbes rejected the Lamarckian doctrine. He maintained that the great majority of his colleagues 'hold the independent creation or calling into being of a protoplast for each species'. He nevertheless argued that 'to stigmatize any other proposition as absurd *a priori* is to talk nonsense'.[3]

To Sedgwick, Miller and Whewell the debate on species was a trench in which to fight for a view of nature and society as providentially organized and constantly acted upon by God. The mechanisms of nature could not be understood because they depended on the mysterious counsels of God. The order of nature revealed features dependent not upon law but upon will. To Baden Powell the attitude of his colleagues again betrayed their incapacity to understand the intellectual change produced by scientific advance. He became increasingly certain that law and not mystery revealed the existence of God. The order of nature and of society was explained and preserved by law, not by will. Thus, it could be argued that Baden Powell's approach to the species question was more similar, albeit opposite, to that adopted by Sedgwick and Miller, than to that of Hooker and Forbes. Baden Powell and his opponents were equally confident that crucial consequences were to be expected from the solution of the species puzzle. They were less concerned with the actual solutions, or lack of them, and concentrated instead on the context of the debate.

It was in the late 1840s that Baden Powell became intimate with Francis Newman and Carpenter. Newman moved to London in 1846, when he was appointed Professor of Latin at University College. In 1847 his close friend William Benjamin Carpenter was promoted to the chair of medical jurisprudence. Robert Chambers, whose sister married a neighbour and friend of Carpenter, was a frequent visitor at the latter's house. Newman, Carpenter, and Chambers had frequent discussions on religious and scientific subjects. There is no direct evidence that Baden Powell took part in these intellectual

[2] Sedgwick, *Discourse* (fifth edn., 1850), pp. xi, cclxxii; H. Miller, *Foot-Prints of the Creator* (1849), p. viii.

[3] J. D. Hooker, *Introductory Essay to the Flora of New Zealand* (1853), p. viii; (E. Forbes), 'The future of geology', *W.R.*, 2 (1852), p. 82. On Forbes and his approach to the question of species see below, and Rehbock, *The Philosophical Naturalists*, 103–13.

gatherings, but from the late 1840s he frequently visited Newman and quoted his works. He knew Carpenter and quoted his works as well. Indeed, the physiological section of the 'Philosophy of Creation' essay was almost written by Carpenter. Finally and significantly, it was in 1848 that Baden Powell first wrote to Robert Chambers, congratulating the author on the sixth edition of the *Vestiges* (16 April).[4]

It is highly probable that Baden Powell discussed science and religion with Carpenter, Chambers and Francis Newman. The few fragments relating to this period of Carpenter's life reveal that in the late 1840s the physiologist was concerned with a variety of theological and philosophical topics remarkably similar to the ones considered by Baden Powell during this time. Each member of the group had strong views on the relationship between science and religion. Newman was to some extent a follower of Baden Powell, as his review of the *Vestiges* proved. Moreover, Baden Powell felt entitled to refer Chambers to his work on the *Connexion of Natural and Divine Truth*, 'where (at page 151) you will, I think, perceive that even at that time I had a strong leaning towards the very views you have since so much more ably expounded, while the whole tenor of my argument I think will be found to stand in striking accordance with yours'.[5]

It is significant that Baden Powell believed his views of 1838 were the very same Chambers put forward in the *Vestiges*, but easy to perceive that this was hardly the case. Nevertheless, Baden Powell felt justified in claiming priority: he had indeed been the first British author to place the question of species in the context of an epistemology and natural theology favouring a naturalistic explanation of the succession of species.

Baden Powell's defence of the main theme of the *Vestiges* was not limited to his personal letter of congratulation. Whately's response to a letter written to him in January 1850 by Baden Powell shows that the latter tried to convince his friend that the *Vestiges* had been considerably improved. Whately had grown more and more impatient with novelty, in particular of the kind the *Vestiges* represented: 'The *Vestiges of Creation* I looked at a few parts, and

---

4 Janet Chambers, the younger sister of Robert, married William Henry Wills (1810–80). Wills had been editor of *Chambers' Journal* from 1846 to 1848, the year in which he moved back to London, to become sub-editor of *Household Words*, the weekly edited by his friend Charles Dickens. Janet Wills was noted in literary and social circles for her soirées and the wide circle of her acquaintances. It would be interesting to study the relationship between the Wills–Carpenter–Newman circle, and the group of intellectuals gathering around John Chapman: the two groups were indeed partially co-extensive.

5 *Vestiges*, twelfth edn., pp. xxx–xxxi; Carpenter, *Nature and Man*, pp. 40–54; V. M. D. Hall, 'The contribution of the physiologist W. B. Carpenter', *Medical History*, 23 (1979), 125–55 I. G. Sieveking, *Memoir and Letters of Francis William Newman* (1909), p. 143. M. Ruse, 'The relationship between science and religion' (1975), argues that 'the exact date of Baden Powell's initial support for Chambersian ideas does not really matter: it happens before the *Origin*', p. 514. It is noted that the chronology of the debate on species before Darwin is of extreme importance to the understanding of the change of mood clearly perceptible in the early 1850s.

certainly thought it could be improved by being mended, like the Irishman's knife, with a new blade and a new handle'. Whately did however acknowledge that he had not anticipated the author's making this needful repair so skilfully.[6]

The closing years of the 1840s were therefore significant ones for Baden Powell's intellectual development and projects. The Tractarian revolt was over, and a spirit of inquiry was abroad in the religious, scientific and philosophical world. Baden Powell's close association with Carpenter, Francis Newman and Chambers, and his friendship with Buckle, Augustus De Morgan, the Baron von Bunsen and other eminent personalities stimulated his ambition of updating, revising, and publicizing views held by him from the late 1830s. In 1849 he wrote the essay on *Necessary and Contingent Truth*, which represented his attempt to come to terms with the philosophy of Whewell and Mill. His project to address his views on the relationship between science and religion, philosophy and theology to a wider audience was however delayed by a series of events, the first of which being his appointment to the Oxford Royal Commission (20 August 1850).[7]

In June 1852 Baden Powell seriously considered the possibility of publishing a series of essays. He thus combined and revised sections of his 1835 book and papers he had contributed to various journals during the previous few years. The three essays originally planned were on 'Induction', 'Creation', and 'Final Causes'. The process of revision was a long one. Entries in Baden Powell's journal record lengthy transactions with publishers and give the impression that the author's election as Vice-President of the Royal Society in December 1853 helped him eventually to find a suitable publisher.[8]

The publication of Whewell's essay on the plurality of worlds in the last months of 1853 again delayed the completion of Baden Powell's book. Longmans probably asked him to contribute to this debate in October 1854. The *Essays on the Spirit of Inductive Philosophy, the Unity of Worlds, and the Philosophy of Creation* appeared in April 1855. Evidence relating to the preparation of the book makes it clear that the original project only included the first and third of the essays in the title, the essay on the 'Unity of Worlds' being added at the last moment. Baden Powell limited his contribution to the topic to reviewing the various ideas put forward by Whewell and Brewster.

The question of how to interpret the debate on the plurality of worlds, or any other scientific debate, Baden Powell had solved from 1838, and perfected when writing his 'Philosophy of Creation' essay. Moreover, recent scholarship has exhaustively explored the plurality of worlds question and its philosophical,

---

[6] Baden Powell Papers, Whately to Baden Powell, January 1850.

[7] We will not discuss Baden Powell's contribution to the Oxford Commission. His ideas on University Reform did not alter significantly from the days of the early 1830s debate; see W. R. Ward, *Victorian Oxford* (1965).

[8] B.P.J., entries for 20 Aug. 1850; 27 Apr. 1852; 7 June 1852; Oct. 1852; Jan. 1853; 6 Dec. 1853; 15 Dec. 1853; 6 July 1854; 17 July 1854; 27 Oct. 1853; Apr. 1853.

scientific and theological implications. In his excellent study, Dr Brooke has also emphasized the crucial points of Baden Powell's views on the subject. It will therefore be possible to concentrate on the section of Baden Powell's work dealing with the species question.

It is significant that Baden Powell's decision to write an essay on the philosophy of creation coincided with the years of his close personal intercourse with Newman, Chambers and Carpenter. His essay was written before the publication in 1853 of the tenth edition of the *Vestiges*. In the early 1850s Carpenter was asked through the publisher to revise the physiological section of the tenth edition. The sequence of events from 1845 to 1853 substantiates the claim that the group comprising Baden Powell, Carpenter, Francis Newman and Chambers considered the question of species and the defence of a naturalistic explanation of natural phenomena as two crucial features of their intervention in contemporary debates.[9]

Attitudes in favour of a naturalistic explanation of the succession of species were rapidly spreading among the young generation of London radical intellectuals. Paradoxically, the reading of Lyell's *Principles* kept convincing many of the reasonableness of Lamarck's research programme. Stanley Jevons remarked in his manuscript journal that 'Lyell makes great fun of Lamarck... but appears to me not to give any good reason against' his doctrine. Herbert Spencer's first approach to Lamarck was also due to Lyell's *Principles*. The *Vestiges* too did their work through successive, improved versions. Alfred Russell Wallace was fired by the book, to the point of determining to take upon himself the task of solving the problem of species. At Oxford, Mark Pattison advised students not to meddle with science, but to be happy with reading the literature of science; he listed Herschel, Humboldt and the *Vestiges* as good suggestions.[10]

Within the *Westminster Review* group, the question of species became a key issue. As noted above, Edward Forbes kept a moderately negative position. Herbert Spencer and George Henry Lewes came decidedly on the side of a lay interpretation of nature, and of the legitimacy of transformism. Spencer published in 1852 his first paper on 'The Development Hypothesis', and Lewes discussed issues relating to transformism in his perceptive articles on Goethe and Etienne Geoffroy Saint-Hilaire. Like Baden Powell, in those years a frequent guest and host of Lewes, the young author considered the doctrine of Lamarck a valuable philosophical speculation, which still required further substantiation and, perhaps, deep revision.[11]

9 Brooke, 'Natural theology and the plurality of worlds. Observations on the Brewster–Whewell debate', *A.S.*, 34 (1979), 221–86. Carpenter knew that Chambers was the author of the *Vestiges*, see *Nature and Man* (1888), p. 42.
10 Stanley Jevons, *Letters and Journals* (1886), p. 23; on Spencer and Lyell, see A. Desmond, *Archetypes and Ancestors*, p. 97; H. L. McKinney, *Wallace and Natural Selection* (1972); L. Atollemanche, *Recollections of Pattison* (1885), p. 3.
11 H. Spencer, 'The Development Hypothesis', *The Leader*, 20 March 1852, in *Essays* (1891), vol. i, pp. 1–7; (G. H. Lewes), 'Goethe as a man of science', *W.R.*, 2 (1852), 475–506 and

The change of mood with respect to transformist conjectures also invested the theological literature, thus preparing the way for the conciliation between cosmological deism or theism and evolution which was going to be one chief characteristic of the evolutionary debate of the second half of the century. Francis Newman and Baden Powell were joined by far less suspect authorities in upholding the apologetic virtues of the development hypothesis. Robert Anchor Thompson, winner of the Burnett Prize for 1854, included his discussion of intuitionism and rationalism, deism and infidelity, the fixity or transmutation of species within the scope of a wide-ranging approach to social and intellectual change: as he explained, 'the country has been already, for several years, in a great state of transition'. Declamations in favour of the conservation of the *status quo* at all cost were better abandoned in favour of a careful and perceptive survey of the new trends emerging at the social and the intellectual levels.[12]

Thompson, like others before him, took Herschel's letter to Lyell, printed in Babbage's *Ninth Bridgewater Treatise*, as an authoritative endorsement of the legitimacy of investigating the secondary means which historically brought about new forms of beings. Thompson had no doubt that men were far from approaching the solution of the mystery. Yet, he could not see where the danger lay for Christianity and theism:

Suppose then it were established, that laws of nature extended to the origination of living species, as well as to their continuance; suppose it were ascertained, that there is a continuity of law and force between the developments of matter and those of vegetable and animal life; and that matter and electricity, and the other dead forces of nature, posesses the power of evolving life under the requisite conditions; what would be the theological effect of this conclusion? Nothing more than this, – to give us an enlarged knowledge of the laws of nature, and to alter our definition of material substance. We should learn that there is a higher energy of Divine Power in the existence of matter, than we have hitherto perceived, but the mystery of the Divine energy would remain as far beyond us as before.[13]

John Tulloch, the winner of the second prize of the Burnett competition, was more moderate and cautious. He quoted Whewell's *Indications of the Creator* and Lyell's *Principles* to assert that variation within the species was a known, but very limited phenomenon. He did however support a developmental interpretation of palaeontological progressionism, and argued against Lyell that the possibility of finding 'vertebrate fishes in the lower Silurian rocks' would not contradict progressionism or *Vestiges*: such a finding 'cannot overturn the idea of a regular procession of species; it only removes the date and verge of that procession further back'. According to Tulloch, the conception of 'Creative Energy' constituted a good alternative to both miraculous intervention and godless transformism: 'Why should such fresh expressions

'Life and doctrine of Geoffroy Saint-Hilaire', 5 (1854), 160–90. See R. E. Ockenden, 'G. H. Lewes, 1817–1878', *Isis*, 32 (1947), 70–86.
[12] R. A. Thompson, *Christian Theism* (1855), vol. ii, pp. 369–75.
[13] Thompson, *Christian Theism*, vol. ii, pp. 197–8.

of Creative Power be supposed to be irregularities, 'interferences', in the great plan of creation – and not, as according to the genuine theistic conceptions they truly are, parts of the development of the Great plan contemplated from the first?'[14]

Once again, Baden Powell's decision to review the debate on 'the philosophy of creation' reflected the change of priorities within the sections of the intellectual élites he looked at with interest and sympathy. It is interesting again to emphasize, however, that Baden Powell decided to write the essay on the species question as a consequence of his discussions with Carpenter, Chambers and Francis Newman. He did not quote Spencer or Lewes, whom he probably regarded as young followers, in the same way in which, years later, he tactfully reproached Darwin for not having acknowledged his pioneering contribution to the solution of the species puzzle.[15]

There is no doubt that Baden Powell was perfectly familiar with the change of mood within metropolitan radical circles: he himself was very active canvassing his friends and relatives to adopt a more enlightened attitude towards the question of species. Yet, as was typical with his late output, the essay on the philosophy of creation was far from original, and did not bear the signs of a deep investigation of the issue. It is also to be emphasized that Baden Powell's approach to the species question in 1855 was a documented and expanded version of the remarks on the succession of species published in 1838 and the article 'Creation' of 1845. As in 1838 and 1845, the main evidence supporting his conclusions derived from geology and physiology.

The discussion of the geological evidence focused on the evaluation of the theory of progression. Baden Powell well knew as did the author of *Vestiges* and Lamarck himself that the series of organic forms could not be represented as following a simple pattern of organic complication. Baden Powell also knew that Lyell was strongly opposed to progressionism. He quoted with respect Lyell's anti-progressionist views, and the latter's 1851 address to the Geological Society when Lyell argued that there was no sufficient evidence of a general inferiority of organic structure in the early periods of the earth's history. Yet, Baden Powell was clearly more sympathetic towards Owen's views on the subject. It is furthermore interesting that Baden Powell quoted extensively from Owen's contribution to the *Quarterly Review* criticizing the views put forward by Lyell in his address. The palaeontologist was convinced that there was evidence of successive and progressive development of the vertebrate skeleton, from an original archetype to the variety of forms now living on earth. Applying to palaeontology the embryological doctrines of Von Baer,

[14] J. Tulloch, *Theism* (1855), pp. 72, 77, 79 and 179.
[15] Gavin de Beer, 'Some unpublished letters of Charles Darwin', *Notes and Records of the Royal Society*, 14 (1959), 12–66.

Owen also argued that the successive development of mammalia was characterized by the 'gradual exchange of a more general for a more special type'.[16]

Baden Powell commented that the investigations conducted by Owen disclosed an important feature of the development of life on earth. Species living at earlier periods combined characters of various higher and lower classes which succeeded them. In the course of ages, species seemed to 'diverge in distinct directions'. Baden Powell did not expand, however, upon the concept of divergence of characters, a key point of later evolutionary debates. His main concern was to emphasize the 'continuity of characters' and the unity of composition displayed by organic forms throughout the history of life. Species succeeded each other, but there was no sudden appearance of totally new forms, unconnected with the previous ones. This consideration brought Baden Powell to discuss the question of the existence of breaks in the series.[17]

The supporters of creationism stressed the presence of gaps in the fossil record which transmutationists were unable to explain. Baden Powell was understandably concerned to find a satisfactory solution to the problem. He relied on his reflections on the role of analogy in the inductive sciences to argue that in every continuous fossil record which had been reconstructed by geologists the transition from one form of life to the following one proceeded 'by *small modifications of species*'. It was therefore legitimate to infer that the gaps were an indication of the long interval of time occurring between the deposition of contiguous species markedly different from each other. The absence of missing links could be explained by taking into account the peculiar geological conditions of the region, probably unfavourable to the preservation of remains.[18]

Baden Powell was aware that his opponents had pointed out strata in which widely different species succeeded each other, and the geological evidence proved the relatively short amount of time involved in the transition from one form to the other. His last resort was to stress the methodological requirements of sound geological investigation. Geologists were not allowed to suppose the existence of a 'real *hiatus* in the continuity of physical laws'. Those who questioned this basic principle put 'all science in danger'. The investigation of organic change must follow the procedures adopted by geologists. Even though the law responsible for the introduction of new species was largely

---

[16] Lyell, 'Presidential Address', *Quarterly Journal of the Geological Society of London*, 7 (1857), pp. xxv–lxxvi; (R. Owen), 'Lyell on life and its successive development', *Q.R.*, 89 (1851), pp. 426, 450. See P. J. Bowler, *Fossils and progress* (1976); A. Desmond, *Archetypes and Ancestors* and 'Designing the Dinosaur: Richard Owen's response to Robert Edmund Grant', *Isis*, 70 (1979), 224–34.

[17] For a suggestive account of the development of the concept of divergence, and its influence on Darwin's thought in the 1850s, see D. Ospovat, *The Development of Darwin's theory* (1981), chs. 7 and 8; D. Kohn, 'Darwin's principle of divergence as internal dialogue', in D. Kohn (ed.), *The Darwinian Heritage*, pp. 245–57.   [18] Baden Powell, *Essays*, pp. 332–5.

unknown, it was not legitimate to invoke extra-natural causes. Geology established the 'broad facts' of the constancy of natural laws regulating changes in organic matter, and the regular succession of beings throughout the strata. There was no reason to believe that changes in organic nature were not brought about by natural laws.[19]

The evaluation of the physiological evidence reached the same conclusion. Baden Powell expanded upon the theory of unity of composition put forward by Geoffroy Saint-Hilaire, though he now acknowledged that the doctrine of the French naturalist was 'a kind of philosophical prophecy'. Reference was also made to the works of the German transcendental anatomist and philosopher Lorenz Oken. The comments on Oken and Geoffroy Saint-Hilaire emphasized the legitimacy of conjectures and hypotheses in science. The progress of discovery brought to light new sets of phenomena. Naturalists who attempted to explain them were bound to proceed through guesses and mistakes. The ideas of Oken and Geoffroy Saint-Hilaire were superseded by the work of Owen and Von Baer. Modern physiologists came nevertheless to realize that their predecessors had inspired new concepts and new ways of looking at phenomena.

When discussing Baden Powell's contribution to natural theology in the 1850s, it was noted that his late works tended to consist of lengthy annotated summaries of theories by contemporary theologians. The same remark fully applies to his discussion of geological and physiological doctrines. The section on the evidence provided by physiologists to the solution of the question of species reviewed theories of Owen, Carpenter and Thomas Henry Huxley. Works by François Jules Pictet, Robert Knox and de Blainville were also mentioned. When discussing points of particular difficulty or relevance to his argument, Baden Powell referred the reader to appendices where he reproduced long passages from contemporary works. He also asked several colleagues to state their views on physiological as well as geological issues.[20]

During the 1850s the debate on species became a highly technical issue. Baden Powell's appeal for help to naturalists from various specialties reflected his awareness of the rapid development of natural sciences. As it had been the case with reference to optics, the technical progress of biology, physiology and palaeontology escaped his grasp. He often found it difficult to focus the relevance of topics he touched upon or to evaluate critically the theories he mentioned. It could even be argued that he did not pay sufficient attention to the precise evidence upon which the theories he referred to were based.

---

[19] *Essays*, pp. 346–9, 355.
[20] *Essays*, pp. 371, 369, and appendices; P. J. Bowler, *Fossils and progress*, pp. 93–122; D. Ospovat, 'The influence of Karl Ernst Von Baer', *J.H.B.*, 10 (1976), 1–28. On Robert Knox, the picturesque and tragic Scottish anatomist who personally knew Cuvier and Geoffroy Saint-Hilaire, see Rehbock, *The Philosophical Naturalists*.

Critics stressed Baden Powell's enthusiasm for theories which totally lacked substantiation, or were at the level of pure speculation.

In his presidential address to the Geological Society, William John Hamilton pointed out that Baden Powell considered the origin of life and of species directly out of inorganic matter a legitimate conjecture. To Hamilton, this was an unjustified and unsupported assertion. Hamilton avoided mentioning, however, that Baden Powell was quoting Carpenter's views on the origin of life and species. Baden Powell's answer to the criticism by Hamilton illustrated his approach to the theories upon which he relied. He conceded that the question of the origin of life was extremely complex and one on which little information was available: 'But I think the extension of sound analogy can only lead us to regard it as just as much a result of some unknown combination of regular physical conditions as any other natural phenomenon'.[21]

There was clearly little originality in Baden Powell's summaries of works by naturalists of the time. Moreover, Hamilton was right in arguing that Baden Powell was uncritical towards theories confirming his own views. The author of the much acclaimed *Essays* was aware of the shortcomings of his approach and of many of the theories he supported. Yet, in his view, his task was to emphasize that the discussion on species involved philosophical questions of which his colleagues appeared unaware. Many opposed transmutationism on account of the inadequacy of the information available. These naturalists failed to realize that 'the question is rather one of general principles of reasoning rather than of precise scientific detail'. It is thus fair to claim that the 1855 essay was not designed to evaluate the details of the theories discussed, but rather their general bearing on the broad debate concerning the interpretation of the succession of beings on earth.

Baden Powell maintained that his discussion of Owen's views represented a significant illustration of the order of priorities he was arguing for. He sent to Owen for approval his summary of the latter's views on vertebrate anatomy. Owen knew that his colleague had a strong leaning towards a strictly naturalistic explanation of the history of life. He therefore invited Baden Powell to insert a paragraph stating that 'Professor Owen...is specially desirous to be understood as applying his conclusions solely to the *order* and *law* of succession, without any attempt to assign a *cause or to trace its origin*'.

Owen, Baden Powell explained, 'anxiously disclaimed' that his theory of progression of life through the historical development of archetypal forms implied direct or indirect support for the development theory. Baden Powell was however pleased to announce that the greatest living palaeontologist did

---

[21] W. J. Hamilton, 'Anniversary Address of the President', *Quarterly Journal of the Geological Society of London*, 12 (1856), cxvi–cxviii. Baden Powell, *Essays*, pp. 408, 422, and second edn., p. 429.

not exclude the possibility of secondary causes regulating the succession of species: Owen simply stated that such causes were 'as yet' unknown.[22]

Baden Powell had no difficulty in accepting Owen's statement as the conclusion of science in general. Naturalists were free to stop where Owen did. It was then the task of the philosopher – his own task – to evaluate whether the result of present investigations represented, as many claimed, the final word on the subject. As far as he was concerned, Baden Powell was convinced that 'the verdict of all inductive philosophy' stressed that '*some* regularly ordained causes' were responsible for the succession and progression of life on earth. Thus, he freely admitted that the Lamarckian theory was faulty, that the views expressed by Geoffroy Saint-Hilaire were 'prophetic', and that the *Vestiges* was wrong on physiological details. This was not all, however: the question at stake involved 'broad philosophical principles'. At that high level, the question of species was solved, even though the details of the solution were still to be discovered.

Science always progressed from the known to the unknown. The condition of progress was the assumption by investigators that '*what we do not know must really be as much under the dominion of laws as what we do know*'. Whatever Sedgwick or Whewell thought on the subject, the results of current geological investigations and the debate on physiological doctrines represented a step forward with respect to the view that the succession of species was a miraculous process. Imperfect conjectures, or even unsupported speculations, were always more favourable to the advance of knowledge than the dogmatic assertion that there was nothing to be known respecting phenomena thought to be brought about by God's direct intervention.[23]

Baden Powell was thus convinced that the broad philosophical evaluation of scientific procedures and results pointed towards a naturalistic explanation of the question of species. His evaluation of the methodological foundation of uniformitarian geology convinced him that a mechanism of organic transmutation was probably responsible for the succession of species. He agreed that naturalists observing the present state of organic arrangements had '*no experience of such a thing as a change of species*'. It was however undeniable that variations did occur in organisms. However slight or temporary, occasional deviations from the parental stock were known and observed facts: 'Thus this known cause,... *conjoined with the influence* of incalculably vast periods of *past time* MAY BE fully competent to give results...remote from those now *every day seen*'.[24]

---

[22] *Essays*, pp. 410–12. Baden Powell quoted R. Owen, *On the Nature of Limbs* (1849), p. 86. In December 1849 Owen had been attacked in the press for supporting pro-transformist views, and was particularly sensitive on the issue: see J. H. Brooke, 'The natural theology of the geologists, (1979), pp. 47–8; on Owen's January 1850 letter to Baden Powell, see Brooke, above, pp. 40–41, and A. Desmond, *Archetypes and Ancestors* (1982), p. 46.

[23] *Essays*, pp. 401, 436, 394–5, 371, 424, 427.   [24] *Essays*, p. 417.

Baden Powell's discussion of the 'philosophy of Creation' reproduced with negligible modification the arguments put forward in his earlier works. He clearly failed to appreciate and was not concerned with the considerable technical development and specialization experienced in the debate on species during the late 1840s and the 1850s. He argued for broad philosophical principles and a general view of nature stressing the regularity of the succession of natural phenomena. The tone of his essay, the priorities he promoted, and his emphasis on the strictly naturalistic interpretation of the history of life made him an effective opponent of the views put forward by Sedgwick, Whewell or Hugh Miller. His disquisitions had however little chance of convincing his Anglican brethren or of impressing naturalists who shared his views of nature, but who wanted arguments more convincing than Baden Powell provided them with.

It is somewhat ironical but not surprising that in the eyes of a dedicated young naturalist like Jospeh Dalton Hooker there was no difference between Baden Powell and his Anglican opponents: 'These parsons are so in the habit of dealing with the abstractions of doctrines as if there was no difficulty about them whatever...that they gallop over the course when their field is Botany or Geology as if we were in the pews and they in the pulpit. Witness the self confident style of Whewell and Baden Powell, Sedgwick and Buckland'.[25]

The situation was clearly more complex than Hooker described, and his view of 'parson' Baden Powell was not shared by all. Alfred Russell Wallace quoted for instance a sentence from Baden Powell's *Order of Nature* as the epigram to one of his notebooks. It was however true that Baden Powell's work belonged to the 1830s and 1840s. His approach was basically unappealing to naturalists involved in research during the 1850s. They enjoyed the consequence of intellectual changes Baden Powell helped to bring about, but considered the wider issues he fought for as already settled.

To the wider public, to the lay reader of the *Vestiges*, to Francis Newman, to the subscribers and the editors of the *Westminster Review*, Baden Powell's essays appeared as a refreshing alternative to the denunciations of Sedgwick, Miller and Whewell. Indeed, to a wide class of readers the question at stake was the definition of a new approach to nature more than the establishment of what was regarded as mere scientific detail.

Baden Powell expanded again on the question of species in his later work on the Burnett prize essays and in the *Order of Nature*. He took advantage of the proof–editing stage of his contribution to the *Essays and Reviews* to introduce a paragraph on Darwin's *Origin of Species*. As might be expected, he was enthusiastic about 'Mr. Darwin's masterly volume', which substantiated the principle of '*the origination of new species by natural causes*'. It is of course to be wondered whether Baden Powell would have accepted the Darwinian theory in all its details, or would have subscribed to the view of chance variation implicit in Darwin's concept of natural selection. It is however impossible not to reflect that Baden Powell's presence at the Oxford British Association meeting of 1860 would have changed the terms of the confrontation Hooker and Huxley had with Bishop Wilberforce.

Hooker commented that Baden Powell 'greedily...has adopted all Darwin has suggested and applied these suggestions (as if the whole were already proved) to his own views'. Hooker's remarks had certainly some foundation. It is however true that Baden Powell's contribution to the debate on species was important, though an indirect one. In the 'Historical Sketch' he added to the third edition of the *Origin*, Darwin spoke of the 'masterly manner with which Baden Powell discussed the question of creation: 'Nothing can be more striking than the manner in which he shows that the introduction of new species is a regular not a casual phenomenon'. It might be argued that it is more striking that already in 1838 Baden Powell had defended the same view and almost in the same terms.[26]

The survey of the debate on species in England during the first decades of the nineteenth century does suggest that the most striking conclusion concerns the extent to which contemporary debates and priorities have been neglected by historians of the period. That Darwin opened his notebook on species in July 1837 or Baden Powell wrote his passages on species in 1838 was not exceptional or unexpected. It would be irrelevant to point out the obvious differences between Darwin and Baden Powell, or between Darwin and the *Vestiges*, the French transformists, Carpenter, Geoffroy Saint-Hilaire and the score of naturalists and natural theologians who discussed the question of the succession of species from a variety of points of view. The close investigation of the Darwinian manuscripts which has characterized scholarship of the last fifteen years has often neglected the wider dimension of contemporary debates relating to natural sciences, as well as to philosophy, natural theology, and broad ideological issues. An integration of the two approaches will probably produce a further step forward in our understanding of this crucial episode in the formation of contemporary scientific and ideological standpoints.

It is not appropriate to discuss in this study the growing pace of pro-, quasi-, and anti-transformist statements from 1855 to the publication of the *Origin of Species*. The years 1855–9 were characterized by the growing awareness that the transformist synthesis many had feared or hoped for since the late 1830s was now approaching. This was the impression Lyell had when reading Alfred Russell Wallace's 'On the Law which has regulated the Introduction of New Species' (1855), a paper which prompted the geologist to open his own notebook on species. This is the impression the reader has,

[26] C. Darwin, *On the Origin of Species* (1859, third edn., 1861), p. xviii.

when perusing English, French, German and Italian works of the period, the periodical literature in particular.[27]

That 1859 was a crucial year in the history of modern biological sciences, no one could ever deny. Yet, the relative and in some case amazing rapidity with which the evolutionary debate – at a biological, as well as a philosophical, theological, and broadly ideological level – fired European culture should alert attention to developments which took place in the 1840s and the 1850s. Historians may study with profit the diffusion of the *Vestiges* in northern European countries, or the permanence of pro- or quasi-Lamarckian options in countries like France and Italy, at different locations of the cultural spectrum: zoology, anthropology, medicine, radical theology and politics. The exercise, far from pleasing lovers of antiquarianism, may throw revealing light on the complex issue of the controversial reception of the *Origin of Species* in England, Europe and the United States. If the *Origin of Species* had little in common with *Vestiges*, or Baden Powell's works, readers approached Darwin's text with a set of convictions which had a lot to do with Chambers and the Oxford Professor, with Lamarck and Geoffroy Saint-Hilaire, with radical anthropological thought and theological debates.[28]

It is important to stress that the reconstruction we have offered in this study was limited to assessing the contribution to the debate on species of a small group of intellectuals. Further investigation would not fail to add new figures and new themes to the narrative here attempted. Yet, though the group composed by Baden Powell, Carpenter, Francis Newman and Chambers himself was a small one, through the writings of its members it mirrored the wide spectrum of issues which contemporaries thought relevant to the species question. The question of species in early Victorian England was not – or not only – the search for an evolutionary truth, natural selection, which needed to be discovered. The problem of interpreting the succession of species concerned a wider audience. It was a feature of a more complex debate on whether providential care or iron laws governed both nature and society. In this debate, Baden Powell emerged as a key protagonist.

[27] For representative standpoints on the problem of species in the years immediately preceding the publication of the *Origin*, see (T. H. Huxley), '*Vestiges of the Natural History of Creation*', *British and Foreign Medical Chirurgical Review*, (1854), 332–43; (H. Spencer), 'Progress: Its Law and Causes', *W.R.*, 11 (1857), 445–85; (G. H. Lewes), 'Hereditary influence', *W.R.*, 10 (1856), 135–62; C. Daubeny, 'Address', Cheltenham Meeting of the B.A.A.S., in *Athenaeum*, n. 1502 (9 August 1856), 997–1002; F. Newman, *Theism. Doctrinal and Practical* (1858); F. R. Ross, 'Philip Gosse's *Omphalos*, Edmond Gosse's *Father and Son*, and Darwin's theory of natural selection', *Isis*, 68 (1977), 85–96; for bibliographical reference to analogous debates in France and Italy, see Corsi, 'Recent studies on French reactions to Darwin' and 'Recent studies on Italian reactions to Darwin', in D. Kohn (ed.), *The Darwinian Heritage* (1985); E. Mayr, *The Growth of Biological Thought* (1982); P. J. Bowler, *Evolution. History of an idea* (1985)

[28] D. Kohn (ed.), *The Darwinian Heritage* (1985), Part III: essays by P. J. Bowler, P. J. Weindling, P. Corsi, F. M. Scudo and M. Acanfora, pp. 641–752 provide useful bibliographical guides to the literature on the reception of Darwin's work. See also J. Moore, *Post-Darwinian Controversies* (1978), on theological debates preceding and following the publication of the *Origin*.

18

Conclusions

The main conclusions of this study have already been expressed when discussing the final phases of Baden Powell's participation in the debates on the methodology of science, natural theology and the question of species. It is therefore appropriate to review briefly the main features of his contribution to contemporary intellectual life and to summarize the significance of his work in the context of nineteenth-century studies.

It has often been noted that several of Baden Powell's ideas could not be described as original or perceptive. As early as 1826 he himself acknowledged that his synthesis of Christian apologetic was indebted to his Oriel teachers and Hackney relatives. In later years his writings concerned with the evaluation of epistemological doctrines, made constant reference to concepts put forward by Stewart, Whately, Copleston and Mill. As far as his scientific interests were concerned, in 1838 Baden Powell wrote to Lubbock that he was anxious to secure correct information on specific experimental issues from experts, upon 'whose labours I should then have the satisfaction of commenting'. Moreover, in his essay on the species question he freely acknowledged his debts towards many colleagues who contributed information to his survey. Yet, Baden Powell's lack of originality is itself a point of considerable interest to historians of nineteenth-century intellectual life. His disregard for details and detailed investigations, his stress on the 'principles', the 'fundamental ideas' involved in various departments of research, introduces the historian to a concept of intellectual activity alien to modern scholarly standards and specialization.

The Anglican intellectual and the Christian apologist were in Baden Powell's eyes gentlemen who devoted leisurely attention to major issues discussed by specialists, and who evaluated the bearing and tendency of current debates with respect to religious beliefs. To some extent, this attitude was characteristic of the great season of nineteenth-century reviews and reviewers, when books were often quoted from extracts included in the *Edinburgh*, *Quarterly*, or *Westminster* reviews. It was however true that Baden Powell's general and often generic approach to intellectual issues derived from his early training at Oriel and his admiration for the Noetic standpoint. Intervention in debates on a wide range of issues, with a view to counteracting developments unfavourable to Christianity and the Church, was the practice characteristic of the apologetic programme developed by the Oriel Noetics in the early decades of the nineteenth century. In this respect, Baden Powell was a faithful disciple of his teachers even in the writings which signified his final departure from the evidential Christian apologetic formulated by Whately.

Having established the point that Baden Powell lacked originality, it cannot be denied that he made the best use of the ideas and conclusions contributed by the intellectual authorities he admired. His first work on *Rational Religion Examined* represented a well-argued and highly interesting synthesis of apologetic priorities within contemporary High Church circles. We have dwelt in some detail upon the interest of Baden Powell's early apologetic for nineteenth-century theological and philosophical studies. Markedly new and original with respect to his intellectual background was his second major book, the *Connexion of Natural and Divine Truth*. The philosophical and theological ideas which characterized the Noetic apologetic approach were applied to solve new and allegedly dangerous developments in science. Baden Powell's defence of geology and of the legitimacy of inquiries into the species issue reached in 1838 conclusions endorsed by few of his Anglican colleagues. The novelty of Baden Powell's ideas on the relationship between science and religion is well illustrated by the fact that twenty years later the principles laid down in the *Connexion* were still regarded by many as a fresh approach to issues debated by naturalists, natural theologians and philosophers. It is therefore fair to conclude that Baden Powell's contribution to the cultural life of the early decades of the century was original in so far as he made use of concepts elaborated by others to draw attention to the implications of developments in specific sectors of intellectual activity for the contemporary worldview.

The detailed analysis of crucial features of Baden Powell's intellectual biography has also emphasized the central role played by broad political and social issues in the reorientation of philosophical and theological priorities. The social and political tensions of the late 1820s and early 1830s persuaded representatives of the Anglican intelligentsia that the critical evaluation of religious beliefs, intellectual approaches, and ecclesiastical policies was an essential condition for survival. A sense of urgency permeated the correspondence of leading Oxford figures and was responsible for Baden Powell's decision to publish his 1832 lecture on the state of scientific education at Oxford and his controversial sermon on the relationship between modern geology and the scriptures. 'The speed with which events march on us', Bowden wrote to Newman in March 1834, required major organizational efforts and effective intellectual answers to the vociferous challenge by the radical and dissenting intelligentsia.

In his early works Baden Powell stressed the Noetic and Hackney belief that the Anglican apologetic represented the only advanced, sophisticated, and reliable approach to religion, philosophy, and science. Events led him to take a very different view. The appeal to authority by the Tractarians and the reluctance of his friends to come to terms with the plurality of intellectual approaches and sources of authority debated in the 1830s and 1840s reinforced his conclusion that the Anglican Church was reacting in the worst possible way to the challenge of the times. He deliberately set out to propose an alternative approach. Anglican apologetic remained the crucial point of reference for his intervention in the debates of the 1840s and the 1850s, though he now viewed the Church as the vehicle for safe intellectual progress. He hoped that the Church would become the tolerant forum for philosophical and theological research, though preserving at the same time its spiritual appeal to the unsophisticated beliefs of the masses.

It was significant of the essentially apologetic approach to intellectual debates adopted by Baden Powell that his philosophical and scientific views underwent little change throughout his career, whereas his theological conclusions were constantly reshaped and reassessed. He remained faithful to basic elements of the philosophy of Stewart and Whately and accepted ideas from Comte and Mill only in so far as the latter two proposed what he regarded as a better formulation of the concepts elaborated by his teachers. As far as modern scientific developments were concerned, by 1829 Baden Powell had reached the conclusion that inductive investigations were bound to alter the traditional religious view of creation in fundamental respects. It seemed counterproductive in the extreme to assess single 'discoveries' or hypotheses against the yardstick of the biblical creation narrative. His emphasis on the evidence for the existence of God in nature, provided by the uniformity and regular succession of natural events, allowed him to apply this simple formula to hypotheses and theories regarded by his Anglican brethren with suspicion and opposed with extreme determination.

It could be said that Baden Powell relied upon his apologetic solution to the point of endorsing every hypothesis which provided a hint as to the possible naturalistic explanation of phenomena. It is noted that his approach to science formed the basis of his support for transformism, as much as for Carpenter's hypothesis of the generation of fully developed species out of inorganic matter.

The scant consideration of technical developments in science and philosophy contrasted with Baden Powell's constant attention to developments in theology and Christian apologetic. We have examined in detail the complex process of revision to which he submitted his apologetic. We have also emphasized the elements of continuity underlying the various phases of his intellectual development. Throughout his career Baden Powell remained persuaded that religious truths could not be judged by human rational standards. The arguments supporting this conclusion were however inevitably expressed in terms governed by criteria of logical consistency and were influenced by the change of intellectual priorities and the advance of human knowledge. It was thus inevitable that the Christian apologist submitted his approach to revision and reassessment.

A member of the social and intellectual élite, Baden Powell addressed himself to the intelligentsia of the country. His early works exhibit the author's distaste for popular religious views. The disturbances of the 1830s and the danger of widespread atheism and social subversion forced him to seek a solution acceptable to all men of all classes. This move appeared to him an effective counterpoise to the democratic threat. When the fear was over, he again concentrated upon philosophical and theological developments discussed by the intellectual élites of the time. In the 1840s and 1850s Baden Powell acknowledged the role of popular religious views in preserving the stability of society. He was however concerned with the question of providing a stable intellectual leadership, capable of securing the peaceful development of a pluralistic society firmly controlled by the social élites.

It is interesting to point out that Baden Powell, as well as Carpenter and Newman, were more worried by the first Chartist outbreak than by the second. Carpenter commented that 1847 and 1848 had been years of great political excitement, but remarked that no major assault upon Christianity had been launched. Secularists and atheists failed to convince socialists and trade unionists that Christianity should be a key target in their campaign for economic and political emancipation. The real threat to the stability of society came from those sectors of the élites which refused to come to terms with the new social and intellectual trends. It was essential to pursue active inquiries into the foundations of religion, science and philosophy in order to master and direct the increased pace of intellectual and social change.

Baden Powell had no intention of embarking upon such a project but he was ready and indeed eager to put forward his views on the matter. He found no difficulty in agreeing with Francis Newman and the *Westminster Review* group that developments in theology, philosophy and science were producing fundamental transformations of man's world view. He was prepared to revise and adapt his apologetic approach to what he regarded as the new priorities of the time. Examination of the complex relationship between Baden Powell's intellectual development and a wide range of social and institutional changes represents an interesting case study of the relationship between the intellectual and the social sphere. Moreover, consideration of Baden Powell's contribution to intellectual debates forces the historian to take into account features of British intellectual life which have so far attracted little attention.

The analysis of debates at Oxford on natural theology, on Christian apologetic and inductive theology, or on the reform of the university and the Church prove that pre-Tractarian Oxford should be as interesting to historians as the much-studied Tractarian phase. A wide range of issues were debated within the Noetic circle. The philosophy of Stewart, the new science of political economy, the popular education movement, the updating of the university curriculum, to mention a few from a much longer list of issues, were topics the Noetics examined with competent thoroughness. It is claimed that the wider group of intellectuals of which Baden Powell was part deserves more attention and further detailed investigation. The same consideration applies to dimensions of British intellectual life of the 1840s and 1850s; the analysis of Baden Powell's writings emphasizes the personal and intellectual links between Baden Powell and Francis Newman, Carpenter, Chambers, as well as our author's contacts with Augustus De Morgan, the *Westminster Review* group of the 1850s and representatives of the radical and liberal intelligentsia of the time.

There is direct and indirect evidence suggesting that this group of intellectuals pursued common intellectual goals and shared many views on the interpretation of new ferments in contemporary society. Their writings and their ideas were of great significance in shaping new approaches. Yet, as we commented when considering Baden Powell's contribution to the species question, later generations failed to acknowledge their debt to intellectuals whose writings were often in advance of the tradition they represented, but were at the same time linked to a concept of intellectual activity out of touch with the increased specialization of theology, philosophy and science. Baden Powell reassured his readers that the advance of knowledge represented no threat to religion and social values, providing adequate steps were taken to update traditional views. From the late 1830s to the 1850s his arguments were appealing to a class of readers who shared his persuasion, but they sounded commonplace to the generation involved in the debate on Darwin's *Origin of Species* or on Bishop Colenso's work and the *Lux Mundi*. It is emphasized that a more balanced assessment of the intellectual scene of the 1840s and the 1850s cannot disregard the significant contribution of Baden Powell and his friends to the reshaping of contemporary values and priorities.

Whatever their shortcomings, or inconsistency, Baden Powell's contributions to natural theology, the methodology of science, and the question of species, represent an important and neglected document of British intellectual life in the first half of the nineteenth century. The excessive – albeit understandable – concentration on such unquestionably key figures as Charles Darwin, John Stuart Mill, Samuel Taylor Coleridge and John Henry Newman, has produced a picture distorted by hagiographical overemphasis on singlehanded achievements. The search for pioneers of late nineteenth-century liberalism, precursors of the Anglican revival, or founders of modern political economy and natural sciences has conspired to the neglect of figures like Baden Powell and many of his colleagues, whose attainments and concerns were less appealing to the priorities of later generations. It has been the aim of this study to contribute an assessment of major aspects of his work and to emphasize the intrinsic importance of Baden Powell's intellectual biography for historians of pre- and early-Victorian England. It is hoped that subsequent studies on figures like Richard Whately and Edward Copleston, Francis Newman and Blanco White, Robert Chambers and William Benjamin Carpenter will add new dimensions to our understanding of a crucial period in the formation of modern culture.

BIBLIOGRAPHY

Note
In view of the considerable number of anonymous contributions to periodicals relevant to the authors discussed in this book, the bibliography of this volume has been organized as follows:

Brackets around an author's name indicate that the work was published anonymously
... indicates a work by the author listed in the previous entry
(...) indicates a work by the same author, published anonymously
[...], ... indicates a work referring to the author listed above, by the author
   ..., or (...) if the contribution is anonymous.

This system allows the unification in logical and chronological order of items referring to the same author or topic.

I REFERENCE WORKS

Biographie Universelle (Michaud) Ancienne et Moderne, 45 vols., new edn., Paris, G. Desplaces, 1854–65.
The British Museum Catalogue of Printed Books. Photolithographic Edition to 1955, 263 vols., London, The Trustees of the British Museum, 1968, and *Supplements*. Now *The British Library Catalogue of Printed Books to 1975*, London and Munich, New York and Paris, Clive Bingley and K. G. Saur, 1975–.
D.N.B. The Dictionary of National Biography, ed. by L. Stephen and S. Lee, 63 vols., London, Smith, Elder and Co., 1882–1900, and *Supplements*.
D.S.B. The Dictionary of Scientific Biography, ed. by C. C. Gillespie, 16 vols., New York, American Council of Learned Societies, Charles Scribner's Sons, 1970–80.
Grand Dictionnaire Universel du XIXe Siècle, ed. by P. Larousse, 17 vols., Paris, Administration du Grand Dictionnaire Universel, 1866–90.
The National Union Catalog. Pre-1965 Imprints, The Library of Congress, 685 vols., London and Chicago, The Library of Congress and American Library Association, Mansell, 1968–80. *Supplement*, vols. 686–754, 1980–1.
Nouvelle Biographie Générale, depuis les temps les plus reculés jusqu'à nos jours, ed. by Dr Hoefer, 46 vols., Paris, Firmin Didot frères, 1854–66.
The Royal Society Catalogue of Scientific Papers 1800–1900, 19 vols., London, H.M.S.O. and Cambridge University Press, 1867–1925.
The Wellesley Index to Victorian Periodicals, ed. by W. E. Houghton, 3 vols., Toronto and London, University of Toronto Press and Routledge and Kegan Paul, 1966–79.

II MANUSCRIPTS

Baden Powell Papers, in the possession of Mr Francis Baden Powell, London.
Bodleian Library, Oxford, 'Examination Statutes – Suggestions, etc.', Ms Top. Oxon d 15.
British Library, Babbage Correspondence.
British Library, Hone Papers.
British Library, Napier Correspondence.
British Library, Peel Papers.
British Library, Wordsworth Papers.
Keble College, Oxford, Keble Papers.
Lambeth Palace, London, Whately Papers.
Liverpool University Library, Blanco White Papers.
Manchester College, Oxford, Blanco White Papers.
Manchester College, Oxford, Francis Newman Papers.
National Library of Wales, Nassau Senior Papers.
Oriel College, Oxford, Hawkins Papers.
Oriel College, Oxford, W. H. Parker Letters.
Oxford University Archives, Hebdomadal Board Minutes, 1823–33.
Oxford University Archives, Register of Convocation 1815–20, 1820–8, 1829–37.
Pusey House, Oxford, Pusey Correspondence.
Royal Society, London, John Lubbock Papers.
Trinity College, Cambridge, William Whewell Papers.
University College Library, London, Society for the Diffusion of Useful Knowledge Papers.

III PRIMARY SOURCES

(Alison, A.), 'On parliamentary reform and the French Revolution' [n.3,5,6], *B.M.*, 29 (1831), 429–46, 745–62, 919–35.
(...), 'Progress of social disorganisation (No. II): the Trades' Unions', *B.M.*, 35 (1834), 331–53.
(...), 'Democracy', *B.M.*, 41 (1837), 71–90.
(...), 'The Chartists and universal suffrage', *B.M.*, 46 (1839), 289–303.
(Anon.), *An Address to the Members of the Lower House of Convocation on the Proposed Examination Statute*, Oxford, W. Baxter, 1830.
(Arnold, T.), *Address to the Members of Convocation*, printed sheet, 1824, Bodleian Library, G. A. Oxon C. 40 (23).
(...), 'Church of England' [Review of R. Whately, *Letters on the Church*], *E.R.*, 44 (1826), 490–513.
..., *The Christian Duty of granting the Claims of the Roman Catholics. With a postscript in answer to the letters of the Rev. G. S. Faber printed in the St. James' Chronicle*, Oxford, W. Baxter, 1829.
..., *Sermons*, 3 vols. London, J. G. and F. Rivington, 1829–34.
[...] (Anon.), 'Arnold's sermons', *B.C.*, 7 (1830), 257–94.
..., *Sermons, with an Essay on the Right Interpretation of the Scriptures*, London, B. Fellowes, 1832.
..., *Principles of Church Reform*, London, B. Fellowes, 1833.
(...), 'The Oxford malignants', *E.R.*, 62 (1836), 225–39.
..., *Sermons, chiefly on the Interpretation of Scripture*, London, B. Fellowes, 1845.
Aspland, R., 'Oration delivered by R. Aspland on laying the first stone of the Gravel-Pit Meeting House in Paradise Field, Hackney', British Library, Hone Papers, Add Ms 40120, f. 84.

..., *A Plea for Unitarian Dissenters: in a letter of expostulation, to the Rev. H. H. Norris, M.A., on that part of his late work against the Hackney Auxiliary Bible Society which relates to Unitarians*, Hackney, Stower and Smallfield, 1813.

Aspland, R. B., *Memoir of the Life, Works and Correspondence of the Rev. Robert Aspland of Hackney*, London, E. T. Whitfield, 1850.

Atollemanche, L., *Recollections of Mark Pattison*, London, C. F. Hodgson, 1884.

Babbage, C., *Reflections on the Decline of Science in England, and on Some of its Causes*, London, B. Fellowes, 1830.

..., *Ninth Bridgewater Treatise. A Fragment*, London, J. Murray, 2nd edn., 1837.

..., *Passages from the Life of a Philosopher*, London, Longman, Green and Co., 1864.

Baden Powell, H. G., *Notices of the Life of the late Rev. Baden Powell, M.A., F.R.S., F.R.A.S., F.G.S.,... with a list of his publications*, London, n.d. [1866].

Bakewell, R., 'Facts and observations relating to the theory of the progressive development of organic life', *Philosophical Magazine*, 9 (1831), 33–7

[J. Barclay] (Anon.), 'Barclay on life and organisation', *B.C.*, 17 (1822), 337–55.

..., *Introductory Lectures to a Course of Anatomy, delivered by the late John Barclay [...] with a memoir of the life of the author, by George Ballingall*, Edinburgh and London, Machlachlan and Stewart, Baldwin, Craddock and Joy, 1827.

Beard, J. R. (ed.), *Voices of the Church in reply to Dr. D. F. Strauss, author of 'Das Leben Jesu', comprising Essays in defence of Christianity, by divines of various Communions*, London, Simpkin, Marshall and Co., 1845.

(...), *Unitarianism exhibited in its Actual Condition: consisting of essays by several Unitarian ministers and others, illustrative of the rise, progress, and principles of Christian Anti-Trinitarianism in different parts of the world*, London, Simpkin, Marshall and Co., 1846.

Belsham, T., *Elements of the Philosophy of the Mind, and of Moral Philosophy. To which is prefixed a Compendium of Logic*, London, J. Johnson, 1801.

[...] (Anon.), 'Belsham's *Elements of the Philosophy of Mind*', *B.C.*, 20 (1802), 601–13; ibid., xxi (1802), 135–47.

..., *A Calm Inquiry into the Scripture Doctrine concerning the Person of Christ; including a brief review of the controversy between Dr. Horsley, and Dr. Priestley, and a summary of the various opinions entertained by Christians upon this subject*, London, J. Johnson, 1811.

..., *A Letter to the Unitarian Christians in South Wales, occasioned by the animadversions of the Right Rev. the Lord Bishop of St. David's. To which are annexed. 1) Letters, before published in the Gentleman's Magazine, in reply to His Lordship's letters to the Unitarians. 2) A brief review of his Lordship's treatise, entitled, 'The Bible and nothing but the Bible, the religion of the Church of England'. 3) An estimate of his Lordship's character and qualifications as a theological polemic*, London, R. Hunter, 1816.

..., *The Present State of Religious Parties in England, represented and improved in a discourse*, London, R. Hunter, 1818.

..., *The Bampton Lectures Considered; being a Reply to the Calumnious Charges of the Rev. C. A. Moysey, D.D., etc., in his late Bampton Lectures against the Unitarians, and especially the Editors of the Improved Version; in letters to a friend, to which is annexed a letter, in reply to the charges of the Very Rev. Dean Magee, in vol. II part II of the Dissertation on Atonement and Sacrifice*, London, R. Hunter, 1819.

..., *Reflections upon the History of the Creation in the Book of Genesis. A Discourse at Warrington August 19, 1821: and published at the Request of the Ministers, and of the Congregation*, London, 1821.

[...], (Anon.), 'Belsham – Translation of St. Paul's Epistles', *Q.R.*, 30 (1823), 79–115.

Bentham, G., *Outline of a New System of Logic, with a Critical Examination of Dr. Whately's 'Elements of Logic'*, London, Hunt and Clarke, 1827.

Bentham, J., *Church-of-Englandism and its Catechism Examined: preceded by strictures on the exclusionary system, as pursued in the National Society's Schools; interspersed with parallel views of the English and Scottish Established and non-Established Churches, and concluding with Remedies proposed for abuses indicated; and an examination of the Parliamentary System and Church Reform lately pursued and still pursuing; including proposed new churches*, London, E. Wilson, 1818.

Blainville, H. D. de, 'Resumé des principaux travaux dans les différentes Sciences Physiques publiés dans l'année 1817', *Journal de physique*, 86 (1818), 4–100.

...., 'Sur le Chameau fossile, et sur le Sivatherium des Sous-Himalayas méridionaux', *Comptes rendus de l'Académie des Sciences*, 4 (1837), 71–6.

Blakey, R., *Historical Sketch of Logic, from the earliest times to the present day*, London, Baillière, 1851.

[...], *Memoirs of Dr. Robert Blakey, Professor of Logic and Metaphysics, Queen's College, Belfast. Edited by the Rev. Henry Miller*, London, Trübner and Co., 1879.

Blanco White, J., *Practical and Internal Evidences against Catholicism; with occasional Strictures on Mr. Butler's Book of the Roman Catholic Church, in six letters*, London, J. Murray, 1825.

...., 'Journals and Reviews', *London Review*, 1 (1829), 1–9.

[...] (Anon.), 'Mr. Blanco White, heresy and orthodoxy', *B.C.*, 19 (1836), 204–24.

...., 'On inspiration and miracles', *Christian Teacher*, 4 (1842), 333–53.

(...), 'The argument from design', *Christian Teacher*, 5 (1843), 137–55.

Blomfield, C. J., 'Copleston. Inquiry into the Doctrines of Predestination', *Q.R.*, 26 (1821), 82–102.

...., *The Duty of combining Religious Instruction with Intellectual Culture. A Sermon preached in the Chapel of King's College, London, at the opening of the Institution on the 8th October 1831*, London, B. Fellowes, 1831.

(Anon.), 'Boué's *Essay on the Geology of Scotland*', *B.C.*, 16 (1821), 651–69.

(Bowden, J.), 'Ecclesiastical Record', *B.C.*, 15 (1834), 233–4.

(...), 'Nolan and Powell', *B.C.*, 15 (1834), 411–34.

Bray, C., *The Philosophy of Necessity, or, the law of consequences; as applicable to Mental, Moral, and Social Sciences*, 2 vols., London, Longman, Orme, Brown, Green and Longmans, 1841).

...., *Phases of Opinion and Experience During a Long Life. An Autobiography*, London, Longmans, Green and Co., 1884.

(Brewster, D.), 'Reflexions on the Decline of Science, and Some of its Causes, by Charles Babbage', *Q.R.*, 43 (1830), 305–42.

(...), 'Whewell's *Astronomy and General Physics*', *E.R.*, 58 (1834), 422–57.

(...), '*Animal and Vegetable Physiology Considered with Reference to Natural Theology*, by Peter Mark Roget', *E.R.*, 60 (1835), 142–79.

(...), 'Life and Works of Baron Cuvier', *E.R.*, 62 (1836), 265–96.

(...), 'Lord Brougham's *Discourse on Natural Theology*', *E.R.*, 64 (1837), 263–302.

(...), 'Mr. Comte's *Cours de philosophie positive*', *E.R.*, 67 (1838), 271–308.

(...), '*Vestiges of the Natural History of Creation*', *North British Review*, 3 (1845), 470–515.

(...), '*Explanations. A sequel to the Vestiges of the Natural History of Creation*', *North British Review*, 4 (1846), 487–504.

...., *More Worlds Than One: The Creed of the Philosopher and the Hope of the Christian*, London, Chatto and Windus, 1874. First edn., 1854.

The Bridgewater Treatises on the Power, Wisdom and Goodness of God as Manifested in the Creation, London, W. Pickering, 1833-6:

Treatise I
Chalmers, T., *On the Power, Wisdom and Goodness of God as Manifested in the Adaptation of External Nature to the Moral and Intellectual Constitution of Man*, 2 vols., London, 1833.
Treatise II
Kidd, J., *On the Adaptation of the External Nature to the Physical Constitution of Man, principally with reference to the supply of his wants and the exercise of his intellectual faculties*, London, 1833.
Treatise III
Whewell, W., *Astronomy and General Physics Considered with Reference to Natural Theology*, London, 1833.
Treatise IV
Bell, Sir C., *The Hand: its mechanism and vital endowments, as evincing design*, London, 1833.
Treatise V
Roget, P. M., *Animal and Vegetable Creation Considered with Reference to Natural Theology*, 2 vols., London, 1834.
Treatise VI
Buckland, W., *Geology and Mineralogy Considered with Reference to Natural Theology*, 2 vols., London, 1836.
Treatise VII
Kirby, W., *On the Power, Wisdom and Goodness of God, as manifested in the Creation of Animals and in their History, Habits and Instincts*, 2 vols., London, 1835.
Treatise VIII
Prout, W., *Chemistry, Meteorology, and the Function of Digestion, Considered with Reference to Natural Theology*, London, 1833.
[Broad Church] (Conybeare, W. J.), 'Church parties', *E.R.*, 98 (1853), 273–342.
[...] (Anon.), 'The Broad Church', *Christian Observer*, 49 (1855), 289–93.
[...] (Newman F. W.), 'Jowett and the Broad Church', *W.R.*, 72 (1859), 41–67.
[...] (Anon.), 'Broad Church theology' [On *Essays and Reviews*], *Christian Observer*, 59 (1860), 375–98.
[...] (Hedge, F. D.), 'The Broad Church', *Christian Examiner*, 69 (1860) 53–66.
[...] Stephen, L. 'The Broad Church', *Fraser's Magazine*, 81 (1870), 311–25.
[...] Gordon, A., 'Historical views of Broad Churchism', *Theological Review*, 10 (1873), 277–309.
[...] (Bartlett R. E.), 'The Broad Church movement', *Fraser's Magazine*, 97 (1878), 353–64.
(Broderip, W. J.), 'Progress of comparative anatomy', *Q.R.*, 90 (1852), 362–413.
Brongniart, A., 'Notes sur la composition de l'atmosphère à diverses époques de la formation de la terre et sur l'opinion de M. le Professeur Parrot relative à ce sujet', *Annales des sciences naturelles*, 20 (1830), 427–41.
(Brougham, H.), [on R. Lloyd] 'High Church national education', *E.R.*, 35 (1821), 509–14.
(...), 'The Consequences of a Scientific Education to the Working Classes of this Country..., by a Country Gentleman', *E.R.*, 45 (1826), 189–99.
..., *A Discourse of the Objects, Advantages, and Pleasures of Science*, London, Baldwin, Cradock and Joy, 1827.
(...), 'Progress of the people – the periodical press', *E.R.*, 57 (1833), 239–48.
..., *A Discourse of Natural Theology, showing the Nature of the Evidence and the Advantages of the Study*, London, C. Knight, 1835.
Brown, T., *Inquiry into the Relation of Cause and Effect*, fourth edn., London, H.G.Bohn, 1835.

(...), 'Villers, *Philosophie de Kant*', *E.R.*, 1 (1803), 253–80.

(...), 'Belsham's *Philosophy of the Mind*', *E.R.*, 1 (1803), 474–85.

[...] (J. Wilson), 'The metaphysician (No. II): Brown on Cause and Effect', *B.M.*, 40 (1836), 122–31.

Buckland, W., *Vindiciae Geologicae, or, the Connexion of Geology with Religion explained...*, Oxford, University Press, 1820.

..., *Reliquiae Diluvianae; or, observations on the organic remains contained in the caves, fissures, and diluvial gravels, and on other geological phenomena, attesting the action of an universal deluge*, London, J. Murray, 1823.

(Anon.), 'Buckland's *Reliquiae Diluvianae*', *B.C.*, 20 (1823), 607–23.

Buckle, H. T., *History of Civilization in England*, 2 vols., London, J. W. Parker, 1857.

..., *Miscellaneous and Posthumous works of Henry Thomas Buckle, edited with a biographical notice by Helen Taylor*, 3 vols., London, Longman, Green and Co., 1872.

Bulwer, E., Lord Lytton, *The Life, Letters and Literary Remains of Edward Bulwer, Lord Lytton, By his Son*, 2 vols., London, Kegan Paul and Trench, 1883.

Bunsen, F., *A Memoir of Baron Bunsen*, 2 vols., London, Longman, Green and Co., 1868.

Butler, J., *The Analogy of Religion, Natural and Revealed, to the Constitution and Course of Nature; to which are added two brief dissertations: I. Of Personal Identity. II. Of the Nature of Virtue*, Clarendon Press edn., Oxford, 1820.

Cairns, J., *Oxford Rationalism and English Christianity*, London, Freeman, 1861.

(Call, W. M. W.), 'Francis Newman and his Evangelical critics', *W.R.*, 14 (1858), 376–425.

Carlile, R., *An Address to Men of Science; calling upon them to stand forward and vindicate the truth from the foul grasp and persecution of superstition; and obtain for the Island of Great Britain the noble appellation of the focus of truth; whence mankind shall be illuminated, and the black and pestiferous cloud of persecution and superstition be banished from the face of the earth, as the only sure prelude to universal Peace and Harmony among the human race, in which a sketch of a proper system for the education of youth is submitted to judgement*, London, R. Carlile, 1821.

..., *Mother Church Relieved by Bleeding; or, Vices and Remedies: extracted from Bentham's Church of Englandism, etc., examined: being matter applying to existing circumstances, and consisting of a summary recapitulation of the vices, therein proved to have place in the existing system, and of the particular of the Remedial System therein proposed*, London, R. Carlile, 1823.

Carpenter, W. B., *Principles of Physiology, General and Comparative*, 1839; third edn., London, Churchill, 1851.

(...), 'Vestiges of the Natural History of Creation', *The British and Foreign Medical Review*, 19 (1845), 155–81.

(...), 'Natural History of Man', *E.R.*, 88 (1848), 429–87.

(...), 'Electro-biology and mesmerism', *Q.R.*, 93 (1853), 501–57.

..., *Nature and Man. Essays Scientific and Philosophical, with an introductory memoir by J. Estlin Carpenter*, London, Kegan Paul, Trench and Co., 1888.

Chalmers, T., *The Evidence and Authority of the Christian Revelation*, Edinburgh, W. Blackwood, 1814.

(Chambers, R.), *Vestiges of the Natural History of Creation*, London, J. Churchill, 1844; sixth edn., 1848; tenth edn., 1853.

[...] (Anon.), '*Vestiges of the Natural History of Creation*: Its Arguments Examined and Refuted, by S. R. Bosanquet', *Athenaeum*, no. 915 (10 May 1845), 460.

(...), *Explanations. A Sequel to 'Vestiges of the Natural History of Creation'*, London, J. Churchill, 1845.

[...] (Anon.), '*Explanations. A Sequel to the Vestiges of the Natural History of Creation*', *Athenaeum*, no. 946 (13 Dec. 1845), 1190–1.

(...), *Some Thoughts on Natural Theology, Suggested by a Work, Entitled 'Vestiges of the Natural History of Creation'*, London, Longman, 1849.

..., *Vestiges of the Natural History of Creation. Twelfth Edition, with an introduction relating to the authorship of the work by Alexander Ireland*, London, W. and R. Chambers, 1884.

Channing, W. E., *The Evidences of Christianity*, Glasgow and London, T. R. Hunter, 1833.

..., *Essays, Literary and Political*, Glasgow, London and Edinburgh, T. R. Hunter, 1837.

..., *Memoir of William Ellery Channing, with Selections from his Correspondence*, London, E. T. Whitfield, 1851.

Chilton, W., *The Oracle of Reason*, 2 vols., London, W. Chilton, 1841–3

Churton, E., *Memoir of Joshua Watson*, 2 vols., Oxford and London, J. H. and J. Parker, 1861.

(Anon.), *A Short Memoir of Archdeacon Churton*, Brochure, n.p., dated July 1874; Bodleian Library, 11126, fol. 9.

Cobbett, W., *A History of the Protestant 'Reformation', in England and Ireland; showing how that event has impoverished and degraded the main body of the people in those countries. In a series of letters, addressed to all sensible and just Englishmen*, London, C. Clement, 1824.

Cockburn, W., *A Remonstrance addressed to the Duke of Northumberland, upon the Dangers of Peripatetic Philosophy*, London, J. Hatchard and Son, 1838.

Cole, H., *Popular Geology Subversive of Divine Revelation! A Letter to the Rev. Adam Sedgwick, Woodwordian Professor of Geology in the University of Cambridge, being a scriptural refutation of the geological positions and Doctrines promulgated in his lately published Commencement Sermon, preached in the University of Cambridge, 1832*, London, Hatchard and Son, 1834.

..., *The Bible a Rule and Test of Religion and Science. A Sermon, preached at St. Mary's Church, in the University of Cambridge, before the Vice Chancellor and the authorities, on Sunday Morning, June 26, 1853*, Cambridge, Hatchard and Son, 1853.

Coleridge, S. T., *Aids to Reflection in the Formation of a Manly Character on the Several Grounds of Prudence, Morality and Religion; illustrated by select passages, from our elder divines, especially from Archbishop Leighton*, 2 vols., London, Taylor and Hessey, 1825; 2nd edn., 1848.

..., *Confessions of an Inquiring Spirit, edited from the author's mss. by Henry Nelson Coleridge*, London, Pickering, 1840.

..., *General Introduction to the Encyclopedia Metropolitana; or, a Preliminary Treatise on Method*, (third edn., London, J.J.Griffin and Co., 1849. First edn., *Dissertation on the science of method; or, the laws and regulative principles of education*, London, J.J.Griffin, 1818.

Comte, A., *Cours de philosophie positive*, 6 vols., Paris, Bachelier, 1832–42.

(Conolly, J.), 'The nervous system', *E.R.*, 47 (1828), 441–81.

Conybeare, W. D., and Phillips, W., *Outlines of the Geology of England and Wales, with an introductory compendium of the general principles of that science, and comparative views of the structure of foreign countries Illustrated by a coloured map and sections*, London, W. Phillips, 1822.

Conybeare, W. D., *Inaugural Address on the Application of Classical and Scientific Education to Theology; and on the evidences of natural and revealed religion. Delivered as introductory to a course for the use of the pupils of Bristol College, being members of the Established Church*, London, J. Murray, 1831.

(Conybeare, W. J.), 'Church Parties', *E.R.*, 98 (1853), 273–342.

(Copleston, E.), *A Reply to the Calumnies of the Edinburgh Review against Oxford. Containing an account of studies pursued in that university*, Oxford and London, J. Cooke and Mackinlay, 1810.

..., *A Letter to John Coker, of New College, Esq., on his Second Edition of Reflections on the Late Election of a Chancellor to the University of Oxford*, Oxford and London, J. Parker and Rivington, 1810.

..., *A Second Letter to John Coker...*, Oxford and London, J. Parker and Rivington, 1810.

[...] (Payne Knight, R., Playfair, J., Smith, S.), 'Calumnies against Oxford', *E.R.*, 16 (1810), 158–87.

(...), *A Second Reply to the Edinburgh Review, by the author of a Reply to the Calumnies of that Review against Oxford*, Oxford and London, J. Cooke and Mackinlay, 1810.

[...] (Davison, J.), 'Replies against the calumnies against Oxford', *Q.R.*, 7 (1810), 177–210.

(...), 'Sir P. Francis on Ricardo on bullion', *Q.R.*, 3 (1810), 151–61.

(...), *A Third Reply to the Edinburgh Review, by the Author of a Reply to the Calumnies of that Review against Oxford*, Oxford, J. Cooke and Parker, 1811.

(..., and Dudley, J. W. W.), 'Reid's *Memoirs of the Life of John Horne Tooke*', *Q.R.*, 7 (1812), 313–28.

(...), *A Letter to the Right Hon. Robert Peel on the Pernicious effects of a Variable Standard of Value*, Oxford, J. Murray, 1819.

..., *An Enquiry into the Doctrines of Necessity and Predestination. In four discourses preached before the University of Oxford, with notes, and an appendix on the seventeenth article of the Church of England*, London, J. Murray, 1821.

[...] (Blomfield, C. J.), 'Copleston – *Enquiry into the Doctrine of Predestination*', *Q.R.*, 26 (1821), 82–102.

[...] (Anon.), 'Copleston on necessity and predestination', *B.C.*, 15 (1821), 561–91.

..., *Remarks upon the Objections made to certain Passages in the Enquiry concerning Necessity and Predestination*, London and Oxford, J. Murray and J. Parker, 1822.

[...] (Anon.), 'Copleston on predestination', *B.C.*, 18 (1822), 1–32.

(...), 'Buckland – *Reliquiae Diluvianae*', *Q.R.*, 29 (1823), 138–63.

..., *Speech of the Bishop of Llandaff in the House of Lords on Tuesday, the 7th of April, 1829, in the debates on the Roman Catholic Relief Bill*, London, 'The Mirror of Parliament', 1829.

..., *A Charge Delivered to the Clergy of the Diocese of Llandaff, in September, 1835*, London, J. G. and F. Rivington, 1836.

... (ed.), *Letters of the Earl of Dudley to the Bishop of Llandaff*, London, J. Murray, 1840.

Copleston, W. J., *Memoir of Edward Copleston, DD, Bishop of Llandaff with selection from his diary and correspondence*, London, J. W. Parker and Son, 1851.

[Cottrell, C. H.] (Anon.), 'Religious Movements of Germany, in the Nineteenth Century, by C. H. Cottrell', *English Review*, 11 (1849), 428–32.

Cousin, V., *The Philosophy of Kant. Lectures by Victor Cousin, with a sketch of Kant's life and writings*, London, J. Chapman, 1854.

Cox, G. V., *Recollections of Oxford*, London, Macmillan and Co., 1868.

Crosse, A., 'On the production of insects by voltaic electricity', *The American Journal of Science and Arts*, 32 (1837), 374–7, and *Annals of Electricity, Magnetism and Chemistry*, 1 (1836–7), 242–4.

..., 'Description of some experiments made with the voltaic battery, for the purpose of producing crystals; in the process of which experiments certain insects constantly appeared', *Transactions and Proceedings of the Electrical Society of London*, 1 (1837–40), 10–16.

Crosse, C. A. H., *Memorials, Scientific and Literary, of Andrew Crosse, the Electrician*, London, Longman, Brown, Green, Longmans and Roberts, 1857.

[...], (Dallas, W. S.), '*Memorials scientific and literary, of Andrew Crosse*', *W.R.*, 9 (1857), 273–6.

Cuvier, F. (ed.), *Dictionnaire des sciences naturelles*, 3 vols. and 2 of plates, Strasbourg, F. G. Levrault, 1804–5. New edn., the first three volumes being a reprint of the 1804–5 edn., 64 vols., Strasburg, F. G. Levrault, 1816–45.

Cuvier, G., *Discours sur les révolutions du globe, et sur les changements qu'elles ont produites dans le règne animal*, third edn., Paris, Dufour and D'Ocagne, 1825.

..., 'Considérations sur les mollusques, et en particulier sur les Céphalopodes', *Annales des sciences naturelles*, 19 (1830), 241–59.

..., 'Considérations sur l'Unité de Composition en général, et sur la structure des Céphalopodes en particulier, lues à l'Académie des Sciences, le 22 février 1830', *Bulletin des sciences naturelles et de géologie*, 20 (1830), 304–11.

Darwin, C., *On the Origin of Species by Means of Natural Selection, or the Preservation of Favoured Races in the Struggle for Life*, London, J. Murray, 1859.

Daubeny, Archdeacon C., *A Guide to the Church, in several Discourses: to which are added two Postscripts: the first to those Members of the Church who occasionally frequent other places of Worship; the second to the Clergy...to which is prefixed some Account of the Author's Life and Writings*, London, Rivington, 1832. First edn., 1798.

[...] (Anon.), 'Daubeny's *Guide to the Church*', *B.C.*, 11 (1832), 288–311.

Daubeny, C. G. B., *An Inaugural Lecture on the Study of Botany, read in the Library of the Botanic Garden*, Oxford, May 1, 1834, London, Whittaker, 1834.

[...] (Anon.), Review of An Inaugural Lecture, *Athenaeum*, no. 344 (May 31, 1834), 401–2.

..., 'Letter of Professor Daubeny on science teaching at Oxford', *Athenaeum*, no. 594 (March 16, 1839), 204.

... 'Sketch of the writings and philosophical character of August Pyramus de Candolle, Professor of natural history at the Academy of Geneva, read at the meeting of the Ashmolean Society, February 13, 1843', *Edinburgh New Philosophical Journal*, 34 (1843), 197–246.

..., 'Address', *Athenaeum*, no. 1502 (9 August 1856), 997–1002.

(...), *A Few Words of Apology for the Late Professor Baden Powell's Essay 'On the Study of the Evidences of Christianity'*, contained in the volume entitled '*Essays and Reviews*', Oxford, J. H. and J. Parker, 1861.

..., *Miscellanies: being a collection of memoirs and essays on scientific and literary subjects, published at various times*, 2 vols., Oxford and London, J. Parker and Co., 1867.

Davies, C. M., *Unorthodox London, or, Phases of Religious Life in the Metropolis*, new edn., London, Tinsley 1876. First edn., 2 vols, 1873–5.

Davies, J., *An Estimate of the Human Mind. Being a philosophical inquiry into the legitimate application and extent of its leading faculties, as connected with the principles and obligations of the Christian religion*, 2 vols., London, J. Hatchard and Son, 1828.

(Davison, J.), *A Short Account of Certain Notable Discoveries in History, Science, and Philology, contained in a recent work, entitled 'Elements of General Knowledge'*, by *Phileleutheros Orieliensis*, Oxford and London, J. Cooke and J. Hatchard, 1803.

..., *Considerations on the Poor Laws*, Oxford, J. Parker, 1817.

..., *Discourses on Prophecy, in which are considered its structure, use, and inspiration: being the substance of twelve sermons, preached in the chapel of Lincoln's Inn, in the Lecture founded by the Right Reverend William Warburton, Bishop of Glouchester*, London, J. Murray, 1824.

[...] (Anon.), 'Davison's *Discourses on Prophecies*', *C.R.*, 7 (1825), 137–65.

Davison, J., *Considerations on the Justice and Wisdom of Conciliatory Measures towards Ireland, addressed to the Electors of the University of Oxford*, Oxford, W. Baxter, 1829.

..., *Remains and Occasional Publications of the late Rev. John Davison*, Oxford, J. H. Parker, 1840.

Davy, Sir H., *Consolations in Travel, or, the Last Days of a Philosopher*, London, J. Murray, 1830.

[De Luc, J. A.] (Anon.), '*An Elementary Treatise of Geology* [...]', *B.C.*, 35 (1810), 497–505.

[...] (Anon.), '*Geological Travels*, by J. A. De Luc', *B.C.*, 37 (1811), 43–6.

De Morgan, A., *A Budget of Paradoxes*, 2 vols. London, Longman, Green and Co., 1915. First edn., 1872.

(De Quincey, T.), 'Kant in his miscellaneous essays', *B.M.*, 28 (1830), 244–68.

(...), 'The French Revolution', *B.M.*, 28 (1830), 542–58.

(...), 'France and England', *B.M.*, 28 (1830), 699–718.

(...), 'On Hume's argument against miracles', *B.M.*, 46 (1839), 91–9.

Douglas, J. M., *The Life and Selections from the Correspondence of William Whewell, Late Master of Trinity College, Cambridge*, London, C. Kegan Paul and Co., 1882.

Duncan, J. S., *Botanical Theology; or, Evidence of the Existence and Attributes of the Deity, Collected from the Appearances of Nature*, Oxford, J. Vincent, 1826.

..., *Analogies of Different Classes of Organised Beings*, Oxford, Collingwood, 1831.

Duncan, P. B., *Essays and Miscellanea*, Oxford, T. Combe, 1840.

Eadie, J. (ed.), *Life of John Kitto, D.D., F.S.A.*, Edinburgh, W. Oliphant and Co., 1857.

(Ellis, F.), 'Whewell's *Mechanical Euclid*', *E.R.*, 67 (1838), 81–102.

Elwin, W. (ed.), *Some Eighteenth-Century Men of Letters. Biographical essays by the Rev. Whitwell Elwin, sometime editor of the Quarterly Review, with a memoir*, 2 vols., London, J. Murray, 1902.

(Empson, W.), 'Principles of belief and expectation as applied to miracles', *E.R.*, 52 (1831), 388–98.

(...), 'On pretended miracles–Irving, Scott, and Erskine', *E.R.*, 53 (1831), 261–305.

Encyclopaedia Londinensis, or, Universal Dictionary of Arts, Sciences, and Literature, 24 vols., London, J.Adlarch, 1797–1829.

Encyclopaedia Metropolitana, or, Universal Dictionary of Knowledge, 26 vols., London, B. Fellowes, 1817–45.

Feuerbach, L., *The Essence of Christianity, translated from the Second German edition by Marian Evans, translator of Strauss's Life of Jesus*, London, J. Chapman, 1854.

Ffoulkes, E. S., *A History of the Church of St. Mary the Virgin, Oxford, the University Church, from Domesday to the Installation of the late Duke of Wellington, Chancellor of the University*, London, Longmans, Green and Co., 1892.

Fitzpatrick, W. J., *Memoirs of R. Whately, Archbishop of Dublin, with a glance at his contemporaries and times*, 2 vols., London, R. Bentley, 1864.

Fleming, J., *The Philosophy of Zoology; or, a general view of the structure, functions and classification of animals*, 2 vols., Edinburgh, A. Constable, 1822.

(...), 'The geological deluge, as interpreted by Baron Cuvier and Professor Buckland, inconsistent with the testimony of Moses and the phenomena of nature', *Edinburgh Philosophical Journal*, 14 (1826), 205–39.

(...), 'Systems and methods in natural history', *Q.R.*, 41 (1829), 302–27.

..., *The Lithology of Edinburgh, edited with a memoir by the Rev. J. Duns* Edinburgh, W. P. Kennedy, 1859.

(Forbes, E.), 'The future of geology', *W.R.*, 2 (1852), 67–94.

Freeman, J., *Life of the Reverend William Kirby, M.A., Rector of Barham*, London, Longman, Brown, Green and Longmans, 1852.

Garbett, J., *The Book of Genesis, and the Mosaical History of the Creation, vindicated from the Unitarian misrepresentation; in a letter to the Lord Bishop of St. David's, and in reply to a recent discourse of Mr Thomas Belsham*, Birmingham, Jabet and Moore, 1821.

Geoffroy Saint-Hilaire, E., 'Sur les êtres des degrés intermédiaires de l'échelle animale, qui respirent dans l'air et sous l'eau, et qui ont à cet effet, dans un medium de développement, les organes respiratoires des deux sortes, principalement sur le mode d'action et sur la composition des organes respiratoires dans le Birgus latro', *Bulletin des sciences naturelles et de géologie*, 6 (1825), 151–7.

..., 'Recherches sur l'organisation des Gavials; sur leurs affinités naturelles, desquelles résulte la nécessité d'une autre distribution générique, Gavials, Teleosaurus, et Steneosaurus; et sur cette question, si les Gavials (Gavialis) aujourd'hui répandus dans les parties orientales de l'Asie descendent, par voie non interrompue de génération, des gavilas antédiluviens, soit des gavials fossiles, dits Crocodiles de Caen (Teleosaurus) soit des Gavials fossiles du Havre et de Honfleur (Steneosaurus)', *Mémoires, Muséum d'histoire naturelle*, 12 (1825), 97–155

..., 'Mémoire où l'on se propose de rechercher dans quels rapports de structure organique et de parenté sont entre eux les animaux des âges historique, et vivant actuellement, et les espèces antédiluviennes et perdues', *Mémoires, Muséum d'histoire naturelle*, 17 (1828), 209–29. See also *Bulletin des sciences naturelles et de géologie*, 20 (1828), 144–7

..., *Principes de philosophie Zoologique, discutés en Mars 1830 au sein de l'Académie Royale des Sciences*, Paris, Pichon et Didier, 1830.

..., 'De la possibilité d'éclairer l'histoire naturelle de l'homme par l'étude des animaux domestiques', *Comptes rendus de l'Académie Royale des Sciences*, 4 (1837), 662–72

..., 'Du Sivatherium de l'Himalaya, comme offrant un cas analogue de terrain et de dégré d'organization à l'elephant mammouth, et comme contribuant à l'enseignement des causes incessantes et graduelles modifiant les formes animales dans les âges de la terre', *Comptes rendus de l'Académie Royale des Sciences*, 5 (1837), 183–94.

..., *Notions synthétiques, historiques et physiologiques de philosophie naturelle*, Paris, Denain, 1838.

Geoffroy Saint-Hilaire, I., *Vie, travaux et doctrine scientifique d'Etienne Geoffroy Saint-Hilaire*, Paris, P. Bertrand, 1847.

Gerando, J.-M. de, *Histoire comparée des systèmes de philosophie, relativement aux principes des connaissances humaines*, 3 vols., Paris, Henrichs, 1804.

Gérard, F., 'De la modification des formes dans les êtres organisés', *Bulletin de l'Académie Royale des Sciences de Bruxelles*, 14 (1847), 25–43.

..., 'De la finalité. Inconciliabilité de cette doctrine avec la philosophie naturelle', *Revue Scientifique*, 13 (1847), 355–75.

Gosse, P. H., *Omphalos: An attempt to untie the geological knot*, London, J. Van Voorst, 1857.

[...] (Dallas, W. S.), 'Omphalos', *W.R.*, 13 (1858), 260–5.

(Grant, R. E.), 'Observations on the nature and importance of geology', *Edinburgh New Philosophical Journal*, 1 (1826), 293–302.

..., *An Essay on the Study of the Animal Kingdom*, London, J. Taylor, 1829.

Greg, W. R., *The Creed of Christendom, its foundations and superstructure*, London, J. Chapman, 1851.

..., *Essays on Political and Social Science, contributed chiefly to the Edinburgh Review*, 2 vols., London, Longman, Brown, Green and Longmans, 1853.

Griffin, J. N., *Seven Answers to the Seven Essays and Reviews*, London, 1862.
Grinfield, E. W., *Cursory Observations upon the 'Lectures on Physiology, Zoology, and the Natural History of Man', delivered at the Royal College of Surgeons, by W. Lawrence, Professor of Anatomy and Surgery to the College, &c &c, in a Series of Letters Addressed to that gentleman; with a concluding letter to his pupils*, London, T. Cadell and W. Davies, 1819.
..., *The Researches of Physiology, illustrative of the Christian Doctrine of the Resurrection. A Discourse delivered at Laura Chapel, Bath, Jan. 30, 1820, to which is added an Appendix, containing strictures on some recent publications in medicine and theology*, London, T. Cadell and W. Davies, 1820.
..., *Vindiciae Analogicae. A Letter to the Rev. Edward Copleston, D.D., Provost of Oriel College, Oxford, &c. &c. &c. on his Enquiry into the Doctrines of Necessity and Predestination*, London, T. Cadell, 1822.
..., *Vindiciae Analogicae. Part the Second. Being a reply to the third section of the Rev. Dr Copleston's 'Remarks on the Objections made to certain Passages in the Enquiry concerning Necessity and Predestination'. To which is added, an Appendix, containing the opinions of some eminent writers on Analogy, &c.*, London, T. Cadell, 1822.
..., *Christian Sentiments Suggested by the Present Crisis:. or, civil liberty founded upon self-restraint. A discourse preached at St. Barnabas Chapel, Kennington, May 1, 1831*, London, C. J. G. and F. Rivington, 1831.
..., *Reflections After a Visit to the University of Oxford on Occasion of the Late Proceedings Against the Regius Professor of Divinity, in a letter to the Rector of Lincoln College*, London and Oxford, B. Fellowes and J. H. Parker, 1836.
(Grove, W.), 'Natural history of man', *B.M.*, 56 (1854), 312–30.
..., *On the Correlation of Physical Forces*, London, Highley, 1846.
(Hamilton, W.), 'Universities of England – Oxford', *E.R.*, 53 (1831), 384–427.
(...), 'English Universities – Oxford', *E.R.*, 54 (1831), 478–504.
(...), 'Admission of Dissenters to the Universities', *E.R.*, 61 (1834), 162–227; 'The University and Dissenters', ibid., 422–45.
..., *Discussions on Philosophy and Literature, Education and University Reform, chiefly from the Edinburgh Review, corrected, vindicated, enlarged in notes and appendices*, 2nd edn., London, Longman, Brown, Green and Longmans, 1853.
Hamilton, W. J., 'Anniversary Address of the President', *Quarterly Journal of the Geological Society of London*, 12 (1856), xxi–lxix.
Hampden, R. D., *Parochial Sermons Illustrative of the Importance of the Revelation of God in Jesus Christ*, London, C. and J. Rivington, 1828.
..., *The Scholastic Philosophy Considered in Its Relation to Christian Theology, in a course of lectures delivered before the University of Oxford in the year 1832, at the Lecture founded by John Bampton, M.A., Canon of Salisbury*, London, Fellowes, 1833.
[...] (Anon.), 'Hampden's Bampton Lectures', *B.C.*, 14 (1833), 125–53.
..., *Observations on Religious Dissent, with particular reference to the use of religious tests in the University*, London and Oxford, Rivington and J. H. Parker, 1834.
[...] (Anon.), 'Extremes in religion: Hampden, Atkinson, Gathercole', *B.C.*, 18 (1835), 201–28.
..., *A Course of Lectures Introductory to the Study of Moral Philosophy*, London, B. Fellowes, 1835.
..., *A Postscript to Observations on Religious Dissent, with particular reference to the persecution of the Regius Professor of Divinity*, London, B. Fellowes, 1835.
(...), *State of Parties in Oxford; from the public prints, with an appendix containing some letters relative to the persecution of the Regius Professor of Divinity*, London, B. Fellowes, 1836.

..., _Introduction to the Second Edition of the Bampton Lectures of the Year 1832_, London, B. Fellowes, 1837.

Hare, J. C. H., _Essays and Tales, by John Sterling, collected and edited, with a memoir of his life_, 2 vols., London, J. W. Parker, 1848.

Harford, J. S., _The Life of Thomas Burgess, D.D., F.R.S., F.A.S., etc. etc., Late Bishop of Salisbury_, London, Longman, Orme, Brown, Green and Longmans, 1840.

Hawkins, E., _A Dissertation upon the Use and Importance of Unauthoritative Tradition As an Introduction to the Christian Doctrines Including the Substance of a Sermon upon 2 Thess. ii 15_, Oxford, J. Parker, 1819.

(...), _Oxford Matriculation Statutes: Answers to the 'Questions Addressed to Members of Convocation by a Bachelor of Divinity' [E. B. Pusey]_, Oxford, B. Baxter, 1835.

..., _An Inquiry into the Connected Use of the Principal Means of Attaining Christian Truth, in eight sermons, preached before the University of Oxford at the Bampton Lectures for 1840_, Oxford, J. H. Parker, 1840.

Hennell, C., _An Inquiry Concerning the Origin of Christianity_, London, Smallfield and Son, 1838.

..., _Christian Theism_, London, Smallfield and Son, 1839, new edn., London, J. Chapman, 1852.

Hennell, S. S., _Christianity and Infidelity. An exposition of the arguments on both sides. Arranged according to a plan proposed by George Baillie Esq._, London, A. Hall, 1857.

..., _Essays on the Sceptical Tendency of Butler's Analogy_, London, J. Chapman, 1859.

Henry, W. C., 'Report on the physiology of the nervous system', _Report of the Third Meeting of the British Association for the Advancement of Science_, London, J. Murray, 1834, pp. 59–91.

Herschel, J. F. W., _A Preliminary Discourse on the Study of Natural Philosophy_, Cabinet Cyclopaedia, London, Longman, Orme, Rees, Brown and Green, 1830; 2nd edn., 1833.

[...] S. S. Schweber (ed.), _Aspects of the Life and Thoughts of Sir John Frederick Herschel_, New York, Arno Press, 1981.

(...), 'Whewell on the inductive sciences', _Q.R._, 68 (1841), 177–238.

..., 'Address', _Report of the Fifteenth Meeting of the British Association for the Advancement of Science_, London, 1846, pp. xxvii–xliv.

..., _Essays from the Edinburgh and Quarterly Reviews, with addresses and other pieces_, London, Longman and Co., 1857.

Hinds, S., _Introduction to Logic: from Dr Whately's 'Elements of Logic'_, London, D. A. Talboys and J. Vincent, 1827.

..., _The History of the Rise and Early Progress of Christianity, comprising an enquiry into its true character and design_, 2 vols., London and Oxford, C. and J. Rivington, J. Parker and Co., 1828.

..., _The Three Temples of the One True God contrasted_, London, B. Fellowes, 1830.

[...] (Anon.), 'The Three Temples [...]', _B.C._, 8 (1830), 369–92.

..., _An Inquiry into the Proofs, Nature and Extent of Inspiration, and into the Authority of Scripture_, London and Oxford, B. Fellowes and J. Parker, 1831.

..., _The Argument for Episcopacy Considered. A sermon, preached at the consecration of Henry Pepys, Bishop of Sodor and Man_, London, B. Fellowes, 1840.

Hitchcock, E., _The Religion of Geology and its Connected Sciences_, Boston, Phillips, Sampson & Co., 1851; new edn., 1861.

[Hobart, J. H.], (Anon.), 'State of the Protestant Episcopalian Church in the United States of America', _B.C._, 17 (1822), 416–24, 540–55, 579–95.

Holden, G., _The Christian Sabbath; or, an inquiry into the religious obligation of keeping one day in seven_, London, C. and J. Rivington, 1825.

(Holland, H.), 'Natural history of man', _Q.R._, 86 (1849), 1–40.

(...), 'The progress and spirit of physical science', *E.R.*, 108 (1858), 71–104.

(...), 'Life and organisation', *E.R.*, 109 (1859), 227–63.

..., *Recollections of Past Life*, London, Longmans, Green and Co., 1872.

Hooker, J. D., *Introductory Essay to the Flora of New Zealand*, London, W. Pamplin, 1853.

Horsley, S., *Biblical Criticism of the First Fourteen Historical Books of the Old Testament; also on the first nine Prophetical Books*, 4 vols., London, Longman, Hurst, Rees, Orme and Brown, 1820.

Hunt, J., *Contemporary Essays in Theology*, London, Strahan and Co., 1873.

..., *Religious Thought in England from the Reformation to the End of Last Century. A Contribution to the history of theology*, London, Strahan and Co., 1873.

(T. H. Huxley), 'Vestiges of the Natural History of Creation', *British and Foreign Medical Chirurgical Review*, 13 (1854), 332–43.

Irons. W. J., *On the Whole Doctrine of Final Causes, a dissertation in three parts, with an introductory chapter on the character of modern Deism*, London, Rivington, 1836.

..., *The Miracles of Christ: being a second series of sermons for the people*, London and Oxford, J. Masters, J. H. and J. Parker, 1859.

..., *On Miracles and Prophecy, being a sequel to the argument of the 'Bible and its Interpreters', with some minor notes*, London, J. T. Hayes, 1867.

Jelf, W. J. (ed.), *Faith and Peace, being answers to some of the Essays and Reviews*, London, Saunders, 1862.

Jenyns, L., 'Report on the recent progress and present state of zoology', *Report of the Fourth Meeting of the British Association for the Advancement of Science*, London, 1835, pp. 143–252.

(Keble, J.), *Tract LXXXIX. Ad Clerum. On the mysticism attributed to the early fathers of the Church*, London and Oxford, D. G. Rivington and J. H. Parker, 1842.

Kennard, R. B., *The Evidences of Religion, natural and revealed, considered in two sermons, with notes*, London, F. and J. Rivington, 1852.

..., *A Protest to the Right Rev. the Lord Bishop of Salisbury on the Appearance of the 'Episcopal Manifesto', with a letter to the Rev. R. Williams D. D. and an appendix containing extracts from each of the Seven Essays and Reviews exhibiting the general character and spirit of the work*, London, R. Hardwicke, 1861.

..., *Essays and Reviews. Their origin, history, general character, significance, persecution, prosecution, the judgement of the Arches Court, review of the judgement*, London, R. Hardwicke, 1863.

Kett, H., *Elements of General Knowledge, introductory to useful books in the principal branches of literature and science, with lists of the most approved authors, designed chiefly for the junior students in the universities and the higher classes in schools*, Oxford, Rivington, 1803.

Kidd, J., *An Answer to a Charge against the English Universities Contained in the Supplement to the Edinburgh Encyclopaedia*, Oxford, University Press, 1818.

..., *An Introductory Lecture to a Course on Comparative Anatomy, illustrative of Paley's Natural Theology*, Oxford, University Press, 1829.

Kitto, J. (ed.), *A Cyclopaedia of Biblical Literature*, 2 vols., Edinburgh, A. and C. Black, 1845.

Knox, R., *Great Artists and Great Anatomists; A biographical and philosophical study*, London, J. Van Vorst, 1852.

Lamarck, J.-B.-P.-A.-M. de, *Philosophie zoologique, ou exposition des considérations relatives à l'histoire naturelle des animaux, à la diversité de leur organisation, et des facultés qu'ils en obtiennent; aux causes physiques qui maintiennent en eux la vie et donnent lieu aux mouvemens qu'ils exécutent; enfin, à celles qui produisent l'intelligence de ceux qui en sont doués*, 2 vols., Paris, Dentu, 1809.

..., *Histoire naturelle des animaux sans vertèbres, presentant les caractères généraux et particulières de ces animaux, leur distribution, leurs classes, leurs familles, leurs genres, et la citation des principales espèces qui s'y rapportent. Précédée d'une introduction offrant la détermination des caractères essentiels de l'animal, sa distinction du végétal et des autres corps naturels; enfin, l'exposition des principes fondamentaux de la zoologie*, 7 vols., Paris, Deterville, 1815–22.

Lancaster, T. W., *An Earnest and Resolute Protestation Against a Certain Inductive Method of Theologizing, which has recently been propounded by the King's Professor of Divinity at Oxford. With other matter*, London, J. G. and F. Rivington, 1839.

Lawrence, W., *An Introduction to Comparative Anatomy and Physiology, being the two introductory lectures delivered at the Royal College of Surgeons on the 21st and 25th of March, 1816*, London, J. Callow, 1816.

..., *Lectures on Physiology, Zoology and the Natural History of Man, delivered at the Royal College of Surgeons*, London, J. Callow, 1819.

[...] (Anon [T. Rennell?]), 'Somatopsychonoologia', *B.C.*, 22 (1824), 225–45.

Lebas, C. W., *The Life of the Right Reverend Thomas Fanshaw Middleton, D. D., late Lord Bishop of Calcutta*, London, C. J. G. and F. Rivington, 1831.

Lee, W., *On Miracles. An examination of the remarks of Mr. Baden Powell on the study of the evidences of Christianity, contained in the volume entitled Essays and Reviews*, London, Saunders, 1861.

Lewes, G. H., *A Biographical History of Philosophy*, 2 vols., London, C. Knight, 1845–6.

... *Comte's Philosophy of the Sciences: being an exposition of the Principles of the Cours de Philosophie Positive of Comte*, London, H. G. Bohn, 1847.

(...), 'Goethe as a man of science', *W.R.*, 2 (1852), 479–506.

(...), 'The life and doctrine of Geoffroy Saint-Hilaire', *W.R.*, 5 (1854), 160–90.

(...), 'Hereditary influence, animal and human', *W.R.*, 10 (1856), 135–62.

Lloyd, R., *Two Letters, addressed to a young Clergyman illustrative of his clerical duties in these times of innovation and schism. With an appendix, containing an account of a recent attempt to institute an Auxillary [sic] to the British and Foreign Bible Society in the Parish of Midhurst*, London, J. Walker, 1818.

..., *An Extensive Inquiry into the Important Questions, what it is to preach Christ: and what is the best mode of preaching Him*, London, L. B. Seely, C. and J. Rivington, Hatchard, 1825.

Lyall. A., *A Review of the Principles of Necessary and Contingent Truth, in reference chiefly to the doctrines of Hume and Reid*, London, C. J. G. and F. Rivington, 1830.

..., *Agonistes; or, philosophical strictures suggested by opinions, chiefly of contemporary writers, by the author of 'A Review of the Principles of Necessary and Contingent Truth'*, London, Rivingtons, 1856.

(Lyall, W. R.), 'Stewart's *Philosophical Essays*', *Q.R.*, 11 (1811), 1–37.

(...), 'Stewart's *Philosophy of the Human Mind*', *Q.R.*, 12 (1815), 281–317.

..., *Propaedia Prophetica: A view of the use and design of the Old Testament; followed by two dissertations. I. On the causes of the rapid propagation of the Gospel among the heathen. II. On the credibility of the facts related in the New Testament*, London, J. G. F. and J. Rivington, 1840.

(Lyell, C.), 'State of the Universities', *Q.R.*, 36 (1827), 216–68.

..., *Principles of Geology; or, the modern changes of the Earth and its inhabitants as illustrative of geology*, 3 vols., London, J. Murray, 1830–3.

..., 'Presidential Address', *Quarterly Journal of the Geological Society*, 7 (1851), xxv–lxxvi.

Lysons, D., *The Environs of London, being an historical account of the towns, villages, and hamlets, within twelve miles of that capital, interspersed with biographical anecdotes*, 4 vols., London, T. Cadell and W. Davies, 1795–6.

..., *Supplement to the First Edition of the Historical Account of the Environs of London*, London, T. Cadell and W. Davies, 1811.

(MacCulloch, J.), 'Penn's *Mineral and Mosaical Geology*', *W.R.*, 4 (1825), 457–95.

MacKay, R. W., *The Progress of the Intellect, as exemplified in the religious development of the Greeks and Hebrews*, 2 vols., London, J. Chapman, 1850.

..., *The Tübingen School and its Antecedents: A review of the history and present condition of modern theology*, London, Williams and Norgate, 1863.

(Mackintosh, J.), 'Stewart's *Introduction to the Encyclopaedia*', *E.R.*, 36 (1821), 220–67.

Mackintosh, R. J., *Memoirs of the Life of the Right Hon. Sir James Mackintosh*, 2 vols., second edn., London, E. Moxon, 1836. First edn., 1835.

Macnaught, J., *Two Sermons: on the external and internal evidences of the Christian religion*, London, Longman, Brown, Green and Longmans, 1856.

Mansel, H. L., *Prolegomena Logica. An inquiry into the psychological character of logical processes*, Oxford, W. Graham, 1851.

..., *Psychology the Test of Moral and Metaphysical Philosophy. An Inaugural Lecture delivered in Magdalen College, October 23, 1855*, Oxford, W. Graham, 1855.

..., *A Lecture on the philosophy of Kant, delivered at Magdalen College, May 20, 1856*, Oxford and London, J. H. and J. Parker, 1856.

..., *The Limits of Religious Thought Examined in Eight Lectures, preached before the University of Oxford, in the year M.DCCC.LVIII on the foundation of the late Rev. John Bampton, M.A., Canon of Salisbury*, Oxford and London, 1858.

[...] (Anon.) 'Mr. Mansel and Mr. Maurice', *C.R.*, 39 (1860), 283–312.

..., 'On miracles', in W. Thomson (ed.), *Aids to Faith. A Series of Theological Essays*, London, J. Murray, 1861.

..., *Letters, Lectures and Reviews, including the Phrontisterion, or, Oxford in the Nineteenth Century*, ed. by H. W. Chandler, London, J. Murray, 1873.

Marsh, H., *An Essay on the Usefulness and Necessity of Theological Learning to Those Who Are Designed for Holy Orders*, Cambridge, 1792.

..., *A Dissertation on the Origin and Composition of the Three First Canonical Gospels; annexed to vol. iii of his translation of Michaelis' Introduction to the New Testament*, Cambridge and London, Deighton and Rivington, 1801.

..., *A Course of Lectures Containing a Descriptive and Systematic Arrangement of the Several Branches of Divinity, accompanied with an account of both the principal authors and of the progress which has been made...in theological learning*, 7 parts, second edn., Cambridge, University Press, 1810–28.

..., *An Inquiry into the Consequences of Neglecting to Give the Prayer Book with the Bible; interspersed with remarks on some late speeches at Cambridge, and other important matter relative to the British and Foreign Bible Society*, London, Rivington, 1812.

[...] (Anon.), 'Election of Herbert Marsh to the See of Llandaff', *Monthly Repository*, 11 (1816), 498.

Martineau, H., *The Positive Philosophy of Auguste Comte*, London, H. G. Bohn, 1853.

Martineau, J., *The Rationale of Religious Inquiry*, London, Whittaker, 1836.

(...), 'Theodore Parker's *Discourse of Religion*', *Prospective Review*, 2 (1846), 83–118.

Maurice, F. D., *Reasons for Not Joining a Party in the Church. A letter to the Ven. Samuel Wilberforce, Archdeacon of Surrey: suggested by Rev. Dr. Hook's letter to the Bishop of Ripon, on the state of parties in the Church of England*, London, Rivington, 1841.

Medway, J., *Memoirs of the Life and Writings of John Pye Smith*, London, Jackson and Walford, 1853

(Merivale, H.), 'Archbishop Whately', *E.R.*, 120 (1864), 372–406.

Mill, J. S., 'Whately's *Elements of Logic*', *W.R.*, 9 (1828), 137–72.

..., *A System of Logic, Ratiocinative and Inductive: Being a connected view of the principles of evidence and the methods of scientific investigation*, 2 vols., London, J. W. Parker, 1843: in J. H. Robson (ed.), *Collected Works of John Stuart Mill*, 2 vols., vols. vii–viii, Toronto, University of Toronto Press, and London, Routledge and Kegan Paul, 1973–4.

Miller, H., *Foot-Prints of the Creator, or, Asterolepis of Stromness*, London and Edinburgh, Johnstone and Hunter, 1849.

..., *The Testimony of the Rocks; or, geology in its bearings on the two geologies, natural and revealed*, Edinburgh, T. Constable, 1857.

Mills, W., *The Duty of Christian Humility as Opposed to the Pride of Science: a discourse preached before the University of Oxford, at St. Mary's, on Sunday, June 24th, 1832*, Oxford, J. H. Parker, 1832.

(Anon.), 'On Miracles', *English Review*, 5 (1846), 395–436.

Morell, J. D., *An Historical and Critical View of the Speculative Philosophy of Europe*, 2 vols., London, W. Pickering, 1848.

..., *On the Philosophical Tendencies of the Age; being four lectures delivered at Edinburgh and Glasgow, in January 1848*, London, J. Johnstone, 1848.

..., *The Philosophy of Religion*, London, Longman, Brown, Green and Longmans, 1849.

Morgan, Sir T. C., *Sketches of the Philosophy of Morals*, London, H. Colburn, 1822.

Mozley, T., *Reminiscences chiefly of Oriel College and the Oxford Movement*, 2 vols., London, Longmans, Green and Co., 1882.

[Mounier, J. J.] (Anon.), '*The Influence Attributed to Philosophers, Free-Masons, and to the Illuminati, on the Revolution of France...*', *B.C.*, 19 (1801), 513–23.

Napier, J., *The Miracles. Butler's argument on miracles explained and defended: with observations on Hume, Baden Powell, and J. S. Mill, to which is added, a critical dissertation by the Rev. H. L. Mansel, B.D., of St. John's College, Oxford*, Dublin, Hodges, Smith and Co., 1863.

Neander, A., *The Theology of Thomas Arnold, its importance and its bearing on the present state of the Church*, Cambridge and London, J. H. Parker and Rivingtons, 1846.

Newman, F., *Lectures on Logic, or on the science of evidence generally, embracing both demonstrative and probable reasonings, with the doctrine of causation, delivered at Bristol College in the year 1836*, Oxford, J. H. Parker, 1838.

(...), '*Vestiges of the Natural History of Creation*', *Prospective Review*, 1 (1845), 49–82.

(...), '*Explanations. A sequel to the Vestiges of the Natural History of Creation*', *Prospective Review*, 2 (1846), 33–44.

..., *The Soul, Her Sorrows and Her Aspirations. An essay towards the natural history of the soul and the true basis of theology*, London, J. Chapman, 1849.

..., *Phases of Faith; or, Passages from the history of my creed*, London, J. Chapman, 1850.

..., *Theism. Doctrinal and Practical; or, didactic religious utterances*, London, J. Chapman, 1858.

[...] (Wilson, H. B.), '*Theism...*',*W.R.*, 13 (1858), 561.

(...), 'The Religious Weakness of Protestantism', *W.R.*, 13 (1858), 132–54.

(...), 'Jowett and the Broad Church', *W.R.*, 16 (1859), 41–67.

..., *Contributions Chiefly to the Early History of the Late Cardinal Newman*, London, Kegan Paul, Trench and Trübner, 1891.

Newman, J. H., *An Essay on the Miracles Recorded in the Ecclesiastical History of the Early Ages*, Oxford and London, J. H. Parker and F. Rivington, 1843.

Noel, B. W., *Remarks on the Revival of Miraculous Powers in the Church*, London, J. Nisbet, J. Hatchard and Seeley, 1831.

Nolan, F., *A Letter to Phileleutheros Orieliensis; occasioned by his short account of certain notable discoveries, contained in a recent work, entitled ' Elements of General Knowledge'*, Oxford, Slatter, 1804.

..., *Objections of a Churchman to Uniting with the Bible Society: including a reply to the arguments advanced in favour of that association*, London, Rivingtons, 1812.

(...), *A Reply to M. Volney's Ruins, or Revolutions of Empires*, London, Printed at the Private Press of the Rev. F. Nolan, T. and W. Boone, 1819.

..., *The Expectation Formed by the Assyrians That a Great Deliverer Would Appear About the Time of Our Lord's Advent demonstrated*, London, T. and W. Boone, 1826.

..., *Observations upon the Consequences Apprehended from Concession to the Roman Catholic Claims, as menacing the security of the Established Church*, London, T. and W. Boone, 1827.

..., *The Time of the Millennium Investigated; and its nature determined on scriptural grounds*, London, T. and W. Boone, 1831.

..., *The Analogy of Revelation and Science Established in a Series of Sermons Delivered before the University of Oxford, in the year M.DCCC.XXXIII on the foundation of the late Rev. John Bampton, M.A., Canon of Salisbury*, Oxford, J. H. Parker, 1833.

..., *The Chronological Prophecies; as constituting a connected system, in which the principal events of the divine dispensation are determined by the precise revelation of their dates; demonstrated in a series of lectures delivered in the Chapel of the Honourable Society of Lincoln's Inn, in the years 1833, 1834, 1835, 1836, on the foundation of the late Bishop Warburton*, London, W. Pickering, 1837.

..., *The Egyptian Chronology Analysed; its theory developed and practically applied; and confirmed in its dates and detail, from its agreement with the hieroglyphic monuments and the scripture chronology*, London, Seeleys, 1848.

Norris, H. H., *A Practical Exposition of the Tendency and Proceedings of the British and Foreign Bible Society Begun in a Correspondence Between the Rev. H. H. Norris and J. W. Freshfield, Esq., relative to the formation of an Auxiliary Bible Society at Hackney, and completed in an appendix, containing an entire series of the public documents and private papers which that measure occasioned, illustrated with notes and observations*, second edn., London, F. C. and J. Rivington, 1813.

[...] (Anon.), 'Norris on the Bible Society', *B.C.*, 2 (1814), 1–21, 149–64, 283–98.

..., *The Origin, Progress and Existing Circumstances, of the London Society for Promoting Christianity amongst the Jews. An historical inquiry*, London, J. Mawman, 1825.

..., *Neutrality in Time of Danger to the Church an Abandonment of the Faith, and Very Short-sighted Worldly Policy. An admonition to the members of the Church of England, delivered in a sermon at South Hackney Church, on Sunday, April 5, 1835*, London, F. Rivington, 1835.

Norton, A., *Two Articles from the Princeton Review, concerning the Transcendental Philosophy of the Germans and of Cousin, and its influence on opinion in this country*, Cambridge, J. Owen, 1840.

[...] (Wilson, H. B.), 'Contemporary Literature', *W.R.*, 9 (1856), 222.

O'Conor, W. A., *Miracles Not Antecedently Impossible. An examination of Professor Powell's argument in Essays and Reviews, being a paper read before the Manchester Clergy Society, and published at their request*, Oxford and London, J. H. and J. Parker, 1861.

Oersted, H. C., *The Soul in Nature. Translated from the original German edition of the author published at Munich, with supplementary contributions from the Leipzig edition, by Leonora and Joanna B. Horner*, London, H. G. Bohn, 1852.

Omalius d'Halloy, J.-B.-J. d', *Eléments de géologie*, Paris, Levrault, 1831.

..., 'Note sur la succession des êtres vivants', *Bulletins de l'Académie Royale des Sciences, des Lettres et des Beaux-arts de Belgique*, 13 (1846), 581–91.

Owen, R., 'Professor Owen on British Fossil Reptiles', *Edinburgh New Philosophical Journal*, 33 (1842), 65–88.

..., *On the Nature of Limbs: A discourse delivered on Friday 9, at an evening meeting of the Royal Institution*, London, J. Van Voorst, 1849.

(...), 'Lyell on life and its successive development', *Q.R.*, 89 (1851), 412–51. 51.

Owen, R., *The Life of Richard Owen by his Grandson*, 2 vols., London, J. Murray, 1894.

Paley, W., *Paley's Natural Theology, with illustrative notes, by Henry Lord Brougham... and Sir Charles Bell...to which are added supplementary dissertations, by Sir Charles Bell*, London, C. Knight, 1836.

Palmer, E., *The Principles of Nature, or, a development of the moral causes of happiness and misery among the human species*, New York 1801; London, R. Carlile, 1820.

Palmer, W., *A Narrative of Events Connected with the Publication of the Tracts for the Time*, Oxford, J. H. Parker, 1843.

... 'On tendencies towards the subversion of faith', *English Review*, 10 (1848), 399–444, and 11 (1849), 181–94.

Parker, T., *A Discourse of Matters Pertaining to Religion*, Boston, 1842; London, J. Watson, 1849.

..., *Theism, Atheism and the Popular Theology. Sermons*, London, J. Chapman, 1853.

(Anon.), 'Theodore Parker and the Oxford essayists', *Christian Observer*, 60 (1860), 467–87.

Pattison. M., *Memoirs*, London, Macmillan, 1885.

[Penn, G.] (Anon.), 'Penn's mineral and mosaical geologies', *B.C.*, 21 (1824), 397–403.

[...] (Anon.), 'Penn on the prophecy of Ezekiel', *B.C.*, 3 (1815), 225–39.

[...] (Wilton, P. N.[?]), 'Misapplication of geology to scripture', *C.R.*, 8 (1826), 208–12.

Penrose, J., *Of the Use of Miracles in Proving the Truth of Revelation*, London, Baldwin, Craddock and Joy, 1824.

Perowne, J. J., and Stokes, L., *Letters, Literary and Theological, of Connop Thirlwall, late Bishop of St. David's*, 2 vols., London, R. Bentley and Son, 1881.

Pictet, F. J., 'Distribution of fossils in the different formations, and succession of animals on the surface of the globe', *Edinburgh New Philosophical Journal*, 40 (1846), 255–80.

Poole, R. S., *The Genesis of the Earth and of Man: or the history of creation, and the antiquity and races of mankind, considered on biblical and other grounds*, second edn., London, Williams and Morgate, 1860.

(Powell, B.), 'Memoirs of the Astronomical Society', *B.C.*, 18 (1822), 160–74.

(...), 'Barrow on magnetic attractions', *B.C.*, 19 (1823), 166–77.

(...), 'Woodhouse's *Treatise on Astronomy*', *B.C.*, 20 (1823), 143–56.

(...), '*Geology of England and Wales*', *B.C.*, 20 (1823), 285–301.

(...), 'Fleming's *Philosophy of Zoology*', *B.C.*, 21 (1824), 148–59.

(...), '*Philosophical Transactions of the Royal Society*', *B.C.*, 21 (1824), 27–36, 244–59.

(...), 'Gurney's *Lectures on the Elements of Chemical Science*', *B.C.*, 22 (1824), 349–63.

(...), 'Davison's *Discourses on Prophecy*', *B.C.*, 22 (1824), 368–89.

(...), 'Davies's *Inquiry into the Just Limits of Reason*', *B.C.*, 22 (1824), 447–58.

(...), '*Life and Remains of the Rev. E. D. Clarke*', *B.C.*, 22 (1824), 504–21.

(...), '*Works of the Rev. Daniel Waterland*', *B.C.*, 22 (1824), 624–38.

(...), 'Hancock on instincts', *B.C.*, 23 (1825), 40–55.

(...), 'Hydrostatics, mechanics, and dynamics', *B.C.*, 23 (1825), 163–74.

(...), 'An examination into the charge of heterodoxy brought against eminent men, in a letter to the editor of the Christian Remembrancer', *C.R.*, 7 (1825), 566–75.

(...), 'Lloyd on preaching Christ', *C.R.*, 7 (1825), 628–40.

(...), 'An examination into the charge of heterodoxy brought against eminent men. On the religious opinions of Locke. In a letter to the editor of the Christian Remembrancer', *C.R.*, 7 (1825), 701–12.

(...), 'State of the Protestant Religion in Germany', *C.R.*, 8 (1826), 65–81.

(...), 'Philosophy and Socinianism. A third letter to the editor of the Christian Remembrancer', *C.R.*, 8 (1826), 105–15.

(...), 'The Christian sabbath', *C.R.*, 8 (1826), 192–208.

(...), 'Observations on Rose's Commencement Sermon', *C.R.*, 8 (1826), 744–7.

..., *The Advance of Knowledge in the Present Times, Considered; especially in regard to religion. A sermon delivered in the Parish Church of Dartford, Kent, on Thursday, April 27, 1826*, London, C. and J. Rivington, 1826.

..., *Rational Religion Examined, or, remarks on the pretensions of Unitarianism; especially as compared with those systems which professedly discard reason*, London, C. and J. Rivington, 1826.

..., *The Elements of Curves: comprising I. The geometrical principles of the conic sections II. An introduction to the algebraic theory of curves. Designed for the use of students the University*, Oxford, University Press, 1828.

(...), 'Elementary mathematical treatises', *London Review*, 1 (1829), 467–86.

..., *A Short Treatise on the Principles of the Differential and Integral Calculus. Designed for the use of students in the University*, 2 Parts, Oxford, University Press, 1829–30.

..., *An Elementary Treatise on the Geometry of Curves and Curved Surfaces, Investigated by the Application of the Differential and Integral Calculus. Designed for the use of students in the University*, Oxford, University Press, 1832.

..., *The Present State and Future Prospects of Mathematical and Physical Studies*, Oxford, 1832.

(..., et al.), *Reasons for the Suggestion of Certain Alterations in the Examination Statutes, Lately Submitted to the Vice-Chancellor and Heads of Houses, by the Public Examiners*, Oxford, W. Baxter, 1832.

[...] (Anon.), *A Short Criticism of a Lecture published by the Savilian Professor of Geometry, by a Master of Arts*, Oxford, W. Baxter, 1832.

..., *A Short Elementary Treatise on Experimental and Mathematical Optics. Designed for the students in the University*, Oxford, D. A. Talboys, 1833.

..., *Revelation and Science: The substance of a discourse delivered before the University of Oxford, at St. Mary's, March VIII, M.DCCC.XXIX, with some remarks occasioned by the publication of the Bampton Lectures for 1833, and other recent works*, Oxford and London, J. H. Parker, 1833.

(...), 'On the admission of Dissenters to the University of Oxford', *Quarterly Journal of Education*, 8 (1834), 79–82.

(...), 'Physical studies in Oxford', *Quarterly Journal of Education*, 7 (1834), 47–54 and 8 (1834), 61–8.

..., *The Cabinet Cyclopaedia – Natural Philosophy: An historical view of the progress of the physical and mathematical sciences, from the earliest ages to the present times*, Cabinet Cyclopaedia, London, Longman, Brown, Green and Longmans, 1834.

..., *A Letter to the Editor of the British Critic, and Quarterly Theological Review, Occasioned by an Article in the Number of that Journal for April, 1834*, Oxford, J. H. Parker, 1834.

(...), 'University education, without religious distinctions', *Quarterly Journal of Education*, 10 (1835), 1–9.

..., *Remarks on a Letter from the Rev. H. G. Woodgate to Viscount Melbourne, Relative to the Appointment of Dr. Hampden*, Oxford, D. A. Talboys, 1836.

..., *On the Nature and Evidence of the Primary Laws of Motion*, Oxford, Ashmolean Society, S. Collingwood, 1837.

(...), *The Magazine of Popular Science and Journal of the Useful Arts: edited under the direction of the Society for the Illustration and Encouragement of Practical Science, at the Lower-Arcade, London*, 2 vols., 1837.

..., 'Recent progress of optical science', in R. D. Thomson (ed.), *British Annual or Epitome of the Progress of Science for 1837*, London, J. B. Baillière, 1837, pp. 162–209.

..., *The Connexion of Natural and Divine Truth; or, the study of the inductive philosophy considered as subservient to theology*, Oxford, J. W. Parker, 1838.

..., 'Remarks on the theory of the dispersion of light', *Philosophical Transactions*, 128 (1838), 253–64.

(...), 'Principles and prospects of University Reform', *Monthly Chronicle*, 2 (1838), 227–38.

..., *Tradition Unveiled, or, exposition of the pretensions and tendency of authoritative teaching in the Church*, London, J. W. Parker, 1839, Philadelphia, 1841.

..., *A Supplement to Tradition Unveiled*, London, J. W. Parker, 1840.

..., *State Education, considered with reference to prevalent misconceptions on religious grounds*, London, J. W. Parker, 1840.

..., 'A supplement to a paper entitled Remarks...', *Philosophical Transactions*, 130 (1840), 157–60.

..., *A General and Elementary View of the Undulatory Theory, as Applied to the Dispersion of Light, and Some Other Subjects Including the Substance of Several Papers, Printed in the Philosophical Transactions, and other Journals*, London, J. W. Parker, 1841.

..., *The Protestant's Warning and Safeguard in the Present Times: the substance of a sermon, preached before the Mayor and Corporation of Oxford, at St. Mary's Church, on Sunday, Nov. 7, 1841*, Oxford, H. Slatter, 1841.

..., *On the Theory of Parallel Lines, read to the Ashmolean Society, May 2, 1842*, Oxford, Ashmolean Society, T. Combe, 1842.

(...), 'Carpenter's *Cyclopaedia of Natural Science*', *Dublin University Magazine*, 22 (1843), 322–35.

(...), 'Anglo-Catholicism', *British and Foreign Review*, 16 (1843), 1–29, 528–59, and 17 (1843), 136–65.

(...), 'Sir Isaac Newton and his contemporaries', *E.R.*, 78 (1843), 402–37.

[...] (Thom, J. H.), '*Connexion*...', *Christian Teacher* 1 (1844), 160–77.

..., 'Creation', *Cyclopaedia of Biblical Literature*, 2 vols. (Edinburgh, 1845), i, 476–87; 'Deluge', i, 542–6; 'Sabbath', ii, 654–9.

(...), 'Life of the Rev. Joseph Blanco White', *W.R.*, 44 (1845), 273–325.

(...), 'Mysticism and scepticism', *E.R.*, 84 (1846), 195–223.

(...), 'The tendency of Puseyism', *W.R.*, 45 (1846), 304–43.

(...), 'The study of the Christian evidences', *E.R.*, 86 (1847), 397–418.

(...), 'Free inquiry in theology the basis of truth and of liberality', *Journal of Biblical Literature*, 1 (1848), 43–73.

..., *On Necessary and Contingent Truth: considered in regard to some primary principles of mathematical and mechanical science*, Oxford, Ashmolean Society, T. Combe, 1849.

..., *The State Church. A sermon preached before the University of Oxford at St. Mary's, on the 5th of November*, Oxford, T. Combe, 1850.

..., *Essays on the Spirit of Inductive Philosophy, the Unity of Worlds, and the Philosophy of Creation*, London, Longman, Brown, Green and Longmans, 1855.

..., *Christianity without Judaism. Two sermons, preached at Her Majesty's Palace at Kensington, on the Epiphany, and on Trinity Sunday (...) 1856*, London, Spottiswood, 1856.

..., *Christianity without Judaism. A second series of essays. Including the substance of sermons delivered in London and other places*, London, Longman and Co., 1856.

(...), 'Sir Isaac Newton', *E.R.*, 103 (1856), 499–534.

(...), 'The life and writings of François Arago', *E.R.*, 104 (1856), 301–37.

..., 'The Burnett Prizes: the study of the evidences of natural theology', *Oxford Essays*, 3 (1857), 169–203

(...), 'Alexander von Humboldt', *Fraser's Magazine*, 60 (1859), 15–23.

..., *The Order of Nature Considered in Reference to the Claims of Revelation*, London, Longmans *et al.*, 1859.

..., 'On the study of the evidences of Christianity', in F. D. Hedge (ed.), *Recent Inquiries in Theology by Eminent English Churchmen being 'Essays and Reviews', reprinted from the second edition*, New York, 1860, 106–62.

Prévost, C., 'Essai sur la constitution physique et géognostique du bassin à l'ouverture duquel est située la Ville de Vienne', *Journal de physique*, 91 (1820), 347–67.

..., 'Note sur an ichtyolite des rochers des Vaches-Noires', *Annales des sciences naturelles*, 3 (1824), in *Bulletin des sciences naturelles et de géologie* 4 (1825), 267–8.

..., 'Mammifères fossiles', *Dictionnaire classique des sciences naturelles*, ed. Bory de Saint-Vincent, 17 vols. (1822–31), vol. x (1826), 127–9.

Prichard, J. C., *Researches into the Physical History of Man*, London, J. and A. Arch, 1813; second edn., *Researches into the Physical History of Mankind*, 2 vols., London, J. and A. Arch, 1826.

[...] (Anon.), 'Prichard's *Physical History of Man*', *B.C.*, 3 (1815), 292–300.

[...] (Anon.), 'Prichard's *Analysis of Egyptian Mythology*', *B.C.*, 14 (1820), 55–69.

[...] (Anon.), 'Prichard's *Physical History of Mankind*', *B.C.*, 7 (1828), 33–61.

..., *A Review of the Doctrine of the Vital Principle, as Maintained by Some Writers on Physiology, with Observations on the Causes of Physical and Animal Life*, London, Sherwood, Gilbert and Piper, 1829.

[...] (Anon.), 'Prichard – *On the Vital Principle*', *B.C.*, 9 (1831), 440–59.

[Priestley, J.] (Anon.), 'Memoirs of Dr. Priestley', *B.C.*, 30 (1807), 267–84, 389–403.

Pring, D., *A View of the Relations of the Nervous System, in Health and Disease, containing selections from the dissertation to which was awarded the Jacksonian Prize for the year 1813 with additional information and remarks*, London, J. Callow, 1816.

..., *General Indications Which Relate to the Laws of the Organic Life*, London, Callow, 1819.

..., *Sketches of Intellectual and Moral Relations*, London, Longman, Rees, Orme, Brown and Green, 1829.

Pusey, E. B., *An Historical Enquiry into the Probable Causes of the Rationalist Character Lately Predominant in the Theology of Germany, to which is prefixed, a letter from Professor Sack, upon...H. J. Rose's discourses on German Protestantism*, London, C. and J. Rivington, 1828.

[...] (Anon.), 'Rose and Pusey – on rationalism', *B.C.*, 6 (1829), 469–85.

..., *Questions Respectfully Addressed to the Members of Convocation*, Oxford, 1835.

(...), *Subscription to the Thirty-Nine Articles: questions addressed to Convocation on the declaration proposed as a substitute for subscription, by a Bachelor of Divinity [E. B. Pusey] with answers by a Resident Member of Convocation [Dr. E. Hawkins] and brief notes upon these answers by the Bachelor of Divinity*, Oxford, W. Baxter, 1835.

Rennell, T., *Animadversions on the Unitarian Translation or Improved Version of the New Testament*, London, J. Hatchard and Son, 1811.

..., 'Lawrence's *Comparative Anatomy*', *B.C.*, 8 (1817), 63–73.

..., *Remarks on Scepticism, especially as it is connected with the subjects of organization and life. Being an answer to the views of M. Bichat, Sir T. C. Morgan and Mr. Lawrence upon those points*, London, F. C. and J. Rivington, 1819. Fifth edn., 1821.

..., *Proofs of Inspiration: or the grounds of distinction between the New Testament and the apocryphal volumes; occasioned by the recent publication of the Apocryphal New Testament by Hone*, London, Rivingtons, 1822.

'A Resident Member of Convocation', *1835 and 1772, The present attack on subscription compared with the last, in a letter to 'A Resident Member of Convocation', occasioned by some remarks in his ' Letter to the Earl of Radnor'*, Oxford and London, J. H. Parker and Rivington, 1835.

Rigg, J. H., 'The modern deists', *The London Quarterly Review*, 3 (1845), 1–42.

..., *Modern Anglican Theology: chapters on Coleridge, Hare, Maurice, Kingsley, and Jowett, and on the doctrine of sacrifice and atonement*, London, A. Heylin, 1857.

(Robinson, D.), 'The Church of England and Dissenters', *B.M.*, 16 (1824), 395–414.

(...), 'The repeal of the Combination Laws', *B.M.*, 17 (1825), 20–31.

(...), 'The Combinations', *B.M.*, 18 (1825), 463–78.

(...), 'Brougham and the education of the people', *B.M.*, 18 (1825), 534–51.

(...), 'The Bible Societies', *B.M.*, 18 (1825), 621–35.

Robinson, W., *The History and Antiquities of the Parish of Hackney, in the County of Middlesex*, 2 vols., London, J.B.Nichols and Son, 1842–3.

Rose, H.J., *The Tendency of Prevalent Opinions About Knowledge Considered. A sermon preached before the University of Cambridge on Commencement Sunday, July 2, 1826*, Cambridge, Deighton, 1826.

[...], (Anon.), 'On systems of instruction', *B.C.*, 1 (1827) 175–211.

..., *The State of the Protestant Religion in Germany; in a series of discourses; preached before the University of Cambridge*, Cambridge, J.Deighton, 1825. Second edn., C.J.G. and F.Rivington, 1829.

[...], (Anon.), 'Rose and Pusey–on rationalism', *B.C.*, 6 (1829), 469–85.

Ryland, J. E., *Memoirs of John Kitto, D.D., F.S.A., compiled chiefly from his letters and journals*, Edinburgh, W. Oliphant, 1856. New York, R. Carter and Brother, 1857.

(Sandford, D. K.), 'Classical education', *E.R.*, 35 (1821), 302–14.

Saunders, A. P., *Observations on the Different Opinions Held as to the Proposed Changes in the Examination Statutes, with the view principally to encourage the study of mathematics in the University, and a plan of examination respectfully submitted to the Committee now appointed to frame the new statute, as well as to members of Convocation Generally*, Oxford, H. Cooke, 1830.

(Anon.), 'On scepticism', *C.R.*, 1 (1819), 427–48.

Sedgwick, A., 'Address to the Geological Society, delivered on the evening of the 18th of February 1831', *Proceedings of the Geological Society of London*, 1 (1831), 281–316.

(...), '*Vestiges of the Natural History of Creation*', *E.R.*, 82 (1845), 1–85.

..., *A Discourse on the Studies of the University of Cambridge*, second edn., Cambridge, J. and J. J. Deighton, 1834; fifth edn., Cambridge and London, J. Deighton and Parker, 1850.

Senior Member of Convocation, *A Letter to a Non-Resident Friend upon Subscription to the Thirty-Nine Articles at Matriculation*, Oxford, 1835; Bodleian Library, G.A. Oxon, 8. 72 (4).

Serres, E. R. A., *Anatomie comparée du cerveau, dans les quatres classes des animaux vertébrés, appliquée à la physiologie et à la pathologie du système nerveux*, 2 vols., Paris, Gabon, 1824–6.

...., 'Explication du système nerveux des animaux invertébrés', *Annales des sciences naturelles*, 3 (1824), 377–80.

...., 'Recherches d'anatomie transcendante sur les lois de l'organogenie appliquées à l'anatomie pathologique', *Annales des sciences naturelles*, 11 (1827), 47–70.

Serres, M. de, 'Lettre adressée à M. de Férussac sur l'époque géologique dans laquelle l'on peut rapporter la separation des mers intérieurs d'avec l'océan', *Bulletin des sciences naturelles et de géologie*, 21 (1830), 185–212.

Sewell, W., *The Attack upon the University of Oxford, in a letter to Earl Grey*, London and Oxford, J. Bohn and D. A. Talboys, 1834.

...., *Thoughts on the Admission of Dissenters to the University of Oxford; and on the establishment of a state religion; in a letter to a Dissenter*, London and Oxford, D. A. Talboys, 1834.

...., *A Second Letter to a Dissenter on the opposition of the University of Oxford to the Charter of the London College*, London and Oxford, D. A. Talboys, 1834.

...., *Thoughts on Subscription, in a letter to a 'Member of Convocation'*, London and Oxford, D. A. Talboys, 1834.

(...), 'Oxford – Tutors and Professors', *Q.R.*, 66 (1840), 162–90.

...., *Memorial Notices of the Rev. William Sewell, D.D.*, Edinburgh, St. Giles, 1894.

Shuttleworth, P. N., *Sermons on Some of the Leading Principles of Christianity*, 2 vols., Oxford, Baxter and Parker, 1827–34.

...., *The Consistancy of the whole scheme of revelation with itself and with human reason*, London, Rivington, 1832.

(Anon.), 'Shuttleworth's on *Consistency of Revelation*', *B.C.*, 12 (1832), 158–66.

(Sikes, T.), *An Humble Remonstrance to the Bishop of London, Vice-President of a new association called the British and Foreign Society. By a faithful minister of the Establishment*, London, Vernon, Hood, Sharpe and Poultry, 1820.

...., *A Discourse on Parochial Communion; in which the respective duties of minister and people are deduced from scripture*, London, F. C. and J. Rivington, 1812.

Smith, J.P., *Letters to the Rev. Thomas Belsham on Some Important Subjects of Theological Discussion, referred to in his discourse on occasion of the death of the Rev. Dr. Priestley*, London, J. Johnson, 1804.

...., *The Scripture Testimony to the Messiah: an inquiry, with a view to a satisfactory determination of the doctrine taught in the holy scriptures concerning the person of Christ, including a careful examination of T. Belsham's Calm Inquiry*, 2 vols., London, R. Fenner, 1812–21.

...., *On the Principles of Interpretation as Applied to the Prophecies of Holy Scripture: A discourse delivered in the Meeting-House in Fetter Lane, February 5, 1829, before the Monthly Association of Congregational Ministers, and published at their request. With Enlargements and supplementary notes*, London, Holdsworth and Ball, 1829.

...., *On the Relation between the Holy Scriptures and Some Parts of Geological Science*, London, Jackson and Walford, 1839; Fifth edn., London, H. G. Bohn, 1854.

(Smith, W. H.), 'Comte', *B.M.*, 53 (1843), 397–414.

(...), '*Vestiges of the Natural History of Creation*', *B.M.*, 67 (1845), 448–60.

Sonnini de Manoncourt, C.S. (ed.), *Histoire naturelle, générale et particulière, par Leclerc de Buffon...Ouvrage formant un Cours complet d'Histoire naturelle*, 127 vols., Paris, F. Dufart, 1798–1808.

(Spencer, H.), 'Progress: its law and causes', *W.R.*, 11 (1857), 445–85.

...., *Essays, Scientific, Political, and Speculative*, 3 vols., London, Williams and Norgate, 1891.

Staël, A. L. G. de, *De l'Allemagne*, 3 vols., Paris, H. Nicolle, 1810. English edn.,
    Germany, 3 vols., London, J. Murray, 1813.
Stanley, A. P., *The Life and Correspondence of Thomas Arnold, D. D.*, London,
    B. Fellowes, 1844; new edn., 1890.
Stephen, L., *Essays on Free Thinking and Plainspeaking. Introductory essays on Leslie
    Stephen and his works by James Bryce and Herbert Paul*, London, Smith, Elder,
    Duckworth, 1907.
Stephens, W. R. W., *Life and Letters of W. F. Hook, DD, FRS*, London, Bentley and
    Son, 1878.
Sterling, J., *Essays and Tales, Collected and arranged, with a Memoir of his Life, by
    Julius Charles Hare, M.A., Rector of Herstmonceux*, 2 vols., London, J. W. Parker,
    1848.
(Stevenson, W.), 'On the reciprocal influence of the periodical publications, and the
    intellectual progress of this country', *B.M.*, xvi (1824), 518–28.
Stewart, D., *Elements of the Philosophy of the Human Mind*, 3 vols., Edinburgh and
    London, A. Strahan and T. Cadell, 1792–1827.
[...] (Anon.), 'Stewart's *Philosophy of the Human Mind*', *B.C.*, 2 (1814), 337–59.
..., *Philosophical Essays*, Edinburgh and London, T. Cadell and W. Davies, 1810.
[...] (Anon.), 'Dugald Stewart's *Philosophical Essays*', *B.C.*, 37 (1811), 537–58 and 38
    (1811), 148–57.
[...] Hamilton, Sir W., *The Collected Works of Dugald Stewart*, 11 vols., Edinburgh,
    T. Constable, 1854–60: vols. 2–4: *Elements of the Philosophy of the Human Mind:*
    vol. 5: *Philosophical Essays*; vols. 8–9: *Lectures on Political Economy*.
Strauss, D. F., *The Life of Jesus Christ Critically Examined*, 3 vols., London, Chapman
    Brothers, 1846.
[...] (Anon.), 'The last German discovery', *British Magazine*, 9 (1836), 612–3.
[...] (Anon.), 'Strauss's theory', *British Magazine*, 10 (1837), 47–9.
[...] (Wicksteed, C.), 'Strauss's *Life of Jesus*', *Prospective Review* 2 (1846), 479–520.
[...] (Anon.), '*Political and theological liberalism*, by D. F. Strauss', *English Review*, 10
    (1848), 199–201.
Sumner, J. B., *A Treatise on the Records of Creation, and on the Moral Attributes of
    the Creator; with particular reference to Jewish history, and to the consistency of the
    principle of population with the wisdom and goodness of the deity*, 2 vols., London,
    J. Hatchard, 1816.
Swainson, W., *A Preliminary Discourse on the Study of Natural History*, Cabinet
    Cyclopaedia, London, Longman, Rees, Orme, Green and Longman, 1834.
..., *On the Natural History and Classification of Quadrupedes*, Cabinet Cyclopaedia,
    London, Longman, Rees, Orme, Brown, Green, Longman and J. Taylor, 1835.
..., *A Treatise on the Geography and Classification of Animals*, Cabinet Cyclopaedia,
    London, Longman, Rees, Orme, Brown, Green and Longman, 1835.
Tayler, J. J., *A Retrospect of the Religious Life of England: or, the Church, Puritanism,
    and free inquiry*, London, J. Chapman, 1845.
Temple, F. (ed.), *Essays and Reviews*, London, J. W. Parker and Son, 1860.
Thom, J. H. (ed.), *The Life of the Rev. Joseph Blanco White. Written by himself. With
    portions of his correspondence*, 3 vols., London, J. Chapman, 1845.
(...), 'Archbishop Whately and the life of Blanco White', *Theological Review*, 4 (1867),
    82–120.
..., (ed.), *Letters Embracing the Life of John James Tayler, B.A., Prof. of Ecclesiastical
    History and Biblical Theology, and Principal of Manchester New College, London*,
    London, Williams and Mergate, 1872.
..., *A Spiritual Faith. Sermons by John Hamilton Thom, with a memorial preface by
    James Martineau*, London, Longmans and Green, 1895.

Thompson, R. A., *Christian Theism: the testimony of reason and revelation to the existence and character of the supreme being*, 2 vols., London, Rivingtons, 1855.

Thomson, T., 'Sketches of the History and Present State of Geology', in R. D. Thomson (ed.), *British Annual or Epitome of the Progress of Science for 1838*, London, J. B. Baillière, 1838, pp. 227–62.

Thomson, W. (ed.), *Aids to Faith. A series of theological essays*, London, J. Murray, 1861.

Tiedemann, F., *Anatomie und Bildungsgeschichte der Gehirns im Foetus des Menschen nebst einen vergleichenden Darstellung des Hirnbaues in den Thieren*, Nürnberg, Steinische Buchandlung, 1816. French Translation, Paris, J. Baillière, 1823; English edn., from the French, Edinburgh, J. Carfrae, 1826.

Todhunter, I., *William Whewell. An account of his writings with selections from his literary and scientific correspondence*, 2 vols., London, Macmillan, 1876.

Tulloch, J., *Theism: the witness of reason and nature to an all-wise and beneficent creator*, Edinburgh and London, W. Blackwood and Sons, 1855.

..., *Theological Tendencies of the Age. An inaugural lecture, delivered at the opening of St. Mary's College on Tuesday, the 28th of November, 1854*, Edinburgh, Paton and Richtie, 1855.

(...), 'The positive philosophy of Mr A. Comte', *E.R.*, 127 (1868), 303–57.

(Anon.), 'Unitarianism in England', *British Magazine*, 3 (1833), 209–10.

Van Mildert, W., *An Historical View of the Rise and Progress of Infidelity, with a refutation of its principles and reasonings. In a series of sermons preached, for the lecture founded by the Hon. Mr. Boyle, from 1802 to 1805*, 2 vols., London, C. J. G. and F. Rivington, 1806. New edn., 1831.

[...] (Anon.), 'Van Mildert's Sermons at Boyle's Lectures', *B.C.*, 31 (1808), 249–58.

... (ed.), *The Works of the Rev. Daniel Waterland, D.D., formerly Master of Magdalen College, Cambridge, Canon of Windsor, amd Archdeacon of Middlesex; now first collected and arranged. To which is prefixed, a review of the author's life and writings by W. Van Mildert, D.D.*, Oxford, University Press, 1823.

..., *Sermons on Several Occasions, and Charges, by W. Van Mildert, Late Bishop of Durham, to which is prefixed a memoir of the author by Cornelius Tues, M.A., Rector of Bradden*, Oxford and London, J. H. Parker and J. G. and F. Rivington, 1838.

Virey, J.-J. (ed.), *Nouveau dictionnaire d'histoire naturelle appliquée aux arts, à l'agriculture, à l'économie rurale et domestique, à la médecine, etc., par une Société de naturalistes et d'agricolteurs*, 24 vols., Paris, Deterville, 1803–4. Second edn., 36 vols. Paris, Deterville, 1816–17.

..., 'Animal', *Nouveau dictionnaire d'histoire naturelle*, vol. i (1803), 419–46; 2nd edn., vol. ii (1816), 1–81.

..., 'Nature', *Nouveau dictionnaire d'histoire naturelle*, vol. xv (1803), 358–414; 2nd edn., vol. xii (1817), 79–81.

..., *Histoire des moeurs et de l'instinct des animaux, avec les distributions méthodiques et naturelles de toutes leurs classes. Cours fait à l'Athenée Royale de Paris*, 3 vols., Paris, Deterville, 1822.

Wade, J., *The Black Book; or, Corruption Unmasked! Being an account of places, pensions, and sinecures, the revenues of the clergy and landed aristocracy; the salaries and emoluments in Courts of Justice and the Police Department; the expenditures of the Civil List (...)*, London, J. Fairburn, 1820.

(Walker, R.), *A Few Words in Favour of Professor Powell, and the Sciences, as Connected with Certain Educational Remarks, (chiefly in the way of extracts), by Philomath: Oxoniensis*, Oxford, Slatter, 1832.

Weekes, W. H., 'Details of an Experiment, in which certain insects, known as Acarus Crossii, appeared incident to the long continued operation of voltaic current upon silicate of potass within a close atmosphere over mercury', *Proceedings of the London Electrical Society*, (1843), 240–57.

..., 'Extracts of Notes describing the non-development of the Acarus Galvanicus, without a voltaic current', *Proceedings of the London Electrical Society*, (1843), 391–5.

(Welsh, D.), 'Archbishop Whately's Works', *North British Review*, 1 (1844), 486–527.

Whately, R., *Essays on Some of the Difficulties in the Writings of St. Paul*, London, B. Fellowes, 1818.

..., *Historic Doubts relative to Napoleon Buonaparte*, London, Hatchard, 1819.

[...] (Anon.), 'Historic Doubts on Napoleon Buonaparte', *C.R.*, 1 (1819), 302–7.

..., *The Christian's Duty with respect to the Established Government and the Laws; considered in two sermons: preached before the University of Oxford*, London, Rivingtons, 1821.

[...] (Anon.), 'R. Whately's Sermons on the Christian Duty', *B.C.*, 15 (1821), 475–88.

..., *The Right Method of Interpreting Scripture in what Relates to the Nature of the Deity, and his Dealings with Mankind, Illustrated, in a Discourse on Predestination, by Dr King, preached at Christ Church, before the House of Lords, May 15, 1705, with notes by the rev. Richard Whately*, Oxford and London, Baxter and Murray, 1821.

..., *The Use and Abuse of Party-Feelings in Matters of Religion, considered in eight sermons preached before the University of Oxford, in the year 1822, at the lecture founded by the Late Rev. John Bampton, M.A.*, Oxford, Clarendon Press, 1822.

..., *Essays on some of the Peculiarities of the Christian Religion*, Oxford and London, J. Murray, 1825.

..., *Elements of Logic, comprising the substance of the article in the Encyclopaedia Metropolitana: with additions, &c*, London, B. Fellowes, 1826; ninth edn., 1852.

(...), *Letters on the Church. By an Episcopalian*, London, Longman and Co., 1826.

..., *Elements of Rhetoric, comprising an analysis of the laws of moral evidence and of persuasion, with rules for argumentative composition and education*, London, J. Murray, 1828; seventh edn., London, J. W. Parker, 1846. Reprint edn., ed. by D. Ehninger, Carbondale, Illinois, Southern Illinois University Press, 1963.

..., 'Oxford lectures on political economy', *E.R.*, 48 (1828), 170–84.

..., *Essays on some of the difficulties in the writings of St. Paul, and in other parts of the New Testament*, London, Fellowes, 1828.

[...] (Anon.), 'Church Reform', *B.C.*, 6 (1829), 267–313.

..., 'Oxford lectures on political economy', *E.R.*, 48 (1828), 170–84.

..., *Thoughts on the Sabbath: being an additional note appended to the second edition of the 'Essays on Some of the Difficulties in the Writings of St. Paul, and in Other Parts of the New Testament'*, London, Fellowes, 1830.

..., *The duty of those who disapprove the education of the poor on grounds of expediency, as well as of those who approve it, pointed out in a sermon preached at Halesworth, Oct. 7, 1830, published by the desire of the subscribers, for the benefit of the Halesworth and Chediston National School*, London, Fellowes, 1830.

..., *The Errors of Romanism Traced to their Origin in Human Nature*, London, Fellowes, 1830.

[...] (Anon.), 'Whately's *Romish Errors*', *B.C.*, 10 (1831), 1–41

..., *Introductory Lectures on Political Economy, being part of a course delivered in Easter Term, MDCCCXXXI*, London, Fellowes, 1831.

..., *Sermons on Various Subjects, delivered in several churches of the city of Dublin, and in other parts of the Diocese*, London and Dublin, Fellowes and Milliken, 1835.

[...] (Anon.), 'Whately's *Sermons*', *B.C.*, 19 (1836), 180–8

..., *Remarks on Some Causes of Hostility to the Christian Religion, which are likely to operate at the present period, being a charge delivered at the Triennial Visitation of the Province of Dublin*, Dublin, Milliken, 1838.

..., *The Kingdom of Christ delineated, in two essays on our Lord's own account of his person, of the nature of his kingdom, and on the constitution, powers and ministry of a Christian Church, appointed by himself*, London, Fellowes, 1841.

..., *Thoughts on Church Government; being the substance of a charge at the visitation of the Diocese and the Province of Dublin, in 1844*, London, Fellowes, 1844.

[...] (Rogers, H.), 'Reason and faith: their claims and conflicts', *E.R.*, 90 (1849), 293–356.

..., *Cautions for the Times. Addressed to the parishioners of a parish in England, by their former Rector*, London, J. W. Parker, 1853.

..., *Remains of the Late Edward Copleston, Bishop of Llandaff. With an introduction containing some reminiscences of his life*, London, J. W. Parker, 1854.

..., *On the Origin of Civilization. A lecture by His Grace the Archbishop of Dublin to the Young Men's Christian Association*, London, J. W. Parker, 1854.

(..., Fitzgerald, W., Elwin, W.), '*Order of nature*', *Q.R.*, 106 (1859), 420–54.

..., (ed.), *A View of the Evidences of Christianity, in three parts, by William Paley, M.A., with annotations by R.W.*, London, J. W. Parker, 1859.

..., *Danger from Within. A charge, delivered at the annual visitation of the Diocese of Dublin and Glandelagh, and Kildare, June 1861*, London and Dublin, Parker and Son, Hodges and Smith, 1861.

Whately, E. J., *Life and Correspondence of Richard Whately, D.D., late Archbishop of Dublin*, 2 vols., London, Longmans, Green and Co., 1866.

(Whewell, W.), 'Lyell's Principles of Geology', *B.C.*, 9 (1831), 180–206.

(...), 'Modern science – inductive philosophy', *Q.R.*, 45 (1831), 374–407.

(...), 'Jones – *On the Distribution of Wealth and the Sources of Taxation*', *B.C.*, 19 (1831), 41–61.

(...), 'Lyell's *Geology*, vol. 2 – Changes in the Organic World now in Progress', *Q.R.*, 47 (1832), 103–33.

(...), 'On the use of definitions', *Philological Museum* 2 (1832), 263–272.

..., *An introduction to Dynamics, containing the laws of motion and the first three sections of the Principia*, Cambridge and London, J. and J. J. Deighton and J. W. Parker, 1832.

..., *On the Free Motion of Points, and on Universal Gravitation, including the principal propositions of books I and II of the Principia*, Cambridge and London, J. and J. Deighton, Whittaker and Arnot, 1832.

..., 'On the nature of the truth of the laws of motion', *Transactions of the Cambridge Philosophical Society*, 5 (1834), 149–72.

..., *Thoughts on the Study of Mathematics as a Part of a Liberal Education*, Cambridge, J. and J. Deighton, 1835.

..., *On the Principles of English University Education*, London and Cambridge, J. W. Parker and J. and J. J. Deighton, 1837.

..., *The Mechanical Euclid, Containing the Elements of Mechanics and Hydrostatics Demonstrated after the Manner of the Elements of Geometry; and including the proposition fixed upon by the University of Cambridge as requested for the degree of B.A., to which is added, remarks on mathematical reasoning and the logic of induction*, Cambridge and London, J. and J. J. Deighton and J. W. Parker, 1837.

..., *History of the Inductive Sciences, from the earliest to the present times*, 3 vols., London, J. W. Parker, 1837; new edn., 1847.

..., *The Philosophy of the Inductive Sciences, founded upon their history*, 2 vols., London, J. W. Parker, 1840.
..., *Of Induction, with especial reference to Mr. J. Stuart Mill's System of Logic*, London, J. W. Parker, 1849.
(...), *Of the Plurality of Worlds. An essay*, London, J. W. Parker and Son, 1853.
(Wilberforce, R. J.), *Considerations Respecting the Most Effectual Means of Encouraging Mathematics*, Oxford, J. L. Wheeler, 1830.
Wild, G. J., *A Brief Defence of the 'Essays and Reviews', showing, by extracts from their work, that similar doctrines have been maintained by eminent divines and living dignitaries of our Church*, London, R. Hardwicke, 1861.
Williams, J., *Memoirs of the Late Rev. Thomas Belsham, including a brief notice of his published works, and copious extracts from his diary*, London, Printed for the Author, 1833.
Wilson, G and Geikie, A., *Memoir of Edward Forbes*, Cambridge and London, Macmillan and Co., 1861.
(Wilson, J.), 'The Dodo and its kindred', *B.M.*, 65 (1849), 81–98.
(...), 'Geographical distribution of animals', *E.R.*, 53 (1831), 328–60.
Wilson, W., *The History of the Antiquities of Dissenting Churches and Meeting Houses in London, Westminster and Southwark; including the lives of their ministers, from the rise of nonconformity to the present time. With an appendix on the origin, progress and present state of Christianity*, 4 vols., London, 1804–18.
(Wilton, P. N.), 'Misapplication of geology to scripture', *C.R.*, 8 (1826), 208–12.
Wiseman, N., *Twelve Lectures on the Connexion between Science and Revealed Religion*, London, C. Dolman, 1836; other edns., 1842, 1859.

IV SECONDARY SOURCES

Aarsleff, H., *The Study of Language in England, 1780–1860*, Princeton, Princeton University Press, 1967.
..., *From Locke to Saussure: essays on the study of language and intellectual history*, Minneapolis, University of Minnesota Press, 1982.
Abbott, E., and Campbell, L. (eds.), *The Life and Letters of Benjamin Jowett*, 2 vols., London, J. Murray, 1897.
Alborn, T. L., 'The York Unitarians: theology, science, and the tensions of modern liberalism', B.A. thesis, Harvard University, 1986.
Allen, D. E., '*The Naturalist in Britain: a social history*' London, Allen Lane, 1976.
Altholz, J. L., 'The Huxley–Wilberforce debate revisited', *Journal of the History of Medicine*, 35 (1980), 313–16.
Annan, N, *Leslie Stephen: his thought and character in relation to his time*, London, Macgibbon and Kee, 1951.
..., 'The intellectual aristocracy', in J. H. Plumb (ed.), *Studies in Social History: a tribute to G. M. Trevelyan*, London, Longmans and Green, 1955, 241–87.
..., 'Science, religion and the critical mind; introduction', in P. Appleman *et al.*, *1859: entering an age of crisis*, Bloomington, Indiana, Indiana University Press, 1959, 31–50.
Appel, T. A., 'The Cuvier–Geoffroy Saint-Hilaire debate and the structure of nineteenth-century French zoology', Ph.D. thesis, Princeton University, 1975; in press, Oxford University Press.
..., 'Henri de Blainville and animal series: a nineteenth-century chain of being', *J.H.B.*, 13 (1980), 291–319.
Appleman, P. *et al.*, *1859: entering an age of crisis*, Bloomington, Indiana, Indiana University Press, 1959.
Aspinall, A., *Politics and the Press, c. 1780–1850*, London, Home and Van Thal, 1949.

Aston, R. D., *The German Idea: four English writers and the reception of German thought, 1800–1860*, Cambridge, Cambridge University Press, 1980.

Balan, B., *L'ordre et le temps: l'anatomie comparée et l'histoire des vivants au XIX siècle*, Paris, Vrin, 1979.

Bamford, T. W., *Thomas Arnold*, London, Cressett Press, 1960.

Barber, L., *The Heyday of Natural History, 1820–1870*, London, Jonathan Cape, 1980.

Barnes, B., and Shapin, S., eds., *Natural Order: historical studies of scientific culture*, Beverly Hills and London, Sage Publications, 1979.

Barthelemy-Madaule, M., *Lamarck ou le mythe du précurseur*, Paris, 1979. English Language Edition, *Lamarck the Mythical precursor: a study of the relations between science and ideology*, Cambridge, Mass., M.I.T. Press, 1982.

Bartholomew, M., 'Lyell and evolution: an account of Lyell's response to the idea of an evolutionary ancestry for man', *B.J.H.S.*, 6 (1973), 261–303.

...., 'The non-progress of non-progression: two responses to Lyell's doctrine', *B.J.H.S.* (Lyell centenary issue), 9 (1976), 166–74.

Barton, R. 'The X Club: science, religion, and social change in Victorian England', Ph.D. thesis, University of Pennsylvania, 1976.

Basalla, G. *et al.* (eds.), *Victorian Science: a self-portrait from the Presidential Addresses of the British Association for the Advancement of Science*, Garden City, New York, Anchor Books, 1970.

Bayne, P., *The Life and Letters of Hugh Miller*, 2 vols., Edinburgh, Strahn and Co., 1871.

Beer, G., *Darwin's Plot: evolutionary narrative in Darwin, George Eliot and nineteenth-century fiction*, London, Routledge, 1983.

Benn, A. W., *The History of English Rationalism in the Nineteenth Century*, 2 vols., London, Longmans, Green and Co, 1906.

Bennett, J. R., 'Francis William Newman and religious liberalism in nineteenth-century England', Ph.D. thesis, Stanford University, 1960.

Berg, M., *The Machinery Question and the Making of Political Economy*, Cambridge, Cambridge University Press, 1980.

Berman, A., 'Romantic Hygeia, Julien Joseph Virey (1775–1846), pharmacist and philosopher of nature', *Bulletin of the History of Medicine*, 39 (1965), 134–42.

Best, G. F. A., 'The constitutional revolution, 1830–32, and its consequences for the Church Establishment', *Theology*, 62 (1959), 226–34.

Biber, G. E., *Bishop Blomfield and his times, an historical sketch*, London, Harrison, 1857.

Bill, E. G. W., 'The declaration of students of the natural and physical sciences, 1865', *Bodleian Library Record*, 5 (1954–6), 262–7.

...., *University Reform in Nineteenth-Century Oxford. A study of Henry Halford Vaughan 1811–1885*, Oxford, Oxford University Press, 1973.

Blanckaert, C., 'Monogénisme et polygénisme en France de Buffon à P. Broca (1749–1880)', 3 vols., Doctoral Dissertation of 3d cycle, University of Paris I, Panthéon-Sorbonne, 1981.

Blomfield, A., *A Memoir of Charles James Blomfield, Bishop of London, with Selections From his Correspondence*, 2 vols., London, J. Murray, 1863.

Bolam, C. G. *et al.*, *The English Presbyterians. From Elizabethan Puritanism to Modern Unitarianism*, London, G. Allen and Unwin, 1968.

Bourdier, F., 'Geoffroy Saint-Hilaire versus Cuvier: the campaign for palaeontological evolution (1825–1838)', in C. J. Schneer (ed.), *Toward a History of Geology*, Cambridge, Mass., M.I.T Press, 1969, pp. 36–61.

Bourl'honne, P., *George Eliot. Essai de biographie intellectuelle et morale, 1819–1854*, Paris, A. H. Champion, 1937.

Bowen, D., *The Idea of the Victorian Church: a study of the Church of England, 1833–1889*, Montreal, McGill University Press, 1969.

Bowler, P. J., *Fossils and Progress: paleontology and the idea of progressive evolution in the nineteenth century*, New York, Science History Publications, 1976.

..., *Evolution. The history of an idea*, Berkeley, University of California Press, 1984.

Brilioth, Y., *The Anglican Revival, Studies of the Oxford Movement*, London, Longmans, Green and Co., 1925.

Brock, M. G., *The Great Reform Act*, London, Hutchinson, 1973.

Brock, W. H., 'The selection of the authors of the *Bridgewater Treatises*', *Notes and Records of the Royal Society*, 21 (1966), 162–79

Brock, W. H., and MacLeod, R. M., 'The scientists' declaration: reflexions on science and belief in the wake of the "Essays and Reviews"', *B.J.H.S.*, 9 (1976), 39–66.

Brooke, J. H., 'Precursors of Darwin', in J. H. Brooke and A. Richardson (eds.), *The Crisis of Evolution*, Milton Keynes, The Open University Press, 1974, 38–43.

..., 'Natural theology and the plurality of worlds: observations on the Brewster-Whewell debate', *A.S.*, 34 (1977), 221–86.

..., 'Richard Owen, William Whewell, and the *Vestiges*', *B.J.H.S.*, 10 (1977), 132–45.

..., 'The Natural Theology of the geologists: some theological strata', in L. J. Jordanova and R. S. Porter (eds.), *Images of the Earth. Essays in the history of the environmental sciences*, Chalfont St. Giles, The British Society for the History of Science, 1979, 39–64.

Brose, O. J., *Church and Parliament. The reshaping of the Church of England, 1828–1860*, London, Oxford University Press, 1959.

Brown, F. K., *Fathers of the Victorians. The age of Wilberforce*, Cambridge, Cambridge University Press, 1961.

Brown, W. E., 'Francis William Newman. A retrospect', Ph.D. thesis, Edinburgh University, 1953.

Buchdal, G., 'Inductivist *versus* deductivist approaches in the philosophy of science, as illustrated by some controversies between Whewell and Mill', *Monist*, 45 (1971), 343–67.

Budd. S., *Varieties of Unbelief. Atheists and agnostics in English society, 1850–1960*, London, Heinemann, 1977.

Bullock, F. W. B., *A History of the Training for the Ministry of the Church of England in England and Wales from 1800 to 1874*, St Leonards-on-Sea, Budd and Gillatt, 1955.

Burkhardt, R. W., 'The inspiration of Lamarck's belief in evolution', *J.H.B.*, 5 (1972), 413–38.

..., *The Spirit of System: Lamarck and evolutionary biology*, Cambridge, Mass., Harvard University Press, 1977.

Burgess, H. J., *Enterprise in Education: the story of the work of the Established Church in the education of the people prior to 1870*, London, National Society, S.P.C.K., 1958.

..., and Welby, P. A., *A Short History of the National Society. 1811–1961*, London, S.P.C.K., 1961.

Burgon, J. W., *Lives of Twelve Good Men*, London, J. Murray, 1888.

Burke, J. C., 'Kirk and causality in Edinburgh, 1805', *Isis*, 61 (1970), 340–54.

Burlingame, L. J., 'Lamarck's theory of transformism in the context of his views of nature, 1776–1809', Ph.D. thesis, Cornell University, 1973.

Burrow, J. W., *Evolution and Society: a study in Victorian social theory*, Cambridge, Cambridge University Press, 1966.

..., *A Liberal Descent. Victorian historians and the English past*, Cambridge, Cambridge University Press, 1981.

Bury, J. B., *The Idea of Progress. An inquiry into its origin and growth*, London, Macmillan, 1920.

Butler, J. R. M., *The Passing of the Great Reform Bill*, London, Longmans, Green and Co., 1914.

Butts, R. E., 'Necessary truth in Whewell's theory of science', *American Philosophical Quarterly*, 2 (1965), 161–81.

..., 'Discussion: On Walsh's reading of Whewell's view of necessity', *Philosophy of Science*, 32 (1965), 175–81.

..., 'Discussion: Prof. Marcucci on Whewell's philosophy', *Philosophy of Science*, 34 (1967), 175–83.

... (ed.), *William Whewell's Theory of Scientific Method*, Pittsburg, University of Pittsburg Press, 1968.

..., 'Whewell's logic of induction', in R. N. Giere and R. S. Westfall (eds.), *Foundations of the Scientific Method. The nineteenth century*, Bloomington, Indiana, Indiana University Press, 1973, 52–85.

Bynum, W. F., 'Time's noblest offspring: the problem of man in British natural historical sciences, 1800–1863', Ph.D. thesis, Cambridge University, 1974.

Cahn, T., *La vie et l'oeuvre d'Etienne Geoffroy Saint-Hilaire*, Paris, Presses Universitaires de France, 1962.

Cairns, D., 'Thomas Chalmers's Astronomical Discourses: a study in natural theology', *Scottish Journal of Theology*, 9 (1956), 410–21.

Cannon, W. F., 'The problem of miracles in the 1830s', *Victorian Studies*, 4 (1960), 5–32.

..., 'The impact of uniformitarianism. Two letters from John Herschel to Charles Lyell, 1836–1837', *Proceedings of the American Philosophical Society*, 105 (1960), 301–14.

..., 'Scientists and Broad Churchmen: an early Victorian intellectual network', *Journal of British Studies*, 4 (1964), 65–88.

..., 'Charles Lyell, radical actualism and theory', *B.J.H.S.*, 9 (1976), 104–20.

Cannon, S. F., *Science in Culture. The early Victorian period*, New York, Science History Publications, 1978.

Cantor, G., 'The reception of the wave theory of light in Britain: a case study of the role of methodology in scientific debate', *Historical Studies in the Physical Sciences*, 4 (1975), 109–32.

..., 'William Robert Grove, the correlation of forces, and the conservation of energy', *Centaurus*, 19 (1976), 273–90.

..., 'The historiography of Georgian optics', *History of Science*, 16 (1978), 1–21.

..., *Optics after Newton. Theories of light in Britain and Ireland, 1704–1840*, Manchester, Manchester University Press, 1983.

Carbery, M., *Assent to God. A discussion of the nature of natural theology according to John Henry Newman*, Rome, Pontificia Studiorum Universitas, Dissertatio ad lauream, Sotto il Monte, 1967.

Carpenter, S. C., *Church and People, 1789–1889; a history of the Church of England from Wilberforce to 'Lux Mundi'*, London, S.P.C.K., 1933.

Chadwick, O., *The Victorian Church*, Part I, London, A. & C. Black, 1966.

..., *The Secularization of the European Mind in the Nineteenth Century*, Cambridge, Cambridge University Press, 1975.

Checkland, S. G., 'The advent of academic economics in England', *Manchester School of Economic and Social Studies*, 19 (1951), 43–70.

Clark, J. W., and Hughes, T. M., *The Life and Letters of the Rev. Adam Sedgwick*, 2 vols., London, 1890; reprinted edn., Farnborough, Gregg, 1970.

Clark, J. W., *Old Friends at Cambridge and Elsewhere*, London, Macmillan, 1900.

Clarke, C. P. S., *The Oxford Movement*, London and Oxford, A. R. Mowbray and Co., 1932.

Clarke, W. K. L., *A Short History of the S.P.C.K.*, London, S.P.C.K., 1919.

Clive, J., *Macaulay. The shaping of an historian*, New York, A. A. Knopf, 1973.

Cockshut, A. O. J., *The Unbelievers: English agnostic thought, 1840–1890*. London, Collins, 1964.

Coleman, W., 'Lyell and the reality of species', *Isis*, 53 (1962), 325–38.

..., *Georges Cuvier, Zoologist: a study in the history of evolution theory*, Cambridge, Mass., Harvard University Press, 1964.

..., *Biology in the Nineteenth Century: problems of form, function, and transformation*, New York, Wiley, 1971.

..., 'Limits of the recapitulation theory. Carl Friedrich Kielmayer's critique of the presumed parallelism of earth history, ontogeny, and the present order of organisms', *Isis*, 64 (1973), 341–50.

Collini, S., Winch, D., Burrow, J., *That Noble Science of Politics. A study in nineteenth-century intellectual history*, Cambridge, Cambridge University Press, 1983.

Collini, S., 'The tendency of things: John Stuart Mill and the philosophical method', in S. Collini *et al.*, *That Noble Science of Politics*, Cambridge, Cambridge University Press, 1983, 127–39.

Cooke, G. W., *George Eliot, a critical study of her life, writings and philosophy*, Boston, J. R. Osgood, 1883.

Cooter, R., *The Cultural Meaning of Popular Science. Phrenology and the organization of consent in nineteenth-century Britain*, Cambridge, Cambridge University Press, 1984.

Cornish, F. W., *The English Church in the Nineteenth Century*, London, Mcmillan, 1910.

Corsi, P., 'The importance of French transformist ideas for the second volume of Lyell's *Principles of Geology*', *B.J.H.S.* 11 (1978), 221–44.

..., 'Sciences in culture', *Isis*, 70 (1979), 593–5.

..., 'Natural theology, the methodology of science, and the question of species in the works of the Reverend Baden Powell', D.Phil. thesis, Oxford University, 1980.

..., 'I gentiluomini della scienza', *Nuovi Argomenti*, n.2 (April–June 1982), 131–5.

..., 'Models and analogies for the reform of natural history. Features of the French debate, 1790–1800', in G. Montalenti and P. Rossi (eds.), *Lazzaro Spallanzani e la Biologia del Settecento. Teorie, esperimenti, istituzioni scientifiche*, Florence, Leo Olschki Editore, 1983, 381–96.

..., '"Lamarckiens" et "Darwiniens" à Tourin (1812–1894)', in Y. Conry (ed.), *De Darwin au Darwinisme. Science et idéologie*, Paris, Vrin, 1983, 49–66.

..., *Oltre il Mito. Lamarck e le scienze naturali del suo tempo*, Bologna, Il Mulino, 1983; *The Age of Lamarck*, English language edition, University of California Press, 1988.

..., 'Lamarck en Italie', *Revue d'histoire des sciences*, 37 (1984), 47–64.

..., 'Recent studies on French reactions to Darwin' and 'Recent studies on Italian reactions to Darwin', in D. Kohn, *The Darwinian Heritage*, Princeton University Press, 1985, 698–711 and 711–29.

..., 'Julien Joseph Virey, le premier critique de Lamarck', in S. Atran *et al.*, *Histoire du concept d'espèce dans les sciences de la vie*, Paris, Fondation Singer Polignac, 1987, 176–7.

..., 'The heritage of Dugald Stewart: Oxford philosophy and the Method of Political Economy, 1809–1832', *Nuncius, Annali di Storia della Scienza*, Istituto e Museo di Storia della Scienza di Firenze, 2, no.2 (1987), 89–144.

Courtney, J. E., *Freethinkers of the Nineteenth Century*, London, Chapman and Hall, 1920.

Crosland, M., and Smith, C., 'The transmission of physics from France to Britain: 1800–1840', *Historical Studies in the Physical Sciences*, 9 (1978), 1–61.

Crowther, W. A., *Church Embattled: religious controversy in mid-Victorian England*, Newton Abbot, David and Charles, 1970.

Darwin, F. (ed.), *The Life and Letters of Charles Darwin, including an autobiographical chapter*, 3 vols., London, Murray, 1887.

Darwin, F., and Seward, A. C. (eds.), *More Letters of Charles Darwin: a record of his work in a series of hitherto unpublished letters*, 2 vols., London, Murray, 1903.

Daudin, H., *Etudes d'histoire des sciences naturelles. I. De Linnée à Jussieu: méthodes de classification et idée de série en botanique et zoologie (1740–1790)*, Paris, F. Alcan, 1926.

...., *II. Cuvier et Lamarck. Les classes zoologiques et l'idée de série animale (1790–1830)*, Paris, F. Alcan, 1926.

Davies, H., *Worship and Theology in England. From Watts and Wesley to Maurice, 1690–1850*, Princeton, Princeton University Press, 1961.

Dawson, C., *The Spirit of the Oxford Movement*, London, Sheed and Ward, 1933.

de Beer, G., 'Further unpublished letters of Charles Darwin'. *A.S.*, 14 (1958), 85–115.

...., 'Some unpublished letters of Charles Darwin', *Notes and Records of the Royal Society*, 14 (1959), 12–66.

De Marchi, N. B., and Sturges, R. P., 'Malthus and Ricardo's inductivist critics: four letters to William Whewell', *Economica*, (1973), 379–93.

De Morgan, S. E., *Memoir of Augustus De Morgan*, London, Longman, Green and Co.

De Smet, W. M., 'L'influence de Butler sur la théorie de la foi chez Newman' *Ephemerides Theologicae Lovanienses*, 39 (1963), 30–49.

Desmond, A., 'Designing the dinosaur: Richard Owen's response to Robert Edmund Grant', *Isis*, 70 (1979), 224–34.

...., *Archetypes and Ancestors: palaeontology in Victorian London, 1850–1870*, London, Blond and Briggs, 1982.

...., 'Robert E. Grant: the social predicament of a pre-Darwinian transmutationist', *J.H.B.*, 17 (1984), 189–22.

...., 'Robert E. Grant's later views on organic development: the Swiney lectures on "Palaeozoology", 1853–1857', *Archives of Natural History*, 11 (1984), 395–413

...., 'Richard Owen's reaction to transmutation in the 1830s', *B.J.H.S.*, 18 (1985), 25–50.

...., 'The making of institutional zoology in London 1822–1836: part I', *History of Science*, 23 (1985), 153–185; 'part II', 23 (1985), 223–50.

Di Gregorio, M., *T. H. Huxley's Place in Natural Science*, New Haven, Connecticut, Yale University Press, 1984.

Distad, N. M., *Guessing at Truth. The life of Julius Charles Hare (1795–1855)*, Shepherdstown, The Patmos Press, 1979.

Dodd, V., 'Strauss's English propagandists and the politics of Unitarianism, 1841–1845', *Church History*, 50 (1981), 415–35.

Edmonds, J. M., and Douglas, J. A., 'William Buckland, F.R.S. (1794–1856) and an Oxford geological lecture, 1823', *Notes and Records of the Royal Society*, 30 (1976), 141–67.

Edmonds, J. M., 'The founding of the Oxford Readership of Geology', *Notes and Records of the Royal Society*, 34 (1979), 33–51.

Egerton, F. N., 'Refutation and conjecture: Darwin's response to Sedgwick's attack on Chambers', *Studies in History and Philosophy of Science*, 1 (1970), 176–83.

Einhorn, L. J., 'Consistency in Richard Whately: the scope of his Rhetoric', *Philosophy and Rhetoric*, 14 (1985), 89–99.

Eiseley, L., *Darwin's Century: evolution and the men who discovered it*, Garden City, New York, Anchor Books, 1959.

Elkana, Y., 'William Whewell, historian', *Rivista di Storia della Scienza*, 1 (1984), 149–97.

Ellegard, A., 'The Darwinian theory and nineteenth-century philosophy'. *Journal of the History of Ideas*, 18 (1957), 362–93.

Ellis, I, *Seven Against Christ. A study of 'Essays and Reviews'*, Leiden, E. J. Brill, 1980.

Engel, A. J., 'From clergyman to don: the rise of the academic profession in nineteenth-century Oxford', Ph.D. thesis, Princeton University, 1975.

...., *From clergyman to don: the rise of the academic profession in nineteenth-century Oxford*, Oxford, Oxford University Press, 1983.

Fey, W. R., 'John Henry Newman, empiricist philosophy and the certainty of faith', D.Phil. thesis, Oxford University, 1977.

Fisch, M., 'Necessary and contingent truth in William Whewell's antithetical theory of knowledge', *Studies in the History and Philosophy of Science*, 16 (1985), 275–314.

Fontana, B. M., *Rethinking the Politics of Commercial Society. The Edinburgh Review 1802–1832*, Cambridge, Cambridge University Press, 1985.

Foote, G. A., 'The place of science in the British reform movement, 1830–1850', *Isis*, 42 (1951), 192–208.

...., 'Science and its function in early nineteenth-century England', *Osiris*, 11 (1954), 438–54.

Forbes, D., *The Liberal Anglican Idea of History*, Cambridge, Cambridge University Press, 1952.

Forrester, D. W. F., 'The intellectual development of Edward Bouverie Pusey, 1800–1850', D.Phil. thesis, Oxford University, 1967.

Frankel, S. J., 'British geology and the universal flood: the diluvial controversy of the 1820s', B.A. thesis, Harvard University, 1986.

Freeman, K. D., *The Role of Reason in Religion: a study of Henry Mansel*, The Hague, Martinus Nijhoff, 1969.

Gale, G. G., 'Darwin and the concept of a struggle for existence: a study in the extrascientific origins of scientific ideas', *Isis*, 63 (1972), 321–44.

Garland, M. M., *Cambridge before Darwin; the ideal of a liberal education*, Cambridge, Cambridge University Press, 1980.

Gash, N., *Mr. Secretary Peel. The life of Sir Robert Peel to 1830*, London, Longmans, 1961.

Giere, R. N. and Westfall, R. S., *Foundations of the Scientific Method. The nineteenth century*, Bloomington, Indiana, Indiana University Press, 1973.

Gilbert, A. D., *Religion and Society in Industrial England. Church, chapel and social change 1740–1914*, London, Longman, 1976.

Gillespie, N. C., *Charles Darwin and the Problem of Miracles*, Chicago, Chicago University Press, 1979.

Gillispie, C. C., *Genesis and Geology: a study in the relations of scientific thought, natural theology, and social opinion in Great Britain, 1790–1850*, Cambridge, Mass., Harvard University Press, 1951; paperback edn., Harper Torchbooks, 1959.

Glass, B., Temkin, O., and Straus, W. L., *Forerunners of Darwin 1745–1859*, Baltimore, Johns Hopkins University Press, 1959.

Goldman, L., 'The origins of British "social science": political economy, natural science, and statistics, 1830–1835', *The Historical Journal*, 26 (1983), 587–616.

Goldstrom, G. L., 'Richard Whately and political economy in school books, 1833–1880', *Irish Historical Studies*, 15 (1966–7), 131–46.

Goodfield-Toulmin, J., 'Some aspects of British physiology: 1740–1840', *J.H.B.*, 2 (1969), 283–320.

Gordon, A., *Addresses, Biographical and Historical*, London, The Lindsey Press, 1922.

Gordon, E. O., *The Home Life of Sir David Brewster*, Edinburgh, D. Douglas, 1881.

..., *The Life and Correspondence of William Buckland*, London, J. Murray, 1894.

Gould, S. J., *Ontogeny and Philogeny*, Cambridge, Mass., Harvard University Press, 1977.

Gow, H., *The Unitarians*, London, Methuen and Co., 1928.

Greene, J. C., *The Death of Adam: evolution and its impact on Western thought*, Ames, Iowa, Iowa State University Press, 1959.

..., 'Reflections of the progress of Darwin studies', *J.H.B.*, 8 (1975), 243–73.

Greenslade, S. L., *The Church and Social Order. A historical sketch.* London, S.C.M. Press, 1948.

Grinnell, G., 'The rise and fall of Darwin's first theory of transmutation', *J.H.B.*, 6 (1974), 259–73.

..., 'The rise and fall of Darwin's second theory', *J.H.B.*, 18 (1985), 51–70.

Gruber, H., and Barrett, P. H., *Darwin on Man. A psychological study of scientific creativity*, London, Wildwood House, 1974.

Guitton, J., *La philosophie de Newman. Essai sur l'idée de developpement*, Paris, Boivin, 1933.

Haight, G. S., *George Eliot and John Chapman. With Chapman's diaries*, New Haven, Yale University Press, 1940.

..., *George Eliot. A biography*, Oxford, Oxford University Press, 1968.

..., (ed.), *The George Eliot Letters*, 9 vols., New Haven, Yale University Press, 1954–78.

Haines, G., *German Influence upon English Education and Science.* New London, Conn., Connecticut College, 1957.

Halevy, E., *History of the British People in the Nineteenth Century*, London, Ernest Benn, 1924; fifth impression, 1970.

Hall, V. M. D., 'The contribution of the physiologist William Benjamin Carpenter (1813–1885), to the development of the principles of the correlation of forces and the conservation of energy', *Medical History*, 23 (1979), 129–55.

Hampden, H., *Some Memorials of Renn Dickson Hampden, Bishop of Hereford*, London, Longman, Green and Co., 1871.

Harris, R. W., *Romanticism and Social Order, 1780–1830*, London, Blandford Press, 1969.

Harrison, J. F. C., *The Second Coming: popular millenarianism 1780–1850*, London, Routledge and Kegan Paul, 1979.

Hendry, J., 'The evolution of William Rowan Hamilton's view of algebra as the science of pure time', *Studies in the History and Philosophy of Science*, 15 (1984), 63–81.

Hilton, B., *Corn, Cash and Commerce. The economic policies of the Tory governments 1815–1830*, Oxford, Oxford University Press, 1977.

Himmelfarb, G., *Darwin and the Darwinian Revolution*, London, Chatto and Windus, 1959.

Herbert, S., 'The place of man in the development of Darwin's theory of transmutation: Part I. To July 1837', *J.H.B.*, 7 (1974), 217–58 and 'Part II', 10 (1977), 155–227.

Hodge, M. J. S., 'The universal gestation of nature: Chambers's *Vestiges* and *Explanations*', *J.H.B.*, 5 (1972), 127–51.

..., 'Darwin and the laws of the animate part of the terrestrial system (1835–1837): on the Lyellian origins of his zoonomical explanatory program', Studies in the History of Biology, 7 (1982), 1–106.

Hollander, S., 'William Whewell and John Stuart Mill on the methodology of political economy', Studies in the History and Philosophy of Science, 14 (1983), 127–68.

Hollis, P., The Popular Press: a study in working-class radicalism of the 1830s, Oxford, Oxford University Press, 1970.

Holmes, S. J., 'Karl Ernst Von Baer's perplexities on evolution', Isis, 37 (1947), 7–14.

Holt, A., A Ministry to the Poor, being the history of the Liverpool Domestic Mission Society, 1836–1936, Liverpool, H. Young and Sons, 1936.

Hooykaas, R., Natural Law and Divine Miracle: historical–critical study of the principle of uniformity in geology, biology and theology, Leiden, Brill, 1959.

Houghton, W. E., The Victorian Frame of Mind, 1830–1870, New Haven, Yale University Press, 1957.

Hughes, E., 'The bishops and reform, 1831–1833: some fresh correspondence', English Historical Review, 56 (1941), 459–90.

Hunt, J., Religious Thought in England in the Nineteenth Century, London, Gibbings and Co., 1896.

Huth, A. H., The Life and Writings of Henry Thomas Buckle, 2 vols., London, S. Low, Marston, Searel and Rivington, 1880.

Huxley, L. (ed.), The Life and Letters of Thomas Henry Huxley, 2 vols., London, Macmillan, 1900.

..., Life and Letters of Sir Joseph Dalton Hooker, 2 vols., London, J. Murray, 1918.

Inkster, J., and Morrell, J. (eds.), Metropolis and Province: science in British culture, 1780–1850, London, Hutchinson, 1983.

Inkster, J., 'Introduction: aspects of the history of science and science culture in Britain, 1780–1850 and beyond', in J. Inkster and J. Morrell (eds.), Metropolis and Province, London, Hutchinson, 1983, 11–54.

Irvine, W., Apes, Angels and Victorians: a biography of Darwin and Huxley, London and Toronto, Weidenfeld and Nicolson, 1955.

Jackson, W. S., An Examination of the Deductive Logic of John Stuart Mill, Oxford, Oxford University Press, 1941.

Jacyna, L. S., 'The romantic programme and the reception of cell theory in Britain', J.H.B., 17 (1984) 13–48.

..., 'Principles of general physiology: the comparative dimension of British neuroscience in the 1830s and 1840s', Studies in the History of Biology, 7 (1984), 47–92.

James, A. J. L., 'The debate on the nature of the absorption of light, 1830–1835: a core-set analysis', History of Science, 21 (1983), 335–68.

..., 'The physical interpretation of the wave theory of light', B.J.H.S., 17 (1984), 47–60.

Jevons, W. S., Letters and Journals, London, Macmillan, 1886.

Johnson, R., 'Educational policy and social control in early Victorian England', Past and Present, n. 49 (1970), 96–119.

Jones, J. K. B., 'Anglican theological thought, 1750–1833, with especial reference to the pre-Tractarians', Ph.D. thesis, Leeds University, 1968.

Jordanova, L. J., 'The natural philosophy of Lamarck in its historical context, Ph.D thesis, Cambridge University, 1976.

..., and Porter, R. S. (eds.), Images of the Earth, Chalfont St. Giles, The British Society for the History of Science, 1979.

Kavaloski, V. K., 'The vera causa principle: an historico-philosophical study of a metatheoretical concept from Newman through Darwin', Ph.D. thesis, Chicago University, 1974.

Ker, J., and Gornall, T., *The Letters and Diaries of John Henry Newman*, 4 vols., Oxford, Oxford University Press, 1978–80.

Kitson Clark, G., *Churchmen and the Condition of England 1832–1885. A study in the development of social ideas and practice from the Old Regime to the modern state*, London, Macmillan and Co., 1973.

Knight, D. M., 'Professor Baden Powell and the inductive philosophy', *The Durham University Journal*, 29 (1967–8), 81–7.

Knights, B., *The Idea of the Clerisy in the Nineteenth Century*, Cambridge, Cambridge University Press, 1978.

Kohn, D., 'Darwin's path to natural selection', Ph.D. thesis, Massachusetts University, 1975.

... (ed.), *The Darwinian Heritage*, Princeton, Princeton University Press, 1985.

Kottler, M. J., 'Charles Darwin's biological species concept and the theory of geographic speciation: the transmutation notebooks', *A.S.*, 35 (1978), 275–98.

Kubitz O. A., 'Development of John Stuart Mill's *System of Logic*', *Illinois Studies in the Social Sciences*, 18 (1932), 1–310.

Laudan, L., 'William Whewell on the consilience of inductions', *Monist*, 55 (1971), 368–91.

Laudan, R., 'The Role of methodology in Lyell's science', *Studies in the History and Philosophy of Science*, 13 (1982), 215–49.

Laurent, G., 'Paléontologie et évolution en France de Lamarck à Darwin', 2 vols., Thèse de Doctorat d'Etat, Université de Paris I, Sorbonne, 1984.

La Vergata, A., 'Images of Darwin: a historiographical overview', in D. Kohn (ed.), *The Darwinian Heritage*, 1985, 901–72.

Lenoir. T., *The Strategy of Life: teleology and mechanics in nineteenth-century German biology*, Dordrecht, Reidel, 1982.

Lepenis, W., *Das Ende der Naturgeschichte. Wandel kultureller Selbstverständlichkeiten in den Wissenschaften des 18. und 19. Jahrhunderts*, Munich, Carl Hanser Verlag, 1976.

Levere, T. H., *Poetry Realized in Nature. Samuel Taylor Coleridge and early nineteenth-century science*, Cambridge, Cambridge University Press, 1981.

Levy, S. L., *Nassau W. Senior*, Toronto, Ryerson, 1943; Newton Abbott, David and Charles, 1970.

Liddon, H. P., *Life of Edward Bouverie Pusey*, 4 vols., London, Longmans, Green and Co., 1893–7.

Limoges, C., *La sélection naturelle: étude sur la première constitution d'un concept, (1837–1859)*, Paris, Presses Universitaires de France, 1970.

Lincoln, A., *Some Political and Social Ideas of English Dissent, 1763–1800*, Cambridge, Cambridge University Press, 1937.

Lindberg, D. C., and Numbers, R. L. (eds.), *God and Nature: historical essays on the encounter between Christianity and science*, Berkeley, University of California Press, 1986.

Lodwick, B. M., 'The Oxford Movement and the Diocese of Llandaff during the nineteenth century', Ph.D. thesis, Leeds University, 1976.

Lonsdale, H., *A Sketch of the Life and Writings of Robert Knox, the Anatomist*, London, Macmillan, 1870.

Losee, J., 'Whewell and Mill on the relations between philosophy of science and history of science', *Studies in the History and Philosophy of Science*, 14 (1983), 113–26.

Lucas, J. R., 'Wilberforce and Huxley: a legendary encounter', *Historical Journal*, 22 (1979), 313–30.

Lurie, E., 'Louis Agassiz and the idea of evolution', *Victorian Studies*, 3 (1959), 87–108.

Lyell, K. M. (ed.), *Life, Letters and Journals of Sir Charles Lyell, Bart.*, 2 vols., London, J. Murray, 1881.

Machin, G. I. T., *The Catholic Question in English Politics 1820 to 1830*, Oxford, Oxford University Press, 1964.

..., *Politics and the Churches in Great Britain 1832 to 1868*, Oxford, Oxford University Press, 1977.

Mackean, W. H., *The Eucharist Doctrine of the Oxford Movement. A critical survey*, London and New York, Putnam, 1933.

Mackenzie, W. M., *Hugh Miller. A critical study*, London, Hodder and Stoughton, 1905.

MacLachlan, H., *The Unitarian Movement in the Religious Life of England*, London, G. Allen and Unwin, 1934.

MacLeod, R. M., 'Evolutionism and Richard Owen, 1830–1868: an episode in Darwin's century', *Isis*, 56 (1965), 259–80.

..., 'Whigs and savants: reflections on the Reform Movement in the Royal Society, 1838–1848', in J. Inkster and J. Morrell (eds.), *Metropolis and Province*, London, Hutchinson, 1983, pp. 55–90.

Macran, F. W., *English Apologetic Theology*, London, Hodder and Stoughton, 1905.

Mallet, E., *A History of the University of Oxford*, 3 vols., London, Methuen and Co., 1924–7.

Manier, E., *The Young Darwin and his Cultural Circle: a study of influences which helped shape the language and logic of the first drafts of the theory of natural selection*, Dordrecht, Reidel, 1978.

Marcucci, S., *L'idealismo scientifico di William Whewell*, Pisa, Università di Pisa, Istituto di Filosofia, 1963.

..., *Henry L. Mansel. Filosofia della coscienza ed epistemologia della fede*, Firenze, Le Monnier, 1969.

Marshall, B. R., 'The theology of Church and State in relation to the concern for popular education in England, 1800–1870', D.Phil. thesis, Oxford University, 1956.

Matthew, H. C. G., 'Edward Bouverie Pusey: from scholar to Tractarian', *Journal of Theological Studies*, 32 (1981), 101–24.

Matthews, W. R., *The Religious Philosophy of Dean Mansel*, Oxford, Oxford University Press, 1956.

Maulitz, R. C., 'Channel crossing: the lure of French pathology for English medical students, 1816–36', *Bulletin of the History of Medicine*, 55 (1981), 475–96.

Mayr, E., *The Growth of Biological Thought. Diversity, evolution and inheritance*, Cambridge, Mass., Harvard University Press, 1982.

Mazumdar, P. M. H., 'Anatomical physiology and the reform of medical education: London, 1825–1835', *Bulletin of the History of Medicine*, 57 (1983), 230–46.

McDowell, R. B., *Public Opinion and Government Policy in Ireland 1801–1840*, London, Faber and Faber, 1952.

McKerrow, R. E., '"Method of composition": Whately's earliest Rhetoric', *Philosophy and Rhetoric*, 11 (1978), 43–58.

..., 'Richard Whately on the nature of human knowledge in relation to ideas of his contemporaries', *Journal of the History of Ideas*, 42 (1981), 439–55.

..., 'Archbishop Whately: human nature and Christian assistance', *Church History*, 50 (1981), 166–81.

..., 'Whately's theory of rhetoric', in R. E. McKerrow (ed.), *Explorations in Rhetoric: studies in honor of Douglas Ehninger*, Glenview, Illinois, Scott, Foresman and Co., 1982.

McKinney, H. L., *Wallace and Natural Selection*, New Haven, Conn., Yale University Press, 1972.
Merz, J. T., *A History of European Thought in the Ninteenth Century*, 4 vols., Edinburgh, Blackwood, 1896–1914.
Metha, V. R., 'The origins of English idealism in relation to Oxford', *Journal of the History of Philosophy*, 13 (1975), 177–87.
Middleton, R. D., *Newman at Oxford. His religious development*, London, Oxford University Press, 1950.
Millhauser, M., 'The scriptural geologists. An episode in the history of opinion', *Osiris*, 11 (1954), 65–86.
..., *Just before Darwin. Robert Chambers and Vestiges*, Middletown, Conn., Wesleyan University Press, 1959.
Mineka, F. E., *The Dissidence of Dissent. The Monthly Repository, 1806–1838*, Chapel Hill, University of North Carolina Press, 1940.
Moore, J. R., *The Post-Darwinian Controversies. A study of the Protestant struggle to come to terms with Darwin in Great Britain and America 1870–1900*, Cambridge, Cambridge University Press, 1978.
..., 'Geologists and the interpretation of Genesis in the nineteenth century', in D. C. Lindberg and R. L. Numbers (eds.), *God and Nature: historical essays on the encounter between Christianity and science*, Berkeley, University of California Press, 1986.
..., 'Crisis without revolution: the ideological watershed in Victorian England', *Revue de synthèse* (1986), 57–78.
Morrell, J. B., 'Professor Robison and Playfair, and the *Theophobia Gallica*; natural philosophy, religion and politics in Edinburgh, 1789–1815', *Notes and Records of the Royal Society*, 26 (1971), 43–63.
Morrell, J. B., and Thackray, A., *Gentlemen of Science: early years of the British Association for the Advancement of Science*, Oxford, Oxford University Press, 1981.
Murphy, H. R., 'The ethical revolt against Christian orthodoxy in early Victorian England', *American Historical Journal*, 60 (1955), 800–17.
Murray, N. U., 'The influence of the French Revolution on the Church of England and its rivals, 1789–1802', D.Phil. thesis, Oxford University, 1975.
Newsome, D., *The Parting of Friends. A study of the Wilberforces and Henry Newman*, London, John Murray, 1966.
Norman, E. R. (ed.), *Anti-Catholicism in Victorian England*, London, G. Allen and Unwin, 1967.
..., *Church and Society in England 1770–1970. A historical study*, Oxford, Oxford University Press, 1976.
Numbers, R. L., *Creation by Natural Law: Laplace's nebular hypothesis in American thought*, Seattle, University of Washington Press, 1977.
Ockenden, R. E., 'George Henry Lewes, 1817–1878' *Isis*, 32 (1947), 70–86.
Ogilvie, M. B., 'Robert Chambers and the successive revisions of the "Vestiges of the Natural History of Creation"', Ph.D. thesis, Oklahoma University, 1973.
..., 'Robert Chambers and the nebular hypothesis', *B.J.H.S.*, 8 (1975), 214–32.
Oldroyd, D. R., 'How did Darwin arrive at his theory? The secondary literature to 1982', *History of Science*, 22 (1984), 325–74.
Oldroyd, D. R., and Hutchings, D. W., 'The chemical lectures at Oxford (1822–54) of Charles Daubeny, M.D., F.R.S.', *Notes and Records of the Royal Society of London*, 33 (1979), 217–59.
Oliver, W. H., *Prophets and Millennialists. The uses of biblical prophecy in England from the 1790s to the 1840s*, Auckland and Oxford, Auckland University Press and Oxford University Press, 1978.

Olson, R., *Scottish Philosophy and British Physics. A study in the foundation of the Victorian scientific style*, Princeton, Princeton University Press, 1975.

Ospovat, D., 'The influence of Karl Ernst Von Baer's embryology, 1828–1859: a reappraisal in light of Richard Owen's and William B. Carpenter's paleontological application of "Von Baer's Law"', *J.H.B.*, 9 (1976), 1–28.

..., 'Perfect adaptation and teleological explanation: approaches to the problem of the history of life in the mid-nineteenth century'. *Studies in the History of Biology*, 2 (1978), 33–56.

..., *The Development of Darwin's Theory: natural history, natural theology, and natural selection, 1838–1859*, Cambridge and New York, Cambridge University Press, 1981.

Outram, D., *The Letters of Georges Cuvier. A summary calendar of manuscript and printed materials preserved in Europe, the United States of America, and Australasia*, Chalfont St Giles, The British Society for the History of Science, 1980.

..., *Georges Cuvier. Vocation, science and authority in post-revolutionary France*, Manchester, Manchester University Press, 1984.

Overton, J. H., *The English Church in the Nineteenth Century 1800–1833*, London, Longmans, Green and Co., 1894.

..., *The Anglican Revival*, London, Blackie and Son, 1897.

Page, L. E., 'Diluvialism and its critics in Great Britain in the early nineteenth century', in C. J. Schneer (ed.), *Toward a History of Geology*, Cambridge, Mass., M.I.T. Press, 1969, 257–71.

Pearce-Williams, L., 'The Royal Society and the founding of the British Association for the Advancement of Science', *Notes and Records of the Royal Society*, 16 (1961), 221–33.

Pfleiderer, O., *The Development of Theology in Germany since Kant and its Progress in Great Britain since 1825*, London, Swan Sonnenschein, 1890.

Pivetau, J., 'Le débat entre Cuvier et Geoffroy Saint-Hilaire sur l'unité de plan et de composition', *Revue d'histoire des sciences*, 3 (1950), 346–63.

Plan, D., *Un Genevois d'autrefois. Henry-Albert Gosse (1753–1816)*, Paris and Geneva, Fischbaker and Kundig, 1909.

Port, M. H., *Six hundred New Churches. A study of the Church Building Commission 1818–1856*. London, S.P.C.K., 1961.

Powell, E., *The Pedigree of the Powell family. To which are added pedigrees of the families of Baden and Thistlethwayte, of Co. Wilts*, London, 1891.

Poynter, J. R., *Society and Pauperism. English ideas on poor relief, 1795–1834*, London and Toronto, Routledge and Kegan Paul, and University of Toronto Press, 1969.

Pullen, J. M., 'Malthus's, theological ideas and their influence on his principle of population', *History of Political Economy*, 13 (1981), 39–54.

Rashid, S., 'Richard Whately and Christian political economy at Oxford and Dublin', *Journal of the History of Ideas*, (1977), 144–55.

..., 'Richard Whately and the struggle for rational Christianity in the mid-nineteenth century', *Historical Magazine of the Episcopal Protestant Church*, 47 (1978), 293–311.

..., 'Edward Copleston, Robert Peel, and cash payment', *History of Political Economy*, 15 (1983), 249–59.

..., 'Dugald Stewart, "Baconian" methodology, and political economy', *Journal of the History of Ideas*, 46 (1985), 245–57.

Reardon, B. M. G., *From Coleridge to Gore: a century of religious thought in Britain*, London, Longman, 1971.

Rehbock, P. F., *The Philosophical Naturalists: themes in early nineteenth-century British biology*, Madison, Wisconsin, Wisconsin University Press, 1983.

Reingold, N., 'Babbage and Moll on the state of science in Great Britain. A note on a document', *B.J.H.S.*, 4 (1968), 58–64.
Restaino, F., *John Stuart Mill e la Cultura Filosofica Britannica*, Florence, La Nuova Italia, 1968.
..., 'La fortuna di Comte in Gran Bretagna. I.', *Rivista Critica di Storia della Filosofia*, ibid., 23 (1968), 171–201; 'II.', 391–409; 'III.', ibid., 24 (1969), 148–78; 'IV.', 374–81.
..., *John Stuart Mill e William Hamilton: confronto e crisi di due filosofie*, Cagliari, Università di Cagliari, Pubblicazioni dell'Istituto di Filosofia, 1983.
Rice, D. F., 'Natural theology and the Scottish philosophy in the thought of Thomas Chalmers', *Scottish Journal of Theology*, 14 (1971), 23–46.
Richards, G. C., 'The Oriel Common Room in 1833', *The Oriel Record*, no. 9 (1933), 335–9.
..., 'Oriel College and the Oxford Movement', *The Nineteenth Century*, no. 676 (1933), 724–38.
Richards, R. J., 'The emergence of evolutionary biology of behaviour in the early nineteenth century', *B.J.H.S.*, 25 (1982), 241–80.
Robbins, W., *The Newman brothers: an essay in comparative intellectual biography*, Cambridge, Mass., Harvard University Press, 1966.
Roberts, M. J. D., 'Private patronage and the Church of England, 1800–1900', *Journal of Ecclesiastical History*, 32 (1981), 199–223.
Robertson, J. M., *History of Freethought in the Nineteenth Century*, London, Watts, 1929.
Role, A., *Un destin hors de série. La vie aventureuse d'un savant, Bory de Saint-Vincent*, Paris, La Pensée Universelle, 1973.
Rosie., G., *Hugh Miller. Outrage and order. A biography and selected writings*, Edinburgh, Mainstream Publishing, 1981.
Ross, F. R., 'Philip Gosse's *Omphalos*, Edmond Gosse's *Father and Son*, and Darwin's theory of natural selection', *Isis*, 68 (1977), 85–96.
Rothblatt, S., *The Revolution of the Dons. Cambridge and society in Victorian England*, Cambridge, Cambridge University Press, 1969.
..., 'The student sub-culture and the examination system in early nineteenth-century Oxbridge', in L. Stone (ed.), *The University in Society*, 2 vols., Princeton, Princeton University Press (1974) vol. i, 247–303.
Royle, E., *Victorian Infidels. The origins of the British Secularist Movement 1791–1866*, Manchester, Manchester University Press, 1974.
Rudwick, M. J. S., 'The strategy of Lyell's *Principles of Geology*', *Isis*, 61 (1970), 5–33.
..., *The meaning of Fossils. Episodes in the history of palaeontology*, London, Macdonald, 1972.
Rupke, *The Great Chain of History: William Buckland and the English school of geology (1814–1849)*, Oxford, Oxford University Press, 1983.
..., 'Richard Owen's Hunterian Lectures on comparative anatomy and physiology', *Medical History*, 29 (1985), 237–58.
Ruse, M., 'Darwin's debt to philosophy: an examination of the influence of the philosophical ideas of John F. Herschel and William Whewell on the development of Charles Darwin's theory of evolution', *Studies in the History and Philosophy of Science*, 6 (1975), 159–81.
..., 'The relationship between science and religion in Britain, 1830–1870', *Church History*, 44 (1975), 505–22.
..., 'The scientific methodology of William Whewell', *Centaurus*, 20 (1976), 227–57.

334   *Science and religion*

..., 'William Whewell and the argument from design', *The Monist*, 60 (1977), 244–68.

..., *The Darwinian Revolution: science red in tooth and claw*, Chicago, Chicago University Press, 1979.

Russell, C. A., *Science and Religious Belief: a selection of recent historical studies*, London, University of London Press and Open University Press, 1973.

Russell, E. S., *Form and Function. A contribution to the history of animal morphology*, London, Murray, 1916; reprint edn., Farnborough, Gregg, 1972.

Ruston, A., 'Radical nonconformity in Hackney, 1805–1845', *Transactions of the Unitarian Historical Society*, 14 (1955), 1–9.

St. Aubyn, G., *A Victorian Eminence. The life and works of Thomas Buckle*, London, Barrie, 1958.

Sanders, C. R., *Coleridge and the Broad Church Movement. Studies in S. T. Coleridge, Dr. Arnold of Rugby, J. C. Hare, Thomas Carlyle and F. D. Maurice*, Durham, North Carolina, Duke University Press, 1942.

Schagrin, M. L., 'Whewell's theory of scientific language', *Studies in the History and Philosophy of Science*, 4 (1973), 231–40.

Schiller, J. (ed.), *Colloque international Lamarck*, Paris, Blanchard, 1971.

..., *La notion d'organisation dans l'histoire de la biologie*, Paris, Maloine, 1978.

Schneer, C. J. (ed.), *Toward a History of Geology*, Cambridge, Mass, M.I.T. Press, 1969.

Schneider, F. D., 'The Anglican quest for authority: Convocation and the imperial factor, 1850–1860', *Journal of Religious Studies*, 139–57.

Schweber, S. S., 'The origin of the *Origin* revisited', *J.H.B.*, 10 (1977), 229–316.

Segerstedt, T. T., *The Problem of Knowledge in Scottish Philosophy (Reid–Stewart–Hamilton–Ferrier)*, Lund Universitets Arsskrift Bd. 31, Lund, C. W. K. Gleerup, 1935.

Sellers, J., 'Political and social attitudes of representative English Unitarians (1795–1850)', B.Litt. thesis, Oxford University, 1956.

Shuttleworth, S., *George Eliot and Nineteenth-century Science: the make-believe of a beginning*, Cambridge, Cambridge University Press, 1983.

Sieveking, I. G., *Memoirs and Letters of Francis William Newman*, London, Kegan Paul, Trench, Trübner, 1909.

Sillem, E. (ed.), *The Philosophical Notebook of John Henry Newman*, Louvain and New York, Nauwelaerts and Humanities Press, 1969.

Simon, B., *Studies in the History of Education, 1780–1870*, London, Lawrence and Wishart, 1960.

Simon, W. M., *European Positivism in the Nineteenth Century, an essay in intellectual history*, Ithaca, N.Y., Cornell University Press, 1963.

Sloan, P. R., 'Darwin's invertebrate program 1826–1836: preconditions for transformism', in D. Kohn (ed.), *The Darwinian Heritage*, Princeton, Princeton University Press, 1985, 71–120.

Smith, C. U. N., 'Charles Darwin, the origin of consciousness and panpsychism', *J.H.B.*, 11 (1978), 245–67.

..., 'Evolution and the problem of mind: Part I Herbert Spencer', *J.H.B.*, 15 (1982), 55–88.

Smith, H., *The Society for the Diffusion of Useful Knowledge 1826–1846*, Halifax, Nova Scotia, 1974.

Snow, D. M. B., 'Hugh James Rose Rector of Hadleigh, Suffolk', B.Litt. thesis, Oxford University, 1960.

Soloway, R. A., *Prelates and People. Ecclesiastical and social thought in England 1783–1852*, London and Toronto, Routledge and Kegan Paul, and University of Toronto Press, 1969.

Stoll, M. R., *Whewell's Philosophy of Induction*, Lancaster, Penn., Lancaster Press, 1929.

Stone, L., *The University in Society*, 2 vols., Princeton, Princeton University Press, 1974.

Storr, V. F., *The Development of English Theology in the Nineteenth Century, 1800–1860*, London, Longmans, Green and Co., 1913.

..., *The Oxford Movement. A liberal evangelical view*, London, S.P.C.K., 1933.

Stoughton, J., *Religion in England from 1800 to 1850. A History with a postscript on subsequent events*, 2 vols., London, Hodder and Stoughton, 1884.

Sulloway, F., 'Darwin and his finches: the evolution of a legend', *J.H.B.*, 15 (1982), 1–53.

..., 'Darwin's conversion: the Beagle voyage and its aftermath', *J.H.B.*, 15 (1982), 327–98.

Taylor, E. R., *Methodism and Politics 1791–1851*, Cambridge, Cambridge University Press, 1935.

Temkin, O., 'The philosophical background to Majendie's physiology', *Bulletin of the History of Medicine*, 20 (1946), 10–35.

..., 'Materialism in French and German physiology of the early nineteenth century', *Bulletin of the History of Medicine*, 20 (1946), 322–7.

..., 'Basic science, medicine and the romantic era', *Bulletin of the History of Medicine*, 37 (1963), 97–129.

Theobald, R. M., *Memorials of John Daniel Morell, M.A., L.L.D., Her Majesty's Inspector of Schools*, London, W. Stewart and Co., 1891.

Thomis, M. I., and Holt, P., *Threats of Revolution in Britain, 1789–1848*, London and Basingstoke, Macmillan, 1977.

Thompson, E. P., *The Making of the Working Class in England*, London, Victor Gollancz, 1963.

Thompson, K. A., *Bureaucracy and Church Reform. The organizational response of the Church of England to social change, 1800–1865*, Oxford, Oxford University Press, 1970.

Trouessart, E.-L., *Cuvier et Geoffroy Saint-Hilaire d'après les naturalistes allemands*, Paris, Mercure de France, 1909.

Tuckwell, W., *Reminiscences of Oxford*, London, 1900. Second edn., London, Smith and Elder, 1907.

..., *Pre-Tractarian Oxford. A reminiscence of the Oriel 'Noetics'*, London, Smith and Elder, 1909.

Tulloch, J., *Movements of Religious Thought in Britain during the Nineteenth Century*, London, Longmans, Green and Co., 1885.

Turner, F. M., *Between Science and Religion: the reaction to scientific naturalism in late Victorian England*, New Haven and London, Yale University Press, 1974.

Valenze, D. M., 'Prophecy and popular literature in eighteenth-century England', *Journal of Ecclesiastical History*, 29 (1978), 75–92.

Walgrave, J.-H., OP, *Newman the Theologian. The nature of belief and doctrine as exemplified in his life and work*, London, G. Chapman, 1960.

Walker, R. B., 'The growth of Wesleyan Methodism in Victorian England and Wales', *Journal of Ecclesiastical History*, 24 (1973), 267–84.

Walsh, H. T. 'Whewell on necessity', *Philosophy of Science*, 29 (1962), 139–45.

..., 'Whewell and Mill on induction', *Philosophy of Science*, 29 (1962), 279–84.

Ward, W. R., *Religion and Society in England 1790–1850*, London, B. T. Batsford, 1972.

.., *Victorian Oxford*, London, F. Cass, 1965.

Waterman, A. M. C., 'The ideological alliance of political economy and Christian theology 1789–1833', *Journal of Ecclesiastical History*, 34 (1983), 231–43.

Webb, K. R., *Harriet Martineau, a Radical Victorian*, New York, Columbia University Press, 1960.

..., *The British Working Class Reader 1790–1848*, London, George Allen and Unwin, 1955.

Webster, A. B., *Joshua Watson. The story of a layman 1771–1855*, London, S.P.C.K., 1954.

Webster, C., *The Great Instauration. Science, medicine and reform, 1626–1660*, London, Duckworth, 1975.

Wellek, R., *Immanuel Kant in England, 1793–1838*, Princeton, Princeton University Press, 1931.

Wells, K. D., 'Sir William Lawrence (1783–1867). A study of pre-Darwinian ideas on heredity and variation', *J.H.B.*, 4 (1971), 319–61.

Wickwar, W. H., *The Struggle for the Freedom of the Press 1819–1832*, London, Allen and Unwin, 1928.

Wigmore-Beddoes, D. G., 'A study of the affinity between Unitarianism and Broad Church Anglicanism in the nineteenth century', Ph.D. thesis, Birmingham University, 1963.

Willam, F. M., *Aristotelische Erkenntnislehre bei Whately und Newman*, Freiburg im Breisgau, Herder, 1960.

Willey, B., *Nineteenth-century studies: Coleridge to Matthew Arnold*, London, Chatto and Windus, 1949.

..., *More Nineteenth-century studies: a group of honest doubters*, London, Chatto and Windus, 1956.

Williamson, E. L., *The Liberalism of Thomas Arnold. A study of his religious and political writings*, Alabama, University of Alabama Press, 1964.

Wilson, D. B., 'Herschel and Whewell's version of Newtonianism', *Journal of the History of Ideas*, 35 (1974), 79–97.

Wilson, L. G. (ed.), *Sir Charles Lyell's Scientific Journals on the Species Question*, New Haven, Conn., Yale University Press, 1970.

..., *Charles Lyell. The years to 1841: the revolution in Geology*, New Haven, Conn., Yale University Press, 1972.

Wills, W. B., 'Ecclesiastical reorganisation and Church extension in the Diocese of Llandaff, 1830 to 1870', M.A. thesis, Swansea University, 1965.

Winch, D., 'The system of the north: Dugald Stewart and his pupils', in S. Collini *et al.*, *That Noble Science of Politics*, Cambridge, Cambridge University Press, 1983, 23–61.

Winsor, M. P., *Starfish, Jellyfish and the Order of Life. Issues in nineteenth-century science*, New Haven, Conn., Yale University Press, 1976.

Woodward, E. L., *The Age of reform, 1815–1870*, Oxford, Oxford University Press, 1938

Yeo, R., 'William Whewell, natural theology and the philosophy of science in mid-nineteenth-century Britain', *A.S.*, 36 (1979), 493–516.

..., 'An idol of the market-place: Baconianism in nineteenth-century Britain', *History of Science*, 23 (1985), 251–98.

Young, R., *Darwin's Metaphor. Nature's place in Victorian culture*, Cambridge, Cambridge University Press, 1985.

..., 'The historiographical and ideological context of the nineteenth-century debate on man's place in nature', in M. Teich and R. M. Young (eds.),*Changing Perspectives in the History of Science*, London, 1973, 344–438.

Yule, J. D., 'The impact of science on British religious thought in the second quarter of the nineteenth century', Ph.D. thesis, Cambridge University, 1976.

INDEX

339